Medieval Ireland

Medieval Ireland is often described as a backward-looking nation in which change only came about as a result of foreign invasions. By examining the abundant but often unexplored evidence available, Downham challenges this popular notion and demonstrates the cultural richness and diversity of medieval Ireland. Starting in the fifth century, when St Patrick arrived on the island, and ending in the fifteenth century, when the English government sought to defend the lands that it ruled directly around Dublin by making the Pale, this up-to-date survey charts the internal changes in the island. Different chapters cover a wide range of areas, with particular focus on land use, economy, society, religion, politics and culture. This concise and accessible overview offers a fresh perspective on Ireland in the Middle Ages and seeks to overthrow some enduring stereotypes.

CLARE DOWNHAM is a senior lecturer in Irish Studies at the University of Liverpool. She did her MA in Medieval History at the University of St Andrews and then completed an MPhil and PhD in Anglo-Saxon Norse and Celtic at the University of Cambridge. In 2004, she was awarded a John O'Donovan scholarship medal in Celtic Studies from the Dublin Institute for Advanced Studies, and her first book, *Viking Kings of Britain and Ireland: The Dynasty of Ivarr to AD 1014*, was published in 2007. She has published more than fifty articles on British, Irish and Viking history.

D1596534

Cambridge Medieval Textbooks

This is a series of introductions to important topics in medieval history aimed primarily at advanced students and faculty, and is designed to complement the monograph series *Cambridge Studies in Medieval Life and Thought*. It includes both chronological and thematic approaches and addresses both British and European topics.

For a list of titles in the series, see www.cambridge.org/medievaltextbooks.

MEDIEVAL IRELAND

CLARE DOWNHAM

University of Liverpool

CAMBRIDGE
UNIVERSITY PRESS

DA
930
.D69
2018

CAMBRIDGE
UNIVERSITY PRESS

University Printing House, Cambridge CB2 8BS, United Kingdom

One Liberty Plaza, 20th Floor, New York, NY 10006, USA

477 Williamstown Road, Port Melbourne, VIC 3207, Australia

314–321, 3rd Floor, Plot 3, Splendor Forum, Jasola District Centre, New Delhi – 110025, India

79 Anson Road, #06–04/06, Singapore 079906

Cambridge University Press is part of the University of Cambridge.

It furthers the University's mission by disseminating knowledge in the pursuit of education, learning, and research at the highest international levels of excellence.

www.cambridge.org
Information on this title: www.cambridge.org/9781107031319
DOI: 10.1017/9781139381598

First published 2018

Printed in the United Kingdom by TJ International Ltd. Padstow Cornwall

A catalogue record for this publication is available from the British Library

Library of Congress Cataloging-in-Publication data
Names: Downham, Clare, author.
Title: Medieval Ireland / Clare Downham, University of Liverpool.
Description: Cambridge : Cambridge University Press, 2017. | Includes bibliographical references and index.
Identifiers: LCCN 2017034607 | ISBN 9781107031319 (hardback) | ISBN 9781107651654 (paperback)
Subjects: LCSH: Ireland – History – To 1172. | Ireland – History – 1172–1603. | Middle Ages.
Classification: LCC DA930 .D69 2017 | DDC 941.501 – dc23
LC record available at https://lccn.loc.gov/2017034607

ISBN 978-1-107-03131-9 Hardback
ISBN 978-1-107-65165-4 Paperback

CONTENTS

———————— • ————————

FIGURES

•

MAPS

———————— • ————————

ACKNOWLEDGEMENTS

Many have helped in putting this work together. I would like to thank Elizabeth Friend-Smith of Cambridge University Press for approaching me to write this book in the first place and to the anonymous reviewers who approved the proposal and provided insightful feedback. The following scholars have kindly read and provided helpful commentary and corrections on individual chapters of the book (presented in alphabetical order): David Dumville, Marie Therese Flanagan, Áine Foley, John Gillingham, Susan Marshall, Raymond Ruhaak and Andrew Tierney. The most important person to thank is Jennifer Dumville. She has constantly reminded me that there are things more important in life than work. This book is dedicated to her with everlasting love and gratitude.

ABBREVIATIONS

———————— • ————————

AClon   *The Annals of Clonmacnoise, being the annals of Ireland from the earliest period to* AD *1408 translated into English A.D. 1627 by Conell Mageoghagan,* ed. Denis Murphy (Dublin: Royal Society of Antiquaries of Ireland, 1896)

AFM   *Annala Rioghachta Eireann: annals of the kingdom of Ireland by the Four Masters, from the earliest period to the year 1616,* ed. John O 'Donovan, 7 vols (Dublin: Hodges and Smith, 1851)

AI   *The Annals of Inisfallen, Rawlinson B503,* ed. and trans. Seán MacAirt (Dublin: Dublin Institute for Advanced Studies, 1951)

AU   *Annala Uladh ('Annals of Ulster'), otherwise Annala Senait ('Annals of Senat'): a chronicle of Irish affairs* from AD 431 to AD 1540, eds and trans. W.M. Henessey and B. MacCarthy, 4 vols (Dublin: Stationery Office, 1887–1901)

CS   *Chronicon Scotorum: a chronicle of Irish affairs from the earliest times to* AD *1135, with a supplement containing the events from 1141 to 1150,* ed. and trans. W.M. Henessey, Rolls Series (London: Longman, Green, Reader and Dyer, 1866)

NHI1   *New History of Ireland. Vol. 1: Prehistoric and early Ireland,* ed. D. Ó Cróinín (Oxford: Oxford University Press, 2005)

NHI2   *New History of Ireland. Vol. 2: Medieval Ireland, 1169–1534,* ed. Art Cosgrove (Oxford: Oxford University Press, 1993)

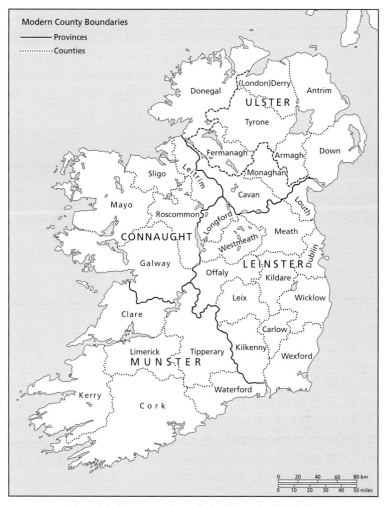

Map 1 Modern county boundaries. Drawn by David Cox.

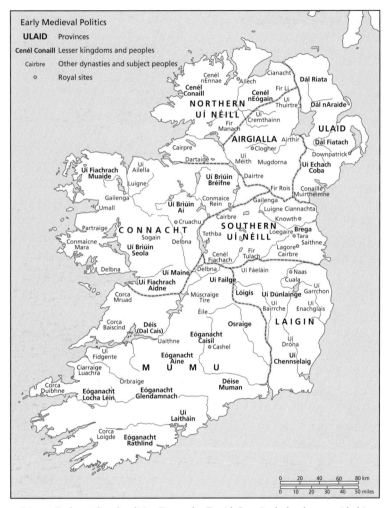

Early Medieval Politics

ULAID Provinces

Cenél Conaill Lesser kingdoms and peoples

Cairbre Other dynasties and subject peoples

o Royal sites

Cenél nEnnae
Ailéch
Cianacht
Dál Riata
Cenél Conaill
Fir Lí
Cenél nEógain
Uí Thuirtre
Dál nAraide
NORTHERN UÍ NÉILL
Uí Cremthainn
Fir Manach
ULAID
AIRGIALLA Ajrthir
Dál Fiatach
Cairpre
Clogher
Downpatrick
Dartaige
Uí Méith
Mugdorna
Uí Echach Coba
Uí Fiachrach Muaide
Uí Ailella
Luigne
Uí Briúin Bréifne
Dairtre
Fir Rois
Conaille Muirtheimne
Gailenga
Conmaice Rein
Gailenga
Umall
Uí Briúin Aí
Luigne Ciannachta
Partraige
Cruachu
Cairbre
Knowth
Sogain
Delbna
SOUTHERN UÍ NÉILL
Brega
Tethba
Loegaire
Tara
C O N N A C H T
Saithne
Conmaicne Mara
Uí Briúin Seola
Cenél Fiachach
Fir Tulach
Lagore
Cairbre
Delbna
Delbna
Uí Fáeláin
Naas
Uí Fiachrach Aidne
Uí Maine
Uí Failge
Cuala
Uí Garrchon
Corca Mruad
Múscraige Tíre
Lóigis
Uí Dúnlainge
Uí Bairrche
Uí Enachglais
Éile
L A I G I N
Déis (Dal Cais)
Osraige
Uaithne
Eóganacht Caisil
Cashel
Uí Dróna
Uí Fidgente
Eóganacht Áine
Uí Chennselaig
Ciarraige Luachra
Órbraige
M U M U
Déise Muman
Corca Duibhne
Eóganacht Locha Léin
Eóganacht Glendamnach
Uí Laitháin
Corca Loigde
Eóganacht Rathlind

0 20 40 60 80 km
0 10 20 30 40 50 miles

Map 2 Early medieval politics. Drawn by David Cox (includes data provided in
T. W. Moody et al. (eds) *A New History of Ireland, IX: Maps, Genealogies, Lists* (Oxford:
Clarendon, 1984), p. 18.

Map 3 Ireland: peoples and politics c. 1100. Drawn by David Cox (includes data provided in S. Duffy (gen ed.) *Atlas of Irish History*, third edition (Dublin: Gill and Macmillan, 2012), p. 31.

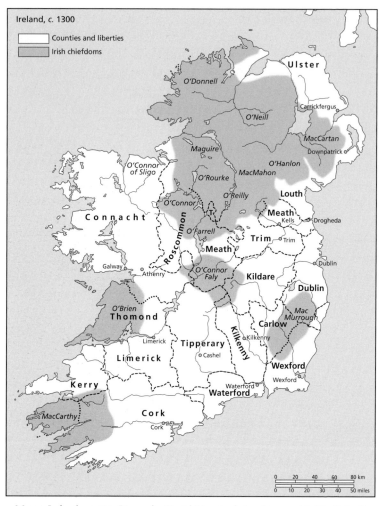

Map 4 Ireland, c. 1300. Drawn by David Cox (includes data provided in S. Duffy (gen ed.) *Atlas of Irish History*, third edition (Dublin: Gill and Macmillan, 2012), p. 41.

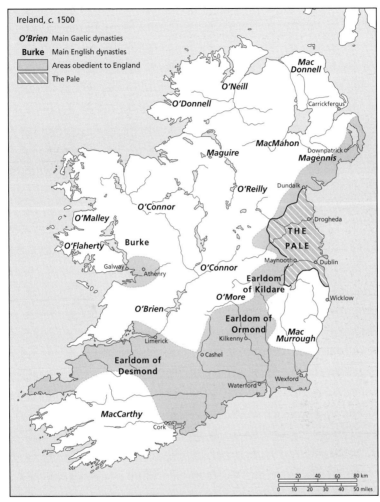

Map 5 Ireland, c. 1500. Drawn by David Cox.

INTRODUCTION

——————— • ———————

ANNALS OF ULSTER, *s.a.* 1041.1

'The events indeed are numerous, killings and deaths and raids and battles. No one can relate them all, but a few of the many are given so that the age in which the various people lived may be known through them'.

CHRONICON SCOTORUM, PROLOGUE

'[T]o make a short Abstract and Compendium of the History of the Gaels only in this copy, leaving out the lengthened details of the Books of History; wherefore it is that we entreat of you not to reproach us therefore'.

Through the history of medieval Ireland, the student can observe the origins of Irish identity, institutions, provinces and political divisions that have shaped modern Ireland. The challenge set by Cambridge University Press to cover 1,100 years of Irish history in a single volume is exacting. The last single-authored textbook to cover Ireland AD 400–1500 was Michael Richter's *Medieval Ireland: The Enduring Tradition*, published in 1988. Richter's book has proved enduringly popular to a general audience as witnessed by numerous reprints and online reviews. However, such a broad treatment did not gain general scholarly approval. It inevitably suffered from uneven coverage and misunderstandings. No author can have an impeccable knowledge of one thousand years of Irish history, and the present work will also have its failings. Nevertheless, given the academic and lay interest in an up-to-date overview of Irish medieval history, this book attempts to provide one.

Scholarship on medieval Ireland has blossomed in the last thirty years. In historiographic terms, the Irish Middle Ages has been a battleground of different perspectives, both political (e.g. nationalist, unionist, postcolonial, postpeace process) and geographical (e.g. Insular, Atlantic-archipelago, European, global comparative). The contemporary relevance of interpretations of the past in Ireland (and across the Irish diaspora) means that debates can be heated and objective. Some decisions in this volume will be controversial. For example, I have chosen to write a history of the island of Ireland rather than writing a history of an ethnic group. As a result, this book contains little about what the Irish achieved abroad (which was considerable), nor do the following chapters maintain a sharp distinction between the activities of the Gaelic Irish and the vikings[1] or English who settled in Ireland.

This brief introduction will provide a map of the work that follows, and will touch on one of the constant elements in Irish history of this period – the physical landscape of mountains, rivers and bogs. Chapter 1 provides an overview of Ireland in the fifth century. The rest of the book is divided into two parts. The first part covers the early Middle Ages. Within this book, the early Middle Ages are defined as the years AD 500–1100. The second part covers the late Middle Ages, AD 1100–1500. The conventional divisions of Irish medieval history of Ireland at AD 800 or 1171 have been avoided. These watersheds are linked to external influences – the arrival of the vikings, and the English invasion. The divisions are to some extent linguistic. For example, Irish history before AD 1171 is often linked with Celtic Studies departments, with sources being predominantly in Irish. Irish history after this period is commonly taught within History departments, with a focus on texts in Latin, French and English. A chronological framework based on externally driven change is not unusual in the historiography of islands. However, it risks obscuring internal change and the roles of indigenous people in shaping events. It can also lead to an overselective use of sources. For example, until the late twentieth century, Gaelic sources were relatively neglected

---

[1] There is debate among scholars as to whether the term 'viking' should have a lower or upper case 'v' as it originally describes an activity rather than an ethnic group.

by scholars in the study of late medieval Irish history. The traditional division of Irish history into the years before and after 800 or 1171 also favours the analysis of history in terms of natives and colonists. We may do a disservice to historical figures if we judge them simply as foreigners or natives, without trying to empathise with the values of their times. One of the aims in this book has been to avoid the analysis of Irish history as a history of invasions and to show something of the internal dynamism and adaptability of Irish society across the centuries.

The themes of landscape and economy, society, politics, religion and the arts are covered in separate chapters for the early and later Middle Ages. Conventional wisdom states that events are shaped by kings and battles. However, visionaries, whether we agree with them or not, have often played a bigger role. This is true of St Patrick in the fifth century and St Malachy in the twelfth century, to name but two examples. Political narrative has a place in this book, but it is not the dominant element; religious matters are given equal attention, and chapters on art provide insight into the mental and cultural world of the Middle Ages. Leaders and visionaries can only succeed if they are in tune with the society that underpins their status. History is also determined by the way that the mass of people interconnected with each other and with their environment and how they sustained themselves through daily toil. To reflect these realities; sections on society, and on landscape and economy are included in this book. While this survey volume errs on the side of breadth rather than depth, I hope readers will use this overview as a portal to further reading and a greater understanding of the rich field of Irish medieval history.

GEOGRAPHY

Landscape has a continuous influence over historical events. Ireland has had a disproportionate impact on world history and culture given its relatively small size. The maximum length of the island from Malin Head to Cape Clear is 280 miles, and its maximum width from Belmullet in Mayo to Ards in County Down is 190 miles. There is a discontinuous rim of higher land around the Irish coasts and relatively isolated mountain ranges in the interior where older, harder rock types protrude through layers of more recently deposited limestone. The main geographical features of Ireland were sculpted by glaciers in successive Ice Ages, the last of which ended 14,000 years ago. The advancing and retreating ice scoured the landscape north of a line running from County Clare to Wexford, leaving a large area of lowland. As glaciers melted, the loose materials that they bore – clays, loams, sands and gravels – were deposited unevenly across central Ireland. This created a series of ridges or eskers running west to east across the central and west midlands. Farther north, the melting ice retreated more rapidly, leaving soil deposits in egg-shaped ridges called drumlins in a belt of territory stretching from County Down to the islands of Clew Bay in County Mayo.

The widest expanse of good agricultural land in Ireland lies between Dublin and Dundalk and stretches as far as the Shannon. This area was accessible from the east through a breach in the highland rim of Ireland between the mountains of Leinster and Mourne. The wealth and accessibility of this zone made it the focus of interest for foreign traders and settlers in the Middle Ages. In the west, the rim of high land is broken by the bays of Galway, Donegal and Clew Bay, as well as the wide estuary of the River Shannon that drains much of the central plain of Ireland. The land here is liable to flooding, and the central lowlands are dotted with lakes and bogs. Beyond the east Midlands, good agricultural lands are found in several areas, including the Golden Vale of North Tipperary and County Limerick in the southwest and the Lagan Valley in the northeast. The northeast region is more mountainous but better drained, with much of the rainfall collecting in Ireland's biggest lake, Lough Neagh. The river valleys of this area drain into the seas adjoining north Britain. The distance from Fair Head in County Antrim to the Kintyre peninsula in Scotland is a mere 13 miles. The geographical proximity of Scotland and the orientation of river valleys encouraged contact and historical connections between northern Britain and Ireland.

Ireland is famous for its humid and mild climate. Its proximity to the Gulf Stream keeps the island more temperate than some other lands at the same latitude. The prevailing winds blow from west to east, bringing warm, damp air from the Atlantic, and leaving the east of Ireland drier and less prone to storms. The climate suits moisture-loving plants and grasses (the abundant greenery has given rise to Ireland's nickname 'the Emerald Isle'). However, the same conditions restrict the range of crops that can be cultivated. Much of Ireland is better suited to grazing than to arable farming. When people first settled Ireland around 7000 BC, most of Ireland was covered with trees. The introduction of farming and the spread of blanket bog, a type of peatland, caused a decline in forest cover, but a major episode of tree clearance appears to coincide with the late Iron Age and early Christian period, and a further decline in woodlands is noted from the late twelfth century. Generally speaking the medieval landscape of Ireland was more thickly forested than today.

--------- Part I ---------

EARLY MEDIEVAL IRELAND AD 400–1100

——————— • ———————

I

IRELAND IN THE FIFTH CENTURY

•

The rhetoric of Ireland, particularly of western Ireland, as an archaic society shielded from foreign influence from the Iron Age until the modern era suited nineteenth-century nationalists and romantic thinkers who advocated the purity of Irish cultural identity. It also suited British imperialists who regarded Gaelic society as primitive. Popular presentations of a backward-looking 'Celtic' society often root themselves in the observation that Ireland lay beyond the boundaries of the Roman Empire. However, this perspective obscures the dynamism of Irish society at the eve of the Middle Ages and downplays the impact of the Roman Empire as a massive power bloc on Ireland's doorstep with which goods, ideas and concepts were exchanged. The decline of the Roman Empire and environmental changes in the fourth and fifth centuries brought instabilities and opportunities for people in Ireland. As a result, the fifth century can be characterised as a period of radical social, technological and religious change.

Ireland's contact with the Roman Empire began as early as the first century AD, as witnessed by archaeological finds of imported goods and references in Latin texts. According to the writer Tacitus, an exiled king from Ireland joined the retinue of the Roman general Agricola who campaigned in Britain.[1] In the second century a geographer working in Alexandria in Egypt, called Ptolemy, charted a recognisable outline of Ireland's coasts and the positions of major river

[1] Freeman, *Ireland and the classical world*, pp. 56–7; J. Cahill Wilson, *Late Iron Age*, p. 129.

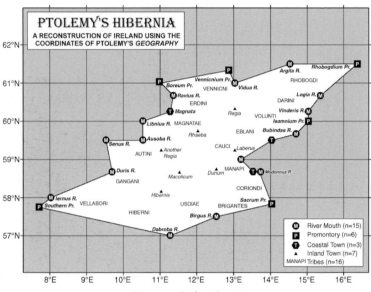

Figure 1.1 Ptolemy's map

mouths, promontories, settlements and islands (see Figure 1.1).[2] This shows that coastal Ireland was relatively well known to outsiders. The presence of a powerful and economically developed empire encouraged a flow of goods to and from the island. Ireland's early exports consisted primarily of raw materials, including hunting dogs, slaves, foodstuffs and perhaps copper.[3] Early imports comprised of manufactured goods including Roman coins, glassware, pottery (perhaps containing olive oil, wine and other foodstuffs) and jewellery. The deposition of Roman coins and jewellery at pagan ritual sites including Tara and Newgrange (Co. Meath) and accompanying furnished burials suggests that Roman exotica were highly valued in Irish society.[4] It may even hint at the imitation of Romano-British ritual practices. Access to Roman goods and culture may have enhanced the prestige of Irish leaders, creating a demand for imports and exchange.

The Irish economy changed significantly during the Roman era, partly in response to climatic change and in part through contacts

[2] Cahill Wilson, *Late Iron Age*, p. 20, cf. Charles-Edwards, *Early Christian Ireland*, p. 154.
[3] Cahill Wilson, *Late Iron Age*, pp. 7, 147, 176.
[4] Bhreathnach, *Ireland*, p. 155; Cahill Wilson, *Late Iron Age*, pp. 35, 39, 129–30, 175.

outside Ireland. Pollen records drawn from a range of archaeological sites indicate that agriculture was in decline from 200 BC–AD 200.[5] A handful of large hillforts flourished between the first century BC and the first century AD at Emain Macha (Navan fort, Co. Armagh), Dún Ailinne (Knockaulin, Co. Kildare), Cruachu (Rathcroghan, Co. Roscommon) and Tara (Co. Meath).[6] Their heyday corresponded chronologically with large-scale nucleated settlements or oppida in northern Europe. While Ireland did not boast large centres of population, the emergence of royal centres suggests that a process of political centralisation was taking place. The Iron Age royal sites are often represented as pagan provincial capitals. It is difficult to surmise too much in the absence of written evidence, but what is clear is that these sites had lost much of their practical status by the fifth century. Of the sixteen population groups named on Ptolemy's map in the second century, only six of these can be identified from early medieval records. While this might reflect problems in the transmission of names, it could also reflect fundamental changes in the political structures of Late Antique Ireland. As large power centres fell out of use, big political units may have fragmented. Certainly, by the time written records emerge in the sixth century, Ireland had a plethora of 150 or more petty kingdoms or *túatha*. These kingdoms tended to be focused around agricultural land, often having a plain (Old Irish *mag*) as their central focus.

From the third century, pollen diagrams record a spread in agriculture and woodland clearance across northern and eastern areas of Ireland. This development continued unabated until the sixth century.[7] Roman farming know-how and the voracious appetite of the late empire for raw materials have been credited with encouraging this period of resource exploitation. New strains of cereal and breeds of livestock were introduced in this period, along with domesticated fowl. A shift in cattle rearing from beef to dairy production allowed an estimated sevenfold increase in calorific output of a herd, allowing greater surpluses of wealth to be generated.[8] From the fourth century, finds of Roman goods appear farther inland and along the western coasts of Ireland, implying an expansion in trade and wider access to

---

[5] Cahill Wilson, *Late Iron Age*, p. 6.
[6] Charles-Edwards, *Early Christian Ireland*, p. 146.
[7] Edwards, 'Archaeology', p. 264.
[8] Halpin and Newman, *Ireland*, p. 2; McCormick, 'Cows', pp. 35–6.

imported exotica.[9] It appears that the island was drawn increasingly within the orbit of the European trading economy.

From the late fourth century, the Roman Empire was in crisis. At this time of instability, a number of Irishmen joined the imperial armies, while others became pirates and warriors who plundered the British coasts.[10] A series of forts were constructed around the western and southern coasts of Britain, which shows growing insecurity. In AD 367, Irish raiders joined Picts and Saxons in a 'barbarian conspiracy' that was aided by a revolt of the Roman garrison stationed on Hadrian's Wall, and the northern parts of Roman Britain were overwhelmed. A Roman relief force successfully defended Britain, but smaller-scale raiding continued. Two silver hoards dating from these troubled times have been recovered from Ireland.[11] The hoard from Balline (Co. Limerick) contains three pieces of silver plate, two complete ingots and parts of two more.[12] The hoard from Ballinrees (Co. Derry) was deposited around AD 425 and contains roughly 1,500 roman coins, 200 ounces of silver ingots, and fine dining ware. Archaeologists have debated whether these large accumulations of silver represent imperial pay for military services or peacekeeping or whether the hoards represent stolen booty.[13] The official stamps found on silver ingots from both hoards favour the view that they were acquired legitimately, but the question remains open.[14] Further evidence of military involvement in Britain, whether in support of or against the empire, can be seen in small items of military paraphernalia found in Ireland dating from the fourth and fifth centuries.[15]

There is direct evidence of Irish activity abroad through the medium of the written word. A Latin panegyric composed for the Roman general Stilicho around the turn of the fifth century recounts that all Ireland was hostile to Britain and 'the sea foamed to the beat of hostile oars'.[16] However, there were also peaceful Irish migrants. In the fifth century an Irishman, named Cunorix, died at Wroxeter

[9] Bateson, 'Roman material', p. 37; Cahill Wilson, *Late Iron Age*, p. 24.

[10] Rance, 'Attacotti'. It should be noted that Rance's theory that the term 'Attacotti' derives from 'aithechthuatha' is linguistically flawed.

[11] Freeman, *Ireland and the classical world*, pp. 9–10.

[12] Ó Ríordáin, 'Roman material in Ireland', p. 45.

[13] Raftery, 'Iron Age Ireland', p. 179.

[14] Cahill Wilson, *Late Iron Age*, p. 176; Swift, *Ogam stones*, p. 5.

[15] Cahill Wilson, *Late Iron Age*, pp. 35, 176.

[16] Freeman, *Ireland and the classical world*, p. 105.

(in Shropshire by the River Severn), and his name was commemorated in Latin script on a reused block of stone.[17] In the same period
a Christian memorial was raised in Trier (Germany) by the wife of
Scottus, a name which in the early Middle Ages referred to Gaelic
speakers from Ireland and Scotland.[18] These inscriptions suggest that
Irish migrants adopted some of the cultural mores and religious values of the late empire.

The practice of raising stones for named individuals was used
throughout the Roman Empire. It was adopted by neighbouring
peoples who developed their own scripts for this purpose; runes in
Scandinavia, and ogam in Ireland and Northern Britain.[19] The ogam
cipher, which was developed by the fourth century, is a series of dots
and dashes that could be carved along the sharp edge of a monument
or on an incised line (see Figure 1.2). This script was not a simple derivative of the Latin alphabet, but developed from knowledge
of how Latin grammarians analysed the sounds of language.[20] Thus
the development of ogam indicates thoroughgoing contact with the
Roman world. An intriguing example is the fourth- or fifth-century
ogam inscription of an Irishman 'Tebicatus' has been found on a col-
umn from a Roman building in Silchester (Hampshire). It is not clear
if the inscription was added in situ as graffiti or as a mark of ownership,
or whether the stone had been removed from its original context and
reused as a funerary monument.[21] It does, however, provide evidence
of assimilation between Irish and Roman culture.

Ogam monuments were raised in Ireland and western Britain from
the late fourth to the seventh centuries. There are around 300 in Ireland, most of which are located in the southwestern counties of Kerry,
Cork and Waterford. Around forty-five ogam inscriptions have been
recovered in western Britain (clustering in south Wales, Cornwall
and the Isle of Man) and twenty-seven have been found in Pictish
Scotland.[22] While the inscriptions in Pictland may date after the sixth
century, those in Wales, Cornwall and the Isle of Man witness Irish
migration to Britain in the fifth and sixth centuries.[23] The ruling line
of Dyfed in south Wales proudly claimed its Irish roots in the early
Middle Ages and the appearance of bilingual inscriptions in Latin and

[17] Wright and Jackson, 'A late inscription from Wroxeter'. [18] Swift, *Ogam*, p. 121.
[19] Charles-Edwards, *Early Christian Ireland*, p. 173. [20] Ibid., pp. 165–6.
[21] Fulford *et al.*, 'An early date for Ogham'. [22] McManus, *Guide to Ogam*, p. 44.
[23] For the argument that Dál Riata was not settled from Ireland in this period, see
Campbell, 'Were the Scots Irish?'

Figure 1.2 Ogam stone at Kilmalkedar, Co. Kerry

Irish show the area to be a melting pot of Roman, British and Irish cultures.[24]

This raises questions regarding the circumstances that caused people to migrate across the Irish Sea. It is tempting to make comparisons

[24] Charles-Edwards, *Early Christian Ireland*, pp. 171–2; Mytum, *Origins*, pp. 163–4; Rance, 'Attacotti', p. 252.

with later medieval migratory processes, including the Viking Age. The Viking Age took place following increased contacts between Scandinavia and more developed European trading economies, at a time of climatic improvement when surpluses in wealth could be generated. These factors encouraged competition among the elites for land and imported luxuries, and expeditions abroad provided a means to acquire both. Were the same processes happening in late fourth- and fifth-century Ireland?

Archaeological and linguistic evidence demonstrate that dramatic changes were taking place in Irish society in the fourth and fifth centuries. Pressure on land ownership may have prompted the emergence of enclosed settlement forms that could display possession of territory, exclusivity and status.[25] Ogam stones were also erected as territorial markers and to commemorate high-status individuals.[26] They commonly recorded a masculine personal name, a male ancestor (with the formula *macci* 'son of' or *avi* 'grandson/descendant of'), and often a group name.[27] The erection of the stones hints at the growing importance of lineages and individual landholders in Irish society.

The oldest surviving population-group names in Ireland tended to be plural or collective names. These might be linked with an animal eponym, occupation or deity. In the fifth century, population-group names beginning with *Cénel* 'kindred of' or *Uí* (a later form of *avi*) 'grandson/descendant of' come to light.[28] This is suggestive of an emergent trend towards territorially and dynastically based power that would continue in later centuries. This change corresponded with a decreasing emphasis on female eponyms from the fifth century. It may be that society in the fifth century was becoming more patriarchal, patrilineal and competitive.

Status was displayed in late fifth-century Ireland partly through access to prestige goods from abroad. Pottery imports came from around the Mediterranean, mainly comprising amphorae that may have carried olive oil, as well as red slipware dining ware. The distribution of these finds naturally focused along the southern and eastern seaways. One of the biggest assemblages of imported pottery from the

---

[25] O'Sullivan *et al.*, *Early medieval Ireland*, p. 65, fig. 3.7.
[26] Charles-Edwards, *Early Christian Ireland*, p. 175; Bhreathnach, *Ireland*, p. 42.
[27] McManus, *Guide to ogam*, pp. 118–20; Charles-Edwards, *Early Christian Ireland*, pp. 97–8.
[28] Mac Neill, 'Early Irish population groups', pp. 60–86.

late fifth century was recovered from a multivallate ringfort at Gar-ranes (Co. Cork), along with evidence of glass imports and skilled craftwork.[29] The ringfort dwellers' importance was displayed through the complexity of their fort, their access to imported items, their control over the production of luxury items, and perhaps the ogam stone located nearby that might commemorate a family member.[30] The finds indicate that the occupants of Garranes enjoyed links with trading communities outside Ireland. More broadly the enthusiasm for imported goods in Ireland led to fashions from the Roman world being imitated and blended with native styles. From the fifth century the influence of Late Antique jewellery, weapons and dining ware can be seen on items made in Ireland.[31]

Among the high-status imports that came to Irish shores in the fifth century were British slaves. They may have been sought out for menial agricultural jobs to improve the agricultural surpluses that funded the lifestyles of the elite. They may also have been valued for their association with Roman culture. Slaves could bring know-how of Roman agricultural and commercial practices and the technology of writing to Ireland.[32] Some of the early Latin loanwords in the Irish language appear to reflect a British pronunciation of Latin. British slaves may have been one medium of transfer of these words, along with Irish travellers to Britain and missionaries.[33] Among the ideas that British slaves helped foster in Ireland was the Christian faith. The Roman Empire adopted Christianity as its official religion in AD 314, and although many other religions continued to coexist within its boundaries, Christianity seems to have been well established among the Romano-British by the fifth century.

The most famous British slave who was transported to Ireland was St Patrick. We are lucky to have two written works by St Patrick. Patrick's 'Confession' outlines his experiences and justifies his missionary work in Ireland. His 'Letter to Coroticus' chastises a British warlord who had seized some of Patrick's recent converts. Patrick's raw emotional narratives reflect upon the unstable circumstances of

---

[29] Bennett, *Excavations 1990*, p. 163; Ó Ríordáin, 'Excavation of a large earthen ring-fort at Garranes'.

[30] Cahill Wilson, *Late Iron Age*, p. 146, cf. Bhreathnach, *Ireland*, p. 163.

[31] Halpin and Newman, *Ireland: an archaeological guide*, p. 22; Earwood, 'Turned wooden vessels', pp. 155–6.

[32] For early finds associated with literacy, see Cahill Wilson, *Late Iron Age*, pp. 180–1.

[33] Freeman, *Ireland and the classical world*, p. 14.

the fifth century. He enumerates himself as one of 'thousands' who were taken into captivity from Britain to Ireland. However, his 'Letter to Coroticus' also demonstrates that British warlords were raiding for slaves in Ireland to take back to Britain. St Patrick was raised as a Christian in a small country estate, somewhere in western Britain. He was snatched as an adolescent and set to work in Ireland as a shepherd, an occupation that gave Patrick time to reflect on his depressed circumstances. Patrick chose to take solace in religion, praying fervently on a daily basis. His renewed faith gave him the courage to escape Ireland, but he soon returned in order to spread the message of Christianity to the pagan Irish. The date and location of Patrick's mission is much debated, but it is known from other sources that he was not the first Christian to enter Ireland.

In AD 431, a bishop called Palladius was sent by Pope Celestine 'to the Irish believing in Christ'.[34] This testifies to the existence of a Christian community in contact with Continental Europe. Palladius was probably the deacon of the same name who had encouraged the pope to send Bishop Germanus of Auxerre to Britain two years before to combat a heresy instigated by a scholar called Pelagius. Pelagius's views on original sin and whether people were predestined to heaven or hell conflicted with those of St Augustine of Hippo. Pelagius argued that divine grace was not necessary to fulfil God's commands, but that individuals had free will to obey the law of God. These views were condemned as heretical at the Synod of Carthage in AD 418. Palladius's appointment to Ireland might have reflected not only the growth in the size of the Christian community (whether of migrants or Irish converts). but also reflect concerns that the Pelagian heresy might spread from Britain to Ireland. There are traditions of pre-Patrician saints in both Munster and Leinster, although there is little credible evidence to support these claims. Nevertheless, Palladiusis seems to have been active in southern Ireland in areas that had direct links to Continental Europe and Britain.[35]

The 'Chronicle of Prosper of Aquitaine' provides a fixed date, 431, for Palladius's arrival in Ireland as a high-profile papal appointment. Scholars are in the dark, however, as to when Patrick arrived with a shipload of disconsolate slaves. Irish chronicles (that are not

[34] Prosper, *Chronicon, s.a.* 431.
[35] Charles-Edwards, *Early Christian Ireland*, p. 205; Hughes, 'Church in Irish society', p. 303.

contemporary accounts of the fifth century) provide a range of dates for his death, including 457, 461 and 493. The latest date may be the most reliable on text-historical grounds, but that does not mean it is accurate.[36] It looks as if attempts were made by chroniclers in the seventh century or later to push back the dates of Patrick's life so that he could claim to be the first successful apostle to Ireland, rather than Palladius, who became increasingly marginalised in medieval accounts of the conversion of Ireland.[37] Patrick's mission is usually linked with Armagh and Downpatrick in medieval hagiography. Only one place is mentioned in Patrick's 'Confession', and that is *silva vocluti quae est prope mare occidentale* or 'the wood of Fochloth which is near the western sea'. This wood has been identified as near Killala (Co. Mayo).[38] Patrick does not mention other Christian communities in Ireland, though he seems to have deliberately ventured into remote areas where his message might be unwelcome. Patrick reports the dangers that he faced including two brief periods of captivity. Despite these setbacks, he claimed to have converted thousands.

The reasons for St Patrick's success need to be addressed. Most of us have encountered street preachers and door-to-door proselytisers who are routinely shunned, so why did people listen to Patrick? Presumably he had personal charisma, but his message must have fitted the spirit of the times. The emphasis of Christianity on individual salvation appealed to different groups. Patrick ranked slaves among his converts and also nobles, in particular he gives an account of a noblewoman who rejected marriage in to devote her life to God. Christianity may have appealed to people who were without power, who suffered as Patrick 'like a stone lying deep in the mud', who had little investment in the existing religious system and may have gained a sense of self-worth through faith in a God who valued them individually. Patrick believed God 'pulled me up and lifted me out' from his misery.[39] Christianity could also appeal to people at the top of the social hierarchy, because it had prestigious connotations of *romanitas* and external links at a time when elites sought out material goods, technological know-how and trading contacts across the sea to boost their status.[40] Christianity had a clear hierarchy of authority, but it also

---

[36] Dumville *et al., Saint Patrick*, pp. 29–36.

[37] Hughes, 'Church in Irish society', pp. 306–7.

[38] Charles-Edwards, *Early Christian Ireland*, p. 217; Thomas, *Christianity in Roman Britain*, p. 310.

[39] Patrick, *Confessio*, ed. Bieler, §12.   [40] Mytum, *Origins*, pp. 44–5.

preached obedience to secular rulers. It may have seemed easier for Irish kings to oversee an emerging Christian hierarchy than to deal with druidic elites who wielded power in Iron Age Ireland. Above all, fifth-century Ireland witnessed radical change, and unsettled times may have encouraged people to innovate in social and cultural practices and to invest hope in a set of religious ideas that were growing in influence across neighbouring countries.

The conversion of Ireland did not happen within a few years or decades, but represented a shift in worldview, social conventions and beliefs that took centuries to embed. It is only in the seventh century that evidence emerges of a comprehensive ecclesiastical hierarchy in Ireland that was powerful enough to deny status to pagan ritualists.[41] The first generations of converts must have faced challenges in organising places of worship. Converts of higher status, such as the sons and daughters of lesser kings referred to by St Patrick, may have established churches near their homes. Those who chose to live a celibate life may have formed small communities based on the lives of the desert fathers, similar to those that flourished in contemporary Gaul and Italy.[42] The earliest phase of church building in Ireland is thought to be represented by place names with *domnach* (from Latin *dominicum*) that focus in the east, midlands and north of Ireland.[43] However, the fourth- and early fifth-century dates assigned to these churches should be questioned, as the name form appeared to have continued in use later.[44]

The new concepts and practices of Christianity necessitated a flow of vocabulary from Latin into Irish to describe them. Many of the fifth century loanwords into Irish were imported from a British dialect of Latin. The forms and practices of early church sites in the north, east and midlands of Ireland may have been influenced by British models.[45] Churches along the southern and western coasts may have also drawn inspiration from the continent. At Caherlehillan (Co. Kerry) a small wooden church was built in the late fifth or early sixth century overlooking the sea. The site included imported pottery, and a table altar with a drain feature for ritual ablutions after mass, which hint at links with the northwestern coasts of the Mediterranean.[46]

---

[41] See the later discussion.   [42] Breathnach, *Ireland*, p. 171.
[43] Ibid., pp. 168–70.
[44] Stancliffe, 'Religion and society', pp. 403–4; Flanagan, 'Summary'.
[45] Charles-Edwards, *Early Christian Ireland*, p. 184.
[46] Sheehan, 'A Peacock's Tale', pp. 196–7.

Later features added to the site at Caherlehillan indicate that links across the Celtic Sea continued into the eighth century. The gradual process of Christianisation can be seen in the landscape of Ireland through the construction of churches, shifts in burial practices, the erection of cross-inscribed stones, and the use of wells for baptism.[47]

Christianity was part of a broader pattern of changes in fifth century. One of the major shifts that is often linked with the emergence of Christianity in Ireland was the rise of a political dynasty called Uí Néill, who would remain significant players in Irish politics throughout the Middle Ages. In early laws, Ireland was seen to be divided into multiple small kingdoms or *túatha*. The existence of these petty kingships in the fifth century is demonstrated in St Patrick's 'Confession' as he describes travelling the countryside with the sons of kings and refers to the conversion of many peoples.[48] Ogam inscriptions witness localised population groups. By the seventh century a hierarchy of kings is recorded: kings of *túatha* recognised the authority of a local over-king, who in turn recognised the power of a provincial ruler.

The term for provinces is *coiceda* or 'fifths', suggesting that Ireland was divided at an early stage into five units.[49] The names of provinces may have developed at different times. They were either plural names referring to the inhabitants (*Laigin* = the people of Leinster; *Ulaid* = the people of Ulster; *Connachta* = the people of Connacht) or represent regional names (*Mumu* = Munster; *Mide* = Meath 'midlands'). *Mide* comprised the most fertile and accessible lands of Ireland, which were hotly contested in the fifth and sixth centuries. Initially rulers from Leinster and Ulster[50] contended over the area. However, in the fifth century a new dynastic group, Uí Néill, appear to have expanded their influence east from Connacht to bid for control in the region.

The origins of Uí Néill are shrouded in myth. Later tales of the dynastic founder Niall of the Nine Hostages and his sons cannot be taken at face value. The claim that the sons of Niall were contemporaries of St Patrick may have some basis. However, the later stories that their personal dealings with the saint determined the success or failure of their descendents bear the hallmark of fiction. These legends

---

[47] Moss, ed. *Art*, pp. 9–11; Bhreathnach, *Ireland*, pp. 135–; O'Brien, 'Pagan or Christian?'
[48] Charles-Edwards, *Early Christian Ireland*, pp. 188–89.
[49] Byrne, 'Tribes and tribalism', p. 135.
[50] Charles-Edwards, *Early Christian Ireland*, pp. 453–4.

recorded from the seventh century elevated the status of St Patrick and bound sections of Uí Néill to the cult of the saint. When Uí Néill emerge into historical light in the sixth century, they were aggressively expanding their power base in the east midlands and northwest of Ireland.[51] The rise of this ambitious group may reflect a more general shift of power into the hands of royal dynasties in fifth- and sixth-century Ireland.

The rise of Uí Néill marks a shift in the politics of northern and midland Ireland. This appears to have been roughly contemporary with political upheaval in southwestern Ireland. On Ptolemy's map, a group called 'Iverni' occupy Munster; this name was rendered as 'Érainn' in the early Middle Ages. Many early population groups in Munster claimed to be affiliated with them, including Corcu Loígde and Múscraige (the power of these two groups was later identified with parts of Co. Cork and Co. Tipperary).[52] In the fifth and sixth centuries, groups called Eóganachta emerged, who claimed descent from a royal ancestor Eógan. They established several branches that came to dominate other groups in the province of Munster until the tenth century. The imposing Rock of Cashel (Co. Tipperary) was their most important royal site. Its name was derived from Latin word *castellum* ('fortress'), which further reveals the changing nature of political power in Ireland around the fifth century.[53]

The notion that early Irish society was archaic and immutable was a fiction peddled from the Middle Ages onwards to suit the interests of different elites. It appears that significant innovations in Irish society, culture, religion and politics were set in train from the third century in response to climatic change and contacts with the Roman Empire. These changes included growing overseas trade, increased cultivation of land and innovations in farming that fostered population growth and the accumulation of wealth. Society placed increasing worth on the territorialisation of power and the leadership of individuals and their dynasties. Growing competition for lands and status encouraged raids and migration into Britain. It also fuelled expressions of power within Ireland through the construction of ringforts, the erection of ogam monuments and the acquisition of prestige goods from abroad.

[51] *AU, s.aa.* 516, 563; cf. Lacey, *Cenél Conaill*, p. 320.

[52] O'Rahilly, 'Origin of the names Érainn and Ériu', pp. 7–9. Cf. McManus, *Guide to ogam*, pp. 73–5.

[53] Charles-Edwards, *Early Christian Ireland*, p. 146.

More Irish people came into contact with Christianity, and the religion was embraced by many. The message and prestigious associations of Christianity may have been appealing in times of rapid social, economic and political change. The political dynamism of fifth-century Ireland is reflected in the rise of new political dynasties including Uí Néill and Eóganachta. The impact of these changes continued through the early medieval period. The themes from this chapter will be pursued in the analyses of early medieval Ireland that follow.

2

LAND USE AND ECONOMY AD 500–1100

—————— • ——————

The student of early medieval Ireland is lucky to have abundant information in early written sources and archaeology. Medieval chronicles are perhaps the best-known historical source from the early Middle Ages. Their focus is on political events, but they also reflect the economic concerns of contemporary society. Law texts surviving from the seventh and eighth centuries reveal much about the Irish landscape and economy, although their interests are arguably skewed towards the concerns of the elite. Saints Lives from the early Middle Ages cast incidental light on the day-to-day economic activities aside from the religious agenda of these writings. Ireland also has a very rich archaeological landscape. The building boom in Ireland that lasted from the 1990s until 2008 led to a massive increase in the number of excavations. Although many sites await publication and further analysis, knowledge on the early Irish economy has grown enormously over the last three decades.

Ireland in the early Middle Ages was not simply a land of self-sufficient farmers.[1] There were social and economic forces that generated surpluses, and there was a need for craftsmen who could produce items for everyday utility with greater efficiency and quality than could non-specialists. There was internal trade for obtaining goods that were bountiful in some areas and lacking in others. There was also a desire for luxuries that stimulated trade across long distances. New scientific techniques in archaeology have revealed that

---

[1] Kerr *et al.*, *Economy*, p. 69.

long-distance trade and travel were more common than scholars have tended to assume. From the ninth to the eleventh centuries, economic change is evident in the deposition of hoarded silver and from the development of towns. By AD 1000, coins were being minted in Dublin, and Irish kings were seeking ways to exploit the wealth of coastal towns and their kingdoms to fund their political ambitions. Ireland was integrated within a European trading economy but during the eleventh century, socioeconomic power shifted away from the Viking Age trading networks of the North Atlantic and Irish Sea towards the coasts of France and southern England. By the twelfth century, Ireland came to be regarded as marginal and underdeveloped by its neighbours.

CLIMATE, FAMINE AND DISEASE

A rich seam of data on weather events is provided by Irish chronicles, which can be compared with the record of tree-ring growth (dendrochronology) as well as records from neighbouring lands, such as Greenlandic ice cores. This evidence of climatic change can be compared with episodes of environmental crisis, but there is no simple pattern. Land use, small-scale fluctuations in weather and regional microclimates may qualify any generalisations.[2] Episodes of colder weather in Ireland have been identified circa AD 540, 690 and 780. These can be linked to occurrences of famine and periods of malnutrition and the consequent spread of epidemics as the population's immunity declined.[3] The Justinian plague of c. 540 affected large swathes of Europe. A series of plagues struck Ireland in the late seventh century, and a famine that lasted three years from AD 700 was said to be so bad that 'man ate man'. Further episodes of famine, pulmonary disease and 'bloody-flux' (a dysentery-like disease that may be linked to malnutrition and suppressed immunity) were recorded in the closing decades of the eighth century.[4] The late eighth century also witnessed a period of harsher winters and wetter summers.[5]

---

[2] Ludlow *et al.*, 'Medieval Irish chronicles'.

[3] Thurston and Plunkett, 'Dynamic sociology', p. 179; Baillie, 'Proposed re-dating'.

[4] Irish chronicles record famines in 538–9, 699–703, 778–9, 793, and 799 and epidemics in 545, 550, 554, 556, 664, 683, 684, 770, 773, 774, 777, 778, 783, and 786. See Charles-Edwards, trans., *The Chronicle of Ireland*.

[5] Kerr *et al.*, 'Making hay', p. 2871.

Throughout the Middle Ages, the farming economy in Ireland was a mix of crop growing and liverstock rearing. An important shift appears to have occurred in eighth-century Ireland away from heavy dependence on dairy cattle towards more grain production. This development has been attributed to various factors, from a climatic downturn that made over-wintering of cattle more diffi-cult, to changing political dynamics towards more centralised power that encouraged the production of storable agricultural surpluses and made the control of land (rather than cattle) more desirable.[6] From the ninth to the twelfth centuries there was a trend towards higher annual temperatures. The term 'Medieval Warm Period' is often used to describe this phenomenon. However, its impact varied over time and place, and the label obscures the harsh realities that shorter peri-ods of climatic decline could bring. For example, poor harvests in the year 963 were so extreme that some fathers felt forced to sell their children to buy food.[7] By the late eleventh century, Irish chronicles show greater concern in charting the impact of weather events on arable crops. This suggests greater dependence on grain cultivation and heightened concerns around food security.[8] Catastrophes were also linked to supernatural forces. Under the year 1084, the 'Annals of Tigernach' reports a plague wrought by three battalions of demons 'as high as the clouds of heaven'.[9] Bad weather in the years 1093–5 led to famine and pestilence across parts of Germany, France and the Low Countries and is thought to have contributed to the Crusad-ing movement.[10] In Ireland in the year 1095, the 'Annals of Inisfallen' record, 'Snow and heavy frost so that the rivers and principal lakes of Ireland were frozen, and a great loss of cattle in this year . . . A great mortality of the men of Ireland, so that it is impossible to enumer-ate all the people that died'.[11] These events may have contributed to apocalyptic thinking in Ireland.[12] The king and the bishop of Dublin were among those who perished, which suggests the greater risk of epidemic spreading in growing centres of population.

SETTLEMENT PATTERNS

The early medieval period witnessed dynamic changes in human set-tlement in Ireland. The upswing in farming activity at the end of the

---

[6] Thurston and Plunkett, 'Dynamic', p. 181.   [7] *AFM, s.a.* 963.
[8] Lyons, 'Weather', p. 38.   [9] AT, *s.a.* 1084.   [10] Slavin, 'Crusaders in crisis'.
[11] AI, *s.a.* 1095.   [12] O'Leary, 'Mog Ruith'.

Figure 2.1 View of a ringfort (by Philip Armstrong)

Roman period was associated with population growth and a building boom, as represented in a wide variety of archaeological features. The most popular and recognisable archaeological feature in the Irish landscape is the ringfort (see Figure 2.1). This label describes a wide range of enclosure forms, and around 45,000 sites have been identified in Ireland. The most common form is an area with an internal diameter of 20–44 metres encircled by an earthen bank with an opening.[13] Stone-walled enclosures were more common in the rocky areas of western Ireland. These enclosures were typically domestic in nature, including houses, farm buildings, pens, areas of craft activity or food processing, and rubbish dumps. Around farmsteads would be enclosed areas for grazing and cultivation. Ringforts are often dispersed rather than clustered in their distribution, with a preference for location on well-drained slopes. A minority of ringforts, roughly one in five, had a more complex construction of two or three rings of defence. It is usually assumed that these marked the homesteads of

[13] Stout, *Irish ringfort*, p. 53.

the elite.[14] Social hierarchy is also hinted at by the increased density of ringforts around some important sites.

Only a small percentage of ringforts have been excavated and dated, but the main period of their construction seems to have been from the sixth to the ninth centuries. Their numerical abundance suggests that they represented the dwelling places of a wide cross-section of society ranging from kings to freemen with their dependants. Their generally dispersed distribution, however, does not mean that the occupants of these enclosures were isolated or entirely self-sufficient. The importance of kin land and co-operative farming in early Irish society would have fostered links between people in neighbouring sites. The enclosures provided a degree of privacy and protection for their inhabitants. However, the popular name 'ringfort' may be misleading as these enclosures seem primarily intended for dwellings rather than serving as fortresses.[15]

The use of ringforts in Ireland had a long history as some sites continued to be occupied into the Early Modern period. That does not mean that settlement forms did not change. For example, a new form of settlement enclosure with a raised interior was in use from the late seventh century. The change in morphology may be attributed to an accumulation of settlement debris (showing the continuity of occupation), although at some sites the platform was built on purpose. The distribution of these sites in good arable lands has been linked with the increasing emphasis on crop production from the eighth century.[16] Their popularity, however, declined in the eleventh century, along with other ringfort forms. Another type of enclosed settlement was the promontory fort. There are approximately 250 of these dotted around the Irish coast; some are prehistoric, but with demonstrable early medieval occupation. They served a defensive or trading function but their use appears to decline towards the end of the first millennium.[17]

Another settlement form associated with early medieval Ireland is the crannóg. This is an artificial or artificially enhanced island in a lake or loch that provided a building platform. Crannógs could be built from layers of brushwood, earth and stone reinforced with

---

[14] Stout, 'Early Christian Ireland', p 96.
[15] O'Sullivan *et al.*, *Early medieval dwellings*, p. 36.
[16] Kerr *et al.*, 'Making hay', pp. 280–1.
[17] Edwards, *Archaeology*, pp. 41–3; O'Sullivan *et al.*, *Early medieval dwellings*, p. 37.

timber revetments to prevent erosion. They vary in size, with most being quite small (8–25 m in diameter). At least 1,200 crannóg sites are known in Ireland.[18] Dendrochronological evidence suggests there was a boom in their construction in the late sixth and early seventh centuries. Like ringforts, some crannógs were occupied for a very long time up to the early modern period, although occupation might more often be seasonal or sporadic given the general challenges of accessibility to these islands.[19] The limited access to these sites may display their social exclusivity. Some crannógs such as that on Lough Ennell in County Westmeath, served as royal dwellings or homesteads of the rich. Some appear to have served as refuges from land-based royal centres and churches. Others are linked with craft activity where there may have been concerns to safeguard products and production techniques.[20]

Underground passages, which are called souterrains, have been found in association with many early medieval dwellings. Approximately 3,500 of these have been identified in Ireland. While they appear to have been constructed throughout the early Middle Ages, the focus of their use was the ninth to the twelfth century. They are often found in ringforts, sometimes as secondary additions, but they also appear in association with other settlement forms including churches and open sites.[21] Their distribution across Ireland is not even, but is focused on Connacht, the north coast of Ulster, the northeast of Mide, and the south and west of Munster. This may reflect regional building practices, but may also point to the utility of these features in certain areas. For example, in coastal areas they might provide cold storage for goods intended for trade, or they could function as defensive refuges in contested border areas. The potential role of these passages in defence is highlighted by inbuilt features at a number of sites, including sudden drops in floor or roof height, obstructions and hidden chambers that might wrong-foot or trick attackers trying to make their way inside in the dark.

It has been argued that there was a drift away from dispersed settlement enclosures from the beginning of the eleventh century. More people may have opted to live in open settlements clustered around high status sites. Unenclosed clusters of houses or huts that

---

[18] O'Sullivan *et al.*, *Early Medieval Ireland*, p. 58.
[19] Edwards, *Archaeology*, pp. 36–7.
[20] O'Sullivan *et al.*, *Early Medieval Ireland*, p. 62.   [21] Ibid., p. 107.

may have once characterised the homes of people of low status may have become a more common feature of Irish settlement. This change is linked with more centralised political authority and the reorganisation of the landscape into administrative units of the *baile* 'townland' and *trícha cét* 'thirty hundreds', which complemented an increasing focus on arable farming in the Irish economy.[22] The development of ecclesiastical settlements appears to mirror these trends. From the tenth century onwards, major church settlements grew in importance. In addition to the churches and their clerical communities, these sites also housed visitors (including pilgrims, travellers and penitents), craftspeople, tenants, and patrons. Some even seem to have served as regional capitals by their royal patrons.

There has been heated debate as to whether vikings were responsible for introducing urbanisation to Ireland. Discussion has often focused on whether settlement clusters associated with large ecclesiastical sites before the ninth century can be defined as urban in terms of population size and density, economic complexity and civic identity. A number of church sites, including at Armagh (Co. Armagh) and Clonmacnoise (Co. Offaly) have been described as 'proto-urban' before the arrival of vikings in Ireland.[23] Churches had a catchment area for religious services and owned lands that brought in a flow of tribute. Shrines also attracted visitors from farther afield, and churches were linked to other institutions in Ireland and abroad. These factors encouraged well-located settlements to become market centres. Nevertheless, it is debatable whether any of the larger ecclesiastical complexes can be regarded as towns before the tenth century.[24]

The earliest unambiguous evidence for a town has been provided by excavations in Dublin that signify that its urban character (in terms of population density, range of economic activities and distinct identity) had developed by the mid-tenth century. It would be mistaken, however, to conclude that vikings 'introduced towns' to Ireland; rather the economic and political development of major ports at Dublin, Waterford, Limerick, Cork and Wicklow resulted from cultural interaction. Both the descendants of viking settlers and the Irish were responsible for their success. The growth of these ports owes as much to the economic strength of their Irish hinterlands as

---

[22] O'Keeffe, 'Rural settlement', p. 147.   [23] Doherty, 'The monastic town'.
[24] Valante, 'Reassessing', p. 5

to the trading activities and strategies of viking settlers.[25] The development of coastal towns and international commerce may have had a knock-on effect, promoting trade, economic specialisation and clustered settlement in their hinterlands. The southeast and central eastern regions of Ireland afford the best evidence for a trend towards settlement nucleation and the declining use of ringforts from the eleventh century.[26]

Vikings are famed as the founders of some of the main coastal cities of Ireland, but they also established a number of camps at strategic coastal and riverine locations throughout Ireland. The term *longphort* ('ship camp') was employed from the 840s as a new word coined to describe viking camps. There were two spates in the foundation of these camps, in the 840s and the 920s, when viking leaders were seeking to establish wider spheres of influence in Ireland through military campaigns. Dublin was one of the earliest bases, founded in 841. Limerick is mentioned in 845 and Waterford in 860. Most of the camps were temporary, lasting from a few days to a few decades; they may have originally been founded for short-term ends, rather than as planned permanent settlements. These camps might assume a number of different forms responding to the needs of a particular campaign and the environment in which warriors and traders found themselves.[27] The meaning of the term *longphort* also broadened over time. By the late tenth century it might refer to 'any military encampment' without connotating links with Scandinavian culture.[28] The change in meaning may be explained by the adoption of viking-style military techniques by the Irish and by more extensive use of encampments in long-distance military campaigns. As with the towns, scholars may have been too keen to emphasise the segregation of Scandinavian and Gaelic populations in Ireland, both at urban centres and at smaller, more ephemeral settlements.

Small, unenclosed settlements dating from the early Middle Ages are hard to trace in the archaeological record, but they tend to be more visible in areas of western Ireland where construction in stone was favoured over wood due to the rocky landscape. The sites that have been studied reveal variety in their forms and dates. Perhaps the most visibly striking are *clochán* or bee-hive-shaped stone structures.

[25] Downham, 'Vikings' settlements'.
[26] O'Sullivan *et al.*, *Early Medieval Ireland*, pp. 78–9.
[27] Ó Floinn, 'Archaeology', p. 164.   [28] Doherty, 'Vikings in Ireland', p. 326.

Those at Barrees Valley and at Coarhabeg on Valentia Island, both in County Cork, have yielded radiocarbon dates between the sixth and eighth centuries. Unenclosed settlements could take a wide variety of forms. For example, these *clocháin* differ from the isolated roundhouse at Blackhills Lower (Co. Cavan) in the north midlands of Ireland. That site has provided a range of radiocarbon dates from the end of the ninth century to the end of the thirteenth century.[29] Unenclosed dwellings may therefore have been a continuous but less prominent feature within the early Irish landscape.

FARMING AND NATURAL RESOURCES

Farming was central to the Irish economy. There were some regional and chronological patterns in the proportion of arable and livestock farming, but the majority of farms combined both activities. In preindustrial societies, the exploitation of resources tends to be regulated by interpersonal relations as well as economic imperatives. A large body of early legal materials illuminates the systems of clientship that existed between lords and farmers. Their terms varied according to the status of the parties involved, but generally comprised loans of cattle and/or other valuables that were granted by a lord to a farmer for a fixed period in return for an annual food rent, manual labour and military service.[30] The bonds of clientship were a political currency, but they also had economic practicality. They provided a means of delegating cattle rearing for a fixed profit and minimised risk (by spreading resources and not hiring farmhands directly). It also prevented inbreeding within herds, making them less prone to genetic defects. The evidence of the laws focuses on the landholding elites in Ireland, but much labour must have been undertaken by landless people, who include the *bothach* and *fuidir* who received land in exchange for services, as well as hereditary serfs and slaves who sat at the bottom of the social hierarchy.[31]

Cattle figured prominently in the early Irish economy. In early Irish laws, the wealth and status of the elites were ranked according to the number of cattle they controlled. Social bonds and hierarchies were forged through exchanges of cattle and the Irish diet was heavily dependent on dairy products, while the consumption of beef was a

---

[29] O'Sullivan *et al.*, *Early Medieval Ireland*, pp. 115–16.
[30] Kelly, *Guide*, pp. 29–31.   [31] Kerr *et al.*, *Economy*, p. 7.

mark of status. The lush pastures and mild winters of Ireland were conducive to stock rearing, and cattle could be maintained through the winter without haymaking. Detailed accounts of Irish cattle are found in Irish law tracts, and archaeological data has been collected from various sites in Ireland. These suggest that while domesticated cattle had been present in Ireland since Neolithic times, new breeds were introduced before AD 1100 from Britain and Scandinavia.[32]

The importance of dairy cows is indicated by their use as a standard unit of currency in early medieval texts.[33] Cows are the most common species of livestock found in medieval bone assemblages.[34] In addition to dairy cows, bulls were reared as studs or for meat, and oxen were maintained as draft animals. The Irish emphasis on cattle differs from contemporary France or England where sheep tended to be the main domestic species.[35] From the tenth century, urbanisation encouraged an increase in meat production, and evidence from Armagh and Dublin suggests that cattle were brought into these settlements on hoof for slaughter. Their carcasses provided raw materials for leather and bone working as well as food.[36]

Pigs were also an important food source. The late eighth- or early ninth-century 'Tale of Mac Datho's Pig' tells of warriors contending at a feast for the most prestigious cut of a great roasted boar. Pig bones are fairly ubiquitous at medieval sites as they were economical to rear. Sows had to be kept near farms while their piglets were young, but they could be fed a wide variety of foods and then let loose to forage in the woods in late summer under the care of a swineherd. Pigs were often kept in towns, where they consumed waste food and turned it into a source of meat. Evidence from viking Dublin suggests that limited space led to greater consumption of piglets, rather than letting them grow to full size. Pigs may have been reared en masse on some farms in order to supply towns, as appears to have been the case at Castlefarm (Co. Meath) near Dublin.[37]

The bones of sheep and goats are hard to distinguish, but they appear as an important factor in early medieval bone assemblages after cattle and pigs. Sheep were primarily raised for wool, with male lambs being slaughtered for food. The breeds reared in medieval Ireland

---

[32] MacHugh *et al.*, 'Early medieval cattle'; Kelly, *Early Irish farming*, pp. 33–4.
[33] Kelly, *Early Irish farming*, p. 27.
[34] Edwards, 'Archaeology', p. 265; Kerr, McCormick and O' Sullivan, *Economy*, p. 13.
[35] Kerr *et al.*, *Economy*, p. 14.   [36] Edwards, 'Archaeology', p. 265.
[37] Kerr *et al.*, *Economy*, p. 14; Kelly, *Early Irish farming*, pp. 79–88.

were smaller and darker than modern commercial breeds, with white sheep being rare in Ireland until the later Middle Ages. Sheep were commercially useful not just for wool but also for sheepskins, horns and milk. They were able to graze on more marginal lands than cattle, which made them particularly important in the uplands and western fringes of Ireland.[38] For example, 40 per cent of the bones recovered from the early medieval stone fort at Dún Eóganachta, in the Aran Islands (Co. Galway) were from sheep.

Other livestock were valued within the farming economy. Hen eggs are frequently mentioned as part of the Irish diet in law texts, with goose eggs regarded as a delicacy.[39] Bee keeping was significant enough to warrant its own law text, *Bechbretha*, which has survived from the seventh century. Honey was valued as a storable food and sweetener that could be fermented to make mead or bragget (a drink made from honey and ale fermented together). Honey also has antibiotic properties that may help explain its prominence in medical texts. Beeswax was valued on church estates for the production of candles and writing tablets.[40]

Some categories of livestock were both economically useful and valued as prestige animals. Horse ownership was usually a badge of status. Textual references indicate that horses were mainly used for transport and racing, and there were religious injunctions against eating horsemeat.[41] Dogs guarded homes and livestock, and special types were bred for hunting or to be lapdogs. The domestic cat was probably introduced to Ireland in the Roman era corresponding with a period of growth in cereal production, as their main economic role was hunting vermin that could plunder grain supplies. However, cats may have also been reared for their pelts.[42]

The importance of cereals within the early medieval diet is often obscured because cattle ownership was associated with noble status.[43] Grains were used for bread, beer, porridge, gruel and animal feed. They had long been cultivated in Ireland, although an upsurge in farming activity is noted in the late Roman era. While most modern Europeans rely on bread wheat for a large component of their diet, this was not so in medieval Ireland. Oats were the most commonly cultivated grain, which suited the cool, damp Irish climate, followed

---

[38] Edwards, 'Archaeology', p. 266.   [39] Kelly, *Early Irish farming*, pp. 104–5.
[40] Ibid., pp. 109–14.   [41] Ibid., pp. 88–101.
[42] Bourke, 'Life in the sunny south-east'.   [43] Edwards, 'Archaeology', p. 265.

by barley and rye.[44] Wheat was regarded as a luxury, and it was best suited to cultivation in the east midlands. The association of wheat with elite consumption may be seen at Lagore royal crannóg (Co. Meath) where wheat straw was recovered from an early medieval context. Charred remains of wheat have also been found at more ordinary ringfort sites, whether produced for consumption by the inhabitants or for their lords.[45] Much time and effort on a medieval farm were devoted to cereal cultivation. It involved ploughing with oxen (often in plough teams that pooled resources of neighbouring farmers), harrowing, sowing, weeding, reaping and processing. Prosperous farmers might have been expected to have their own barn or storage for grain while lesser farmers owned shares in one.[46] The amount of grain production in Ireland was not constant over time, but tended to increase in significance from the late eighth century until the thirteenth century. These developments responded to climatic changes, population growth and socioeconomic demands to generate surpluses for trade and elite consumption.

The range of vegetables grown in Ireland increased through contact with the Roman Empire. Cabbage, peas, leeks and onions may have come to Ireland at that time.[47] Scandinavian settlers appear to have introduced an improved type of bean, giving rise to the Irish word *pónair* (loaned from Old Norse *baunir*).[48] Peas and beans could be cultivated on land that had previously grown grains as they helped restore soil fertility. The evidence that bean cultivation increased during the tenth and eleventh centuries may be indicative of crop rotation and intensification in agriculture. Other vegetables were grown in enclosed gardens near the farmhouse, and fruit trees were also maintained, whether in orchards or along field boundaries. The significance of apples as a food source is witnessed in many literary references from early medieval Ireland. In the tale *Echtra Chondla* ('The Adventure of Connla'), the love-struck hero lives for a month on nothing but a magic apple thrown to him by an otherworldly woman.[49] Crops were also grown for textile production, including flax for linen. Its cultivation appears to have been a male preserve, while processing it was a female one. The early Irish laws on

---

[44] Kelly, *Early Irish farming*, pp. 19–27.   [45] Edwards, 'Archaeology', p. 267.
[46] O'Sullivan *et al.*, *Early Medieval Ireland*, p. 199.
[47] Kelly, *Early Irish farming*, pp. 250–9; Mason, *Food culture in Great Britain*, p. 6.
[48] Greene, 'Influence', p. 79.   [49] Oskamp, ed., 'Echtra Condla'.

Irish divorce are careful in specifying the entitlements of husband and wife at different stages of flax cultivation, preparation and cloth manufacture.[50] Plant-based dyes were used to enhance the look and prestige of garments. Woad pods for the production of blue dye have been recovered from the raised rath at Deer Park Farms (Co. Antrim) and madder cultivation for red dye is witnessed at the ringfort at Boho (Co. Fermanagh).[51]

In addition to farming, the early medieval Irish were dependent on the exploitation of natural resources from the landscape. The use of different food sources provided a degree of food security, and foreign commentators tended to view Ireland as a land of natural abundance and good health.[52] The importance of woodland in providing foodstuffs in the form of wildlife, nuts, wild fruit and vegetables, and animal fodder was noted in early literature, alongside its provision of firewood and building and craft materials. The woodlands were protected from over-exploitation in the early Middle Ages by strict laws, which included the protection of certain tree species including oak, hazel and holly.[53] Deer hunting was a high-status activity that was a popular topic for depiction on early medieval crosses, usually involving men on horseback and dogs. Those of humbler rank collected the shed antlers of deer for craftworking. Other species that dwelt in the woods were useful for their meat or fur.

Coasts and rivers also provided food in the form of fish, shellfish and edible weeds. Early Irish laws show that by the eighth century, fishing rights were closely guarded and belonged to landowners whose properties adjoined river banks and coasts. Weirs were established in tidal waters and early medieval examples have been found on the Shannon estuary and Strangford Lough.[54] Shellfish was not highly prized in the Irish diet, but it could be essential in times of famine. Seabird eggs were systematically collected in some areas and seals and birds were also hunted for their meat.[55] At Dooey (Co. Donegal) and Iniskea (Co. Mayo) there is evidence that dog whelks were collected

---

[50] Kelly, *Farming*, pp. 269–70.

[51] Kerr *et al.*, *The economy of early medieval Ireland*, p. 31.

[52] Colgrave and Mynors, eds., *Bede: Ecclesiastical history*, I: 1; Forester, trans., *Giraldus Cambrensis: The topography of Ireland*, I: 5, 25.

[53] Ó Cróinín, *Early Medieval Ireland*, p. 86.

[54] O'Sullivan and Breen, *Maritime Ireland*, p. 132.

[55] Kelly, *Farming*, pp. 104, 282–300.

to produce an expensive purple dye for high-status clothing that could have been traded inland.[56]

The tools for farming required the extraction of metals and stone from land through mining and quarrying. These activities may have been seasonal rather than full-time occupations. Bog iron was relatively abundant and relatively easy to extract from the central lowlands, while small-scale quarrying and copper mining were well established along the east and south coasts. The importance of natural resources is illustrated in an eighth-century law text, *Tír Cumaile*. It primarily ranks land according to its farming potential, but also mentions factors such as access to an estuary, the proximity of woodland, or the presence of a mine for copper or iron.[57]

CRAFT AND INDUSTRY

The resources of the Irish landscape gave rise to many crafts and industries. The most important was food processing, for it allowed food to be stored and accumulated for trade, tribute, or as a safeguard against famine. The dampness of the Irish climate meant that grain often had to be dried before it could be stored, and drying also speeded the milling process. Small amounts of grain could be dried in a domestic setting over a fire or on heated stones. From the Late Iron Age drying kilns were used in Ireland for large quantities of corn. These varied in shape and size but basically consisted of a furnace and a flue that led to a drying chamber. Several hundred of these have been identified from the early Middle Ages, mostly in the grain-growing regions of Ireland. From the fifth century to the eighth century kilns became more abundant, which complements the pollen evidence in indicating increases in grain cultivation. From the eighth century, fewer kilns were used, but they were larger and more sophisticated. This hints that grain processing became more centralised in the eighth century, and landlords may have exerted more pressure on their tenants to transport corn to their kilns.[58] As milling technology and climatic conditions improved during the tenth and eleventh centuries, kilns may have also become less useful.

Before the sixth century, the only technology available in Ireland to turn grain into meal or flour was grinding by hand using quernstones.

[56] O'Sullivan and Breen, *Maritime Ireland*, p. 119.
[57] Mac Niocaill, ed., 'Tír Cumaile'.
[58] O'Sullivan *et al.*, *Early Medieval Ireland*, pp. 199–202.

Figure 2.2 Cutaway of the seventh-century mill, Nendrum, Co. Down
(by Philip Armstrong)

The most efficient method was to use a rotary quern that comprised
two small millstones with a handle and a central hole for pouring
in corn. This was time-consuming labour that was often allocated to
female slaves. The lowly connotations of the work are reflected in
medieval Irish satire, comparing a person to a worn-out lower quern
stone.[59] Hand milling continued through the Middle Ages, but from
the late sixth or early seventh century, watermills were introduced
to Ireland. The Church may have been an agent of change as the
Old Irish word for a mill, *muilenn*, comes from the Latin *molina*. The
island church of Nendrum in Strangford Lough (Co. Down) boasts
the earliest known watermill in Europe, which dates from AD 619 (see
Figure 2.2).[60] More than a hundred water mills have been identified
from early medieval Ireland. There was a boom in their construction
in the late eighth and early ninth centuries.[61] This scale of investment may reflect a shortage of labour for hand milling and increasing

[59] Kelly, *Early Irish farming*, p. 245; McLaughlin, *Early Irish satire*, pp. 154–5.
[60] McErlean and Crothers, *Harnessing the tides*.
[61] Rynne and Manning, 'How early Irish horizontal-wheeled mills really worked';
O'Sullivan *et al.*, *Early Medieval Ireland*, pp. 207–8.

demands for bulk food production. Relatively few querns have been recovered from coastal towns in Ireland, which suggests that grain was often processed into meal or flour before being sold in the ports.

Grain, meal and flour were processed into a variety of foods. Brewing and baking were jobs associated with women in a domestic setting. In wealthier church settlements, a professional male baker may have been employed. Bread baked on a griddle was an important feature of the monastic diet. The Old Irish 'Rule of Ailbe' specifies that a monk's daily ration included a loaf of thirty ounces. Bread made with wheat was clearly associated with high status; barley or oats were more common ingredients.[62] Drink was also brewed from partially fermented husks from barley or oats. Grains were also malted for beer, and beer was consumed by all ranks of society. It may have been a particularly important food source during the winter. Large churches and royal households employed professional brewers to ensure that the quality and quantity met their requirements.[63]

Milk could be used to make a wide variety of foods. Rennet was added to make coagulated milk and cheese from cows, goats and sheep. Salting, drying and pressing helped make foods that could be kept longer. Preserved rounds of cheese must have been a familiar sight, for in the early medieval saga 'The Destruction of Da Derga's Hostel' the buttocks of a hideous giant were memorably described as the size of cheeses.[64] Milk was also churned to make butter that could be stored in cool damp souterrains or bogs.

Meat was preserved either in cuts or combined with other ingredients in sausages and puddings. Bacon was the most popular cured meat, and a common component of food rents. The twelfth-century 'Vision of Mac Con Glinne' imagines a world made of wonderful foods. Its glories include a bacon house with forty ribs, wattled with tripe, and a fortress protected by stakes of old bacon topped with fried lard. Other animal components of this visionary world are meat puddings and sausages, lard, tallow and beef fat.[65] The essential work of processing food for immediate consumption and storage clearly pleased the imagination as well as the stomach. Tallow, skins and bones were also extracted from carcasses to support crafts such as candlemaking and leatherworking and comb making.

---

[62] Lucas, 'Irish food', pp. 10–12.   [63] Kelly, *Early Irish farming*, p. 333.
[64] Lucas, 'Irish food', pp. 23–6; Koch *et al.*, trans. *Celtic heroic age*, p. 173 (§38).
[65] Meyer, ed. and trans., *Aislinge Meic Conglinne*.

Professional craftworkers produced or repaired goods on a full-time basis. Their trades tended to be hereditary, with sons being apprenticed to learn the skills of the father. Occasionally a woman might inherit the status of a professional craftworker if her father had no male heirs. The eighth-century law text *Uraicecht Becc* lists the main groups of professional craftworkers in early medieval Ireland and assigns them varying levels of status.[66] Craftspeople of all ranks tended to cluster around elite settlements where a regular stream of customers for their goods might pass by. This clustering also allowed secular or ecclesiastical lords to benefit from, or regulate, their production.

The lower ranks of craftspeople worked on the raw materials yielded by animal carcasses. Leatherworkers were involved in the messy business of scraping, soaking and tanning animal skins using tree bark or tormentil. Tormentil was a plant used to give a red hue to leather, traces of which were discovered at the raised ringfort at Deerpark Farms (Co. Antrim) where shoes were made and repaired.[67] The activities of a leatherworker are also well attested in different phases at Ballinderry crannóg (Co. Westmeath) where more than 250 fragments of leather along with leatherworking tools have been found.[68] In addition to shoes, leatherworkers made a wide array of everyday objects including scabbards, bags, straps and belts. A set of specialist skills were required to produce vellum for manuscripts. This work must have been undertaken in larger church settlements. As vellum was usually made from the skins of young or foetal calves, the raw materials could be expensive, and care had to be taken to scrape, pumice and stretch the skins without damaging them. The 'Book of Kells' used the skins of approximately 185 calves, which entailed a great cost even before the folios were inscribed with coloured inks and beautiful artwork.[69]

Other animal products used in crafts were bone, antler and horn. A quarter of excavated early medieval sites have yielded evidence for the production of bone and antler artefacts.[70] The most commonly produced items were combs, pins and gaming pieces. The raw materials were easy to obtain, and an early legal text *Bretha Nemed Tóisech* mocks the comb maker who frequents dunghills or competes

[66] Kelly, *Guide*, pp. 61–3.   [67] Edwards, 'Archaeology', p. 279.
[68] O'Sullivan *et al.*, *Early Medieval Ireland*, p. 236.
[69] Meehan, *Book of Kells*, p. 86.   [70] Kerr *et al.*, *Economy*, pp. 30–1.

with dogs for his materials.[71] Antlers from red deer could be gathered in winter and early spring. Despite the contempt shown for
comb makers in literature, their work did require skill. Early combs
were of two types, either a single piece of antler with teeth on one
side or a composite object with a tooth plate with riveted side plates.
Within coastal towns a fashion for longer and thinner combs developed, and these were imported to inland sites; thus Scandinavian-style
combs have been found at Lagore and Knowth (Co. Meath).[72] The
mass production of antler combs in Dublin and Waterford is attested
through large deposits of antler waste. Bone objects that were made
in Dublin include needles, spools, strap ends, handles, ice skates and
gaming pieces.[73]

Woodworking ranked among one of the more prestigious crafts
in early Irish law texts. Bridge builders, church builders, shipwrights,
millwrights and masters in yew carving could obtain a status equivalent to a physician or judge. Lower-grade carpenters included
chariot-wrights, house builders, relief carvers, shield makers and
turners.[74] Not much early medieval woodwork has survived except
in waterlogged environments. At the large riverside church complex
at Clonmacnoise (Co. Offaly), the work of a master craftsman was
revealed with the discovery of parts of a bridge that could be dated
from the tree rings in the wood to the early ninth century.[75] A good
body of data has survived on the construction of medieval watermills
from rivers in Ireland, while crannóg sites have yielded evidence of
domestic vessels. At Moynagh Lough (Co. Meath), stave planks and
lathe-turned waste suggest that bowls and buckets were being manufactured on site.[76] Discarded items from crannógs include barrels,
tubs, platters and baskets, which give a rich insight into the medieval
home. Woodworking was also well represented in the archaeological finds from Dublin, which include houses, furniture, pathways,
drains, fences, ship repairs, waterfronts, revetments and a plethora of
household objects. Wood was commonly used for food vessels, and
there is limited evidence for pottery production in Ireland. In the
northeast of Ireland coarse pottery was produced between the eighth
and the twelfth century similar to contemporary Hebridean types.

[71] Kelly, *Guide*, p. 63.   [72] Edwards, 'Archaeology', p. 281.
[73] Wallace, 'Archaeology of Ireland's Viking-Age towns', p. 832.
[74] Kelly, *Guide*, p. 61.   [75] King, 'Economy and industry', p. 334.
[76] Edwards, 'Archaeology', p. 277.

These coil-built vessels called 'souterrain ware' lacked specialist skill and were probably homemade.[77]

In early medieval Ireland, the Church seems to have been encouraged the development of skills of masons in building churches and erecting carved monuments. While the majority of early churches were built of wood, some, particularly in the west of Ireland, were masonry built from the seventh century. Large ecclesiastical settlements were the biggest patrons of stonemasons, which is well evidenced at Clonmacnoise. A range of stone churches are visible at the site dating from the ninth to the twelfth century. The cathedral was originally built in the early tenth century.[78] In addition to these buildings, more than seven hundred early medieval carved slabs and six high crosses have been identified at the site. The carvings attest to a workshop of skilled masons whose memorials could be commissioned by wealthy patrons, who must have been a significant source of income to the church. More mundane stone objects were also produced at Clonmacnoise, including querns, whetstones, bowls, net weights and spindle whorls.[79] Some secular sites also specialised in the production of stone objects.[80] For example, whetstones were manufactured in the ringfort at Cahercommaun (Co. Clare). The simplest stone objects such as net weights were probably fashioned by non-specialists in a domestic setting.

One of the most common crafts in early medieval Ireland was smithing: nearly two-thirds of excavated early medieval sites have yielded evidence of ironworking.[81] A medieval farm could not operate without iron tools. These were produced by blacksmiths, but law tracts imply that farmers also acquired basic skills to repair items.[82] The work of processing and smelting iron tended to take place close to woodlands (for fuel) and water (for cooling metal and reducing fire risks). Mass production of iron from ore is witnessed at some sites including Johnstown (Co. Meath), where two tons of iron slag were recovered along with evidence of bowl furnaces. At Bofeenaun crannóg (Co. Mayo) large-scale smelting and smithing coexisted.[83] Vikings may have introduced new metalworking techniques to Ireland for weaponry, but evidence from Dublin suggests

---

[77] Ibid., p. 74.   [78] King, 'Economy and industry', p. 334.
[79] Ibid., pp. 339–41.   [80] Ibid.   [81] Kerr *et al.*, *Economy*, p. 13.
[82] Carlin, 'Ironworking', pp. 109–11.
[83] O'Sullivan *et al.*, *Early Medieval Ireland*, pp. 221–6.

that native ironworking practices also continued with some conces-sion to imported styles.[84]

Copper alloy, lead, tin, silver and gold were used to produce luxury items by craftsmen of the highest ranks. Nonferrous-metal smiths tended to practise their art more exclusively on high-status settlements.[85] Copper alloy was widely used for cast orna-ments including ringed pins, penannular brooches and horse har-ness mounds. Sheet bronze was also used for decorative bowls and bucket plates.[86] One of the more famous objects to be cast in sil-ver was the 'Tara Brooch'. This small but magnificent penannular brooch that was made around AD 700 showcases the finest skills that metalworkers attained in medieval Ireland.[87] From the ninth century, the style of metalwork in Ireland became plainer and the volume of precious metals circulating in Ireland increased. Ring pins, penannu-lar brooches and kite-shaped brooches were made in Dublin, which were traded widely and imitated outside Ireland. Imported glass was recycled into studs, beads and armlets. On a number of early medieval excavated sites, it appears that glass and enamel workers plied their craft alongside fine-metal smiths.[88]

Textile production can also be ranked among the most impor-tant crafts and industries in medieval Ireland. Archaeological evidence for this work is limited as cloth rarely survives, and wooden looms leave little trace. Spindle whorls are nevertheless a common find on early medieval sites. Spinning and weaving tended to be regarded as female activities.[89] Specialised cloth production took place at some high-status sites. Large numbers of spindle whorls have been recov-ered from the cashels at Cahercommaun (Co. Clare) and Carraig Aille (Co. Limerick). Clothing was important in medieval displays of status. Laws even governed the colours of clothing that different ranks were permitted to wear: purple and blue for royalty; red, grey and brown for nobility; and yellow, black, white or dun for commoners. Medieval Irish sagas describe royal characters wearing cloaks and tunics cov-ered or bordered with embroidery. The otherworldly woman in the Middle Irish tale 'The Wooing of Becfhola' wore a tunic covered in red and gold embroidery and a purple cloak. The political and social

---

[84] Blakelock, 'Early medieval cutting', I: 221–5.
[85] Kerr *et al.*, *Economy*, p. 13.   [86] Edwards, 'Archaeology', p. 285.
[87] Whitfield, 'More like the work of fairies'. See the later discussion.
[88] O'Sullivan *et al.*, *Early Medieval Ireland*, pp. 399–406.
[89] Kerr *et al.*, *Economy*, p. 13; Edwards, 'Archaeology', pp. 281–2.

significance of wearing ornamented cloths endowed them with significant economic value. One early legal text compares the profits of embroidery to the wealth of queens.[90] Humbler textile skills were needed in coastal communities for making and repairing fishing nets and sails. This must have become a minor industry in urban ports during the tenth and eleventh centuries.

COMMERCE AND COMMUNICATIONS

People travelled for many different reasons, and there were a variety of roads and paths that traversed the Irish landscape. A law tract of c. 700 identifies five types of road, from highways wide enough for two chariots to pass to cow tracks that were wide enough for two cows and their offspring. Narrower paths comparable to modern footpaths are also mentioned in medieval writing.[91] The 'Metrical Dindshenchas' claims there were five ancient roads in Ireland that reached Tara. This brings to mind the fiction of four royal roads in England.[92] The heavy labour involved in road building is recognised in the saga 'The Wooing of Étaín'. One of the miraculous feats performed by fairy folk overnight included the building of a trackway over a bog. This myth may have been used to explain the origins of the Iron Age trackway at Corlea (Co. Longford), parts of which have been preserved. Where mythological characters were not available, the construction and maintenance of roads was a public duty.[93] They were important for diplomacy and war, contact between churches, and trade.

One important route dictated by physical geography was the *Slighe Mór* or 'Great Way' which used a series of eskers crossing the midland bogs of Ireland to link Dublin and Galway.[94] Saints' Lives and sagas provide incidental information about route ways when describing the itineraries of their characters. The existence of local roads is witnessed in distribution of finds including millstones from the Wicklow mountains across Leinster. The growth of towns encouraged the development of route-ways to transport goods to and from surrounding settlements. For example, the archaeological data from Dublin suggests that cattle, timber, milled flour and fruits were among

---

[90] Whitfield, 'Dress and accessories', p. 9.
[91] Doherty, 'Road well travelled'.
[92] Ó Lochlainn, 'Roadways in ancient Ireland'; Cooper, 'The king's four highways'.
[93] Comber, 'Trade and communication', p. 74.
[94] Meyer, ed. and trans., *Triads*, p. 6.

the many items brought to the town for market, while manufactured goods and imports were traded back.[95] The technology for haulage was limited. Many items were simply carried on foot. A legal commentary implies that slaves were useful for this purpose.[96] Livestock could be herded to market, and packsaddles were used on horses and oxen. Four-wheeled carts were also used, drawn by oxen or horses. Royalty and leading churchmen needed to travel in style, so they rode on two-wheeled vehicles pulled by a pair of horses and operated by a professional charioteer. A chariot of this type is depicted on the ninth-century 'Cross of the Scriptures' at Clonmacnoise (Co. Offaly).[97]

There are many references to boats in early Irish literature, which shows that the natural routes of rivers and coasts were well used. Eleven dugouts were found submerged near the bridge at Clonmacnoise. These were simply fashioned from hollow tree trunks.[98] Other boats that are well known from early literature are coracles and currachs that were made by stretching hides over a wooden or wicker frame. Despite their apparent fragility these craft are very buoyant and are suitable for rivers and seas. 'The Voyage of St Brendan' describes a vessel with a ribbed wooden frame covered with tanned hides smeared with butter and possessing a central mast and sails.[99] Other ships were built with planks. The technology of these improved during the tenth and eleventh centuries through viking influence. A number of nautical terms were borrowed into Irish from Old Norse. Timbers and nails have been recovered from Dublin, which witness the construction and repair of ships taking place on site.[100] The most stunning discovery has been the remains of a warship recovered from Roskilde fjord in Denmark that had been made and repaired with Irish oak during the eleventh century. This vessel ('Skuldelev 2') was more than 29 metres long and was equipped for sixty oarsmen.[101]

Many transported goods were perishable, but the journeys of some items along Ireland's rivers and coasts can be traced in the archaeological record. The sandstone that was used to make carved slabs at Clonmacnoise was presumably taken by river on a journey of five miles

[95] Wallace, 'Economy and commerce'.   [96] Kelly, *Farming*, p. 499.
[97] Ibid., pp. 497–8.   [98] King, 'Economy and industry'.
[99] J. O' Meara, trans., *Navigatio Sancti Brendani*, trans., §4.
[100] Wallace, 'Archaeology of Ireland's Viking-Age towns', p. 832.
[101] Bill, *Welcome on board!*

or more, while finished products appear at other sites in the Shannon basin.[102] At the ecclesiastical complex of Nendrum (Co. Down), millstones were brought in from Bloody Bridge valley in the mountains of Mourne, which required a sea voyage of fifty miles.[103] Internal trade is also reflected in the finds of souterrain ware from northeastern Ireland in Dublin, while coins, jewellery and other items manufactured in Dublin have been discovered throughout Ireland.

Throughout the early Middle Ages, royal dwellings and churches were local centres for the collection of tribute. Goods were often manufactured on these sites. The production and distribution of prestige items may have been carefully guarded by the elite in an economic system that involved social bonds of reciprocity and clientship. The exchange of goods through political rather than economic ties is represented in the 'Book of Rights', which was probably compiled around AD 1100.[104] According to this text, foreign imports, agricultural goods and manufactured items were exchanged between local dynasties, provincial kings, and the most powerful king of Ireland.[105]

Seasonal fairs and markets were an important feature of the Irish trading economy that predated the advent of towns and continue into the present day. Clusters of archaeological finds at seaside locations may witness the existence of beach markets. Pre-viking examples include Bettystown (Co. Meath) where the magnificent 'Tara Brooch' was discovered, Dunnyneil island in Strangford Lough (Co. Down) and Dooey (Co. Donegal).[106] Other sites such as Lambay (Co. Dublin), Dalkey (Co. Dublin) and Cork harbour retained their significance for trading into the Viking Age. Islands or headlands may have been particularly valued as early trading centres, not merely because of their accessibility but because they represented safe places that traders could defend or withdraw from. This element of security or trust was essential for commerce to flourish.

Commerce was a natural adjunct to any large gathering of people. In early medieval Ireland, one of the most important types of assembly was called an *óenach*. These meetings were called by kings, normally a provincial king or a king of Tara, although many *túatha* may have originally held their own. Large ecclesiastical settlements whose status might rival that of a small petty kingdom also came to hold their

---

[102] King, 'Economy and industry', pp. 340–1; Swift, 'Sculptors', p. 117.
[103] Kerr *et al.*, *Economy*, p. 61.   [104] Charles-Edwards, '*Lebor na Cert*', pp. 16–19.
[105] See the later discussion.   [106] Kerr *et al.*, *Economy*, p. 47.

own *óenaig* by the tenth century. The *óenach* had a legal or judicial role, but plenty of other activities went on as well. The best recorded conventions were those held at Teltown (Co. Meath), which were associated with the kingship of Tara. A number of *óenaig* are mentioned here from the sixth to the twelfth century.[107] The eleventh-century place-name lore of Carmun (perhaps Carnalway, Co. Kildare) gives the fullest description of what an *óenach* might entail.[108] According to this story, the event at Carmun took place the first week of August (corresponding to the ancient festival of *Lugnasad*). It was used to promulgate laws and judgements and to discuss dues and tributes. Alongside these events were seven days of horseracing, music, storytelling, and three busy markets; one of food, one of livestock and one of foreign ('Greek') traders. These lively events must have encouraged not only merrymaking but also the formation of social bonds and commercial deals, including future orders for goods and organisation of payments. Records of *óenaig* decrease from the tenth century, although these assemblies did not cease. Their economic role may have been usurped by permanent settlements, and it has been noted that by the eleventh century the term *óenach* became interchangeable with *margad* ('market') a word that was borrowed from Old Norse.[109]

The arrival of vikings on Irish coasts in the 790s was clearly damaging to the economic fortunes of many churches. Coastal churches were their first targets. Iona (Scotland), Inishmurray (Co. Sligo), Inishbofin (Co. Galway) and *Rechru* (either Lambay, Co. Dublin or Rathlinn, Co. Antrim) bore the brunt of attacks in 795. The amount of plunder that was carried back to Scandinavia from early raids is witnessed in the metalwork recovered from viking graves in western Norway in the ninth century.[110] Apart from theft, the earliest economic activity of vikings in Ireland was the gathering of tribute, perhaps as protection money.[111] By the 840s vikings were gathering ransoms for captives and establishing a series of camps along coasts and river banks.[112] The inability of different viking groups to conquer large swathes of lands meant that their settlements stayed near the

---

[107] Swift, 'Óenach Tailten', pp. 118–19. See the later discussion.
[108] Ó Murchadha, 'Carmen'; Stokes, ed. and trans., 'The prose tales in the Rennes dindshenchas', I: 314; Gwynn, ed. and trans., *Metrical Dindshenchas*, III: 25–6.
[109] Simms, *From kings to warlords*, p. 62; Doherty, 'Exchange and trade', p. 81.
[110] Wamers, 'Insular finds'.   [111] *AU, s.a.* 798; *AClon, s.a.* 795.
[112] Downham, 'Vikings' settlements', pp. 2–3.

coast. The vikings' control of the seaways, advanced shipping technology and networks overseas enabled them to excel as middlemen in Irish foreign trade. While vikings continued to plunder churches after the ninth century, their raids became increasingly tactical. A militarised economic policy developed that involved viking groups striking at political enemies and economic centres that were outside their immediate trading network.[113] The economic hinterland of Dublin is revealed in a range of silver hoards of the ninth and tenth centuries that cluster in the Irish midlands and north Leinster.[114] Silver hoards also mark an economic hinterland around Limerick and Waterford. The hoards may not only reflect increased wealth being generated in Ireland during the Viking Age but also a growing gap between the rich and poor. An increasing amount of raw materials produced by those of lower social echelons were exported, rather than being redistributed in Ireland, in exchange for foreign luxuries and silver that were hoarded by the elite.

Larger ecclesiastical centres including Armagh and Clonmacnoise appear to have developed an urban economy by the eleventh century.[115] At Clonmacnoise, paved streets and regular plot divisions have been noted along with small-scale industrial activity. Two single coin finds and a hoard of the late eleventh century, which included thirty coins minted in Dublin, a bronze ingot and fragment of gold ornament, have been recovered from Clonmacnoise.[116] At Armagh, a sizeable settlement is attested in 1090, when 100 houses were destroyed by fire.[117] Six single finds of coins and two hoards ranging in date from the late eighth to the early eleventh century have also been recovered from the settlement, and there is evidence of industrial activity on the site.[118] The written and archaeological evidence highlights the role of churches, kings and seasonal markets in the early medieval economy. From the eighth to the eleventh centuries communication improved, permanent markets were established and overseas trade increased. While vikings loom large in this picture, it can be argued that some of the economic trends were in place before their arrival.

[113] Downham, 'Viking camps', p. 110.
[114] Sheehan, 'Early Viking Age silver hoards', p. 174.
[115] Doherty, 'Exchange and trade', pp. 82–3.
[116] Kenny, 'A hoard of Hiberno-Norse coins from Clonmacnoise'.
[117] *AU*, *s.a.* 1090.   [118] Woods, 'Monetary activity', p. 305.

OVERSEAS TRADE

Ireland was not isolated in the early Middle Ages, and recent research has highlighted the long distances that people sometimes travelled. Minerals preserved in the tooth enamel of skeletons indicate the geological origins of the drinking water consumed in childhood. Where the data from tooth enamel does not match the geology where the skeleton is found, it is an indicator of mobility. The method is not perfect in identifying regions of origin as results may be confused if a child was highly mobile in his or her early years, and the same set of mineral traits can be linked to a range of different locations. A male skeleton excavated at Bettystown (Co. Meath) yielded a proposed origin in North Africa or southern Portugal. This individual arrived in Ireland at some point between the fourth and seventh century. Other skeletons from the fifth, sixth and seventh centuries in Ireland cast light on immigration from Britain and Central Europe.[119]

The travels of Irish monks abroad during the early Middle Ages are widely known, but traders were also involved in networks between churches. The seventh-century 'Life of St Philibert of Noirmoutier' refers to the arrival of an Irish ship loaded with cargo at the island monastery off the northwestern coast of France.[120] When the controversial Irish monk, St Columbanus, was expelled from Gaul, he went to board a ship in Nantes where Irish goods were conveyed.[121] The role of kings in negotiating overseas trade is hinted at in a pre-Viking Age wisdom tract 'The Testament of Morann'. It described the benefits that a truthful king could bring to his people, including access to a merchant ship laden with valuables. From the ninth century, Ireland's major ports on the island were drawn into viking maritime networks that spread northwest across the Atlantic and southeast to the Caspian Sea. Dublin's fame as an international marketplace is represented in two Arabic accounts. The first penned in Sicily around AD 1154 drew from earlier reports and identified Ireland as a place where amber and coloured stones could be purchased. The other, based on the work of Al-'Udhri, a Spanish Muslim geographer of the eleventh century, identifies Ireland as a viking land where the nobles wear expensive hooded mantles adorned with pearls.[122]

[119] Cahill Wilson, *Late Iron Age*, ed. pp. 131, 139–44.
[120] Levison, ed., 'Vita Filiberti', V: 603.
[121] Doherty, 'Exchange and trade', p. 77; Krusch, ed., 'Vita Columbani', IV: 97.
[122] James, 'Two medieval Arabic accounts'.

The main categories of imports to early medieval Ireland were slaves and horses, foodstuffs, pottery and other vessels, textiles and raw materials for jewellery and accessories. The buoyancy of the slave trade on both sides of the Irish Sea in the fifth century is attested in the writings of St Patrick. Not only was he brought to Ireland with many others, but years later when he was a missionary, a British warlord (possibly based in Strathclyde) stole some of his recent converts. Not all slaves who dwelt in Ireland during the Middle Ages were from abroad. Prisoners of war, criminals, debtors and the impoverished could be enslaved. During the Viking Age, Dublin became a renowned slave market both for importing and exporting people. In 871, the viking king Ivar returned in triumph from Britain with '200 ship of slaves of Angles, Britons and Picts'.[123] This was presumably booty accumulated from campaigns in Northumbria, Strathclyde and Pictland. Dubliners continued to acquire human booty from abroad until the twelfth century. This was illustrated in 1098 when the Dublin fleet was tempted away from an alliance with the people of Anglesey by the English with the promise of Welsh captives.[124]

Horses were another import. Foreign steeds were especially valued. They are listed as suitable compensation for injury in the law text *Bretha Déin Chécht*.[125] In 1029 the ransom that was paid by the Dubliners to secure the release of the king's son from the men of Brega included 60 Welsh horses, 1200 cows, 60 ounces of gold and a ceremonial sword.[126] The term *gaillit*, a derivative of *gall* 'foreign', referred to good-quality mares.[127] Newly imported horses are among the entitlements that kings of Coille Fallamain and Fir Tulach claimed from the king of Tara as their stipend in the 'Book of Rights'.[128] Well-bred horses were therefore a luxury import that might be used for racing, riding or pulling the chariots of kings in early medieval Ireland.

Fragments of pottery are durable in archaeological contexts and provide a wealth of information on early medieval imports. In the last quarter of the fifth century and the first quarter of the sixth century, pottery was imported to Ireland from the east Mediterranean. Items included amphorae (B ware) from Greece, Carthage and the north Mediterranean, which may have contained oil or wine, and

[123] *AU, s.a.* 871.   [124] Downham, 'Viking slave'.
[125] Binchy, ed. and trans., 'Bretha Déin Chécht'.   [126] *AU, s.a.* 1029
[127] Kelly, *Early Irish farming*, p. 91.   [128] Dillon, ed., *Lebor na Cert*, pp. 98–9.

red slipware bowls (A ware) from Asia Minor and North Africa.[129] As wine and oil were both important in Christian ceremonies, the Church may have been an agent in encouraging these imports. Secular rulers may have also wanted exotic foodstuffs in order to offer lavish hospitality. In the later sixth and early seventh centuries the focus of pottery imports shifted to Gaul. The most popular goods from this later period were wheel-made jars, bowls and cooking pots (E ware), which have been recovered from than twenty-five sites in Ireland including humbler ringforts and high-status sites. They have a broad pattern of distribution in the southwest, midlands and northeast of Ireland.[130] Pottery imports declined in the eighth century, but reemerged with the growth of coastal towns. Cooking pots and wheel-made bowls were imported from Chester, Stamford, Bristol and Crowland in England during the tenth and eleventh centuries. After the Norman conquest of England, more pottery was imported from northern France, including grey ware, red painted wares and glazed Andennes ware. Soapstone and schist vessels were also imported through trade links with the viking world. A schist bowl from Begenish (Co. Kerry) probably came from Norway, while soapstone vessels found in Dublin may have come from the Shetland islands.[131]

Pottery and other vessels may have accompanied other goods into Ireland. Wine was a prominent import to Ireland throughout the Middle Ages whether imported directly or indirectly. The Irish word *fín* was borrowed from Latin *vinum* during the period of contact with the Roman Empire. The amphorae that came to Ireland in the sixth and seventh centuries may have contained wine or oil. As trade shifted from Mediterranean to northwest Europe in the seventh and eighth centuries, wine may have come in barrels.[132] The 'Life of St Ciaran of Clonmacnoise' refers to merchants bringing wine along the River Shannon from Gaul.[133] Vikings may have assumed control over much of the wine trade to Ireland from the tenth century. The Middle Irish word for a wine ship *Fíncharb* contains the second element –*carb*, borrowed from Old Norse *Karfi*. Walnuts and plums were among the foods imported to Dublin during the Viking Age as witnessed by

---

[129] Edwards, 'Archaeology', p. 290; Comber, 'Trade and communication', pp. 82–3.
[130] Laing, *Archaeology of Celtic Britain*, p. 141; Edwards, 'Archaeology', p. 292.
[131] Wallace, 'Economy and commerce', pp. 217–18; Edwards, *Archaeology*, p. 32.
[132] Kerr *et al.*, *Economy*, p. 49.
[133] Doherty, 'Exchange and trade', p. 77; Comber, 'Trade and communication', p. 82.

the contents of cesspits.[134] Other goods imported for culinary purposes included salt from England (probably Cheshire). Wheat was
also imported to Ireland in the early Middle Ages.[135]

Imported textiles were worn by people of high status in Irish
society. Mention is made of a bishop who wore foreign vestments
by Cogitosus in his seventh-century 'Life of St Brigit'.[136] A wealth
of textile fragments has been recovered from Viking Age Dublin.
These include high-quality worsted fabrics that may have come from
England or farther afield, more than 130 fragments of silk from the
eastern Roman Empire and Islamic centres, along with silver and
gold braids from Continental and Islamic centres.[137] Fragments of
silk have also been found at Lagore crannóg.[138] These fine cloths may
not have come to Ireland directly from their producers, but may have
been traded via other ports. The luxurious cloths traded by Hiberno-
Scandinavians were clearly objects of desire among neighbouring
peoples. According to the twelfth-century saga, 'The War of the Gaels
and Foreigners', when Limerick and Dublin were plundered by the
people of Munster in the late tenth century, many coloured cloths
were among the objects that were looted.

Items of antler, bone, and ivory are another category of imports.
The presence of roe deer antlers in Waterford shows that bulky
items of relatively low value were economical to import from abroad.
Walrus ivory was imported from the North Atlantic and may have
accompanied furs that have been lost in the archaeological record.[139]
Walrus ivory pins and gaming pieces have been found in Dublin.
Other materials that came from abroad were glass, amber and jet.
In the early Middle Ages glass was imported to Ireland from the
Continent, and fragments of vessels have been found in a few high-
status secular and ecclesiastical sites including Clogher (Co. Tyrone),
Cathedral Hill (Co. Down) and Dublin.[140] Imports of amber pre-
date the Viking Age as shown by the Tara Brooch. Early amber
imports may have come from the Baltic via Britain. In the Viking Age
significant amounts were brought directly, as suggested by the

---

[134] Wallace, 'Economy', p. 215.
[135] Kerr, McCormick and O'Sullivan, *Economy*, p. 51.
[136] Comber, 'Trade and communication', p. 82.
[137] Wallace, 'Economy', pp. 219–20.
[138] O'Sullivan *et al.*, *Early Medieval Ireland*, p. 238.
[139] Wallace, 'Economy', pp. 216, 220.
[140] Edwards, 'Archaeology', p. 291; Comber, 'Trade and communication', p. 84.

large-volume debris from amber working found at Fishamble St, Dublin.

Metals were another import used for practical and ornamental purposes. Tin was needed for bronze, which was an important element in jewellery and ornamental metalwork. Tin was probably imported from Cornwall or Brittany. Only a small regular supply was needed to keep Ireland's bronze smiths employed. The rarity of gold before the Viking Age encouraged Irish metalsmiths to excel in the art of gilding and producing intricate items from gold wire and granules, which worked their limited supply of the precious metal to maximum effect. Mercury was used in gilding and may have come to Ireland from Italy or Spain.[141] The discovery of a hoard of gold of ten gold arm-rings on Hare Island (Co. Westmeath), and five gold arm-rings from Vesnoy (Co. Roscommon) suggests that vikings imported gold as well as silver to Irish ports.[142] To date more than 130 silver hoards of Viking Age date have been recovered from Ireland, as well as many single finds. While Ireland has its own sources of silver, the style of a number of objects in the hoards and limited metallurgical analysis suggest that much arrived in Ireland through viking trading networks.[143] Imported coin and silver objects were often chopped up and used as bullion, or melted down to make other items in Irish workshops.[144]

Manufactured metal items that were imported to Ireland include base metal jewellery and mounts, which were not all consigned to the melting pot. Anglo-Saxon origins have been assigned to a gilt copper alloy mount from Knowth.[145] English and Pictish terms for brooches are found in the eighth-century law text *Bretha Nemed Toísech*, which hints that brooches were acquired from across the sea.[146] In the Viking Age, disc brooches were imported from England and Germany. Weapons were also imported. The first generation of viking settlers in Ireland brought weapons with them, as witnessed by early furnished burials. Later imports include a late Saxon example found at Fishamble St, Dublin and tenth-century blades from Lough

[141] Comber, 'Trade and communication', p. 83.
[142] Graham-Campbell, 'Viking Age gold hoard'; Sheehan, 'A Great Famine'.
[143] Wallace, 'Economy and commerce', pp. 216–17.
[144] Sheehan, 'Ireland's early Viking Age silver hoards', p. 53.
[145] Ó Floinn, 'Anglo-Saxon connection', p. 237.
[146] Etchingham and Swift, 'English and Pictish terms'.

Gur (Co. Limerick) and Ballinderry crannóg (Co. Westmeath).[147] The Ballinderry sword is particularly fine, with a silver-mounted handle and blade inlaid with the label 'Vlfberht', which was synonymous with high-quality swordsmithing in the Rhineland.

The appetite for imported goods had to be fed through a balance in trade. Ireland's exports throughout the early Middle Ages included slaves, animal products, textiles and metalwork. Ireland has already been mentioned as an importer of slaves, but they were also exported from the island. The 'Life of St Germanus of Paris', written in the sixth century, refers to the sale of Gaelic slaves in Marseilles along with people with other nationalities.[148] Slaves were raided and trafficked across boundaries. The foreignness of slaves may have added to their cache as a luxury item, but their 'otherness' also contributed to their vulnerability and may have made it easier for slave-owning societies to dehumanise them. Slave-raiding activities by vikings are documented in Irish chronicles, including the capture of 280 people from Kildare in 886 and 710 people from Armagh in 895.[149] Individual tales of slavery show that individuals of relatively high status could end up being sold abroad. St Findan of Rheinau was a nobleman from Leinster who was captured by Vikings, but escaped and made his way to the Continent where he pursued an illustrious career in the Church. In the early eleventh century, it was claimed that an Irish poet called Moriuht arrived in Normandy as a slave.[150] Attitudes towards the slave trade changed in the eleventh century, eventually leading to its banishment in Ireland the late twelfth century.

The export of agricultural products and textiles from Ireland is hard to trace. These items do not survive well in the archaeological record. The historian is therefore reliant on incidental references. According to a letter from the 640s, Irish butter was eaten by monks at the monastery of Bobbio (Italy) founded by St Columbanus.[151] It is unlikely that this product was only sent to one location, so a wider foreign market may be assumed. Wheat was also exported from Ireland from the late Viking Age. Meat was a major component of the tribute demanded by Irish lords and kings, and some was

---

[147] Wallace, 'Economy and commerce', pp. 218–19.
[148] Krusch, ed., *Venanti Honori Clementiani Fortunati Presbyteri Italici Opera*, p. 193 (§72).
[149] Holm, 'Slave trade', pp. 321–2; *CS, s.a.* 886; *AU, s.a.* 894.
[150] McDonough, trans., *Moriuht*.   [151] Kerr *et al.*, *Economy*, p. 57

probably sold abroad or exchanged for other goods.[152] Furs, leather and textiles were exported from Ireland. The aforementioned seventh-century 'Life of St Philibert of Noirmoutier' refers to Irish exports of shoes and clothes. Woollen cloaks were prominent in the tribute demanded by Irish kings, and the surpluses that were generated would have been well suited for export. The woodlands of Ireland also abounded with furry creatures. The export trade in marten skins is noted in the Domesday book account of Chester.[153]

Metalwork is the most easily traceable export from Ireland. The great skill of early Irish metalworkers has already been touched on. While the basic form of the penannular brooch was imported to Ireland from late Roman Britain, metalworkers soon adapted it to create something distinctively Gaelic. Some of these brooches were traded across the Irish Sea, and pre-Viking Age examples have been found at Llandewi Castle on the Gower peninsula, Llys Awel (Denbighshire) and High Down (Sussex).[154] Eighth-century mounts from shrines and caskets have also been found at a few sites along the western shores of Britain. Ornate hanging bowls that may have been produced in Ireland from the eighth century have been found in England and Scandinavia.[155] The volume of exported metal objects appears to have increased significantly in the Viking Age. Bronze ringed pins and stickpins were mass produced in Hiberno-Scandinavian workshops and widely distributed around the North Atlantic. Strap ends with zoomorphic ornament were also found along viking trade routes around Britain and Ireland. Silver circulated through the medium of purpose-made broad-band arm-rings that were produced in Ireland around AD 850–950. These often exhibit lines of stamped decoration. Hiberno-Scandinavian arm-rings followed trade routes and political links outside Ireland. More than two hundred complete and incomplete examples have been found in Britain. These focus in northern England (127 pieces were recovered from the magnificent Cuerdale hoard in Lancashire), the northern coasts of Wales and the islands and western coasts of Scotland.[156] Examples have also been found in Denmark and Norway.

[152] O'Donovan, ed. and trans., *Circuit of Ireland*, pp. 32–5.
[153] Round, *Feudal England*, pp. 465–7.
[154] Redknap, 'Glitter', p. 299; Griffiths *et al.*, *Meols*, p. 63; Youngs, 'Anglo-Saxon, Irish and British relations', p. 214.
[155] Youngs, 'Anglo-Saxon, Irish and British relations', pp. 228–30.
[156] Sheehan, 'Hiberno-Scandinavian', pp. 94–5.

Commentaries on Irish laws refer to imported and exported goods that could be washed up ashore after a shipwreck, including hides, iron, salt, foreign nuts, horns, wine and honey. This reveals the precarious but lucrative nature of early medieval trade. The legal list is restricted to items that could be salvaged and represent the tip of the iceberg of the range of goods that were imported and exported through the Irish coast.

CURRENCY

The primary means of exchanging goods in early medieval Ireland was through barter. Units of wealth were used to estimate value as a yardstick for such transactions. Ironically given his former condition, St Patrick evaluated the amount of wealth he had given away in Ireland to aid his mission as equivalent to fifteen slaves.[157] In Irish law tracts of the seventh and eighth centuries, female slaves are commonly mentioned as a unit of wealth, and so are dairy cows (with three dairy cows being cited as equivalent to one female slave in glosses). Smaller units of assessment were sheep, fleeces and sacks of grain.

The economies of gift, barter, sale and bullion overlapped in early medieval Ireland. St Patrick states that he rejected gifts of jewellery proffered by women. While these were intended as gifts or votive offerings, it suggests that jewellery was a portable form of personal wealth that men and women were free to dispose of. Law tracts refer to *sét* (a treasure or jewel) as a standard unit of value in the seventh and eighth centuries. Reference is also made to silver bullion. The loan of the words for an ounce (*ungae*) and a scruple (*screpal* or a twenty-fourth of an ounce) from Latin suggests that the principles of a bullion economy may have been adopted from the Roman Empire. Glosses on early Irish laws indicate that one dairy cow was equated with an ounce of silver.[158]

Law tracts established fixed prices for compensation and payments for marriage, fosterage and clientship, and some services. One could question whether this attempt at price fixing represented the actions of the elite who had (or wanted) control over economic policy, or whether it was social regulation intended to prevent extortion by the wealthiest in society. It can be questioned whether the laws provide a record of well-established mores or a conservative act at a time

[157] Patrick, *Confessio*, ed. Bieler, §53. [158] Kelly, *Guide*, p. 116.

of flux, or did they embrace and firm up a set of changes that had recently occurred? Earlier generations of scholars have often assumed that the laws had a timeless character. However, the evidence of social changes and the growing power of the Church in the seventh and eighth centuries may hint that they were written down in response to changing times.

From the ninth century, growth in overseas trade led to the hoarding of wealth. More than 100 silver hoards found in Ireland are dateable to the ninth and tenth centuries.[159] They contain status objects and currency in the form of ornaments, currency rings, hack-silver, ingots and coins. Twenty-six of these hoards are comprised only of complete ornaments and so may reflect gift or tribute payments rather than commerce. The most common component of Irish hoards is chopped-up items (whether ornaments, currency rings, ingots or coins), which is suggestive of economic exchange as bullion. Ingots and currency rings were produced within Ireland, mainly within the time frame AD 850–950. The weight of Hiberno-Scandinvian arm-rings tends to fall in the range of 24–26 grams, a range that is linked to the Scandinavian *ore*. In the tenth and eleventh century weights used in Dublin tend to be slightly heavier (around 26.5 grams), perhaps reflecting the influence of Anglo-Saxon systems of weights.[160] These changes may reflect shifting patterns of trade away from Scandinavia and towards England.

Before the Viking Age, coin finds are rare in Ireland. Frankish coins have been found at Maryborough (Co. Laois) and Trim (Co. Meath). Individual coins of Offa of Mercia (AD 780–96) have been found at six locations. Small numbers of Arabic coins came to Ireland indirectly through viking hands, but circulated in their original form because of the high-quality silver they represented. Their exotic inscriptions were, in effect, badges of quality. Kufic dirhams have been found at seventeen sites in Ireland.[161] Early viking coinages minted in East Anglia and York in the late ninth century also found their way to Ireland, but the bulk of imported coins were tenth-century Anglo-Saxon issues.[162] The mints represented in these coins included Chester, London, York, Lincoln, Derby, Norwich, Oxford, Barnstable and Exeter.[163] Under the influence of trade contacts with

159 Sheehan, 'Ireland's early Viking Age silver hoards', p. 49.
160 Wallace, 'Archaeology of Ireland's Viking-Age towns', p. 837.
161 Woods, 'Monetary activity', p. 313.   162 Kenny, 'Coins', p. 843.
163 Wallace, 'Archaeology of Ireland's Viking-Age towns', p. 838.

England and farther east, Irish traders engaged in a hybrid economy, incorporating coin into their systems of exchange. This flexibility was an advantage given the wide range of trading partners
with Ireland.[164] An influx of coin to Ireland in the 980s may have
encouraged the foundation of a mint in the 990s in Dublin by King
Sitric Silkenbeard. These coins were based on those minted by King
Aethelred II of England, and Anglo-Saxon dies were used for some
of the coins that may have been acquired through raids or diplomacy.
It could be argued that the establishment of a mint was a political
as much as an economic act. It conferred a degree of control over
exchange to King Sitric and his successors, and it allowed them to
tax moneyers working in the town. The success of the early Dublin
coinage is shown by its wide distribution. Dublin coins have been
found in Iceland, Faeroe islands, Norway, Denmark, Sweden, Finland,
Russia, North Germany, Frisia and Rome. After 1035 the utility of
the Dublin coins decreased. Their quality declined and circulation
became more localised. Nevertheless, the mint in Dublin continued
to operate into the twelfth century.[165]

TAX, TRIBUTE AND RENDERS

As mentioned earlier, freemen in early medieval Irish society were
bound to their lords on receipt of a fief (often comprising cattle),
for which they had to provide an annual food rent, hospitality and
manual labour.[166] These payments were in proportion to the size of
the original fief and depending whether or not the client was free
to terminate his contract at will. If a client evaded his obligations, his
lord could requisition goods by force.[167] The compilation *Míniugud
Senchusa fer nAlban* (a tenth-century text that includes eighth- and
ninth-century materials) relates the military obligations of communities in British Dál Riata to provide two seven-bench ships from every
twenty households or a variable number of fighting men.[168] From the
ninth century, kings levied exactions from their people with less reference to individual ties of dependence.[169] The poem on the *óenach*
of Carmun indicates that royal assemblies served as venues where
tribute was negotiated between a king and his people. As the role of

---

[164] Kenny, 'Coins', p. 845.   [165] Kenny, 'Coins', pp. 838, 842, 848.
[166] See the earlier discussion.
[167] Charles-Edwards, *Early Christian Ireland*, p. 526.
[168] Dumville, 'Ireland and North Britain'.
[169] Gerriets, 'Economy', p. 43; O'Keeffe, ed., 'Dál Caladbuig'.

the *óenaig* appeared to decline, a more uniform system of land-based assessment emerged. The *trícha cét*, which contained a notional figure of thirty *baili* (Anglicised as 'townlands'), is witnessed as a territorial unit of taxation and military levy in the eleventh century.[170] All of Ireland had been divided into around 185 *trícha cét* by the early twelfth century.

Law tracts identify three layers of kingship in Ireland. A *rí túaithe* ('king of a people') was a petty king, the smallest unit of royalty. He might be ruled over by a king of several kings (*ruiri*), who was in turn overseen by a *rí coiced* (a provincial king).[171] The nature of the relationship between kings could be couched in terms of 'free' and 'base', mirroring the relationship of clients to lords. In genealogical terms, free population groups (*sóerthúatha*) claimed kinship with the people of their over-king. Their subjection was seen to be more honourable and voluntary than a 'base-client people' (*aithechthúath*), who were obliged to pay food renders and a share of judicial fines to their over-king.[172] From the ninth century the power of provincial kings over petty kings increased. They secured the obedience of under-kings not only by taking hostages but also by giving gifts. By the eleventh century provincial kings were leading more ambitious military expeditions, which placed a greater fiscal burden on their under-kings. As a sweetener to this arrangement, over-kings granted stipends (*túarastal*) to subject peoples. According to the 'Book of Rights' the stipends included prestige items and luxuries. In return, under-kings gave agreed amounts of tribute, military support, manpower and hospitality to over-kings.

The demands of a new over-king over his people may be illustrated in chronicle accounts of the subjection of the town of Dublin to Máel Sechnaill, over-king of the Southern Uí Néill in AD 989. On that occasion he was said to levy a tax of one ounce of gold for every garth or tenement in Dublin, which was to be collected annually at Christmastime. Nine years previously Máel Sechnaill had freed the Southern Uí Néill from claims of tribute by the people of Dublin. Subsequent raids made by Máel Sechnaill on Dublin may be interpreted as punishment for nonpayment of their dues.[173] Máel Sechnaill also levied extraordinary taxes on Mide in 986 and 1007,

---

[170] MacCotter, *Medieval Ireland*, pp. 15, 22, 254–6.
[171] Charles-Edwards, *Early Christian Ireland*, pp. 130–2.   [172] Ibid., pp. 546–50.
[173] Valante, 'Taxation'; *AFM*, *s.aa.* 980, 989.

which were paid to win the support of the powerful ecclesiastical communities of Armagh and Clonmacnoise.[174] It appears then that, by the late tenth century, provincial over-kings were able to levy direct taxes over a wide area, and a land-based system of taxation was developed to facilitate this.

The relationship of the Church to its people, like that of a lord to his people, was conceived as a legal contract. Services of baptism, communion, requiems and masses were given in return for dues, which maintained the clergy and the temporalities of the church. In the period of conversion dues may have been conceived of as a series of individual payments or gifts, but as the power of the Church increased, regular payments of tithes were established in return for religious services. Initially it was the tenants of church lands and those who willingly entered the clientship of the church, whose payments and labour were the backbone of the ecclesiastical economy. Beyond this group pastoral provision and payments to churches were initially less generalised. In the 'Rule of Patrick' composed around AD 800 the laity were entitled to receive the religious services of an ordained cleric in return for tithes, death duties, labour services and bequests.[175] As the Church became more powerful in Irish society from the eighth century, lords were encouraged to pledge payments from their people to the church. Over time, ecclesiastical taxes became more of a matter of compulsion than choice.

Urban centres were a rich source of revenue for both king and church. Their growth in the tenth century may have spurred innovations in taxation. A poem in the 'Book of Uí Maine' lists the dues of craftsmen and traders in Dublin to their king. They include

> A horn of mead from every vat
> A comb from every comb-maker
> A sandal from every shoe maker
> A vessel from every glorious silversmith
> A scruple from every moneyer . . .

Irish traders who came to the port had to pay dues in malt, salt meat, firewood and candles, while foreign traders paid 'a cowl from every merchant's ship' in tolls.[176] The same poem lists a tax paid by the people of Dublin to Armagh. This may contextualise the composition to

---

[174] Ó Corráin, 'Nationality', pp. 24–35; *AFM, s.a.* 986; *CS, s.a.* 1007.
[175] Ó Corráin, 'Ireland c. 800', pp. 594–5; O'Keeffe. ed. and trans., 'Rule of Patrick'.
[176] Valante, 'Taxation', pp. 249–50.

the years AD 1106–29, when Cellach, archbishop of Armagh, sought
to bring Dublin under his jurisdiction.[177] The tax was presumably in
return for clerical provision and consisted of 'an ounce of gold, and
ounce for each nose thus, a scruple of gold for each man'. At face
value this does not make much sense, for each man has a nose and
yet must pay a scruple, rather than an ounce. The inconsistency may
be explained by other references to a 'nose tax' in Irish and Scandinavian literature. Bishops in western Norway were paid an annual due
of 9 grams of silver for each fortieth nose (5.4 scruples of silver per
person) in the eleventh century, which compares well with the Irish
account.[178] The principle of a nose tax may have been introduced
to the Irish Church through Scandinavian influence in the eleventh
century.[179] In early medieval Ireland there seems to have been considerable development in systems of tax, tribute and renders over time.

CONCLUSION

The perception of early medieval Ireland as a land of self-sufficient
farming communities has been subject to significant criticism in
recent years.[180] Clearly, there were economic surpluses and specialisation from the fifth century that encouraged long-distance trading
networks. From the tenth century, some coastal ports grew in size and
influence through contact with viking trading networks. The development of a handful of towns at coastal sites and at major church sites
stimulated the growth of a more market-oriented economy.

　　Irish rulers were keen to reap the profits of economic expansion.
While economic relations between rulers and subjects were initially
defined by agreements between individuals, they became increasingly
generalised and regularised by the eleventh century. This allowed
power to become centralised into the hands of provincial over-kings
and the greater churches, but it also generated increased competition
over resources and the tenth and eleventh centuries may have paved
the way for growing inequalities of wealth in Irish society.

[177] *AU*, s.a. 1121.
[178] Andersen, 'When was regular, annual taxation introduced?' p. 76.
[179] *Cogadh*, ed. Todd, p. 51; Stokes, ed. and trans., *Lives of Saints from the Book of Lismore*,
　　p. 245.
[180] Edwards, 'Archaeology', p. 295.

3

SOCIETY AD 500–1100

•

Despite popular stereotypes that early Celtic-speaking societies were more egalitarian, our sources reveal early medieval Ireland had a highly stratified society. The surviving laws provide a fairly comprehensive, if somewhat abstract, guide to early medieval Irish society, which is complemented by the evidence of sagas and chronicles. The titles of more than one hundred Old Irish law tracts composed AD 650–750, are known. Roughly a quarter are concerned with status and social categories. Status even figures prominently in law tracts that were ostensibly written on other topics.[1] Early Irish lawyers devoted much time to the classifications of rank and its concomitant entitlements. They provided a tally of compensation due to a victim of insult or injury, which was to be paid by the criminal or his family. Each person had a body price according to his or her rank and also had an honour price. The honour price was a form of compensation if someone was publicly insulted (e.g. through damage to his or her property). People might forfeit their honour price by acting in a manner inappropriate for their station, for example if a king performed manual labour with a spade. The laws portray a society that obsessed over status and codes of behaviour. A crime against someone of high rank brought a much greater penalty than a crime against someone of low rank. Similarly, the oath of someone of high rank automatically outweighed the oath of someone lower down the

---

[1] Breatnach, *Companion*, pp. 160–321; Kelly, *Guide*, pp. 267–71.

pecking order. Across the board, the law gave greater rights to those at the top of the hierarchy.

The purpose of early Irish law was not to be fair, but to limit violence and disorder in a society that lacked strong state institutions. The law operated primarily through private arbitration between kin groups rather than public enforcement. The status of an individual was linked to his or her family, which was quite broadly defined as the descendants of a common great-grandfather. The kin group might be entitled to receive or pay legal compensation, which gave it a vested interest in exacting justice if one of its members was a victim of crime. Similarly, it gave the kin group an economic incentive to discourage members from wrongdoing. A family of low status received little compensation if its members were the victims of a crime, for they had little means to stir up trouble if they were dissatisfied with a legal decision, whereas a powerful family could wreak havoc. The harsh consequence of this system was that families lower down the social scale were at risk of being attacked with relative impunity by those of high status. The social rules therefore motivated vulnerable classes to seek the protection of elites through clientship or other contracts. There was also an incentive for people to try and enhance their social status, but this was not easily done. Even if a person overcame the disadvantages of his birth and acquired significant wealth or influence above his rank, the elevated position needed to be maintained for three generations before the increase in social rank was recognised in law.[2] The laws, to a large extent, served to protect the exclusivity of the elite.

THE UNFREE

More legal literature was written about the various classes of freemen than about their legal dependants and the unfree who must have made up the bulk of Irish society. At the bottom of this social hierarchy was the slave. Recent studies have highlighted the role of slavery in societies with a strong warrior ethos, where the enslavement of people, particularly females, is a strategy of war.[3] The capture of people was a way of demoralising rivals. It also provided a crude demonstration of power by accumulating people who could be humiliated through menial labour or tortured by various methods including rape. The

[2] Kelly, *Guide*, p. 28.   [3] Wyatt, *Slaves*.

availability of slaves increased during times of war and famine when people might enter slavery voluntarily or sell offspring for food. The slave trade in Ireland also increased as a result of involvement in viking trading networks in the tenth and eleventh centuries.[4] While literary accounts of slavery tend to focus on the seizure of captives, many slaves were born to other slaves or entered that condition as a result of a judicial penalty.

Slavery seems to have been accepted in early medieval societies as an economically useful and long-standing institution. It was useful because labour obligations that lords could command from their clients were relatively limited, leaving a shortfall in labour supply.[5] Slaves could be forced to fulfil any task under the threat of physical abuse. There is no evidence for large-scale gang labour; rather they might work individually or in small groups as farmhands or domestic servants. The socially embedded nature of slavery is indicated in literature. In the saga *Echtra mac nEchdach Mugmedóin* ('The Adventures of the sons of Eochaid Mugmedón'), the mother of Niall of the Nine Hostages, progenitor of the powerful Uí Néill, was said to have been a foreign captive. She not only bore the child of her owner but also contended with the jealousy of his wife, who tried to make her existence as miserable as possible.[6] The ubiquity of slavery is also reflected in legal references to the *cumal* or 'female slave' as a standard moveable unit of value, along with the dairy cow. Slaves might escape their condition through manumission by their owners, escape, or by accumulating private wealth, but for the majority it must have been a lifelong condition.

Above the level of slaves were the half-free. These were individuals of free descent, but who lacked an honour price or land and so they lacked self-sufficiency.[7] Their lord had legal responsibility over them and was liable for their fines, but he was also entitled to their compensation. Thus, the half-free were unable to make legal contracts without their lord's permission. The lord could also impose any labour requirement upon them. Within this category were 'tenants at will' (*fuidri*). According to one legal text there were ten different types of *fuidir*.[8] These fine gradations suggest that the *fuidir*

---

[4] See the earlier discussion.
[5] Charles-Edwards, *Early Christian Ireland*, pp. 79–80.
[6] Koch *et al.*, trans., *Celtic heroic age*, pp. 203–8.
[7] Charles-Edwards, *Early Christian Ireland*, p. 71.
[8] Thurneysen, ed. and trans., *Irisches Recht*, pp. 62–7.

encompassed a large number of people. Some grades were able to leave their lord on making a payment, although in practice, it must have been hard to raise the necessary resources and move elsewhere. If the family of a *fuidir* remained in place for three generations, they became hereditary serfs (*senchléithe*) bound to the land they worked, and they could no longer claim a right to leave. The classification of half-free also included servants who were entirely dependent on their lords for sustenance.

FREE FARMERS

Irish laws were mainly concerned with the position of freemen. To be free required a basic level of wealth. According the Old Irish law text, *Críth Gablach* ('branched purchase'), the *ocáire* or low level of freeman had his own house and outhouse, land worth 7 *cumala* (equivalent to twenty-one dairy cows) and livestock to the total value of seven cows and a bull, seven pigs, seven sheep and a horse. He also had to possess a share in a plough team, a kiln, a mill and a barn.[9] At the upper end of the scale, the *mruigfher* possessed the means to farm independently, including having a plough team and a share in a mill that allowed him to grind his own corn. The high-ranking freeman was thus defined by self-sufficiency. A man of freeman status who had not yet inherited property was in a more precarious position. He was the lowest rank of freeman and did not possess the full entitlements of his more independent peers.[10] For some, the anticipation of an inheritance might never be realized, and so the status might become a permanent condition.

Freemen were expected to enter into contracts of clientship. They could have more than one lord, as long as their primary allegiance was identified. In return for an advance of land or stock and legal support, the client provided food rent and services, as well as contributing to his lord's status. The law defines two types of contract between a lord and a client, which might vary in duration. Base clientship could not be terminated prematurely without penalty. It involved a range of obligations including manual labour. Free clientship was more prestigious and could be terminated by either party at any time. It did, however, involve steeper payments to the lord. According to the law tract *Cáin Shóerraith* ('law of the free fief') if a lord granted three cows,

---

[9] Kelly, *Guide*, p. 10.　　　[10] Patterson, *Cattle lords*, pp. 197–8.

the free client would over seven years return nine cows (the original amount plus a cow each year for six years), as well as providing services of attendance and providing labour.[11] In many situations the client must have been paying out for his affiliation with someone of higher rank. While legal texts were important guides to lawyers (as witnessed by the copying and glossing of texts), the detailed prescriptions relating to social rank varied from region to region. It is hard to believe that the terms of agreements were not subject to negotiation between individuals, with preferential terms to be given to a client of good standing or a kinsman or with adjustments made according to economic conditions. According to the text *Cáin Aicillne* it was considered preferable for lords and clients to be kinsmen.[12]

A woman born to free parents generally did not have the same rights as a man. According to the Old Irish tract on *dire* ('honour price') 'her father has charge over her when she is a girl, her husband when she is a wife, her sons when she is a [widowed] woman with children . . . she is not capable of sale or purchase or contract or transaction without the authorization of one of her superiors'.[13] While the woman was assigned an inferior position, there were exceptions to this statement. A woman had control of her own personal property and she could inherit a life interest in lands if she had no brothers (on her death the land would revert back to the kin group). A female landowner shared some of the same rights as a male counterpart. She was allowed to veto contracts of her husband if they seemed unwise. A woman could also rise to high position independently from a husband through the Church as an abbess, or through practising a craft or skill. For the most part, though, the laws assume a woman to be married and to undertake farm work as well as child rearing.

NON-FARMING CLASSES

The law tracts also dealt with classes of society apart from those who worked the land and those who owned it. These included professionals whose vocation was passed down through generations. The learned classes comprised lawyers, clerics and poets. The lines between these vocations could sometimes be blurred. According to

[11] Kelly, *Guide*, p. 32.
[12] Charles-Edwards, *Early Irish and Welsh kinship*, pp. 360–3.
[13] Thurneysen, ed. and trans., *Irisches Recht*, p. 35.

Uraicecht Becc ('small primer'), the highest grade of judge needed to possess expertise in traditional law, poetry and canon law.[14] A judge might be one trained within the Church or a secular law school. There seems to have been an official judge for every *túath* who was chosen by its king and always in his company. In addition, there were secular judges or advocates who could be hired for a fee to adjudicate or arbitrate in legal matters. Clerics had recourse to canon law, but their status is also recorded in secular tracts, which may reflect ecclesiastical influence on Irish law. In the tract *Uraicecht Becc* the archbishop is assigned a status equivalent to a provincial king, while an expert in ecclesiastical learning is given the same honour price as the king of a *túath*. There is an interesting symmetry in the laws between the hierarchy of clerics and that of the secular poets. The late eighth-century law tract *Uraicecht na Ríar* ('primer of stipulations') lists seven grades of *fili* or learned poets and three subgrades. This follows the structure of seven grades of clerics and three subgrades found in *Collectio Canonum Hibernensis* and in various forms across Latin Europe.[15]

The skilled poet was defined by the term *fili*, which literally means 'seer'. The term reflects a perceived overlap in early medieval societies between learned and supernatural powers. While the druids were purposefully denied status in early Irish laws (but their continued existence is hinted at in early texts), the role of *fili* in Irish society adapted to the new order.[16] Poets held important social functions in Christian society, including the praise of kings, storytelling, and memorisation of genealogy and history. Their position was often complementary rather than antagonistic to the Church. Members of the learned classes were able to ascend their respective career structures through study and merit, although family connections helped.[17] Poets, like clerics, were able to cross political boundaries and maintain their status.[18] This freedom of movement was important for the spread of knowledge, and it meant that these members of those professions often served as ambassadors as they travelled between royal courts.

Poets could also be classed as entertainers. The main difference between the high-ranking *fili* and the lower-level bards was that the former were scholars and the latter were not.[19] At the lower end of the

---

[14] Kelly, *Guide*, p. 52.   [15] Flanagan, *Transformation*, pp. 60–2.
[16] Kelly, *Guide*, pp. 59–61.   [17] Breatnach, ed. and trans., *Uraicecht na Ríar*, pp. 96–7.
[18] Charles-Edwards, *Early Christian Ireland*, p. 103.
[19] Breatnach, ed. and trans., *Uraicecht na Ríar*, p. 99.

poetic ranks were those who composed satire. Their performances then, as now, were irreverent and could threaten political and clerical elites. For this reason, early Irish law evinced disapproval of their arts. Particular censure is reserved for female performers of illegal satire. Women poets are occasionally mentioned in laws and chronicles. However, such women appear to have been in a minority and generally excluded from higher ranks. It was perhaps the generally low status of female poets that made their satire seem particularly derogatory to those in power.[20] Other entertainers mentioned in law and literature were musicians, jugglers, jesters, acrobats and the professional farter who presumably performed for comedic effect. Lucky and talented performers may have held celebrity status, performed at the most prestigious royal courts and won positions of influence. At the other end of the scale, those with less luck or talent presumably had a more precarious existence, struggling to find patrons who would support them.

Practical professions ranged from physicians to smiths and these had obvious social worth. While these tasks occupy different social niches today, they were classed together in early Irish legal texts as *nemed* or sacred, along with poets, jurist, clerics and nobles. It is likely that physicians, like poets and jurists, were awarded higher status the greater their learning and expertise, although the laws do not provide clear evidence of this.[21] High-ranking and clerical physicians might have been expected to acquire scientific learning from foreign manuscripts and to combine it with knowledge of folk medicine. As with the role of poets, there is evidence of women achieving recognised status in this field. The law text *Bretha Crólige* makes specific reference to 'the woman-physician of the *túath*' whose main task may have been midwifery, but who also might have been an expert on herbal lore.[22] The high value of craftspeople is recognised in *Uraicecht Becc* where the most skilled of carpenters commanded an honour price greater than the highest grade of judge. According to the laws, the honour price of metalsmiths did not exceed more than half of that of the most skilled carpenter. However, the blacksmith was also an important figure. In a pre-tale to the famous saga *Táin bó Cúailnge* ('The Cattle Raid of Cooley') the smith Culann was of sufficient

[20] Kelly, *Guide*, pp. 49–50, 64–5.
[21] Binchy, ed. and trans., 'Bretha Déin Checht', pp. 6–7.
[22] Kelly, *Guide*, p. 77, n. 66.

standing to invite the king of Ulster to a feast. Folklore and mythology surrounds the character of skilled craftspeople in many early cultures. Lowly manufacturers such as leatherworkers and comb makers are also mentioned in laws. Their suggested honour price was equivalent to a yearling heifer.[23]

Craftspeople worked on commission, but also sold their wares from their premises. However, merchants and porters also played a part in medieval society, transporting goods from source to market and dealing with overseas trade. In early medieval society, the social significance of trade often rivalled its economic purpose. Trade often took the form of reciprocal gift exchange or barter. Coin circulation remained limited even after a mint opened in Dublin in the 990s. Exchange therefore required social interaction and negotiation. The laws encouraged members of a kin group to offer goods for sale to each other first, to help promote each other's prosperity.[24] Lords could also expect first choice of goods offered for sale by their clients. In pre-viking Ireland, access to exotic items or luxuries was a prerogative of the elites. Overseas trade was controlled by royalty or by churches that could distribute imports to favoured subjects or allies. Messengers and carriers could also be commissioned to take goods over longer distances. Traders received little mention in Irish laws of the seventh and eighth centuries. However, in the tenth century merchants acquired wealth and social influence as overseas trade grew in significance. Hiberno-Scandinavian ports grew in size to handle this trade. Their bi-cultural identity was an asset for it eased access to Norse-speaking communities abroad and the use of Scandinavian shipping technology. Hiberno-Scandinavian merchants might have also been less enmeshed with the social ties of Irish *túatha* so that their exchanges could focus more on profit.

In addition to their reputation as traders, Hiberno-Scandinavians were often alluded to in Irish literature as warriors. From as early as the mid-ninth century, vikings became entangled in the disputes of Irish kings, as well as with each other. The political instability of the ninth, tenth and eleventh centuries may have led to greater use of mercenaries; the Middle Irish word for a warrior *súaitrech* is derived from an Old Norse word *svartleggja* meaning 'blackleg'. Nevertheless, fighting men held an important place in Irish society well before the Viking Age. Laws refer to royal bodyguards who helped protect the

[23] Ibid., pp. 61–3.   [24] Patterson, *Cattle lords*, p. 228.

court and the king's body from harm. Saints' Lives and sagas also refer, often disapprovingly, to warrior fraternities who lived on the margins of society and lived by plunder or through offering service as merce-naries. The taking of arms was a rite of passage and sign of free status. For young men of free stock who had not received their share of kin-land, the warrior lifestyle offered a transitional stage between youth and entry into respectable membership of the *túath*.[25] Warrior bands may have also provided career paths for outlaws, renegades and out-siders. It was a high-risk choice, but potentially it offered high rewards. The mobility, risk-taking and violence of the warrior made him a popular figure in literature as shown by the stories of Cú Chulainn and Finn mac Cumaill (Finn McCool).[26] Talented warriors could elevate their status from commoner to a low grade of lord by being appointed to oversee blood feuds between *túatha*.[27]

Another means of increasing social rank was for a wealthy individ-ual to take on the role of hosteller. This was a non-military role that required a man to maintain a house on a public road that offered hos-pitality to all, according to rank, as frequently as it was commanded. If the hosteller owned twice the property of a lord, he obtained equal status. Hostels must have served an important role as meeting-places. They are the setting for dramatic conflicts in *Scéla Mucce mac Dathó* ('The Tale of MacDatho's Pig') and *Togail Bruidne Da Derga* ('The Destruction of Da Derga's Hostel'). This may reflect on the real risk of bandits and brawls in such places. To run a hostel may have been an expensive, demanding and sometimes risky enterprise, but it offered a route for social climbers in a highly stratified society.[28]

LORDS, KINGS AND CONSORTS

Early Irish laws placed more emphasis on economic productivity as a means of enhancing wealth and social rank than on fighting and raiding. This predisposition may reflect clerical influence, for war-fare posed economic and moral dangers to the Church.[29] If a non-noble freeman accumulated sufficient wealth to distribute fiefs and acquire clients, he could secure noble status for his male descendants. According to the law text *Críth Gablach*, the lowest grade of lord was

---

[25] McCone, 'Werewolves'.   [26] See the later discussion.
[27] Binchy, ed., *Críth Gablach*, pp. 70–2, *s.v. aire échta*.   [28] Kelly, *Guide*, pp. 36–9.
[29] Patterson, *Cattle lords*, p. 200.

a man who had a minimum of ten clients (five in free clientship and five in base clientship). The highest grade of lord had forty clients.[30] However, the possession of wealth and clients over several generations was not the only characteristic of lords. They might also hold public office or exercise military duties. The privileges of lordship included the collection of food renders and control over the labour of others. The demesne lands of a lord were worked by slaves, hereditary serfs, tenants at will and base clients, rather than by his own hands. A lord held status within his *túath* such as the right to act as a surety and lead his own retinue in battle. He had the economic means to offer hospitality to people of equal and higher rank, which could help build alliances, and the privileges of a good education and a noble marriage for his offspring.

The number of ranks of lords varies between law texts. Originally there seem to have been three grades, with an additional grade 'lord of superior testimony' (*aire forgill*) developed by the late eighth century. The reason for this addition may have been that the lordly class was expanding due to downward mobility from royal lineages. This could be the result of multiple royal unions creating large numbers of offspring whose status could not be maintained. It may have also resulted from a restriction in the number of lineages that held royal office as power became more centralised. Leading noble lineages could hold the honorary title *rígdamna* or 'royal material', which suggests their royal ancestry. While some of these lineages may have been contenders for royal status, over time this title seems to have become a consolation prize for those excluded from power.[31]

At the top of the social hierarchy were kings. Their power was said to extend beyond society into the realms of the supernatural. To unlawfully unseat a king might therefore cause natural disaster, but also the king himself had to follow rules and respect inherited taboos to keep the natural order in place. This overlap between myth and law was most clearly demonstrated in legends concerning the kingship of Tara (see Figure 3.1).[32] The origin of these myths relate to the idea of the king as the symbolic spouse of the goddess who represents his kingdom. This sacred marriage is a phenomenon

---

[30] Kelly, *Guide*, pp. 27–8.

[31] McLeod, 'Interpreting early Irish law (Part 1)', pp. 62–3; McLeod, 'Interpreting early Irish law (Part 2)', p. 54.

[32] See the later discussion.

Figure 3.1 Hill of Tara, Co. Meath

with Indo-European parallels. However, the sacral role of early Irish kings was also linked to Old Testament examples including David and Solomon. The king was not free to act as he pleased, as his rule was hedged around by supernatural and social prescriptions. In Ireland, the king did not write the laws. This was the job of clerics and professional lawyers. The king nevertheless held an important legal role in approving the judgements of courts and adjudicating in difficult cases.[33] A king could issue new laws in a state of emergency, be it political, environmental or moral. A number of these laws were linked to the Church. Examples include *Cáin Dar Í*, which sought to prohibit cattle raiding at a time of social disorder in the early ninth century.[34]

Different grades of kingship were recognised in early Irish law. The lowest grade of king was the ruler of a single community (*túath*) who commanded an honour price of 7 *cumala* (female slaves); at the top end was a provincial over-king whose honour was rated at 14 *cumala*. The notion of a high king of all Ireland was recognised in literature from the late seventh century, but it does not find expression in the laws.[35] Like the 'Bretwalda' (Britain-ruler) of Anglo-Saxon

[33] Kelly, *Guide*, pp. 23–5.
[34] Ó Corráin, 'Ireland c. 800', pp. 583–4. See the later discussion.
[35] Breatnach, '*Ardrí* '; Kelly, *Guide*, p. 18.

history, the title might be flatteringly applied to the most powerful provincial rulers. These were kings in a position to intimidate their rivals, but their claims to kingship over all the Irish lacked political substance. Ireland did not possess a centralised monarchy in the early Middle Ages. During the period under discussion, the lowest layer of kingship (based on *túatha*) lost some authority to kings of higher rank (*ruirí* and *rí cóicid*), sometimes serving as their agents and becoming akin to the level of lords in other parts of Europe. The number of lineages that aspired to kingship also decreased over time. During the eleventh century, a handful of provincial royal lineages competed to unite Ireland under their rule, but no single dynasty held power long enough to make this a reality.

The title *rígan* ('queen') began to appear in annals from the mid-eighth century. The 'Annals of Ulster' consistently gives death notices of queens of Tara from the late eighth century, and it occasionally mentions others. These women were identified by their patronym or the name of their husband or simply by their title. Each of these women may be identified as the *cétmuinter* or legal spouse of the king. Only one queen is listed for each king, although he may have been known from other sources to have plural legitimate or illegitimate unions. The policy of identifying one spouse may reflect the interests of the Church in promoting marriage as a lifelong commitment. The records may also suggest the growing importance of queenship in medieval Ireland. As Uí Néill kings contended for control throughout Ireland from the eighth century, the choice of legal spouse (*cétmuinter*) was an important way to build a lasting allegiance with a powerful family. This made the queen an important ally in the king's power-building strategy.

A list of royal consorts dating from the early Middle Ages is also provided by the twelfth-century *Banshenchas* ('Lore of Women'). This gives a different picture from the 'Annals of Ulster'. It has been convincingly argued that the *Banshenchas* account of royal wives was drawn from a list of the mothers of kings.[36] Thus while only one spouse is often assigned to each of the important kings who are listed, that spouse is sometimes a different partner from the one recorded in the annals. From AD 1000 the record of the *Banshenchas* becomes fuller, and often multiple consorts of kings are recorded. This may reflect a change in sources, which allowed more detail to be included,

---

[36] Connon, 'Banshenchas'.

and it may provide a more accurate reflection of the sex lives of kings. The intense competition between provincial over-kings in the eleventh and twelfth centuries may have encouraged rulers to build up a wider network of alliances through their choice of wives and mistresses.[37]

The marital practices of royalty might be mirrored on a more modest scale by the nobility. A king or lord might choose a *cétmuinter* from the family of an important ally. He might also have less formal partnerships with women from families of lesser allies, or simply have sex with women of low status based on amorous rather than political interests. In northern Europe, laws of primogeniture and legitimacy were not strictly enforced until the eleventh century. Although the son of a legitimate spouse might be prioritised in matters of inheritance, any sons whom a leader recognised, born to a free woman, might gain a share of his wealth or his position. This may have heightened the jealousies that could arise between wives and mistresses, as their offspring might compete for favour and power.[38] Some leaders avoided such domestic disharmony through chastity or by embracing celibacy. For married women however, fidelity was expected. The consequences of a perceived breach in conduct could be fatal, as illustrated in the execution of Órlaith, wife of Donnchad, son of Flann, king of Tara in 941. She was accused of having illicit sexual relations with her stepson Óengus.[39] This did not prevent Óengus from succeeding to the kingship three years later. It is possible that a political motive was involved in this complex relationship: Óengus may have been seeking to usurp his father, or Donnchad may wanted to slight the royal dynasty of Dál Cais to which Órlaith belonged. The social anxieties that arose over the sexual propriety of elite women were expressed as themes in Irish sagas.[40]

In a number of instances, a new ruler married the widow, former wife or daughter of a previous king or lord. These acts might be construed as crude assertions of power over women formerly under the authority and protection of other men. However, these marriages could also reduce conflicts over succession to power by offering a degree of continuity in life at court, or they might help maintain a political alliance between the wife's family and successive rulers. It is also worth considering the value of wives as advisors. Elite women

---

[37] Connon, 'Banshenchas', p. 108   [38] Bhreathnach, *Ireland*, p. 87.
[39] *CS, s.a.* 941.   [40] See the later discussion.

presumably acquired a working knowledge of the politics of the kingdom or lordship they dwelt in, its allies, and the leading personnel. This knowledge would be of great use to a new ruler. The important role of the queen in this respect may be seen in the law text *Críth Gablach*, which assigns the king's consort the equivalent place to his judge in the layout of the royal household.[41] The duties of a royal or aristocratic wife might extend to diplomacy and overseeing hostages who were retained at her husband's court. *Bretha Crólige* identifies women who were of particular value in a *túath*, including 'the hostage ruler' and 'the woman who turns back the streams of war'.[42]

MARRIAGE

Elite men and women were often political pawns in the marriage market. Women in particular might be obliged to enter into a series of unions until they were past child-bearing age. The woman's right to select her own partner in marriage is recognised in law, but in reality, women across social ranks seemed to have limited freedom in choosing their partners. The laws seem to expect girls over fourteen years and men over twenty years of age to enter into sexual unions. The main alternative for those who did not wish to marry, or who did not wish to marry again, was to seek refuge in the Church.[43] Early canon laws suggest that clerics could also marry, although sexual relations might be forbidden for priests or higher-ranking clergy.[44] In the late eleventh century, the influence of papal reforms, which demanded clerical celibacy, was felt in Ireland. However, that proved to be a difficult rule to enforce. There was evidently some divergence between what the Church and secular laws might define as marriage. The 'law of couples' (*Cáin Lánamna*) identifies nine forms of union, ranging from a 'marriage of joint property' between partners of equal rank, to sex between two people who are insane and therefore incapable of raising a child. There was a distinction between having a legal spouse (what the Church would recognise as a marriage) and other forms of sexual union that might produce offspring.[45] These alternative unions were legislated for in secular law so that the woman and her children received some legal protection.

[41] Bhreathnach, *Ireland*, p. 83.   [42] Binchy, ed. and trans., 'Bretha Crólige'.
[43] Kelly, ed. and trans. *Marriage disputes*, p. 2; Ní Dhonnchadha, 'On Gormfhlaith'.
[44] Kelly, *Guide*, p. 40.   [45] Eska, ed. and trans., *Medieval law*, pp. 22–3.

The laws presented the picture of the ideal marriage as a monogamous union between partners born of families of equal rank.[46] However, there was little equality within marriage. In *Cáin Lánamna* the relationship between a husband and wife is likened to that between a teacher and a pupil, a church and its monks, or a lord and his base client.[47] Thus the male head of a household legally wielded authority over his wife, his children and his slaves. While partners may have been born of equal wealth and status, the honour price of a wife was half that of her husband; that of a concubine was a quarter. The type of union between a man and a woman determined the level of association that remained between a woman and her kin. In the case of a legal spouse (*cétmuinter*) one-third of any fines went to her family.[48] If a woman was abducted against the will of her family, all assets that she was entitled to went to her family, and all liabilities fell to her abductor. This included the duty to provide for her children. In the case of a prostitute, all liabilities and entitlements fell to her own kin group.

In secular law, marriage was perceived as a contract involving rights, responsibilities and property. As part of this contract, a man was expected to pay a bride price to the father or guardian of his intended spouse before witnesses. The woman was entitled to keep a share of her bride price. Her family was also expected to contribute property, and normally the woman was expected to move into the man's household. If the couple split without blame, the bride price was kept by the bride and her family, as was the share of property she brought to the union. The man retained his property, and the profits of joint labour within the marriage were split. These rulings reveal different expected gender roles, with the wife being more involved in the tasks of milking, food processing and cloth manufacture and the husband's role relating more to the cultivation of crops and the care of livestock.[49] The household economy of medieval Ireland thus bound man and wife in a mutually dependent relationship. In addition to its economic utility, the main purpose of marriage was the production of offspring. Where grounds of divorce are discussed in legal texts, these often relate to matters of fertility and child-rearing, or the insult to a partner through theft, slander or infidelity. Where one party is seen to carry the blame for a

[46] Breathnach, *Ireland*, pp. 83–4.   [47] Kelly, *Guide*, p. 27.   [48] Ibid., p. 14.
[49] Charles-Edwards, *Early Christian Ireland*, p. 110.

divorce, the share of property that partner takes away from the union is reduced. In the late eleventh century, the secular laws came under criticism from Church reformers who wished to ban most grounds for divorce and to make all forms of union, apart from the first official wedding, illegitimate.[50]

INHERITANCE

The importance of family as defining individual status and providing legal protection has already been touched upon. It also determined access to kin-land in wealthier families. The Old Irish law text *D'fodlaib cineoil tuaithi* ('on the divisions of the kin groups in the *túath*') describes four family groups. The smallest is the *gelfine* ('bright kin') referring to those related within three generations (i.e. descended from a common grandfather), and the largest is the *indfine* ('end kin'), which comprises a group related through the male line within six generations. The rules of inheritance are laid out as follows. When a man dies the land is divided between his sons. If he has no offspring his land is shared between members of the *gelfine*; if there are no relatives related within three generations, then three-quarters of the land is divided between relations within four generations (*derbfhine* 'true kin'), and the remaining quarter is shared between those related within five and six generations.[51] A daughter could share a life interest in lands if she had no brothers, but this property would revert to the male members of the kin group on her death. Land was such an important resource within farming societies that clear rules of inheritance were needed to prevent bitter conflicts from arising.

Scholars have debated the mechanisms of kinship and inheritance, but the evidence of *D'fodlaib cineoil tuaithi* may be best interpreted as following the principle that the *gelfine* was a kin group that comprised up to three generation of living adults. Membership of a kin group changed through an individual's lifetime, just as the family we are born into differs in its membership from the one that exists when we die. A man might expect to belong to three different *gelfine* during his lifespan. When he came of age he would join the *gelfine* defined by common descent from his grandfather. When his sons reached maturity, his *gelfine* would be defined by those sharing common descent from his father. When his grandchildren reach maturity, he became the defining figure of his *gelfine*, binding all men descended from him

[50] Eska, ed. and trans., *Medieval law*, p. 23.   [51] McLeod, 'Kinship', pp. 1–2.

in three generations. If a man lived to see his grandsons mature, his total kindred extended to the maximum extent recognised by law. This is the 'end-kin' defined by six generations, comprising all the living descendants of his great-grandfather, extending down to the generation of his grandchildren. The importance of kin groups in defining land inheritance is reflected in the names of places in the Irish landscape. Thousands of townlands still bear the names of families who once owned them.[52]

Regarding the division of land, the principle was that sons took an equal share of the lands that had belonged to their father. However, sons of dubious paternity or who were bad sons could be excluded. Daughters would usually only receive a share of moveable goods so that kin-land was retained in a line of patrilineal descent. The Church seems to have favoured eldest sons in matters of inheritance, and an Old Irish legal commentary assigned the paternal house and farm buildings to the eldest son; however, this might not have always been observed in practice.[53] The laws also allowed for a share of property to be granted to the Church. Naturally there was a risk that through population growth in successive generations the shares of kin-land would be whittled down to the point where families risked losing wealth and status. This was in part compensated by the redistribution of lands within the kin group when one of their male members died without offspring. It could also be offset by the acquisition of more land. Land purchase is not well documented in early medieval Ireland. Communal memory may have often been sufficient to confirm transactions. However, a pan-European trend towards greater use of written documentation in the eleventh century encouraged the use of charters in Ireland. One example, copied into the 'Book of Kells', records the purchase of land around AD 1092 in the parish of Donaghmore (Co. Meath) by an Ua Bresláin, priest of Kells, and his kinsmen.[54]

As well as land and moveable goods, professions and offices were often hereditary. Any male members of an office holder's *derbfhine* might inherit the title, which could give rise to a large number of contenders. This could lead to conflict between candidates, particularly in relation to the office of kingship. These rules worked to help ensure that professional and official dynasties did not die out

---

[52] Kelly, *Early Irish farming*, p. 402.
[53] Charles-Edwards, *Early Christian Ireland*, p. 87.
[54] Herbert, 'Charter material from Kells'.

and that from a pool of eligible candidates, that the most worthy might succeed. In relation to kingship, some laws sought to limit the sexual activity of kings, perhaps in a bid to limit the number of off-spring. For example, a king might not go out alone, lest a woman claim that he had fathered a child on her. Laws also favoured the position of the king's official wife (*cétmuinter*), and by granting her greater esteem, this may have given some advantage to her offspring in matters of succession. If the *cétmuinter* came from a powerful family this would improve the chances of her son succeeding to power. The risk of violent succession disputes was also diminished when a royal heir was chosen during the king's lifetime. Succession often favoured the oldest male son or grandson of a previous ruler. Older candidates had had the opportunity to acquire relevant life experience and build up their own network of supporters. A royal candidate also had to be publicly recognised for his personal excellence (Old Irish *febas*) and charisma.[55]

Where two or three branches of a royal kindred were well matched in strength, the kingship might alternate between them.[56] This arrangement could be long lasting. A prime example of this is the Uí Néill kingship of Tara, which alternated between the dynasties of Clann Cholmáin and Cenél nEógain in the ninth and tenth centuries. This method of power sharing between royal branches would often be preferable to waging a zero-sum war where one family might lose everything. Some royal candidates might also choose to opt out of succession to become allies and courtiers of the next king. This might be a safer choice for a weaker candidate, for it was not uncommon for unsuccessful contenders to be killed or maimed. It was common for an unsuccessful claimant or excluded lineage to be compensated with a position in the Church. While early Irish royal succession is often portrayed as chaotic, there was a clear rationale to the system, which sought to elevate the most able candidates to power, although it was not always successful in limiting conflict between rivals.

FOSTERAGE AND ALLIANCES

To mitigate the risks of conflict or downward social mobility, alliances could be formed across kin groups. It seems to have been normal

---

[55] Charles-Edwards, *Early Christian Ireland*, pp. 91–2.
[56] Warntjes, 'Regnal succession', pp. 401–3.

practice among the wealthier classes to send children away from a young age to a foster family or church. This practice helped form alliances by building intimate links between the children's family and the households or communities that received them. The institution was also regarded as beneficial to the child's education. Furthermore, it could reduce emotional tensions in households where children from one father but different mothers might otherwise live together. The period of fosterage began before a child reached seven years of age and continued until the age of fourteen or seventeen, according to different accounts. The fosterage arrangement could be undertaken either free of charge (on the grounds of affection between two families) or for a fee that was calculated according to the gender and rank of the child. The foster parents were required to educate and maintain the foster child accordingly. For example, the daughter of a noble is taught sewing, but the daughter of a high-ranking farmer is taught bread making.[57] The importance of links between foster kindred is a recurrent theme in Irish sagas and hagiography, and this must to some extent mirror social realities. One of the most poignant scenes in the saga *Táin bó Cúailnge* ('The Cattle Raid of Cooley') is when the warrior Cú Chulainn is forced to kill his foster brother Fer Diad and utters a poetic lament over his dead friend. Fosterage and marriage were forms of artificial kinship that could bind families across political boundaries, but these relationships could also be strained by the changing course of events.

Alliances between families or polities might be formed for a temporary goal, such as a military campaign against a common enemy. Relations could also be formalised by treaties. Chronicles give many instances of agreements being made to end or prevent wars. Taking the second decade of the tenth century as an example, peace was made between Aéd, over-king of Ulster, and Niall Glúndub, over-king of the Northern Uí Néill, in 914. In the following year, Niall exacted a pledge from the sons of Flann Sinna, over-king of the Southern Uí Néill, that they would end the rebellion against their father. In 918 the king of northern Brega made an alliance with vikings in a bid to protect his kingdom, but this failed and he died fighting the men of Dublin, alongside Niall Glúndub in the following year.[58] A fragmentary law text on treaty relationships, called *Bretha Cairdi*, gives some insights into cross-border agreements, including

---

[57] Kelly, *Guide*, p. 87.   [58] *AU, s.aa.* 914, 915, 918, 919.

protection for the subjects of each polity and rules regarding crimes
that were committed by members of one group in the territory of
another.[59]

CONCLUSION

Early medieval Ireland was a highly stratified society. There is abundant evidence in surviving law tracts that gives insight into the many
shades of social distinction. The laws are mainly concerned with the
elite in Irish society. It appears that a large share of agricultural and
servile work was undertaken by ranks of unfree and semi-free people.
Being free, however, did not bring liberty from obligations. People
of free status had responsibilities towards neighbours, kin and allies.
They were also bound to provide services and economic support to
those of higher rank through clientship, fosterage and tribute giving. In return, the elites provided protection and favours. Opportunities for social advancement were limited. However, it was possible
through the accumulation of wealth, professional talent or military
skill to climb the greasy pole. Downward social mobility was a challenge for many. Among royal kindreds, the proliferation of heirs and
the centralisation of royal authority forced a number of families to
lose status, which may have brought a downward social pressure to
other ranks. The intense competition over status within the highest
echelons of Irish society led to frequent conflict. As a result, the Irish
chronicles provide a dizzying tally of violent deaths among the male
upper classes.

[59] Bemmer, 'Early Irish hostage surety'.

4

POLITICS AD 500–1100

•

Ireland is lucky in the richness and variety of sources that allow analysis of early medieval politics. These include chronicles, law texts and genealogies. The nature and practice of kingship were the focus of much literary composition. There were a plethora of kings operating at any one time in early medieval Ireland as power remained fairly localised. Therefore, the island's political development is best discussed through the lens of different provincial histories. An overarching theme during the early Middle Ages was the rise of the Uí Néill dynasty and their subsequent failure to secure an over-kingship of all Ireland. The rise of the Dál Cais of Munster who sought (and nearly won) control of all Ireland under Brian Boru at the start of the eleventh century shattered the ambitions of Uí Néill. By the late eleventh century, the over-kings of Connacht and Leinster were also competing in the race to win island-wide control. At the end of the eleventh century, the most powerful king of Ireland was the Munster dynast, Muirchertach Ua Briain, who sought to increase his power and prestige through cultivating contacts abroad. The growing links between Ireland and its neighbours would set the scene for the political developments of the twelfth century and beyond.

THE HIERARCHY OF KINGS

Kingship in early medieval Ireland was a multilayered affair with petty kings being tied in relationships of dependence to greater kings. At the bottom of the scale were the kings of one *túath*. The legal definition of a *túath* was a small but distinct community with its own king, its own church, a poet and an ecclesiastical scholar.[1] There were more than 150 *túatha* operating in Ireland at any time between the fifth and twelfth centuries. Above the petty kings of the *túath* was an over-king of plural *túatha* who wielded power through his recognised position of lordship over lesser kings. At the top of the scale were provincial over-kings.

Ireland was divided into provinces that, in the early medieval period, comprised Munster, Leinster, Ulster, Connacht, Mide, Brega and lands in the northwest of the Island under the power of Uí Neill dynasts. In the sixth century, Uí Néill extended their power over the east midlands and divided into two branches: the Southern Uí Néill in Mide and Brega, and the Northern Uí Néill, in the northwest. There was also an over-kingship of Northern and Southern Uí Néill, and the remaining provinces had their own over-kings. The ruler over both branches of Uí Néill was regarded as the most powerful king in Ireland. The Uí Néill over-kingship was associated with the ancient site of Tara (Co. Meath). The legend was developed by Uí Néill that there had once been a mythical kingship of all Ireland based here and they were its rightful heirs. It was an ideal which coloured legends and political ambitions right through the Middle Ages. The extent of the power wielded by the historical kings of Tara is debated. At times, they could wield authority over other provincial kings, but they never achieved direct rule across all Ireland.

Power in Ireland was mediated by the language of kinship and personal ties. Genealogies could be rewritten as power changed hands and fictional relationships were projected into the distant past in order to justify the status quo. The origin and relationship of Irish provinces in the early Middle Ages were thus defined through tales of kinship. The Old Irish 'Saga of Fergus mac Léti' identifies three free peoples of Ireland: the Ulaid (people of Ulster), Laigin (people of Leinster) and Féni.[2] The leading dynasties of Connacht, Uí Néill and Eóganacht of Munster, were said to belong to the Féni. More prestige was thus accorded to the descendants of the Féni when the tale was written. A plethora of early tales concerned the ancestors of different provincial over-kings explaining in heroic or moral terms why one branch of a royal dynasty would succeed and why others did not.

To help maintain their position, over-kings relied on client kings who might belong to subbranches of their own family or were rulers

---

[1] Charles-Edwards, *Early Christian Ireland*, p. 13.   [2] Ibid., p. 580.

of unrelated peoples within their sphere of influence. Ultimately royal power rested on the number of clients one had, rather than direct control of land, and this fact explains a number of features of early Irish society. It meant that kingship was seen in a contractual rather than an absolute manner. Therefore there was pressure on early Irish rulers to continually justify and uphold their authority.

THE PRACTICE OF POWER

The nature of kingship can be explored through early medieval chronicles, biblical literature, laws, gnomic literature, sagas and poetry. Power was displayed in public events, most symbolically in the act of inauguration at royal sites, but also at assemblies and through the exercise of royal prerogatives such as exacting hospitality from clients and making legal judgements. The king also relied on his retinue and the work of poets and craftsmen to make his court a centre of cultural and political life. The Church played an important role in winning public support for secular leaders, and relations between kings and churches were often cemented through networks of allegiance. It is no surprise that the rhetoric and imagery of kingship in Ireland (as elsewhere in Europe) were heavily influenced by Christian ideologies. From the eighth century, it is evident that the legal independence of *túatha* was being eroded with a concomitant rise in power of provincial over-kings. The elevated power of provincial kings required more elaborate practical and ritual underpinnings. This is best illustrated in portrayals of the kingship of Tara, which represented the pretensions of Uí Néill over-kings to exercise power across all Ireland.

The Hill of Tara was a strategic site, overlooking fertile lands in the kingdom of Brega and with impressive views across the midlands of Ireland. The low-lying hill hosts a prehistoric complex of monuments that were associated with ancient deities. The local rulers Síl nÁedo Sláine had been ousted from using this site, and made do with a seat at Ráith Airthir (Oristown, Co. Meath). The more impressive site at Tara became the ceremonial focus for the most important Uí Néill kings, who bore the title 'king of Tara'. In common with other important royal inauguration sites (like Cashel in Munster and Rathcroghan in Connacht), the rich archaeological landscape at Tara endowed kings who were inaugurated there with an aura of ancient respectability.[3]

---

[3] Bhreathnach, *Ireland*, p. 56.

There is no detailed account of the inauguration of a historical king at Tara, although tales of king-making ceremonies here are enshrined in medieval sagas. These associate the inauguration of a king with the celebration of a feast and the demonstration of worthy qualities of military power, generosity, truth and good judgement. In literature, the royal inauguration represented a union between a king and his kingdom; thus the leader was presented as a mediator between the society he ruled and the natural forces of his territory. Sometimes this was characterised as a marriage between the king and a goddess who embodied the sovereignty of the land. In the reign of a good king, it was believed, the forces of society and nature would be in harmony and there would be abundance and prosperity.

As institutions of kingship became more Christianised, the pagan and prehistoric associations of Tara were marginalised. In the 'Life of St Patrick' penned by Muirchú in the seventh century, Tara was presented as the site of a dramatic confrontation between Saint Patrick and the druids of Lóegaire mac Néill, king of Tara, where the saint was victorious. From the seventh century, another site at Teltown, north of Tara, was favoured for assemblies.[4] This prehistoric mound lay near Donaghpatrick, an important early church named after St Patrick. The meeting at Teltown aspired to be an annual event. It was noted in the 'Annals of Ulster' when the assembly was not held in the years 873, 876 and 878.[5]

Assemblies were integral to the workings of early Irish kingdoms. According to the eighth century law text *Críth Gablach*, an assembly or *óenach* was where a king could form treaties, issue edicts and order military levies. These gatherings became a magnet for other activities including sports, entertainment and trade. The Old Irish word *óenach* has given rise to modern Irish *aonach* meaning a 'fair', reflecting its social and economic dimensions. These assemblies could operate at the level of a *túath* or a major province. The one at Teltown was the most famous.[6] Meetings between kings also happened at a provincial or national level. An important example is the royal assembly (*rígdál*) held at Birr in 697 at the border between Munster and the lands of Uí Néill. This was combined with a synod at which kings and clerics co-operated in the promulgation of an edict *Cáin Adomnáin* or *Lex Innocentium*, 'Law of the Innocents', which sought to protect

---

[4] Ibid., p. 59. [5] Charles-Edwards, *Early Christian Ireland*, p. 19.
[6] Swift, 'Óenach Tailten'.

non-combatants in war and to boost the authority of the church of Iona.[7] In the mid-ninth century, the Uí Néill over-king Máel Sechnaill mac Maíl Ruanaid used royal assemblies as a diplomatic method to extend his authority across the northern half of Ireland and into Munster.[8] Assemblies (*óenaig* and *rígdála*) were thus not only a demonstration of royal power but also a means of resolving political tension and avoiding conflict.

Assemblies were occasions where laws might be promulgated. The word *rechtge* described a legal enactment by a king made in special circumstances. The term could cover royal and religious edicts to legal pronouncements intended to strengthen existing laws at times of social stress. *Rechtge* could bind all those under the authority of the king, and sometimes they reflected the relationship between a king and a church in promoting the laws of a particular patron saint.[9] Kings had legal functions beyond the issuing of edicts, although these were limited in scope compared to the legal prerogatives of Carolingian or Anglo-Saxon kings. A king could afford legal protection to subjects who came to his court seeking sanctuary, and his testimony had the highest status in a legal case. The king's household also acted as a court of appeal for his subjects. He could settle disputed legal matters directly by acting as a judge, or he might defer cases to a professional judge or advisor. The fairness of a king's judgement was treated as an essential feature of his leadership in literature about kingship. Ill consequences of a natural, human or supernatural variety said to result from bad judgement.[10]

A variety of sagas, law tracts and wisdom literature highlight the importance of royal justice (*fír flathemon*) that will bring not only harmony to his people but also good luck and abundance in the natural world. The notion of justice extended beyond legal judgement to other aspects of a king's conduct. There were taboos that certain kings must not break, indicating expectations of royal conduct and endowing the figure of a king with a supernatural mystique. The law tract *Críth Gablach* is even specific enough to outline what a king should do on each day of the week: judging legal cases on Mondays and Saturdays, drinking ale on Sundays, playing board games on

---

[7] Ó Néill and Dumville, eds and trans., *Cáin Adomnáin*; Ní Dhonnchadha, 'Guarantor List'.

[8] Bhreathnach, *Ireland*, pp. 71–2; *AU, s.aa.* 851, 859.

[9] Charles-Edwards, *Early Christian Ireland*, pp. 560–4.

[10] Ó Croinín, *Early Medieval Ireland*, pp. 75–81; Kelly, *Guide*, pp. 23–5.

Tuesdays, hunting on Wednesdays, sex on Thursdays and horseracing on Saturdays.[11] In practice it seems unlikely that the life of a king was so neatly compartmentalised. The laws prohibited kings from losing their honour by engaging in manual work, fleeing from a battle, or engaging in or tolerating other acts that could damage their reputation. It was also incumbent on a king to never be alone.[12]

Kings relied on the support of kinfolk, advisors, allies and subjects to succeed. These relationships were exercised through mutual exchanges of gifts and goods, services and protection. The reciprocity was not, however, equally balanced. Those at the top of the hierarchy bound those of lower status into a contract where they expected to receive more over the long term than they gave. The resulting accumulation of wealth, labour and military resources underpinned royal power. To exact their share of the bargain, kings and their retinues did not reside in one place, but travelled on circuits. Their subjects provided hospitality, which provided the royal household with its day-to-day needs. Laws attempted to regulate what the king and his retinue were entitled to receive. However, there is a lack of consistency in written accounts, which suggests that these obligations were negotiated from time to time. According to the law text *Críth Gablach* the king of a *túath* should be entertained with up to twelve men while travelling on public business, while a provincial king might have a retinue of thirty. The Old Irish poem on the Airgíalla (a group of dynasties whose power was focused around Monaghan, Armagh, Tyrone and Derry) limited hospitality given to kings of Tara to a hundred followers.[13] The arrival of a royal retinue must have been a significant economic burden to their hosts, especially during the winter months.

As kings travelled they would stay at royal forts, either their own, or those of a client. The fort or *dún* was a place where food renders were collected or where an army might be assembled. It also acted as a royal court and centre of public life where the people could visit their ruler. The maintenance of forts and the roads that led to them was another obligation that a king could impose on his clients, thus creating a network of royal sites. While kings might follow a circuit around client kingdoms, travel was also a way that he could display

---

[11] Charles-Edwards, 'Contract'.   [12] Kelly, *Guide*, pp. 18–19.
[13] Charles-Edwards, *Early Christian Ireland*, p. 526; O Daly, ed. and trans., 'A poem on the Airgialla'.

and enforce power over areas that had been recently subjected. A king might also subject an intransigent or disobedient people by entering their land by force and exacting tribute in cattle or other goods. In 1005, Brian Boru of Munster set out on an expedition to cement his authority as over-king of Ireland, travelling to Teltown (Co. Meath) and then to Armagh. He camped at the royal site of Navan fort (Co. Armagh) and visited the royal seat of Rathmore (Co. Antrim), where he received the submission of local kings, demonstrating his dominion over the farthest province of Ireland from his own turf. Each of the royal sites Brian visited was symbolic of his ambitions.[14]

Wherever the king travelled, key members of the royal household travelled with him. They included not only family, servants and guards but also selected clients, political hostages, entertainers, clerics and administrators. Some royal agents, such as the poet, crossed categories. The poet could perform as an entertainer, but also acted as a royal spin doctor or advisor. Others might accompany the household in a temporary capacity to serve a specific function. The complexity of royal administration seems to have increased from the eighth to the eleventh centuries as over-kings sought to extend their power. The eighth-century text *Frithfolad ríg Caisil fri tuatha Muman* depicts the court of an over-king of Munster staffed by officials from subordinate kingdoms.[15] The *rechtaire* (an official who might serve as a steward or revenue collector) is mentioned in law texts. From the eleventh century, the *rechtaire* was important enough to be mentioned in chronicles.[16] They could also act as royal agents outside of the royal household, presiding over a town or fort. Advisors (*comairli*) for kingdoms are also recorded, as are *muirig*, whose duties might include overseeing royal property, enforcing agreements and holding hostages. A *muire* could also act as a remote agent of royal authority, operating in a specific district.[17] Sometimes these offices were combined with high ecclesiastical positions. For example, Muiredach, son of Domnall, is recorded as deputy abbot of Armagh, chief steward (*ard maer*) of Southern Uí Néill and chief counsellor (*cenn adcomairc*) of Brega at his death in 924.[18]

From the ninth century, over-kings might appoint a deputy to wield authority during periods of absence from their home

[14] Duffy, *Brian Boru*, pp. 138–9.
[15] Charles-Edwards, *Early Christian Ireland*, p. 542.
[16] Byrne, 'Ireland and her neighbours', p. 873; Kelly, *Guide*, p. 65.
[17] Byrne, 'Ireland and her neighbours', pp. 875–6.   [18] *AU, s.a.* 924.

kingdom. The term *airrí* is first recorded from 960 as a title for the viceroy. By the twelfth century the term was shifting to identify petty kings who could be treated as hereditary local governors for their over-king.[19] As the power of over-kings grew, they increasingly interfered in the affairs of their sub-kings. For example, they might take executive decisions in matters of succession or dividing territories. In the mid-ninth century, Máel Sechnaill mac Maíl Ruanaid laboured to turn the ideal pan-Irish hegemony of the legendary king of Tara into a realistic ambition. His military interventions in Munster and Ulster in the 850s extended the power of Uí Néill. Nevertheless, the failure of future Uí Néill kings to secure tight control over Munster, Connacht and the rich resources of the coastal towns ruled by viking dynasties heralded their eventual decline. At the end of the tenth century, a Munster over-king, Brian Boru, would take on the ambition of former kings of Tara, and he succeeded briefly in uniting Ireland under his rule. After 1022 the title of the king of Tara ceased to connote pretensions to island-wide power, but merely denoted the over-king of Mide. In the eleventh and twelfth centuries over-kings of different provinces would battle it out to be 'king of Ireland'.

WARFARE

Military prowess was one of the essential qualities demanded of a medieval king. It was incumbent upon him not only to defend his people but also to use the threat of force to prevent feuds among his subjects. The warrior whose failure or success reflected on his king was an esteemed figure in Irish society. Such men play a prominent role in myths, legends and accounts of battle. Just as modern newspapers are filled with records of violence, so too are medieval chronicles. Texts risk giving an exaggerated view of endemic warfare, but archaeology tells its own story. About 140 early medieval cemeteries have been excavated in Ireland (c. AD 400–1200). Evidence of weapon trauma on skeletons has been recovered from eighteen sites. A few appear to have suffered very grisly deaths indeed.[20] Many other bodies could have suffered violence without it showing signs on the skeleton. Disproportionately the individuals who suffered heavy blows from sharp implements were adult men. A number of these

[19] Byrne, 'Ireland and her neighbours', pp. 877–8.
[20] Geber, 'Comparative study', p. 261.

appear to have been trained warriors with shoulder problems that could reflect repetitive stress from spear thrusting and javelin throwing. At Mount Gamble cemetery (Co. Dublin), the skeletons that exhibited weapons trauma belonged to men of above-average stature and health.[21] It seems that kings and warriors could pay a high price for their status.

Archaeology and art history provide insights into the weapons that were used in the early Middle Ages. Illustrations of warriors are found in manuscripts such as the 'Book of Kells' and in sculpture, as at White Island, Co. Fermanagh. These show a small round shield and a spear to be the standard equipment of warriors.[22] Spears were suited for both throwing and for hand-to-hand combat. Elite fighters might be expected to arrive at battle on horseback and fight with swords. Over time, the technology of war changed as state-of-the-art weapons and tactics were introduced.[23] The Viking Age witnessed the adoption of the battleaxe as a weapon that was suited to close combat but was cheaper to produce than a sword. Archery also increased in significance from the ninth century.[24] From the mid-tenth century arrowheads were used of a type designed to pierce armour. This suggests that armour became increasingly common in battle, at least among the Hiberno-Scandinavians. Swords also improved in quality. These changes reflect increasing investment in warfare over time as royal resources increased and large-scale military campaigns became more common.

At the beginning of the period under discussion, the mobility of Irish warriors at sea was well known due to their attacks on post-Roman Britain. The British writer Gildas refers to them travelling in coracles.[25] The military levies recorded in *Míniugud Senchusa fer nAlban* (a text compiled in the tenth century from seventh- or eighth-century materials) suggest that the ability to mobilise troops by sea remained important in Gaelic coastal communities, and occasional references to fleets are found in Irish chronicles during the seventh and eighth centuries.[26] Scandinavian settlement in Ireland in the ninth century brought advanced maritime technology. A plethora of records from the 830s to the 850s suggest that longships frequented the coasts and inland waterways of Ireland.[27] Each of the coastal fortresses

---

[21] Bhreathnach, *Ireland*, p. 98.   [22] Charles-Edwards, 'Irish warfare', p. 27.
[23] Halpin, 'Weapons', p. 125.   [24] Ibid., pp. 126, 129.
[25] Charles-Edwards, 'Irish warfare', p. 27.   [26] *AFM, s.aa.* 612, 728
[27] *AFM, s.aa.* 836, 838, 841, 847, 850, 858.

established by vikings seems to have had its own fleet.[28] This development may have spurred Irish kings on to improve their own naval capacity not only against vikings but also in the field of interprovincial warfare.[29] The increasing use of naval warfare among the Irish is noted from the late tenth century.[30] The construction of Scandinavian-style ships in Ireland in the mid-eleventh century is indicated by the find of the warship 'Skuldelev 2' scuttled in Roskilde Fjord, which was found to be built from Irish oak. The fleet of Dublin was probably the best in Ireland, and during the eleventh century it would be engaged from time to time in overseas campaigns. The resources needed to maintain these ships were a significant drain on the economy, although the costs might be alleviated by slave taking, plunder and mercenary ventures. The introduction of the Norse word *leiðang* into Irish by the eleventh century may indicate that a Scandinavian system of raising fleets and crews had been introduced to the island to help manage the rising costs and activities of fleets.[31]

Throughout the early Middle Ages, warfare on land often took the form of raids, carrying away portable wealth and causing a level of destruction that could weaken a rival king and bring death, enslavement or famine to his people. A king could call on his retinue to support him in battle. This was a diverse group of men bound to a ruler through personal ties. Military obligations were also placed upon royal subjects and client peoples to supply campaigns with goods and men. A poem dated to around AD 700 outlines the relationship between the Airgíalla (a people whose territory lay between Ulster and Mide) and their Uí Néill overlords. The text indicates that contingents were supplied and led by kings of client peoples.[32] As over-kings became more powerful from the ninth century, the potential size and reach of their campaigns increased. Professional warriors or mercenaries might also be employed to gain an advantage in battle. These included viking warriors. Relations between Hiberno-Scandinavian ports and Irish kings were conditioned by the latter's need for military resources. The fleets and militias of Limerick and Waterford aided the rise of the Munster over-king Brian Boru in the late tenth and early eleventh centuries. The emergence of new terms – *óglachas* to describe warrior service and *tuarastal* and *inarrad* as payments given for military service – by AD 1100 suggests the increasing specialisation of military

[28] *AFM, s.aa.* 864   [29] *AFM, s.aa.* 902, 905, 908.
[30] Etchingham, 'Skuldelev 2', p. 89.   [31] Holm, 'The naval power', p. 77.
[32] Charles-Edwards, *Early Christian Ireland*, p. 464

activity.[33] The eleventh century also witnessed increasing investment in fortress building and bridge building to secure lines of communication and defence in large-scale wars.

Violence was often part of a wider strategy for political control that could include alliances against an enemy, assassination of high-status opponents, interference in dynastic succession and winning the support of powerful ecclesiastical figures. The threat of violence could bring rival parties into a treaty, and churchmen sometimes served as negotiators in these agreements.[34] The Church in Ireland had a mixed relationship with violence. On the one hand, it issued regulations intended to inhibit violence and the moral chaos that could result. The best known of these is *Cáin Adomnáin* or *Lex Innocentium*, which was issued in 697. The purpose of this law was to help protect women, children and clerics from violence by imposing fines on their killers. On the other hand, rivalry between religious houses was also a cause of armed conflict.[35] The stereotype that churches were unarmed targets for viking aggression from the late eighth century should be qualified. Battles took place between churches particularly during the late eighth and early ninth centuries, including the conflict between the supporters of Clonmacnoise (Co. Offaly) and Birr (Co. Offaly) in AD 760.[36] The wars may have reflected the growing wealth of the Church and increased competition, perhaps induced by the working out of a system of territorial jurisdiction (*paruchiae*).[37] As churches were bound up with political order, they also became embroiled in the conflicts of kings. The raiding of churches is a recurrent feature of Irish warfare during the early Middle Ages: it was not an innovation introduced by vikings. In the growing scale of interprovincial warfare in the eleventh century, leading churchmen, including the abbot of Armagh, became powerful allies and arbiters of peace.

LOCAL HISTORIES

Uí Néill

Uí Néill claimed descent from a semi-legendary figure 'Niall of the Nine Hostages'. According to later myths, Niall was abandoned as a

---

[33] O' Keeffe, 'Rural settlement', p. 145.
[34] Charles-Edwards, 'Irish warfare before 1100', pp. 32–3.
[35] Ó Corráin, 'Ireland c. 800', p. 600.
[36] Hughes, 'The Church in Irish society', p. 316.
[37] Ó Corráin, 'Ireland c. 800', pp. 600–1.

child and raised by a poet. Once his true parentage is revealed, he competes against his brothers in various feats. In one of these competitions, the brothers must draw water from a well presided over by a monstrous old woman who demands a kiss from each of them. Only Niall complies enthusiastically with her request, and the woman is transferred into a beautiful lady representing the sovereignty of Ireland.[38] Niall may have been a figure of the fifth century.[39] In legend, his sons are represented as contemporaries of Saint Patrick, but this may be a fiction. Stories of Patrick's favour or disfavour towards different sons were used retrospectively to explain why their descendants succeeded or failed politically.[40] The label Uí Néill can be no older than the sixth century, and yet by the end of that century Uí Néill had emerged as the dominant dynasty in the northern half of Ireland. By the eighth century their lands extended from Donegal to Dublin, excluding the province of Ulster.

A significant theme in early chronicle records is the struggle for control of the midlands between the descendants of Neill and the rulers of Leinster. It is claimed that Brega was won by Coirpre, son of Niall, from the Leinstermen in the 490s. The plain of Mide was then taken from Leinster by Fiachu, son of Niall, at the battle of Druim Derg (near Downpatrick, Co. Down) in 516.[41] Their conquests were consolidated by the great-grandsons of Niall – Túathal Máelgarb and Diarmait mac Cerbaill – in the sixth century. The descendants of Diarmait retained power in the midlands of Ireland as kings of Southern Uí Néill. They were split into two main groups that dominated the east midlands, namely Síl nÁedo Sláine and Clann Cholmáin. In the northwest of Ireland, two other branches of Niall's descendants wielded power: Cenél Conaill and Cenél nEógain controlled the kingship of Northern Uí Néill. Various related and unrelated groups were brought under the overlordship of Northern and Southern Uí Néill within this wide arc of territory. From the 730s until the tenth century, Clann Cholmáin in the south and Cenél nEógain in the north alternated in holding the over-kingship of all Uí Néill. The breakdown of this relatively stable arrangement preceded the decline of Uí Néill as the most powerful rulers in Ireland.

---

[38] Koch *et al.*, trans., *Celtic heroic age*, pp. 203–8.
[39] Charles-Edwards, *Early Christian Ireland*, pp. 441–50.
[40] Ibid., p. 458.   [41] Ibid., pp. 450–1.

Figure 4.1 Grianan of Aileach, Co. Donegal

Northern Uí Néill

The heartland of Northern Uí Néill came to comprise the areas of the modern counties of Donegal, Tyrone and Londonderry. Initially their territories lay west of the River Foyle, and their main royal seat was at Aileach on the Inishowen peninsula where the impressive stone fort of Grianán still stands (see Figure 4.1). Three main dynasties presided over Northern Uí Néill – Cenél Conaill, Cenél nEógain and Cenél nÉnnai – claiming descent from three brothers.[42] From the sixth until the eighth century, Cenél Conaill were the most powerful group. Their power also extended to ecclesiastical politics, for St Columba (d. 597) and subsequent abbots of Iona belonged to this dynasty. The supremacy of Uí Néill in the north of Ireland was established at the Battle of Mag Roth (Moira, Co. Down) in 637 when Domnall mac Áedo of Cenél Conaill defeated the forces of Ulaid and Dál Riata.

In the 730s, Cenél nEógain challenged the power of Cenél Conaill in a series of battles over the land of Mag nÍtha (Co. Donegal). Cenél nEógain emerged victorious, and their king Áed Allán asserted his power over all Uí Néill. He defeated the Ulaid at the battle of Faughart (Co. Louth) in 735, taking the strategic lands of Conaille Muirthemne on the east coast.[43] In 738 he also won a great victory over Leinster at Áth Senaig (Ballyshannon, Co. Kildare).[44] Áed's successors continued to maintain the supremacy of Cenél nEógain in

---

[42] Ó Corráin, *Ireland*, p. 16.   [43] Charles-Edwards, *Early Christian Ireland*, p. 571.
[44] Byrne, *Irish Kings*, p. 209.

the north, winning a further victory over Cenél Conaill at the battle of Clóitech (Clady? Co. Tyrone) in 789.[45]

Cenél nEógain continued to pursue their ambitions to wider hegemony in Ireland, alternating in the kingship of Tara with their Southern Uí Néill counterparts. In 804, their king, Áed Oirdnide harried Leinster and in the following year brought an army to the northern borders of the province and proceeded to divide it between two kings.[46] Áed's son Niall Caille also extended the power of the dynasty by winning a major victory over the Airgíalla and Ulaid in 827. This brought Cenél nEógain the over-kingship of lands around the important church of Armagh, of which they became major patrons.[47] From the late ninth century, vikings added an element of instability into the political strategies of Cenél nEógain. The reign of Áed Finnlíath (d. 879) witnessed periods of alliance and defiance of different viking groups. His son Niall Glúndub would fall in battle against the Dubliners, and another son Muirchertach was slain in battle against the same enemy, despite his earlier victories against them. Muirchertach's death in 943 helped trigger a succession dispute over the kingship of Northern Uí Néill and the kingship of Tara. A candidate from Cenél Conaill, Ruaidrí ua Canannáin, would briefly rise to power before Cenél nEógain were able to reassert their supremacy in the north under Domnall ua Néill, son of Muirchertach. His reign witnessed a struggle with Southern Uí Néill, paving the way for the decline of the kingship of Tara.[48] At the eve of the eleventh century Cenél nEógain sought to resist the rise of the Munster king Brian Boru with limited success. The fortunes of the dynasty improved under the kingship of Domnall Ua Lochlainn at the end of the eleventh century. He managed to establish authority across the north of Ireland and Southern Uí Néill, but his achievements would be limited by Brian Boru's grandson, Muirchertach Ua Briain.[49]

Southern Uí Néill

Two great dynasties would come to dominate the lands of Southern Uí Neill that comprised the east midland territories of Brega, Mide and Tethba. These were Síl nÁedo Sláine in Brega in the east and Clann Cholmáin in Mide in the west. The royal sites of Síl

[45] Ó Corráin, *Ireland*, p. 17.   [46] Charles-Edwards, 'Irish warfare', pp. 32–3.
[47] Ó Corráin, *Ireland*, p. 16.   [48] Ibid., pp. 118–20.
[49] Ó Cróinín, *Early medieval Ireland*, pp. 278–9.

nÁedo Sláine included Oristown (Ráith Airthir) and Lagore (Loch nGabor) and from the ninth century were associated with a hill-fort at Knowth (Cnogba) in a landscape of prehistoric tombs. Clann Cholmáin presided over the Hill of Uisneach, an archaeological land-scape that was regarded in Irish mythology as the meeting point of all the ancient provinces of Ireland. Other sites included Cró-Inis on Lough Ennell, and Rathconnell, near Mullingar (Co. Westmeath).[50]

Despite their common descent from Diarmait mac Cerbaill, the two dynasties of Síl nÁedo Sláine and Clann Cholmáin were already opposed by the early seventh century. They fought on opposing sides at the great Battle of Mag Roth in Ulster.[51] Initially Síl nÁedo Sláine was the dominant dynasty in Southern Uí Néill, but power shifted west in the early eighth century, when a feud within Síl nÁedo Sláine led to a series of killings.[52] Clann Cholmáin was able to capitalise on their rivals' bloodshed and rise to power. Clann Cholmáin would continue to wield authority over Southern Uí Néill for much of the early Middle Ages.

The growing power of Uí Néill led to an attempt by Máel Sech-naill mac Maíl Ruanaid of Clann Cholmáin (d. 862) to bring all the provinces of Ireland under his lordship. In 845 Máel Sechnaill defeated local rivals and then took on the growing threat of viking invasions by capturing and drowning one of their leaders, Tuirgeis, who had been raiding along the River Shannon and having him ritually drowned. In the following year, Máel Sechnaill succeeded the Cenél nEógain over-king of Tara, Niall Caille. He spent the rest of his days labouring to turn the aspiration of a Uí Néill kingship of Ireland into a realistic ambition. Máel Sechnaill won further victories over vikings in 848 and 849, and in 851 he executed Cináed, a king of Brega who had allied with the vikings of Dublin against him. By 860, Máel Sech-naill wielded authority over much of southern Ireland. However, the Dubliners continued to be a thorn in his side during his campaigns against Áed Finnlíath of Cenél nEógain. On Máel Sechnaill's death in 862 he was commemorated as 'king of Ireland'.[53] He had achieved much and helped establish a secure position for his son and successor, Flann Sinna. Flann would enjoy a remarkably long reign as over-king of Southern Uí Néill (and later king of Tara) until his death in 916.

---

[50] Byrne, *Irish kings*, p. 87.   [51] Charles-Edwards, *Early Christian Ireland*, p. 497.
[52] Ibid., p. 571.   [53] Ó Corráin, *Ireland*, p. 100.

A great rivalry arose between the sons of Flann Sinna. This
caused a rebellion prior to Flann's death. It is tempting to link these
chaotic political events to the deposition of silver hoards around
Lough Ennell, which date to the reign of Flann. Maybe a slighted
father had refused to tell his offspring where the family treasure was
hidden.[54] Donnchad mac Flainn succeeded to rule as king of Tara
in 919 and clung to power until 944, blinding one brother, treacherously murdering another and disposing of a nephew in the process.[55]
A succession crisis followed Donnchad's death, and a candidate from
Síl nÁedo Sláine was able to seize power. This was Congalach mac
Maíl Mithig, who ruled as over-king of Southern Uí Neill and king
of Tara from 944 to 956. He was able to maintain his position against
the Northern Uí Néill king, Ruaidrí ua Canannáin, by forging an
alliance with Olaf Cuarán, king of Dublin. On Congalach's death the
alternating succession of Clann Cholmáin and Cenél nEógain to the
kingship of Tara was restored.

Máel Sechnaill mac Domnaill of Clann Cholmáin would be the
last king of Southern Uí Néill to wield significant power in Ireland.
In 980, Máel Sechnaill hastened the end of the reign of Olaf Cuarán,
king of Dublin, by defeating him in battle at Tara. For the next decade,
Máel Sechnaill may have wielded influence in Dublin while it was
ruled by his brother-in-law Glún Iairn. When Glún Iairn was killed
when drunk by one of his slaves in 989, Máel Sechnaill attacked the
port in a bid to bring it under his control.[56] The major challenge in
Máel Sechnaill's reign was the rise of Brian Boru, over-king of Munster. Máel Sechnaill was a vigorous ruler and master of grand political
gestures. In 982 he invaded Brian's political heartland and cut down
the royal inaugural tree of his people at Magh Adair (Co. Clare) and
had it turned into firewood. Some years later in 999, Máel Sechnaill
took the 'Stone of Ailbe', the most important monument of Síl nÁedo
Sláine and converted it to millstones.[57] Máel Sechnaill also sought to
build a causeway across the River Shannon at Athlone so that he
might use his troops to outmanoeuvre Brian Boru, but his tactics
failed. From 1002, Máel Sechnaill was subject to the Munster over-
king.[58] Although Máel Sechnaill could claim to be the most powerful
king of Ireland for the years between the death of Brian Boru in 1014
and his own demise in 1022, future kings of Southern Uí Néill were

---

[54] Downham, 'Vikings in Southern Uí Néill'.   [55] Doherty, 'Donnchad Donn'.
[56] *AU, s.a.* 989.   [57] *CS, s.a.* 982; *AU, s.a.* 999.   [58] *AU, s.aa.* 1001, 1002.

unable to achieve a position of political prominence. For the remainder of the eleventh century, the rulers of Munster, Connacht and Northern Uí Néill would hold greater power in Ireland.

Ulster

The province of Ulster was said to have dominated the northern half of Ireland in prehistory. The story of its former greatness, reaching as far south as the River Boyne, was preserved in saga. The province appears to have diminished in size through the growth of Uí Néill power from the sixth century. The early medieval province was very different in its geographical scope from the modern one. There were three main political groups in Ulster. Dál Fíatach occupied the east coast (eastern Co. Down) with their political centre at Downpatrick. This group supplied many of the early medieval over-kings of the province. Another group, the Cruithni, comprised several peoples, notably Dál nAraidi based in Mag Line (Moylinny, Co. Antrim) and Uí Echach Cobo (western Co. Down). Finally, there were the Dál Riata who held territory along the north coast of Ulster (north Co. Antrim) and in Argyll.[59]

The early history of the province was characterised by resistance to the growing power of Uí Néill, complicated by rivalries between different groups within Ulster. One of the famous early over-kings was Báetan mac Cairill (d. 582). Báetán sought to offset the expansion of Uí Néill by extending his power overseas. He attempted the conquest of Dál Riata in Britain and the Isle of Man.[60] In the immediate aftermath of Báetán's death, Dál nAraidi were able to win control of Ulster. A coalition then developed between Dál nAraidi and Dál Riata to confront Uí Néill. This led to a battle at *Mag Roth* (Moira, Co. Down) in 637 where the Ulster forces were defeated and their over-king, Congal Cáech, was killed.[61] The significance of this event was commemorated in three Middle Irish sagas: *Fled Dúin na nGéd*, *Cath Maige Rátha* and *Buile Shuibne*. The over-kingship of the province then swapped between rival groups of Dál Fíatach and Dál Riata, with Dál Fíatach often holding the upper hand. Nearly a century later, a Dál Fíatach over-king, Áed Róin, suffered another major defeat against Uí Néill at Faughart (Co. Louth) in 735. Nevertheless,

[59] Charles-Edwards, *Early Christian Ireland*, p. 54.
[60] Byrne, *Irish kings*, pp. 109–11.   [61] Ibid., p. 114.

Áed and his son Fiachnae were able to make some territorial gains at the expense of their northern neighbour Dál nAraidi.[62] The struggle with Uí Néill over the southern borderlands of Ulster continued into the ninth century, with the Ulster forces under Muiredach mac Eochada being dealt another blow by the king of Tara, Niall mac Áeda, at the battle of Leth Cam in the lands of Airgíalla in 827.[63]

In the eighth century, the ambitions of kings of Ulster were contained by Uí Néill along their landward borders. Across the North Channel, the growth of Pictish power would also curtail the power of Dál Riata in North Britain. Scottish Dál Riata stretched from Eigg to Kintyre and inland to the mountains called Druim Alban ('the Spine of Britain'). The area was 'hammered' by Óengus son of Fergus, king of the Picts in the year 741. At the same time Indrechtach, king of Dál nAraidi, attacked the Irish lands of Dál Riata, and it may be from this point that the Scottish and Irish parts of Dál Riata came under separate rule.[64] The arrival of Scandinavian pirates at the end of the eighth century would have further consequences as large parts of Dál Riata were settled by vikings.

The coasts of northeast Ireland were vulnerable to seaborne attack. In 811, an early victory is recorded by the Ulaid against vikings, but this did not prevent further attacks. A series of raids in the 820s and 830s culminated in the foundation of short-lived viking camps at Strangford Lough, Carlingford Lough and Lough Neagh. Viking wars were recorded in the region in the 870s, and a further period of intense activity is noted from the 920s to the 940s.[65] Nevertheless, kings of Ulster were successful in resisting territorial conquests. Dál nAraidi grew in strength during the ninth century, perhaps as a consequence of the decline of Dál Riata and the warfare between Dál Fíatach and the vikings. Dál nAraidi seized control of the overkingship of Ulster several times during the late ninth and early tenth centuries. However, Dál Fíatach power was firmly reestablished during the long reign of Eochaid mac Ardgail (972–1004), and his dynasty ruled the province thereafter.[66]

---

[62] McErlean *et al.*, *Strangford Lough*, p. 59.

[63] Charles-Edwards, *Early Christian Ireland*, p. 557.

[64] Downham, 'The break up', p. 190.

[65] *AU, s.aa.* 811, 823–5, 831–3, 839–42, 852, 866, 871, 877, 879, 886, 913, 924–7, 937, 942, 970.

[66] Byrne, *Irish kings*, pp. 286–7.

From the late tenth century, Ulster would come under pressure as both Uí Néill and Dál Cais sought to establish their dominance in Ireland. In 1003 Brian Boru led the forces of Munster, Mide and Connacht against Ulster and the Northern Uí Néill. In 1004, Eochaid was killed in a major battle against the Northern Uí Néill at the inauguration site of Cráeb Telcha (Crew Hill, Co. Antrim).[67] In the following year, Brian Boru came to Armagh in order to win the support of that famous church. At the same time, he took hostages from Ulster.[68] The province was further weakened by internecine conflict between members of Dál Fíatach during the early eleventh century. In the late eleventh century, over-kings of Ulster adopted the tactic of allying with the Munster over-kings, Toirdelbach and Muirchertach Ua Briain, to offset the threat posed by the Northern Uí Néill. However, this policy would force the province into a damaging war between Muirchertach Ua Briain and Domnall Ua Lochlainn of the Northern Uí Néill .[69]

Connacht

During the early Middle Ages, the lands of Connacht were bounded by Galway Bay in the south and the Drowes estuary (Co. Donegal) in the north. The River Shannon as far as Lough Ree formed the eastern boundary. The province takes its name from the Connachta, a group of dynasties that professed descent from a legendary king, Conn Cétchathach ('Conn of the Hundred Battles'). They claimed common ancestry with Uí Néill, who were said to have originated in the province. One branch of Uí Néill, Cenél Coirpri Dromma Clíab continued to reside within the northern borders of Connacht during the early Middle Ages. A number of other peoples, both related and unrelated to the Connachta, dwelt in the rest of the province. In the sixth and seventh centuries, the most powerful group of Connachta were Uí Fíachrach. By the seventh century they were divided into two main groups: Uí Fíachrach Aidne who resided in the south and Uí Fíachrach Muaide who held territory around Moy estuary in the north.[70] From the eighth century, another Connachta people, Uí Briúin, would rise to prominence. Uí Briúin was divided into several

[67] *AU*, s.a. 1004; Macdonald, 'Archaeological evaluation'.
[68] Ní Mhaonaigh, *Brian Boru*, p. 36. [69] Ó Corráin, *Ireland*, p. 147.
[70] Charles-Edwards, *Early Christian Ireland*, p. 39.

subgroups, the most powerful of which held the fertile lands of Mag nAí in eastern Connacht. This plain included Crúachu (Rathcroghan, Co. Roscommon), a focus of prehistoric monuments and a site of royal inaugurations.

The earliest chronicle accounts of Connachta are coloured by their relations to the growing power of Uí Néill. In 561 a battle was fought near Connacht's northern border with Uí Néill at Cúl Dreimne. In this conflict, Áed mac Echach, king of Uí Briúin Aí, was allied with the Northern Uí Néill and won a victory against the Southern Uí Néill king of Tara, Diarmait mac Cerbaill.[71] The location of the battle suggests Diarmait was the attacker. Áed's grandson Rogallach would help consolidate the fortunes of the Uí Briúin Aí dynasty in the early seventh century. However, Uí Fíachrach remained a power to be reckoned with in Connacht history. Guaire Aidne of the southern Uí Fíachrach was one of their best-known rulers. In 649, he was defeated by the king of Tara, Diarmait mac Áedo Sláine, in battle at Carn Conaill in Connacht (near Gort, Co. Galway). The event was the topic of a later saga *Cath Cairnd Chonaill*. Other literature about Guaire suggests he was involved in the politics of northern Munster and had established a reputation for piety.[72]

Uí Briúin Aí rose to greater prominence in the eighth century. In 704, their aged king, Cellach mac Ragallaig, successfully defended the province against an invasion by Loingsech mac Óengusso, king of Tara. Thereafter Uí Briúin Aí gradually won the allegiance of many other peoples in Connacht, and from 773 they were able to block Uí Fíachrach from winning the over-kingship of the province.[73] At the end of the eighth century rivalry between different dynasties within Uí Briúin led to conflict, with Muirguis mac Tommaltaig emerging victorious from the battlefield in 799. His reign, which ended in 815, was characterised by vigorous efforts to impose more direct rule over the peoples of Connacht.[74] In the years before his death the shores of southwest Connacht were subject to viking attacks, but the brunt of these was borne by local population groups Fir Umaill and Conmaicne.[75]

During the late ninth century, kings of Uí Briúin Aí often worked in allegiance with kings of Tara. The grandson of Muirguis, Conchobar mac Taidg Mór, participated in the campaign of Máel Sechnaill of

---

[71] Ibid., p. 294.   [72] Byrne, *Irish kings*, pp. 239–42.   [73] Ibid., p. 247.
[74] Ibid., p. 251.   [75] *AU, s.aa.* 812, 813.

Southern Uí Néill against the Northern Uí Néill in 860. Three years later Conchobar was brought under the subjection of the Northern Uí Néill king of Tara, Áed Finnlíath, whom he had formerly opposed. He then allied with Áed to campaign against Brega. In the early tenth century, the continued efforts of Uí Néill to impose authority over Connacht led to two invasions during the reign of Cathal mac Conchobuir; the first, which was led by Niall Glúndub in 913, was successful. The second, led by Donnchad Donn in 922, took place while the borders of Connacht were under viking attack, but the Connachta prevailed.[76] In the late tenth century, Connacht would become a battleground for the competing ambitions of Máel Sechnaill mac Domnaill, king of Tara, and Brian Boru of Munster, with Brian gaining the upper hand.[77]

Uí Briúin Bréifne in the northeast of Connacht had extended their territory into the northwestern midlands by the late ninth century. They wielded power over minor peoples who dwelt between the boundaries of Northern and Southern Uí Néill.[78] By the late tenth century, their power was sufficient to challenge the hegemony of Uí Briúin Aí by raising one of their own kings, Fergal Ua Ruairc, to the over-kingship of the province. After Fergal's death, Uí Briúin Aí raised their own candidate Conchobar. The rivalry between their descendants, the Uí Ruairc and the Uí Chonchobuir, continued through the eleventh century. Another group, Uí Briúin Seóla, who held land east of Lough Corrib, also contended for power and raised their own provincial over-king Flaithbertach Ua Flaithbertaig, who died in 1098. From 1102, Uí Chonchobuir of Uí Briúin Aí once again held the monopoly on the provincial over-kingship. To compensate, the Uí Ruairc sought to extend their power in Mide, taking advantage of the decline of the Southern Uí Néill during the eleventh century. Both groups, Uí Chonchobuir and Uí Ruairc, would play a significant role in the history of twelfth-century Ireland.

Munster

The borders of Munster ran from Slieve Bloom (Co. Laois) in the northeast to the Burren (Co. Clare) in the northwest, and comprised the southwest coasts of Ireland.[79] From the sixth century

[76] *AU, s.a.* 913; *CS, s.a.* 922.   [77] Duffy, *Brian Boru*, pp. 114–15, 120.
[78] Ó Corráin, *Ireland*, p. 10.   [79] Cf. *AU, s.a.* 858.

Figure 4.2 Rock of Cashel, Co. Tipperary

until the mid-tenth century, the province was dominated by families that claimed a common prehistoric ancestor, Eógan 'the Great'. These Eóganachta were divided into several groups spread throughout the province, none of which were able to monopolise the over-kingship of the province. The more prominent groups included Eóganacht Glendamnach, who dwelt in the Upper Blackwater valley in the south, and Eóganacht Chaisil, who dwelt around the impressive Rock of Cashel (Co. Tipperary), which was a provincial royal site in eastern Munster (see Figure 4.2). A handful of kings were raised from Eóganacht Glendamnach from the late sixth century until the early ninth century. Eóganacht Chaisil were more successful in raising a number over-kings in the late seventh, late ninth and tenth centuries.[80] The provincial over-kingship nevertheless remained open to other Eóganacht groups in Munster. There were also multiple non-Eóganacht peoples who were excluded from the over-kingship until the tenth century, including Fir Maige Féne of Fermoy, Éli in the north, Osraige in the east and Déisi in the south.[81] There is a relatively limited body of chronicle information from Munster to tell us about developing relations between these groups in the sixth and seventh centuries.

[80] Byrne, *Irish kings*, pp. 176–7, 278.   [81] Ibid., p. 180.

From the eighth century, Munster kings competed with the growing power of Uí Néill and sought to extend their influence in Leinster. In 721, the recently ordained king of Eóganacht Glendamnach,
Cathal mac Finguine, attacked Brega in alliance with the over-king of
Leinster, Murchad mac Brain. During the 730s, Cathal campaigned
against Brega and Leinster.[82] These actions led to a royal meeting
between Cathal and Áed Allan, a Cenél nEógain king of Tara, at Ter-
ryglass (Co. Tipperary) in 737. The event was presumably intended to
diminish the risk of open conflict, but it did not stop both kings from
waging separate wars against Leinster in the following year.[83] Cathal's
bid to limit the influence of Uí Néill along the eastern borders of
Munster had limited success. Nevertheless, he would later be revered
as one of the more powerful over-kings of Munster.

The competition between the over-kings of Munster and Uí Néill
drew in ecclesiastical politics. In 793, the Munster over-king Artrí
mac Cathail was ordained by the abbot of Emly (Co. Tipperary).
This ceremony of royal ordination, which raised the status of a king
to God's anointed, was new in Ireland. Not to be outdone, the Uí
Néill over-king Áed mac Néill was ceremonially ordained a few years
later and was later known as Áed Oirdnide (Áed the Ordained). The
charismatic union of religion and politics was further exemplified
in the reign of Feidlimid mac Crimthainn, who succeeded Artrí to
the over-kingship of Munster in 820. Feidlimid was a cleric linked
with the ascetic movement of the Céli Dé, and in some later mar-
tyrologies he was considered a saint. Despite these pious associations,
Feidlimid used violence against churches that opposed his power. He
also attacked important religious establishments beyond Munster in
a bid to extend his power in Ireland, even briefly holding Forannán,
abbot of Armagh, captive in 836.[84] The challenge Feidlimid posed
to kings of Tara led to royal meetings with Conchobar mac Donnchada (of the Southern Uí Néill) and his successor Niall Caille (of
the Northern Uí Néill). One of Feidlimid's more outlandish insults to
Uí Néill power was the capture of Gormflaith, daughter of a former
king of Tara and the wife of the current king of Tara, Niall Caille,
in 840. In the following year Niall Caille faced Feidlimid in battle
near Cloncurry (Co. Kildare), which may have successfully limited
Feidlimid's ambitions in Leinster.[85]

[82] Ibid., pp. 207–8.　[83] Ó Cróinín, 'Ireland, 400–800', p. 227.
[84] Ó Corráin, *Ireland*, pp. 97–8.　[85] Byrne, *Irish kings*, p. 225.

The death of Feidlimid in 847 hearkened a period of political decline in Munster as the province was beset by viking attacks; there were short-lived reigns of three Munster over-kings during the 850s. These circumstances aided the rising power of Osraige along the eastern borders of the province. In 859 Máel Sechnaill, king of Tara, alienated Osraige from the control of Munster over-kings and subjected it to his own authority. The ambitions of Munster would rise again during the reign of Cormac mac Cuilennáin, who campaigned in Mide, Connacht and finally in Leinster where he met his death at the Battle of Ballaghmoon (Co. Kildare) in 908. Cormac failed to staunch the decline of Eóganacht power, and his successor in the provincial over-kingship, Flaithbertach, may have been from a non-Eóganacht people.[86] During the 920s and 930s, Munster over-kings had limited success in countering and manipulating the growing power of the fortresses of Waterford and Limerick.[87] In 939 Cellachán of Cashel, over-king of Munster, allied with the army of Waterford to attack Mide, but he spent several years in captivity as a result of his opposition to Uí Néill over-kings. Later in Cellachán's reign we hear of the emerging power of a formerly obscure group who took the name Dál Cais, from northern Munster. The Dál Cais king Mathgamain mac Cennétig rose in power to seize Cashel in 964 and sack Limerick in 967.[88] His son, Brian Boru, achieved even greater fame by briefly establishing himself as over-king of all Ireland.

Brian's rise to power was dramatic. First, he subdued rivals in Munster and then waged war against Máel Sechnaill, king of Tara. In 997, Máel Sechnaill seems to have recognised Brian as supreme king in southern Ireland. Brian won control over Dublin two years later and then led further campaigns against Máel Sechnaill, who offered his submission in 1002. Only the Northern Uí Néill and Ulster continued to hold out against him, but both recognised his over-kingship by 1013. Brian's supremacy over Ireland was complete, however, it was short-lived: he would fall at the Battle of Clontarf in Easter 1014.[89] The battle has often been portrayed as an epic struggle, with Brian Boru as the saintly victor against pagan foreigners. These dramatic contrasts make for good stories, but have little basis in fact. Brian's forces at Clontarf included warriors from Hiberno-Scandinavian ports, and his enemies included many Irishmen. The

---

[86] Ibid., p. 204.   [87] *AI, s.aa.* 922, 927; *AFM, s.aa.* 921[=923], 937[=939].
[88] Ó Corráin, *Ireland*, pp. 114–17.   [89] Ibid., pp. 121–7.

conduct of Brian's life was less than saintly, and the Dubliners by 1014 were not overtly pagan.[90] Nevertheless the propaganda potential of Clontarf was fully utilised by later authors, not least through the patronage of Brian's descendants who continued to wield power over Munster in the eleventh and twelfth centuries.

Brian's grandson Toirdelbach followed his ambition in attempting to establish himself as the high-king of Ireland. Toirdelbach was the most powerful ruler in Ireland from 1072 until his death in 1086. His tactics included provoking civil war in Connacht, arranging the death of opponents, supporting the Church and improving communications by building two bridges across the Shannon. His son Muirchertach ascended to a contested throne, but eventually came to dominate Ireland despite sustained opposition from Domnall Mac Lochlainn, king of the Northern Uí Néill, and Ruaidrí Ua Conchobuir of Connacht.

Leinster

Before the sixth century, Leinster included midland territories of Mide and Brega that were seized by Uí Néill. By the seventh century, its boundaries extended from the Liffey valley in the north and the boglands of Offaly (Uí Failge) to Slieve Bloom in the west, then across to Slieve Margy and down to the Barrow estuary to the south. The long coast of Leinster faced towards Britain and France, which gave its ports a position of influence in terms of overseas trade and cultural contacts. Early kings of the province had their power focused in the fertile plains of Liffey and Kildare. They included rulers of Uí Garrchon; Uí Enechglais, who lost power in the sixth century; and Uí Mail in the seventh century. They were eventually displaced by the powerful dynasties of Uí Dúnlainge. Uí Dúnlainge occupied the fertile plain of Kildare and claimed the ancient hillfort of Knockaulin (Co. Kildare) as their ceremonial seat. The *óenach* of Leinster was associated with Carmun (probably Carnalway, Co Kildare). From the eighth century Uí Dúnlainge was subdivided into three subgroups (Uí Dunchada, Uí Fáeláin and Uí Muiredaig), which alternated in their control of the kingship of Leinster from 738 until 1033.[91] Leinster was naturally divided in two by the watershed between the Rivers Slaney and Liffey. In the south, the Uí Chennselaig were the main

---

[90] Downham, 'Battle of Clontarf'.   [91] Byrne, *Irish kings*, p. 150.

political dynasty. They had been rivals of Uí Dúnlainge in the early eighth century, but were thereafter excluded from the over-kingship of Leinster until the eleventh century.

During the late eighth century, Uí Néill succeeded in imposing their authority over Uí Dúnlainge. In the early ninth century, Feidlimid mac Crimthainn, over-king of Munster, sought to limit the power of Uí Néill in Leinster, but this effort was somewhat undone after his death.[92] During the tenth century, Uí Dúnlainge were often embroiled in wars against Dublin. In 902, an alliance between Cerball mac Muirecáin, over-king of Leinster, and Máel Finnia, king of Brega, succeeded in expelling viking leaders from the port, but Cerball's successor failed to stop their return to Dublin in 917. In 944, Bráen, son of Máel Mórda, king of Leinster, made another alliance with Brega to sack Dublin, but Uí Dúnlainge failed to bring the port under their sway. From the late tenth century, intermittent alliances were formed between the Dubliners and different branches of Uí Dúnlainge. The most famous alliance was between Máel Mórda mac Murchada, over-king of Leinster, and Sitric, king of Dublin. Their troops fought side by side against Brian Boru at the Battle of Glenn Máma in AD 999 and the Battle of Clontarf in AD 1014. According to the saga 'War of the Gaels and the Foreigners', Máel Mórda was goaded into war against Munster by his sister Gormflaith, the beautiful but vengeful ex-wife of Brian Boru. The reality is that an alliance between Leinster, Dublin and their overseas allies posed a significant challenge to Brian's ambitions to dominate all Ireland. The defeat and death of Máel Mórda at Clontarf were significant blows to the power of the north Leinster over-kings, helping other dynasties' attempts to win control of the province.[93]

There was an external bid to the over-kingship of Leinster from the royal line of Osraige in the early eleventh century. These peoples dwelt west of the River Barrow, almost acting as a buffer state between the provinces of Leinster and Munster. In 859, Máel Sechnaill mac Maíl Ruanaid had drawn Osraige away from the sphere of Munster influence. Osraige grew in strength during the kingship of Cerball mac Dúnlainge (d. 888) who allied with the Loígis in the borderlands of Leinster against different viking groups and won some notable victories.[94] The declining power of Eóganacht in Munster

[92] Ibid., p. 225.   [93] Downham, *Viking kings*, pp. 26–60.
[94] Downham, 'Career of Cearbhall'.

and Uí Dúnlainge in Leinster as a consequence of the growing ambitions of Dál Cais and Uí Néill provided further opportunities for Osraige to expand their authority in the eleventh century. Cerball's great-great-grandson Donnchad mac Gilla Pátraic, king of Osraige, was able to hold sway over Leinster for a brief period from 1033–9. Uí Dúnlainge briefly re-established their sway after his death during the reign of Murchad mac Dúnlainge, but thereafter their hegemony was broken.

In 1042, the Uí Chennselaig dynast, Diarmait mac Maíl na mBó, succeeded as over-king of Leinster. His rise to power was helped by his family ties as a grandson of Gilla Pátraic mac Donnchada, king of Osraige. He also established a formidable military reputation and wielded power over the coastal towns of Waterford and Wexford. Although Diarmait married the daughter of Donnchad Ua Briain, king of Munster, he spent much of his reign battling against his father-in-law's ambition to be over-king of Ireland. In 1052, Diarmait also brought Dublin under his sway, and he became drawn into the politics of the Irish Sea, even providing refuge for the sons of Harold Godwineson, the last Anglo-Saxon king of England in 1066. In Diarmait's later years he had a powerful ally in Toirdelbach Ua Briain, king of Munster and grandson of Brian Boru, but his long reign ended during an attack on Mide in 1072.[95] His descendants were nevertheless able to maintain their position as provincial over-kings of Leinster, shored up by control of the important coastal ports of Dublin, Wexford and Waterford, until the English invasion.

VIKING KINGS

Scandinavian raids on coastal ecclesiastical communities are documented from the 790s. Nevertheless, vikings and their descendants continued to be regarded as 'foreigners' (*gaill*) in Irish society until the twelfth century. In medieval and modern historiography vikings have been blamed for many things, including the decline of the Uí Néill, the demise of the Church and debasement in arts and learning. On the other hand, they have been praised for establishing towns and developing overseas trade. However, their impact may have been exaggerated. Hiberno-Scandinavian kings were not the main drivers in Irish politics during the 'Viking Age', although they did make a noticeable contribution.

[95] Ó Corráin, 'Career of Diarmait'.

The first record of viking activity was in 794 when 'devastation of the islands of Britain' is recorded in the 'Annals of Ulster'. A series of raids against the Irish coasts are recorded in the following year. The attackers became more ambitious in successive years, engaging in combat (with limited success) against Irish population groups and picking on wealthy inland targets such as the churches of Glendalough (Co. Wicklow) in 834 and Armagh in 832.[96] We cannot draw a neat distinction between a ninth-century phase of viking raiding driven by greed or blood lust and a tenth-century phase that was more calculated. From an early stage viking raids in Ireland display a political dimension. This is illustrated in the year 832 when the most important church in Ireland, Armagh, was sacked three times in one month. There was not much portable loot left to plunder on the third occasion. It may be that vikings group were competing with each other to attack the site, but it seems more likely that the viking armies were deliberately slighting Uí Néill as protectors of the Church and highlighting their impotence. The first identified viking leader in Irish records is Saxólfr 'lord of the foreigners' who was killed by the Cianachta of eastern Ireland in 837.[97] The mention of a name is indicative of communication between vikings and Irish. It is around this time that records emerge of viking camps established in Ireland. Most famously Scandinavians first over-wintered at Dublin in 841.[98] Soon after, political alliances are recorded between viking warbands and Irish.[99] As vikings became a permanent feature of the Irish political landscape, they established coastal bases and competed among themselves for power.

Two kings, Ivar and Olaf, emerged as the most powerful vikings in Ireland in the 850s. These rulers allied together and led active careers in Britain as well as Ireland. In 871, they transported their accumulated wealth from their British campaigns – '200 ships and a great booty of people, of English and Britons and Picts' – back to Ireland.[100] Ivar's departure from Britain seems to have prompted a story to circulate in England that he had been killed by divine vengeance, but his death is recorded in Irish chronicles in 873 as 'king of the Northmen of all Britain and Ireland'.[101] It is likely given the record of Ivar's death in Irish sources that he died in Ireland. In contrast, his associate Olaf, who was killed in Alba (North Britain) the following year, is not

---

[96] *AU, s.aa.* 832, 834.   [97] *AU, s.a.* 837.   [98] *AU, s.a.* 841.   [99] *AU, s.a.* 842.
[100] *AU, s.a.* 871.   [101] Winterbottom, ed., *Three lives*, pp. 67–87; *AU, s.a.* 873.

mentioned in Irish chronicles. His death was reported in the 'Chronicle of the Kings of Alba'.[102] As there is no surviving English record of Ivar's death in 873 there has been some doubt that the Ivar mentioned in Irish and English sources are the same. However, the chronology of Ivar's recorded activity in both islands, his high profile, and references to his English captives and British campaigns in Irish annals make a compelling case that there was one rather than two kings called Ivar operating in Britain and Ireland in the 860s and early 870s. The historical sources are complemented by early archaeological evidence of the links between vikings active in Northumbria and Ireland.[103]

Ivar's family continued to play an important role in Ireland. At least three sons and one brother survived him. His descendants would rule over Dublin and other viking settlements in Britain and Ireland for generations. Their power was, however, subject to constant challenge. Ivar's grandsons suffered a major defeat in 902, when the political elite of Dublin was driven out by a coalition between the over-kings of Brega and Leinster. Archaeological evidence suggests that not all of the port's population left.[104] Dublin's elite escaped 'half dead' across the sea. The political refugees ended up in different destinations: northwest England, Scotland and northern France. Events in 902 are credited to have brought swathes of territory in northwest England, the Isle of Man and western Scotland into viking hands. However, we only have historical evidence to suggest that Wirral in Cheshire was newly colonised by vikings from Dublin in 902, and there was a failed attempt to take land in Anglesey.[105] Other areas may have been colonised at different times. The estuaries of the Dee and the Mersey would be a natural landfall for people leaving Dublin. It is debateable whether the vikings of Dublin had the numbers or resources to make wide-ranging territorial conquests after their ignominious expulsion. It seems more likely that Hiberno-Scandinavian exiles settled among existing viking communities, so it could be argued that vikings had

---

[102] Hudson, ed. and trans., 'The Scottish Chronicle', pp. 148, 154.

[103] See for example Graham-Campbell, 'An early medieval horse-harness', pp. 247–50. Abbo identifies that a contingent of the 'great army' that fought in England in the 860s came from 'the north', which would tie in Olaf's recorded activities in Pictland: *AU, s.a.* 866.

[104] Simpson, 'Forty years', p. 25.

[105] Downham, *Viking kings*, pp. 206–7. Archaeological evidence suggests the increased influence of vikings from Ireland in Anglesey at this time.

settled in parts of Lancashire and Cumbria before 902. The distribution of the Gaelic place-name -airge ('sheiling') in viking settlements in the Irish Sea region and the North Atlantic suggests that
settlers came to northwest England from the Hebrides as well as from
Ireland.

The dynasty of Ivar returned to Ireland in the second decade of the
tenth century and retook the ports of Waterford and Dublin.[106] The
same family held York during the 920s and 930s. These decades witnessed the political zenith of Hiberno-Scandinavian power. Dublin,
Waterford and Limerick developed as towns in the tenth century,
and a series of viking camps were established at coastal and inland
sites as urban centres competed to secure their economic hinterlands
and spheres of influence. The rivalries between the leaders of Dublin
and Limerick reached a climax in 937 when the Limerick king Olaf
'Scabbyhead' was killed by his Dublin opponents. The wars between
viking rulers also entangled Irish dynasties. For example, Muirchertach, son of Niall of the Northern Uí Néill, opposed Dublin in the
930s, but his rival Matudán, over-king of Ulster, allied with them.[107]

Dublin's power would be compromised by successive attempts
of the dynasty of Ivar to shore up their fortunes in Northumbria
from the late 920s. In 937, Olaf Guthfrithsson of Dublin was heavily
defeated alongside forces from Alba and Strathclyde in the Battle of
Brunanburh in northern England. The victor was King Aethelstan,
the first ruler to unite England. Sensing weakness, the over-kings of
Northern and Southern Uí Néill allied to attack Dublin in 938, but
they failed to take it.[108] York was bought back under Wessex control
in 939, but held with some difficulty. In 944 a coalition of the over-
kings of Leinster and Brega sacked Dublin – the same year that the
dynasty of Ivar was driven out from Northumbria. In 948, Dublin
was attacked again when the Dubliners again failed again to hold
York. The canny manoeuvres of Irish kings to exploit the Dubliners' moments of political weakness marked the beginning of political
decline for the dynasty of Ivar. It also compromised their position in
Northumbria, which was permanently brought under the control of
Wessex in 954.

The late tenth century witnessed greater successes by Irish dynasties to reduce the political ambitions of Hiberno-Scandinavian towns.
In 967, King Mathgamain of the Dál Cais dynasty defeated the vikings

---

[106] Ibid., pp. 31–2.   [107] Ibid., p. 40.   [108] Ibid., pp. 41–2.

of Limerick at Solloghed (Co. Tipperary). Ten years later the port was brought under the direct control of Mathgamain's brother and successor Brian Boru, who was over-king of Munster and later achieved temporary over-kingship over all Ireland. The last viking king of Limerick and his sons were executed on Scattery Island on Brian's orders.[109] The port of Waterford chose to ally with the Dál Cais against Dublin. In 975, Máel Sechnaill, over-king of Southern Uí Néill, marked his accession by attacking Dublin. Five years later he would win a significant victory over Olaf Cuarán, king of Dublin, at the battle of Tara in 980. The alliance of Ireland's two most powerful kings, Máel Sechnaill and Brian Boru, brought further defeat for Dublin at the Battle of Glenn Máma in 999.

During the early eleventh century, Dublin and Waterford continued to operate with a degree of autonomy, but the political influence of Hiberno-Scandinavian rulers was in decline. The Battle of Clontarf between the forces of Brian Boru and Dublin in 1014 is often seen as a decisive victory over the Hiberno-Scandinavians, but the story is longer and more complex. After the battle, Dublin continued to maintain a degree of independence during the long reign of King Sitric Silkenbeard (c. 995–1036). Thereafter Dublin was increasingly subject to provincial over-kings and contenders for the over-kingship of Ireland. By 1052 Waterford had been brought under the direct control of kings of Leinster, although Dublin retained local kings until 1171.

The practice of kingship in Hiberno-Scandinavian towns was similar to that of Irish rulers. Olaf Cuarán bears an epithet 'of the sandal', which may refer to an inaugural rite involving a shoe that has comparisons with Gaelic kingship rituals. We also have a praise poem in Irish that refers to this king. However, the eclectic culture of the coastal ports may have also given a distinct character to aspects of Hiberno-Scandinavian kingship. There is reference to 'a ring of Thorir' and 'the sword of Carlus' serving as emblems of royal authority in Dublin in the tenth century.[110] Swords and rings are associated with kingship in Irish literature, but the personal names linked with the Dublin insignia seem to derive from a non-Irish context. The assembly site or 'Thing' mound of Dublin that once stood near College Green represents a Scandinavian form of government. This is where the kings, royal heirs, viceroys, and law-speakers who were

[109] Ibid., p. 55.   [110] Ibid., pp. 7–8.

mentioned with reference to the government of the town would have held public assemblies on legal and military matters.[111] An innovation imported from England, rather than Scandinavia, was the minting of coins, which began in Dublin in the 990s. The production, regulation and imagery of these coins would serve political as well as economic ends and cast light on relations between England and Dublin during the reign of Sitric Silkenbeard.

Ireland's coastal towns were connected with a widespread Scandinavian-speaking community that brought an eclectic mix of cultural influences to Ireland. Hiberno-Scandinavian kings controlled Ireland's major coastal ports and developed navies, which made them brokers in international trade and mercenary fleets. There is evidence of foreign alliances between Dublin, Alba and Strathclyde in the tenth century. In the reign of Sitric Silkenbeard an alliance was developed with Cnut, king of England, Denmark and Norway. Cnut seems to have encouraged Dubliners to attack Wales and develop a base in Anglesey to serve his interests in Wales.[112] As Irish kings increasingly controlled affairs in Hiberno-Scandinavian towns they were drawn into the sphere of English politics. During the reign of Edward the Confessor of England, the over-king of Leinster, Diarmait mac Maíl na mBó, presided over Dublin, and the port became a haven for English aristocrats who had fallen from royal favour. The exile Harold Godwineson raised a fleet of nine ships from Ireland in 1052, which helped restore his family to power in England. In the aftermath of the Battle of Hastings in 1066, two of Harold's sons fled to Diarmait, where they led abortive attempts to reconquer England from Ireland.[113] The role of Hiberno-Scandinavian ports as a conduit for external political connections would continue during the twelfth century.

CONCLUSION

By the end of the eleventh century, the identity of the different provinces of Ireland had been firmly established. Their political divisions, leading dynasties and major churches continued to exert influence over the politics of Ireland into the later Middle Ages. The most significant political theme to emerge from the early Middle Ages was

---

[111] Downham, 'Viking settlement'.   [112] Downham, 'England', p. 64.
[113] Ibid., p. 67.

the inability of any single royal dynasty to establish overarching power in Ireland. This heralded the continued political division of Ireland and competition over resources in later centuries. The notion of a unified Ireland that was developed from an early time by the kings of Uí Néill would nevertheless have a lasting place in Irish political discourse.

5

RELIGION AD 500–1100

Perceptions of early Irish churches have been greatly influenced by romantic notions of 'otherness'. Ireland's place on the margins of Europe has led its early Church to be regarded as separate from the mainstream, with greater continuity of pagan traditions and possessing a less worldly outlook than the Church in other lands.

Such stereotypes can only be maintained through a very selective and partial reading of the primary sources. A contrary view can be put forward that Irish churches were greatly concerned with orthodoxy and they maintained strong and meaningful links with churches abroad. Ecclesiastical institutions were not staffed solely by ascetic recluses, but there was an all-embracing model of church organisation in which pastoral care and the administration of temporalities were fundamental aspects of ecclesiastical life. While churches aspired to be gateways to the otherworld, their everyday concerns would always be firmly anchored in the social, political and economic realities of the world around them.

CHRISTIANISATION

Saint Patrick was an important figure in the conversion of Ireland. However, Ireland was not entirely pagan when his mission began, nor was the work of conversion completed when he died. The role of Patrick's predecessor Palladius was acknowledged but also downplayed by later writers. In the late seventh century, Tírechán claimed that Palladius was martyred, while Muirchú asserted that he had abandoned his mission. The truth is not known, but writers who championed St Patrick were keen not to let Palladius's reputation interfere with the glory of their patron.[1] Patrick's *Confessio* referred to the religious enthusiasm of his converts, but it does not say much about the foundation of churches.[2] Patrick also described the ongoing dangers of his mission in a land that was largely heathen. There are medieval stories concerning those who continued the work of conversion immediately after St Patrick. The names of Secundinus and Auxillius whose missions were linked with Dunshaughlin (Co. Meath) and Killashee (Co. Kildare) may be translated as 'Second' and 'Auxiliary'. This combination of names hints at invention.[3] Irish chronicles preserve contemporary records of events from the late sixth century. By that time the Church had made significant headway in Ireland. Nevertheless, the processes of conversion and Christianisation were complex and long term. Our earliest sources reflect a society in transition between spiritual worlds.

Older belief systems coexisted with Christianity for a long time, both in Ireland and elsewhere in Europe. Early texts witnessed the struggle of Christianity for spiritual dominance. The 'First Synod of St Patrick', which may be dated to the sixth century, prohibits Christians from swearing oaths before soothsayers in the manner of pagans and exhorts Christians to take disputes to a church rather than a judge and not to receive alms from a pagan.[4] The segregation of Christian practices from those of secular law indicates that the rulings reflect a time when Christianity was a minority religion. The continued activity of druids as religious practitioners is witnessed into the early eighth century when Christianity became the dominant faith. The law tract *Bretha Crólige* sought to deny druids any privileges of sacred status. The near-contemporary *Collectio Canonum Hibernensis* stigmatises druidry, *díberg*, satire and heresy as activities contrary to the church.[5] It is worth exploring this list more fully. Druidry was banned because of its pagan connotations, but the other activities are

---

[1] Charles-Edwards, *Early Christian Ireland*, p. 235.

[2] Bieler, ed., *St Patrick's Confessio*, §§41–2.

[3] Dumville *et al.*, *Saint Patrick*, pp. 89–105. The use of proper names that allude to the personality or role of characters is not uncommon in fictional writing.

[4] Ibid., pp. 175–8; Bieler, ed. and trans., *Patrician Texts*, pp. 54–9.

[5] Binchy, ed., 'Bretha Crólige', §51; cf. Etchingham, *Church organisation*, p. 302.

not inherently pagan. Heresy represented Christian beliefs contrary
to the teachings of the church. *Díberg* described marauding violence,
sometimes with diabolical associations, which operated outside the
moral code of the church. Satire may have been opposed because it
undermined authority, but *Collectio* may also reflect a belief in the
efficacy of the malevolent words of satirists to cause physical harm.
The texts of the eighth century suggest society was largely Christian, in which lingering heathen practices were classed along with the
heinous crimes of bad Christians. Druids were the focus of Christian
denunciation as a religious caste whose status challenged the status of
the church.

Not all features of heathen society could be done away with.
Druids were suppressed, but the pre-Christian roles of judge and poet
were adapted to Christian society. The 'First Synod of St Patrick'
attempted to segregate native law from Christian law, but by the time
of the seventh-century *Canones Hibernensis*, the concept of 'natural
goodness' is used to justify laws inherited from a pagan era.[6] Although
satire was condemned, the art of the *filid* ('learned poet' or literally
'seer') was accepted within a Christian milieu. A key part of their
role was to praise and legitimise the deeds of kings. These spin doctors of the early Middle Ages were too important to lose, but their
work was also more profound and entertaining. They were guardians
and transmitters of oral culture who could tell stories of the past and
were credited with powers to see into the future.

The Church continued to legislate against practices that might
hearken back to pagan rituals or that represented unorthodox beliefs.
A seventh- or eighth-century poem that praised the rise of the church
of Kildare denounced the worship of auguries and use of spells that
predict death. Similarly, penitentials condemned beliefs in witches and
werewolves or the concoction of potions to excite love.[7] The ancient
festivals that marked the change of seasons continued to be celebrated as important markers in the farming year. These were Samain
(1 November), Imbolc (1 February), Beltaine (May Day) and Lugnasad (1 August). The year was also divided into a routine of Christian
holy days. In the medieval conceptualisation of time, Christian festivals jostled for space alongside older commemorations and sometimes
displaced them, such as the celebration of St Brigit's day on Imbolc.

---

[6] Charles-Edwards, *Early Christian Ireland*, p. 197.   [7] Borsje, 'Rules'.

THE RELIGIOUS LANDSCAPE

Just as the division of time was negotiated and appropriated by the new religion, so too was the organisation of the physical landscape. Place names have preserved the pre-Christian veneration of rivers, wells, mountains, trees and megalithic monuments as abodes of the Gods in a polytheistic religion that was intimately entwined with the experience of physical place. The stories of these sites were perpetuated and developed in medieval lore along with the triumph of Christian sites in the landscape. The rise of great churches while nearby centres of pagan power declined is a theme pursued in poetry.[8] Early churches may have been deliberately situated close to existing centres of authority where their patrons may have resided. Some may have been intended to displace the significance of earlier cult sites. At Armagh, the name of the hill (*Ard Macha* or 'the Height of the Goddess Macha') is suggestive of its pre-Christian significance that was overidden by Ireland's most famous saint.[9] The ability of saints to convert the landscape, along with the people in it, is reflected in Saints' Lives. At the well of Slán in Findmag (Co. Mayo), St Patrick was said to have encountered a pagan shrine that he dismantled. He then used the water to baptise 'many thousands'.[10] The saintly dedication of many features in the Irish landscape represented the Christianisation of space, and this moulded the experiences of those who moved through it.

While the Christian God is regarded as omnipresent, the cult of relics that developed in the early Middle Ages channelled divine power into material objects. The construction of shrines and reliquaries to house relics is well attested in Ireland from the seventh century.[11] Relics included the bones of saints and objects that they had worn or used in their lifetime that were thought to convey miraculous power. In Ireland, non-corporeal relics tended to be more popular. Churches that owned prestigious relics became centres of pilgrimage and accumulated wealth and status as a result. By the eighth century, Armagh had sought to boost its prestige by importing relics from Rome, including those associated with Saints Peter, Paul, Stephen, and Lawrence and Christ. While pilgrims were encouraged to visit shrines, relics could also be taken on tour. Their itineraries marked the

[8] Stokes, ed., *Félire Óengusso*, p. 24.   [9] Sharpe, 'St Patrick'.
[10] Bieler, ed. and trans., *Patrician Texts*, pp. 154–5.   [11] See the later discussion.

areas of jurisdiction claimed by a church. The journeys were intended
to boost the power of the church and encourage devotion among
the laity.[12] They were another way of marking God's place in the
landscape.

The cult of relics had an important consequence in the medieval
landscape, bringing burials into churchyards. The Irish name for a
churchyard is *reilig*, which is taken from the Latin *reliquiae* 'relics'. The
belief developed that burial close to holy people brought protection
on the Day of Judgement, when all people would rise together from
their graves. In the Iron Age, cremation was often used to dispose of
the dead. From the late fourth to the sixth century this rite was gradually displaced by inhumation. This shift may reflect the adoption of
Roman habits as much as Christianisation. The additional orientation
of graves east to west (so that the incumbent would stand facing the
rising sun on the Day of Judgement) is a stronger reflection of Christian ideas.[13] Special graves in the Iron Age were marked by mounds
or *ferta*. In the legal text *Din Téchtugud* ('On legal entry'), a claim to
landownership included crossing the *ferta* that stood at the boundaries of the land. It may be understood that the ancestral owners
of the territory in the grave mounds acted as its spiritual guardians.
The practice of inserting selected burials (both male and females)
into mounds continued until the eighth century. These might be
natural features of reused prehistoric tumuli, often located in prominent positions near natural boundaries. The inclusion of grave goods
with some early medieval burials may hint at the continuity of earlier
rites. At Parknahown (Co. Laois), an infant who died at some point
between the seventh and ninth centuries was interred with an antler
bone, a perforated horse tooth and a quartz pebble.[14] From the sixth
century the idea began to take hold in medieval Christendom that
the faithful should be buried away from the heathen graves of their
ancestors, and the dead were more fully integrated into the world of
the living through burial at churches that stood at the heart of the
community.[15]

Initially, burial close to a church was a privilege of monks and
nuns, monastic tenants and church benefactors. The early eighth-
century *Collectio Canonum Hibernensis* urged the general populace to

---

[12] Bhreathnach, *Ireland*, pp. 231–2.   [13] O'Brien, 'Pagan or Christian?' p. 136.
[14] Bhreathnach, *Ireland*, pp. 138–9.
[15] Iogna-Prat, 'Churches in the landscape', p. 376.

be interred in churchyards, but this was burial for a fee. Internment in consecrated ground became normative from the eighth century. This demonstrates not only the growing authority of the Church but also the evolution of new categories of social inclusion and exclusion. To be buried outside consecrated ground or in a deviant fashion suggested that an individual held a liminal position in Christian society and that his or her immortal soul was in peril. Two deviant burials dated to the eighth century were found side by side at Kilteasheen (Co. Roscommon), each with a large stone blocking their mouths. These finds may hint at a fear of revenants, which is attested in contemporary penitential literature and later Saints' Lives. The deviant burials at Kilteasheen correspond chronologically to deviant burials in Anglo-Saxon England.[16] As well as offering mediation between this world and the next, burial practices reveal anxieties and segregation within Christian communities concerning death and salvation.

As churches came to be regarded as sacred spaces, it was necessary to mark their boundaries. Churches on islands had their outer boundaries marked by the ocean, and these places of retreat loom large in modern imagery of the early Irish church. Well-known examples include Skellig Michael (Co. Kerry), Scattery Island (Co. Clare), Inishmurray (Co. Sligo) and Iona (Argyll). Early Irish churches often had more than one boundary, marking out levels of sanctity within the church settlement. At Iona, the sea acted as an outer boundary regulating entry to the island, a ditch defined a middle boundary, and the church and cemetery formed an inner zone from which members of the public were excluded. The majority of early ecclesiastical enclosures in Ireland are 90–120 metres in diameter.[17] At some sites the enclosures were reworked as the settlement grew or contracted. Multivallate enclosures have been uncovered at some church sites, including Nendrum (Co. Down) and Clonfad (Co. Westmeath) and Fenagh (Co. Leitrim). This pattern may have been modelled on the biblical description of Ezekiel's temple with its outer court for public visitors, an inner court for the virtuous and the central temple. The layout might have also been based on high-status ringforts that had up to three rings of banks and ditches, defining their social exclusivity as well as providing defence.[18]

---

[16] Cf. Reynolds, *Anglo-Saxon deviant burial customs*.
[17] O'Sullivan *et al.*, *Early medieval Ireland*, p. 147.
[18] Bitel, *Isle of the Saints*, pp. 58–9.

TYPES OF CHURCHES

The rapid growth in the number of Irish churches in the fifth, sixth and seventh centuries required a degree of organisational adaptation to local circumstances. Thus, Irish political structures and settlement patterns influenced the development of ecclesiastical provision and hierarchy. Place names of ecclesiastical origin, including elements such as *Cell, Domnach, Dísert, Tempall*, and names that were often associated with sites of worship, including *Tech* and *Cluain*, suggest that one was never far from a church in medieval Ireland. Textual and archaeological evidence has been used to estimate that there were more than five thousand pre-1170 churches in Ireland. These would not have all been in use at the same time, as each century witnessed new foundations and the failure of less well-established or less fortunate institutions. Many of the churches constructed before the ninth century were small wooden structures that have disappeared from view.[19] From the tenth century larger church sites proclaimed their status through cathedrals and round towers in stone, and a number of these can still be seen in the Irish landscape.

The earliest churches may have been private foundations of high-class converts. This would mirror the early villa communities of fifth-century Gaul and Italy.[20] They might be lifetime endeavours supported by the resources of kin-land. More permanent churches may have been endowed with gifts or kin-land by consent of relatives, on the understanding that family members would continue to control positions in their foundation. Genealogical literature refers to a myriad of proprietary churches that were associated with a particular dynasty, and the records themselves may have had the status of being charters of ownership.[21] In the seventh century, the writer Tírechán envisioned many of Ireland's earliest churches being founded through grants of land from kings to clerics. Saint Patrick would then arrive to bless them and take them under the protection of Armagh. The idea that Patrick visited all these sites seems to be an anachronistic claim to Armagh's superiority over them.[22] Other churches were assigned separate origins or taken under the control of other large church settlements.

---

[19] Stout, 'Distribution of early medieval ecclesiastical sites'.
[20] Bhreathnach, *Ireland*, p. 171.   [21] Ó Corráin, 'Early Irish churches', pp. 338–9.
[22] Bieler, ed. and trans., *Patrician Texts*, pp. 123–67.

In addition to private estate churches, reference is made in early texts to a communal church for each *túath*. The eighth-century law text *Bretha Nemed Tóisech* envisages that each *túath* should have a church served by a priest and a scholar. The 'Old Irish Penitential' charges clerics or nuns who dwell in such a communal church to grant any excess wealth they might accumulate to the poor of the church. Place names with the element *domnach* (from Latin *dominicum*) may refer to early foundations that were the main church of a *túath*. More than one hundred places bearing *domnach* names can be identified. These cluster in the central east and north of the island. An example of a *domnach* site is Donaghpatrick in the royal landscape of Teltown (Co. Meath), perhaps replicating a pattern found across Europe of churches being located near sites associated with their secular patrons.[23]

Tírechán asserted that every *civitas* founded by a bishop in Ireland should owe allegiance to Armagh. This was based on the claim that God gave St Patrick jurisdiction over all the island of Ireland. It seems to have been envisaged at one stage that each *túath* would have an episcopal church, but as power structures in Ireland became more centralised, only larger churches might boast an episcopal seat. Larger churches or *civitates* were multifunctional sites with a cluster of buildings.[24] They sometimes attracted secular settlements outside their precincts for landless clients, craftspeople and visitors. According to the law tract *Bretha Nemed Tóisech*, the qualities of a good church were to have incumbents who were following an active and contemplative life, as well as visitors performing penance. Such a church was expected to provide services of baptism, communion, and mass; prayers for death; and hospitality.[25] These duties required various functionaries including a priest, scribe, a steward, and male or female coenobites.

One of the larger church settlements of medieval Ireland was at Kildare. Its founder Brigit was said to have died in the 520s. There is debate among scholars as to whether she was a real woman or a pagan goddess transmuted into a Christian saint. Nevertheless, evidence for a pre-Christian cult of Brigit in Kildare is lacking, and the earliest hagiography was written less than 150 years after her supposed

---

[23] Bhreathnach, *Ireland*, p. 170. [24] Sharpe, 'Churches', p. 106.
[25] Breatnach, ed. and trans., 'The first third of *Bretha Nemed Tóisech Tóisech*', §§3, 6, 12.

death: these details favour the view that she was a real person.[26] By
the early seventh century the church had a community of nuns
headed by abbess and a bishop. The writer Cogitosus described the
great wooden church at Kildare in the mid-seventh century and the
throngs that visited. He also mentions that the treasures of kings were
kept here. Although Brigit's kin group, the Fothairt, had little political significance other than through their link to the church, Kildare
had close links to the Uí Dúnlainge kings of Leinster.[27] Brigit's great
house and oratory are referred to in 964 when the clerics of the
church were ransomed from the vikings. A stone church had been
built at Kildare by 1050, and a round tower dating from the twelfth
century (although perhaps replacing an earlier monument) still stands.
The church maintained its significance as an episcopal seat throughout the Middle Ages, despite suffering numerous military attacks. To
maintain its position, the church must have held considerable landed
resources and had the support of powerful lay figures.

THE CULT OF SAINTS

Saints were key figures in the Christianisation of Ireland; their dedica-
tions and relics redefined the landscape and their feast days marked the
passage of time. Saints are regarded as holy people who could perform
miracles through the grace granted to them by God in life and after
their death. Until the twelfth century, sainthood was conferred by
popular acclaim rather than through ecclesiastical procedures. Many
charismatic founders of churches in the sixth and seventh centuries
were enthusiastically endorsed as saints. These included Comgall of
Bangor (Co. Down), Cíarán of Clonmacnoise (Co. Offaly), Finnian
of Clonard (Co. Westmeath), and Columba of Durrow (Co. Offaly)
and Iona (Argyll). A myriad of local cults developed alongside those
of major saints, either reflecting founders of small churches or variant
forms of larger cults. In this way, the imported religion of Christianity
soon became embedded within local heritage and identities.

From the mid-seventh century, written accounts of the deeds of
saints became popular in Ireland. Saints' Lives were prominent in
hagiographic literature, but litanies, hymns and poems reveal the
attributes that the early Christian laity sought in their saints. Their
qualities were often modelled on biblical accounts of Christ and Old

---

[26] Harrington, *Women*, pp. 63–7.   [27] Bhreathnach, *Ireland*, p. 174.

Testament prophets. In the Old Irish 'Life of Saint Brigit', the saint created a stream by striking a staff in the ground in the manner of Moses and turned water into beer in imitation of Christ's transmutation of water into wine at the wedding at Cana.[28] Motifs used in Saints' Lives were also drawn from Continental hagiography, classical stories and native folk tales. These literary attributes made Saints' Lives into an entertaining and memorable written genre. Miracles involving healing, raising the dead and providing food account for the majority of narrative episodes.[29] Their prominence also tapped into fears of ill health, starvation and death that stalked the lives of the medieval laity. Sometimes sublime and mundane matters occupied the same folios. Visions and prophecies might condemn or elevate the fortunes of a political lineage, or a saint might struggle with a king over property rights or legal matters. In competition for lay patronage and donations, saints also needed to have their unique selling points. St Brigit, for example, was famous for her hospitality, while St Brendan's miraculous journey across the ocean made him a patron of seafarers. Saints both male and female were also shown to be inveterate travellers in order to link them personally to many different places.[30] Competition between cults could also lead to sharp practices among hagiographers. The Latin 'Life of St Cainnech' drew episodes from an earlier 'Life of St Columba', not as one might expect, to celebrate the earlier saint, but to portray Cainnech as a superior alternative.[31]

Hagiographic literature throws into relief fundamentally different ways of understanding the world in medieval thought. There was a human need to explain and seek to control natural hazards, but without a modern scientific understanding, the invisible worlds of natural science were interpreted as driven by the forces of good and evil. In the Latin 'Life of Saint Columba' penned by Adomnán, the saint was miraculously able to see demons who wished to inflict illness on the monks of Iona, and he expelled them from the island.[32] On another occasion Columba saw rainclouds bearing disease coming towards the island, and he blessed bread to be distributed as a cure. The blighting of foodstuffs and failure of crops were attributed to malevolent spirits.[33] While saints and holy people had powers to

[28] Ó hAodha, ed. and trans., *Bethu Brigte*, §§15, 28.
[29] Bray, 'Study of folk-motifs', p. 272. [30] Harrington, *Women*, pp. 54, 60.
[31] Herbert, '*Vita Columbae* and Irish hagiography', pp. 33–6.
[32] McDonald, 'Aspects of the monastic landscape', pp. 24, 28.
[33] Carey, 'Varieties of supernatural contact', pp. 50–8.

banish them, popular remedies also developed, drawing on the power
of holy words into herbal treatments or amulets.[34] Holy words thus
had the ability to channel divine power along with invocations to the
saints. These beliefs are illustrated side by side in an eleventh-century
prayer that calls upon the protection of Irish female saints against
demons and evil people, sickness and lies, cold, hunger, plague and
monsters.[35]

PENITENCE AND ASCETICISM

According to the seventh-century 'Alphabet of Piety' the rite of baptism brought renunciation of the world, the devil and passions of
the flesh. When this renunciation slipped, penitence was required to
secure entry into the heavenly kingdom.[36] By this definition, to sin is
to embrace worldliness, the temptations of the devil and the passions
of the flesh. It was not simply a matter causing harm to others; crimes
of thought as well as deed could separate a soul from God. In the sixth
century, Pope Gregory the Great adapted the work of a fifth-century
writer to compile a list of 'seven deadly sins' that are still familiar
in popular culture. Early Christianity advocated public confession
followed by punishment for sin, but the idea quickly developed in
Ireland to promote rehabilitation of the sinner by private means, rendering spiritual compensation for the crime to God overseen by a
bishop. In effect sin was seen as a spiritual debt that could be paid
off by self-improvement, almsgiving or self-mortification. The Irish
approach may be seen to mirror that of Gaelic secular law, where
crimes could be resolved by private negotiation and compensation
overseen by a judge.

The need to provide an equitable tariff of self-mortification led to
the development of penitential texts. The earliest surviving example
was penned by St Finnian in the sixth century. Other penitentials and
texts relating to penance have survived from early medieval Ireland,
which may have led west European thought on this issue. The segregation of the world into categories of holy and unholy, worldly and
unworldly may have been a major change in world view introduced
by Christianity. The pleasures of food and sex came to be regarded

---

[34] Best, ed., 'Some Irish charms'; Borsje, 'The second spell'.
[35] Plummer, ed. and trans., *Irish litanies*, pp. 92–3.
[36] Etchingham, *Church organisation*, p. 312.

as spiritual pollutants that should be overcome through fasting and abstinence. The 'Penitential of Finnian' accepted that pious people who were married could enter the kingdom of God, but sex was prohibited on holy days.[37] Separation from the things one loved in the world was thought to aid unworldly contemplation. For this reason, penance could also involve separation from home and family. Penitents could become temporary members of religious communities, completing their period of penitence under the guidance of an abbot. The seventh-century *Liber Angeli* records that penitents were entitled to hear the gospel preached each Sunday in the northern church of Armagh, along with devout people, virgins and those who served the church in lawful matrimony.[38] Some might choose to leave their worldly existence for good in a state of permanent pilgrimage to atone for earlier sins.[39]

Monks and nuns might also choose to live under a penitential regime in a search for spiritual advancement or as a form of self-martyrdom. Some of Ireland's most famous sixth-century saints – Columba, Comgall and Columbanus – represented the social elite of ascetic idealists who would have been familiar with each others' endeavours. The writings of Columbanus and Finnian reveal concerns over the stability of monks who were enthusiastic to seek out a harsher monastic regime.[40] The idea of testing one's spiritual endurance to superhuman limits remained a popular theme in Irish religious writings. The ninth-century 'Monastery of Tallaght' relates a tale of a virgin Copar who took on an increasingly harsh diet to the point where if a needle was thrust into her hand no blood would come out.[41] In notes that were added to the 'Martyrology of Oengus' we have a tale of St Scothine of Tisscoffin (Co. Kilkenny) who was said to have slept blamelessly each night between two attractive virgins so 'that the battle with the devil might be greater'. More often places of retreat were sought out away from the temptations offered by lay communities. The rigours of monastic retreat are vividly revealed at the island of Skellig Michael, which rises from the sea like a twin peaked mountain off the west coast of Kerry (see Figure 5.1). On the northern summit are two small stone oratories, six beehive huts, a graveyard and a small garden, which might be enough

---

[37] Harrington, *Women*, p. 41.   [38] Etchingham, *Church organisation*, p. 293.
[39] Ibid., p. 296.   [40] Stancliffe, 'Religion and society', p. 405.
[41] Gwynn and Purton, eds. and trans., 'Monastery of Tallaght', §60.

Figure 5.1 Skellig Michael, Co. Kerry, beehive cells and Small Skellig

to contain a small community of monks. On the southern pinnacle was a hermitage that can only be reached by rock climbing. Here stood a simple oratory and water-collecting basin on a barren and windswept ledge.[42]

THE IRISH ABROAD

Some monks in search of a penitential life left Ireland altogether. This act of self-exile mirrored one of the harshest penalties in secular law. Some of these *peregrini* would become famous church founders and scholars who gave Ireland its reputation as an 'Island of Saints and Scholars'. Saints Columba and Columbanus are perhaps the most famous examples. Columba was a member of the Uí Néill dynasty of Cenél Conaill. He was educated in Ireland and studied scripture with Bishop Finnian who may be the author of the penitential mentioned earlier.[43] Columba set out towards Britain in 563, and he was granted the island of Iona on which he founded his first church. Columba courted controversy in his lifetime, and he was temporarily excommunicated at a synod held at Teltown (Co. Meath). His evangelical work among the Picts was nevertheless successful and is touched

---

[42] Stancliffe, 'Religion and society', p. 411.   [43] Ó Riain, 'St. Finnbarr'.

upon in the eulogy *Amra Choluim Chille*, which was composed soon after his death in 597. One of Columba's successors, Ségéne, sent a mission to Northumbria, and the Irish mission was later extended to Mercia and Essex. However, opposition arose in seventh-century Britain regarding the traditions of the church of Iona that differed from those at Canterbury, which had been evangelised from the Continent. As a result, the influence of Irish churchmen in Britain waned from the late seventh century.[44] Despite the decline in Iona's influence, Columba's biographer Adomnán was able to write of the fame of the saint in Britain, Spain, Gaul, Italy and Rome around 700.[45]

Columbanus was a near contemporary of Columba. He was the son of a Leinster nobleman who received his education at Bangor (Co. Down) and left for the Continent around 591. We have a rich testimony of Columbanus's deeds through his own writings including letters, sermons, monastic rules, poetry and a penitential, as well as a Life of the saint written within a generation of his death. Columbanus won support in Burgundy to found monasteries at Annegray and Luxeuil. During his career Columbanus ran into disagreements with some of his monks over the strictness of his monastic regime and with Frankish bishops over the calculation of Easter. When Columbanus chastised Theuderic II of Burgundy regarding his sexual morals, he was obliged to leave the kingdom. Columbanus eventually settled in Lombardy where he died at his foundation at Bobbio in 615.[46] Columbanus's writings show him to be highly skilled and widely read author, as well as a devoted ascetic. These qualities reflect on the education he received in Ireland and on his experiences abroad.

The quality and prestige of Irish scholarship led a number of Irish clerics to be recruited to the courts of European rulers. Emperor Charlemagne recruited some of the best scholars in Europe to his court.[47] He gave patronage to a number of Irish men, including the astronomer and poet Dúngal of Bobbio and the hagiographer and poet Donatus of Fiesole.[48] Charlemagne's successors continued in this vein, providing support to the poet Sedulius Scottus, the geographer Dícuil and the philosopher John Scottus Eriugena. Dícuil also refers to the existence of nameless exiles who sought out remote hermitages

---

[44] Herbert, *Iona, Kells and Derry*, pp. 44–6.
[45] Anderson and Anderson, eds. and trans., *Life of Columba*, III: 3 and 23.
[46] Stancliffe, 'Columbanus's monasticism'.
[47] Thorpe, trans., *Einhard*, p. 67.   [48] Eastwood, 'Astronomy'; Young, 'Donatus'.

in the northern seas until their activities were curtailed by vikings. The religious enthusiasm of some travellers is witnessed in a record in the 'Anglo-Saxon Chronicle' for the year 891. It reports that three clerics had set out in a boat from Ireland made of only two and a half animal hides and with no oars, but had landed in Cornwall and made their way to the court of King Alfred. The condition of their self-imposed exile tallies with the procedure of 'setting adrift' in Irish law. This entailed an offender being sent out in a small boat with limited provisions so that his fate could be determined by God.[49] Other Irish men and women travelled in more comfort as pilgrims. The activities of early medieval Irish *peregrini* helped establish the cult of Gaelic saints across Europe.

DEALING WITH DIFFERENCE: THE EASTER DEBATE

The Easter controversy that plagued the careers of Columbanus and the successors of Columba demonstrates that, as the Church became bigger and more interconnected in Western Europe, divergence in local practice became less acceptable. Differences in religious practice had theological and political implications. Throughout the Church, Easter was to fall on a Sunday during the third week of the first lunar month of the year. The cycle of Easter calculation in Ireland allowed Easter to be celebrated between the fourteenth and twenty-first day of the first lunar month, but the cycle adopted in Rome in the early sixth century only allowed Easter to be celebrated between the fifteenth and twenty-first day. There was also debate as to when the paschal month began.[50] In practice, Easter was often celebrated on the same day by both reckonings, but where divergence happened between communities in contact, it threatened the unity of the Church.

A cycle of nineteen years for calculating Easter was adopted by much of southern Ireland and Irish churches on the Continent in the early seventh century. Northern parts of Ireland and churches founded in Britain by the Irish held onto their inherited traditions of calculating Easter (which may have originated in Gaul in the fifth century) according to an eighty-four-year cycle.[51] In Northumbria matters came to a head at the Synod of Whitby in 664 when the older

---

[49] O'Neill, '*Peregrinatio*'.   [50] Charles-Edwards, *Early Christian Ireland*, p. 392.
[51] McCarthy, 'Origins of the *Latercus* paschal cycle', pp. 38–44.

method of calculating Easter was rejected. This was a major blow to the influence of the church of Iona in Britain.[52] The dispute raged on between Gaelic churches until Iona adopted the Dionysian calculation of Easter in 716. However, the damage caused by the dispute contributed to the decision to expel Columban clergy from Pictland in 717. Other differences of practice within Gaelic churches would also come under criticism, including forms of tonsure and monastic rules. Ireland eventually chose to adopt the regular form of tonsure (shaving the top of the head and allowing hair to grown in a ring around the side), and Irish churches on the Continent adhered to the 'Rule of St Benedict'. However, diversity in practice of the religious life persisted at a local level in Ireland. Despite the success and high standards of many Irish churches, wider institutional intolerance of their differences would have harsh consequences.

EPISCOPAL JURISDICTION

The relationship that a church had with surrounding communities is defined by the words *paruchia* and *familia*, whose exact meaning has excited debate regarding the organisation of the early Irish church. The eighth-century Northumbrian author Bede referred to a peculiar custom at Iona that the church was headed by an abbot rather than a bishop. This comment has been mistakenly generalised into a model for the Church in Ireland, dominated by monasteries. Closer evaluation of seventh- and eighth-century texts has made it clear that bishops consistently held a central role in Irish churches. They commonly dwelt at churches that also had a coenobitic community.[53] The term *paruchia* found in Irish texts was a variant spelling of Latin *parochia* (origin of the English word 'parish'). It was an earlier term of pastoral jurisdiction defining the area subject to an episcopal church. It might correspond geographically with a secular unit of government, whether a *túath* or group of *túatha* under the rule of an over-king. If the size of the diocese increased, assistant bishops or *chorepiscopi* might help minister at a local level.

Collectio Canonum Hibernensis, which was compiled in the eighth century, presents a view of episcopal hierarchy that complements that

---

[52] Colgrave, ed. and trans., *Life of Bishop Wilfred*, §8; Colgrave and Mynors, ed. and trans., *Bede's ecclesiastical history*, III: 25; V. 19.
[53] Charles-Edwards, *Early Christian Ireland*, pp. 241, 258.

of kings. There are three grades of bishop.[54] The lowest level may be associated with a *civitas*, and the middle level with a sub-province wielding authority over a small number of minor bishops. At the top of the hierarchy was a provincial bishop who may be regarded as the ecclesiastical equivalent of a provincial over-king (*rí cóiced*). Annalistic references tend to define bishops by their church rather than their territorial sphere. However, in the tenth and eleventh centuries definitions of jurisdiction are more common and provide more insight into the ecclesiastical hierarchy. Lower-rank bishops were equated with small kingdoms in which the church was situated. Middle-rank bishops might include the bishops of Síl nÁedo Sláine (Brega, Co. Meath) and Thomond (North Munster). Provincial bishoprics are referred to for Munster, Connacht, Leinster and Uí Néill.[55] Primacy of honour among provincial bishops was accorded to the see of Armagh as the successor of St Patrick, apostle of Ireland.

From the seventh century, Armagh sought to turn this honour into jurisdictional power over all the churches of Ireland.[56] The ambition was opposed by St Brigit's church of Kildare. Kildare seems to have been the most powerful see in southern Ireland in the central decades of the seventh century and an advocate of the Roman calculation of Easter. Kildare claimed all Ireland as its *paruchia* in the mid-seventh century. Armagh's adherence to the older eighty-four-year paschal cycle was becoming a barrier to its ambitions for supremacy in Ireland.[57] Wilfred, bishop of York, may have used the matter of noncompliance with Rome as justification to claim some sort of authority over churches in northern parts of Ireland in 680.[58] After Armagh adopted the Roman Dionysian calculation of Easter in the 680s, the see of St Patrick asserted its metropolitan claims in Ireland more vigorously through hagiographic writings in the closing decades of the seventh century.[59] A counter-rhetoric developed to oppose these claims. For example, in Munster, the church of Emly claimed that its patron St Ailbe had ministered before St Patrick, and therefore that Armagh should not have precedence over Emly.[60] These assertions of jurisdictional authority were important as they had political ramifications.

---

[54] Etchingham, *Church organisation*, pp. 148–68.   [55] Ibid., pp. 178–83.
[56] Sharpe, 'Armagh and Rome'.   [57] Bhreathnach, *Ireland*, pp. 200–3.
[58] Charles-Edwards, *Early Christian Ireland*, p. 416.   [59] Ibid., p. 438–40.
[60] Ó Riain-Raedel, 'Question'.

Armagh sought secular support for its ambitions through a series of astute alliances. These alliances offered to the secular patron a level of spiritual endorsement and influence through the agency of the church. In the early ninth century, the bishop of Armagh made common cause with Feidlimid mac Crimthainn, over-king of Munster. Feidlimid allowed the 'Law of Patrick' to be proclaimed in Munster, and he attacked the church of Clonmacnoise whose ambitions had clashed with Armagh.[61] In the tenth century Armagh initially allied with the over-kings of Southern Uí Néill and later shifted allegiance to the Munster dynasty of Dál Cais. Armagh famously endorsed the claim of the Dál Cais over-king Brian Boru to be 'emperor of the Gaels'.[62] Despite these efforts, Armagh's claims to archiepiscopal supremacy in Ireland encountered further resistance in the eleventh century. The matter would only be resolved with the restructuring of the Irish Church in the twelfth century.

CHURCH OFFICES

While the term *paruchia* denoted territorial jurisdiction, *familia* described the community associated with a church. Given the significance of kin in Irish society, the terminology is appropriate. Positions in the Church were often hereditary whether as landowners, office holders or patrons. A *familia* could refer to the personnel of one church or of a group of churches that were linked by a dynasty, cult or ownership. The *familia* of Saint Columba included members of the churches founded by the saint and his successors. These included Iona, Durrow, Derry, Kells and Skreen. The term *familia* also overlapped with *paruchia* as it could refer to the heads of churches within a larger jurisdictional unit, such as those subject to Armagh or Kildare.[63] Connections between churches were underpinned by visitations and hagiographic writings that claimed links between founding saints as friends, relatives or pupils. In these relationships, a presiding church might exact tribute from a dependent church or provide the leader for a church where a local candidate was lacking.[64]

[61] Bhreathnach, *Ireland*, p. 189; Charles-Edwards, *Early Christian Ireland*, pp. 252–4.
[62] *AU, s.aa.* 924, 927, 973, 986, 1005; Bhreathnach, *Ireland*, p. 212.
[63] Charles-Edwards, *Early Christian Ireland*, p. 275; Etchingham, *Church organisation*, pp. 126–30.
[64] Bhreathnach, *Ireland*, p. 228.

The leadership of a church might rest in the hands of an abbot, bishop or coarb. The term 'coarb' is derived from Old Irish *comarba* meaning the heir of a saint. It is sometimes used interchangeably with the term 'erenagh' (*airchinnech*) or church leader. These were overseers of the temporalities in large institutions. They were not required to be in holy orders, although they were often tonsured as a sign of their ecclesiastical office, and their positions could often be hereditary.[65] The interchange in leadership of churches between abbots, bishops and coarbs indicates the multifunctional aspects of church settlements. The prominence of monastic, clerical and administrative roles could vary from church to church. Sometimes the duties of leadership were combined, so that abbots might also serve as bishops. In larger institutions, there might be greater specialisation; thus at the church of Armagh from the tenth century the role of coarbs or erenagh tended to be distinct from the bishops. Coarbial duties included routine administration and travelling to represent the church as a negotiator and to gather tribute.[66] These tasks might be taken on by a bishop or abbot. However, the primary role of the abbot was to focus on care of monks and penitents, while the bishop was responsible for ministry and pastoral care. Church offices were incorporated into the Irish legal system of status, comparable to secular grades. However, a single ecclesiastical hierarchy was not envisaged, but rather three parallel structures: the priesthood (from bishop to doorkeeper), scholarship (from master to pupil) and administration (from erenagh to cooks, millers or gardeners).[67] It was not uncommon for a cleric to hold more than one office. The combination of roles was often complementary; for example, expertise in religious law was practical for a bishop or abbot, while periods of spiritual withdrawal as an anchorite could support their role as spiritual directors.[68]

The pillars of active and contemplative religious life were priests and monks. Priests were essential figures in pastoral ministry, and a shortage of priests was a concern of texts in the eighth century.[69] Priests often lived within the communities they ministered to. As entry to the priesthood occurred late in the medieval life cycle, many had wives and children before they took holy orders. The Church

---

[65] Holland, 'Were early Irish church establishments under lay control?'

[66] Etchingham, *Church organisation*, pp. 83–8.

[67] Breatnach, ed. and trans., *Uraicecht na Ríar*, pp. 84–5.

[68] Charles-Edwards, *Early Christian Ireland*, pp. 274–6.

[69] Ó Corráin, 'Ireland, c. 800', pp. 603–4.

allowed them to remain with their families in a state of celibacy, and a priest's wife might be a respected figure in society. Nevertheless, Irish religious literature displays concern over rumours of sexual misconduct and the spiritual impurity associated with unchaste priests. It was only in the eleventh century that clerics were ordered to send their wives away, although such regulations were widely flouted.[70] When it comes to defining monks in early medieval Ireland the terminological waters are muddied by the adoption of ecclesiastical words into secular life. For example, the Irish word for household (*muinter*) is taken from Latin *monasterium*, and the service of a client to his lord was *manchuine* derived from Latin *monachus*, 'a monk'. Such borrowings attest to the impact of the early Church on Irish society. In a similar way, the term *manaig* 'monks' did not only describe coenobites. It described a broad category of people subject to the jurisdiction and protection of a church leader, regardless of whether they were laymen or clerics or were bound to a monastic rule.[71] The lay clients of the church were themselves a diverse group whose members could range in status from servile retainers and rent payers to aristocratic adherents. The feature common to early Irish *manaig* was their socioeconomic relationship to a particular church.

A range of texts makes clear that a category of *manaig* lived communal lives according to monastic rules. In common with monks and nuns across Christendom, these rules included poverty, chastity and obedience. The monastic day was structured around canonical hours for the chanting of psalms, hymns and prayer. Other times between meals and sleep were dedicated to study, prayer and labour (which could be manual, administrative or scholarly). Irish monks and nuns followed practices common throughout western Europe, but with some local variations regarding ascetic practices of silence, fasting and periods of solitude. There also seems to have been less segregation on church sites between male and female religious than was seen elsewhere in Europe from the ninth century.[72] While the 'Rule of St Benedict' became standard for coenobitic life across much of western Europe in the tenth century, there was continued adherence in Ireland to ideals and practices that were often attributed to founder

[70] Swift, 'Early Irish priests', pp. 33–4; Harrington, *Women*, pp. 250–1, 261–5. See earlier discussion.
[71] Charles-Edwards, *Early Christian Ireland*, p. 121.
[72] Warren and Stevenson, *Liturgy*, p. xliv; Harrington, *Women*, p. 107.

saints. The monastic rules that have survived from early medieval Ireland often consist of precepts and moral advice rather than detailed regulations. They may be regarded as guides to inner life more than as rules for outward observance.[73]

ASSEMBLIES AND LAWS

Synods are ecclesiastical assemblies convened to deal with administrative issues or resolve disputes relating to faith, church discipline or law. Usually synods in the early Middle Ages were composed of bishops, but in Ireland nonepiscopal heads of churches and leading scholars also participated. This reflects the threefold nature of the Church hierarchy discussed earlier. Assemblies were important venues for communication in a landscape of dispersed church settlements. Annalistic references suggest that synods were held at both a provincial and an inter-provincial level depending on the nature of the issues discussed. The debate over the celebration of Easter in the early seventh century appears to have prompted meetings for the northern half of Ireland and the southern half. The meeting of a synod might sometimes correspond with that of an *óenach* (lay assembly) or *rígdal* (meeting of kings) that was attended by clerics. For example, in 789, Donnchad Midi, king of Tara, 'dishonoured' the relics carried by the abbot of Armagh during an *óenach* at the royal seat of Ráith Airthir (Oristown, Co. Meath).[74]

The law tract *Críth Gablach* states that a king could pledge a *cáin* (edict) on his people at an assembly.[75] The promulgation of a *cáin* was an important legal development, for it meant that certain crimes were not matters to be resolved privately simply by the payment of compensation, but they were crimes of public interest. A number of edicts were associated with the church. The 'Law of Adomnán' (*Cáin Adomnáin*) issued in 697 made the penalty for killing or wounding a child, woman or cleric significantly greater than the sliding scale of private compensation payments recommended in contemporary secular law. The *cáin* was less mindful of status, as payments were at a fixed rate regardless of the status of the victim. Some of the punishments also involved the public spectacle of penitence. As well as giving the

---

[73] Hughes, *Early Christian Ireland*, pp. 90–4; Kenney, *Sources*, pp. 197–8, 315, 397, 471–4.
[74] Charles-Edwards, *Early Christian Ireland*, p. 278.
[75] Ibid., p. 280.

church extra legal authority, *Cáin Adomnáin* served to raise revenues for the community of Iona, which received a share of the fines.[76]

Cáin Adomnáin was one of a series of ecclesiastical ordinances issued in Ireland from the late seventh to the early tenth centuries. They reinforced the jurisdiction of major churches, helped to impose a moral code the laity, and were an opportunity to make profit. They reflected the powerful position the Church had obtained in Irish society by the late seventh century. The promulgation of church laws at assemblies had declined by the tenth century, perhaps corresponding with the decline of *óenaig* as political assemblies.[77] By the early tenth century, ecclesiastical jurisdictional spheres and tribute gathering had settled into a more organised system that made the ad hoc issue or reissue of church ordinances less useful. Meanwhile the centralisation of royal power may have led to a decline in the political importance of the secular assemblies at which these laws had been communicated.

FUNDING

A *cáin* was one of many methods adopted by the Church to raise revenues for its maintenance and ministry. Other streams of income may be defined in categories of gifts and endowments, one-off payments and pastoral contracts. From the time of conversion, devotees presented gifts of moveable goods and land to the church. For example, Saints' Lives not infrequently show pious individuals submitting themselves and their lands to a church or saint, to be held by their descendants in lease.[78] Through such donations, churches quickly became landowners and accumulated stock. Another form of funding was to charge for each service a cleric performed. This idea is witnessed at an early stage in the sixth-century 'Penitential of Finnian', where a cleric is entitled to seek alms for his services. A range of other early medieval religious and legal texts refer to payments, alms or refection being given to priests for fulfilling specific services, including preaching or performing mass, baptism, communion and last rites.[79] This 'pay as you go' system may have operated in times and places where more regular contracts between the laity and the church were lacking.

---

[76] Ó Néill and Dumville, eds. and trans., *Cáin Adomnáin*.
[77] Etchingham, *Church organisation*, pp. 194–205.   [78] Ibid., pp. 437–8.
[79] Ibid., pp. 242–8.

In the sixth century, the idea of paying an annual tithe (a tenth of one's property) developed in Latin Europe. In return for such regular payments, the church was expected to provide ongoing pastoral support. In texts from seventh- and eighth-century Ireland, there is some disagreement as to how tithes should be calculated. This may reflect a system in its infancy where the practicalities were still being ironed out, or it may be that different churches favoured different interpretations of a general rule. There is some debate as to how widely tithes were applied in Ireland. *Manaig* (church dependants) by choice or circumstance were more firmly tied into the system. Payments made by *manaig* included an annual tithe of livestock and tillage. To this was added 'firstlings', which often meant the first male offspring of humans and animals, and 'first fruits', which could mean the first share of each crop and the first offspring of each species of livestock each year. A death due could also be charged. Labour services were also expected, but might vary according to the status of each *manach*.[80] The church's ability to control manpower may explain why labour-intensive practices of arable farming tended to be more associated with church settlements than with ringforts. In return for all these payments, it is stated that the laity were entitled to baptism, communion, prayers for the dead, preaching and mass. Texts from the eighth century espouse the ideal that the laity in general should be obliged to pay tithes, but this seems to have been more aspiration than reality. In the ninth and tenth centuries, secular authorities on the Continent and in England enforced the general payment of tithes.[81] However, the centralising power of these kings exceeded that of their Irish counterparts. It is not clear how widely the payment of tithes, first fruits, and firstlings was applied in Irish society beyond those classed as *manaig*.

An alternative to calculating tithes was to levy a regular ecclesiastical tax on the laity. There is better evidence for the general application of this model in texts dating from the tenth, eleventh and twelfth centuries. Ecclesiastical taxes could apply to the people of a region or of regions with the cooperation of their kings. In the Middle Irish 'Life of St Naile' a band of noble youths are baptised by the saint. In return, their leader Luan son of Írgalach vows that his people will pay ecclesiastical taxes thereafter.[82] The event is said to have taken place in the

---

[80] Ibid., pp. 409–10.   [81] Godfrey, *Church in Anglo-Saxon England*, p. 326.
[82] Plummer, ed. and trans., *Miscellanea Hagiographica*, pp. 110–14, 136–40.

sixth century, but the episode may have been invented to provide a historic justification for contemporary fiscal claims. Similarly, in his Latin 'Life', St Fínán of Kinnitty demands that the king of Munster hand over the tax (*census*) of his people; otherwise his residence would be burned with heavenly fire. The text may be dated from the end of the eighth century to the beginning of the tenth century.[83] From the ninth century there are references to church officials called *maer* who collect revenues from a *cáin* or *cís/census* in a particular district. They may have also travelled around the areas of their jurisdiction to administer church laws.[84] The aspiration of the church of Armagh to levy an ecclesiastical tax on the citizens of Dublin around 1100 is witnessed in a poem found in the 'Book of Rights' and 'Book of Uí Maine'. An ounce of gold was levied for every twenty-four men: 'a screpall for each nose'. The idea of a 'nose tax' may have come to Ireland through contact with other churches in the North Atlantic.[85] A similar tax is mentioned in relation to Munster churches in the 'Book of Lismore'. The version of the poem in the 'Book of Uí Maine' also claims one-tenth of all the goods that arrived in Dublin for St Patrick. It may be deduced that secular leaders co-operated with the Church in ensuring the payment of regular dues throughout Ireland by AD 1100. This secured a level of pastoral care for the people and assisted kings in their own bid to secure more political and economic control over their subjects.

The Church in early medieval Ireland was funded by various methods. There were donations of land and gifts thatcould be used as endowments. Alms and payments were also received on an ad hoc basis in return for services. Regular payments of tithes, first fruits and firstlings were levied from *manaig*, and there was the aspiration that all the laity should make these payments. Over time, larger churches were successful in obtaining a significant share of their revenue from subject churches in return for their protection and management. Powerful churches also issued religious edicts to raise revenues from the late seventh to the ninth centuries. These arrangements may have been displaced by the payment of regular ecclesiastical taxes that were implemented with the co-operation of kings. The system of gathering revenue and apportioning responsibilities of pastoral care would

---

[83] Heist, ed., *Vitae sanctorum*, p. 158; Szaciłło, 'O'Donohue Group'; cf. Etchingham, *Church organisation*, p. 93.

[84] Etchingham, *Church organisation*, pp. 211–12.   [85] See the earlier discussion.

have also been a spur to parochial organisation and the reorganisation of Irish diocese witnessed in the twelfth century. The broad
range of funding sources used by Irish churches placed them in a
powerful position. The wealth of individual institutions gave them
resilience in the face of famines, pestilence and hostile attacks, which
were recurrent threats in the early Middle Ages.

THE VIKING IMPACT

The impact of vikings on the Irish Church is a topic that has
excited the imagination of historians from the Middle Ages to the
present. The contrast in image between marauding heathens dedicated to bloodshed and ascetic monks could not be more stark.
In twelfth-century Saints' Lives, reformers hailed the rebuilding of
the Church, both physically and morally, which they thought had
regressed through viking influence. The long-held idea that vikings
were responsible for the progressive secularisation and moral corruption of the Church has been effectively critiqued in recent decades.
Medieval reformers appear to have exaggerated a picture of the
Church in decay that suited their political and cultural agenda in
calling for change. The question of viking impact can be approached
by analysing violence towards churches, assessing economic changes
and religious conversion, and taking a broader view of institutional
developments in the medieval Church.

As a result of their political and dynastic links, churches in Ireland
were mired in local power structures and therefore political violence
before the vikings arrived. A series of battles between powerful
ecclesiastical settlements and between churches and Irish kings are
recorded from the 760s to the 840s.[86] This demonstrates that churches
were able to put armies in the field to protect their power and that
they were not simply havens of prayer. These conflicts may reflect
growing rivalry between powerful churches or increasing lay influence, or they may even reflect a period of climatic decline that led
to greater competition over diminishing resources. The late eighth-
century economic downturn has also been seen as a contributory
factor to viking raids in Europe. It has been demonstrated that in the
ninth and tenth centuries the Irish attacked churches as often as the
vikings.[87] This does not mean that there were no differences in their

---

[86] Ó Corráin, 'Ireland c. 800', pp. 600–1.   [87] Lucas, 'Plundering and burning'.

attacks. The first viking attacks are recorded in the 790s, and these naturally struck churches on islands first. Iona (Argyll), Inishbofin (Co. Galway) and Inishmurray (Co. Sligo) were among the churches raided in 795. Heathen vikings feared the Christian God less than the Irish, and their desecration of holy places appalled contemporaries. In 824 viking raiders shook the relics of St Comgall of Bangor from their shrine. The reliquary may have been transported back to Scandinavia along with other pieces of Insular ecclesiastical and secular metalwork, many of which have been recovered from viking graves in western Norway. Clerics were also captured for ransom or sale overseas. Others, including Étgal, seized from the island church of Skellig Micheal in 824 died in viking hands.[88] The individual trauma inflicted by viking raids should not be downplayed, but their impact on the Church, as a whole, is less than clear. From the 840s it was not unusual for vikings to work in concert with Irish allies to attack the churches of their political rivals. The conversion of vikings to Christianity over time may have ameliorated the violence against holy relics, but it did not diminish the number of raids on church settlements or the seizure of captives. It appears that economic and political strategies went hand in hand, regardless of religious scruples.

As noted earlier, ecclesiastical settlements were the main economic centres in pre-viking Ireland: they were foci of arable production, technological development, manufacturing and trade.[89] The attempt of the eighth-century *Collectio Canonum Hibernensis* to ban prostitutes, thieves and pedlars from ecclesiastical precincts illustrates some of the less desirable exchanges that took place at these sites. The Church was also involved in overseas trading networks, as suggested by the wheat, beer and wine sent from Nantes to Ireland as a gift to St Columbanus, and the cloaks and shoes conveyed to the church of Noirmoutier in Irish ships.[90] It can be argued that vikings did not simply raid churches as stores of wealth, but used their economic potential for their own ends. Viking bases were commonly found in or near eccle- siastical sites. The churches at Dublin, Linn Duachaill (Annagassan, Co. Louth) and Limerick appear to have been driven out of business when they were seized by vikings in the 840s. Other churches sur- vived despite being used as viking camps, including Clondalkin (Co.

---

[88] *AI, s.a.* 824.   [89] See the earlier discussion.
[90] O'Sullivan *et al.*, *Early Medieval Ireland*, pp. 263, 265.

Dublin) and Cork.[91] Powerful churches were often situated within reach of communication routes and varied landscape resources. These attributes suited vikings who used their bases for raiding and trading. The finds of weights, coins and silver at the ninth-century camp at Woodstown show that economic engagement with local people must have taken place at an early stage of viking colonisation.[92]

Vikings in Ireland failed to make any wide-ranging territorial gains. Their survival strategy was to use their skills and their overseas connections to thrive as craftsmen and traders. This led to the development of towns at Dublin, Limerick and Waterford. Vikings may have attacked some churches as economic rivals, just as viking settlements clashed with each other. However, viking settlements also needed to develop positive trading links with the Irish polities and to tap into existing economic networks in order to flourish. A series of alliances between Irish and vikings kings asattested from the mid-ninth century aided this process. The 150 or so silver hoards deposited in Ireland that can be dated from the mid-ninth to the mid-tenth century illustrate trading networks. Often the biggest churches profited from involvement in viking trading networks. Silver hoards have been recovered from the most powerful church settlements, including Armagh, Glendalough (Co. Wicklow), Durrow (Co. Offaly) and Clonmacnoise (Co. Offaly). Each of these sites was raided more than once by vikings. As long as churches maintained their landed possessions and continued to attract artisans, traders and visitors they seemed able to recover from the trauma inflicted by military attacks. Churches that had grown in significance during the eighth century often accumulated greater power and wealth during the Viking Age. They may have built more powerful connections with secular patrons for their defence. Clonmacnoise is a good example (see Figure 5.2). The settlement experienced a boom and considerable expansion from the ninth to the eleventh century. It housed busy workshops producing items from antler, bone, metal and glass, and more than 700 cross slabs were carved at the site. Excavations in the urban landscape of Armagh provide similar evidence of settlement expansion from the ninth century.[93]

While the quality of Irish manuscript art and fine metalwork decreased somewhat during the Viking Age, the amount of wealth

---

[91] Clarke, 'Conversion', p. 24.   [92] Russell and Hurley, eds., *Woodstown*.
[93] Lynn, 'Recent archaeological excavations', p. 277.

Figure 5.2 Clonmacnoise, Co. Offaly

invested in religious art and architecture increased. The pages of the 'Book of Kells' were illustrated as the first viking raids struck Ireland, but its pages were never intended for mass consumption. High crosses, stone churches and round towers are monuments that flourished in the Viking Age. These accomplished works were harder to destroy and were meant to be appreciated by many. In the eleventh and twelfth centuries, high-quality reliquaries, crosiers and crosses were created that combined Scandinavian and other imported art styles with Irish form and design. Literature also flourished, and the vitality of Viking Age artistic production may reflect the greater amounts of wealth in circulation as a consequence of growing overseas trade.

The conversion and christianisation of vikings may have begun soon after they settled in Ireland. Archaeological evidence suggests that heathenism and Christianity existed side by side in tenth-century Dublin. Finds from this period include a Thor's hammer pendant and a small bone cross.[94] The gradual cessation of furnished burial by the mid-tenth century may be taken as evidence of Christianisation, while the names of elite members of Dublin society indicate that they had adopted the cults of Irish saints. For example, Gille Pátraic, 'Servant of St Patrick', who may be a member of the royal dynasty of

---

[94] Downham, 'Religious and cultural boundaries'.

Dublin, fell in battle in 983.[95] King Olaf Cuarán of York and Dublin was baptised in England in 943, and he was an enthusiastic devotee of St Columba. Olaf gave patronage to the church at Skreen (Co. Meath) and he died in pilgrimage at the church of Iona in 980. Olaf may have championed St Columba because the geographical range of the saint's cult matched his political ambitions. Iona had historical connections in Northumbria, and the church held jurisdiction over parts of North Britain, the kingdom of the Isles and Ireland.[96]

Vikings drew upon a network of trading contacts with church settlements in the interior of Ireland. They may also have worked with ecclesiastical networks abroad. A number of churches in Britain are dedicated to Irish saints. Some of these were founded in the Viking Age or received renewed interest in their cults at that time. Maps of the cult of St Brigit, St Patrick and less well-known saints in Britain complement the distribution of Hiberno-Scandinavian metalwork finds. They may provide insight into trading routes across the Irish Sea. A church dedicated to St Brigit in eleventh-century London has been attributed to the activities of Hiberno-Scandinavian traders. The cult of a more obscure saint, Bega, appears to link Dalkey Island south of Dublin with St Bees on the Cumbrian coast and the Cumbrae islands in the Firth of Clyde and Dunbar in Lothian in the Middle Ages. It is intriguing given the possible association between economic and cultic links that the now-lost relic of St Bega at St Bees was a silver arm-ring with a cross marked on its summit. Perhaps this was a Hiberno-Scandinavian currency ring, as they commonly have a saltire cross impressed on the top of the ring. In a world that lacked modern levels of regulation or safety for international trade, shared values and trust between traders was important. Co-worship helped in providing the social nexus for trade, and it has been demonstrated that there was popular demand for churches to be established at market locations in tenth-century England.[97] It is perhaps ironic that vikings, who were famed for plundering churches in Ireland, may have been the agent of promoting the cults of Irish saints abroad.

The evidence suggests the impact of vikings on Irish churches was far from one of simple destruction. Church settlements could both benefit and suffer from their dealings with raiders and traders. Large church settlements weathered viking attacks well. Examples include the churches of Louth, Clonard (Co. Meath) and Glendalough

---

[95] *AU, s.a.* 983.   [96] Clancy, 'Iona v. Kells', p. 91.   [97] Stocker, 'Aristocrats'.

(Co. Wicklow). These lay within raiding distance from Dublin and were attacked on more than one occasion, but they have a continuous set of obits for ecclesiastical leaders throughout the Viking Age. Middle-rank churches at Clondalkin, Finglas, and Tallaght, all within a short distance of the largest viking-ruled settlement in Dublin, also endured. It is possible that many smaller and medium-sized churches that receive sporadic or no mention in chronicles went out of business as a result of viking attacks. Further archaeological research may shed light on this issue. The small church excavated at Caherlehillan (Co. Kerry) seems to have been in use from the early sixth century until the late eighth century, but there is no evidence to link vikings to its demise. Recent excavations at Clonfad (Co. Westmeath) appear to correlate the demise of a medium-sized church with its violent desecration by Fir Tulach, the local population group who may have objected to the church's alignment with a political rival.[98] The decrease in smaller and middling churches at the expense of larger ones may be characteristic of broader changes in Irish society in the Viking Age.[99] The period also witnessed the depression of minor political units and the centralisation of power into the hands of regional over-kings. Within these broader patterns of political change, vikings may have been mere catalysts, rather than major agents of change.

A contested area of viking impact on Irish churches relates to institutional organisation and moral standards. Vikings have long been blamed as agents of secularisation within the Irish church. Nevertheless, this paradigm has come under increasing criticism. The Irish Church before the Viking Age was characterised by small proprietary churches and larger multifunctional ecclesiastical sites led by a bishop, abbot or coarb. Whether or not there were fixed territorial dioceses before the Viking Age is a matter of debate.[100] It may be argued that dioceses were determined by the allegiances of people, and their boundaries might fluctuate with political circumstances. Episcopal jurisdictions like those of kings appear to have been well defined, as rules were in place against one bishop intruding in the sphere of authority of another.[101] There was also some flexibility where the seat of a diocese lay. The adaptable and decentralised character of Irish ecclesiastical structures gave them resilience during

---

[98] Stevens, 'Clonfad'.   [99] Johnston, *Literacy*, pp. 73–4.   [100] Ibid., p. 61.
[101] Etchingham, *Church organisation*, pp. 177–94.

times of crisis. The Church in Ireland did not experience the large-scale appropriation of ecclesiastical lands or the centralised reforming agenda encountered in England from the tenth to the twelfth century. While the Church in England developed a more rigid, uniform and hierarchical system that segregated the functions of monastic and secular churches, churches in Ireland continued to have localised and multifunctional systems of organisation. The institutional differences of the Irish Church, compared to England or northern France, were regarded as an aberration by reformers in the twelfth century. Nevertheless, this administrative decentralisation did not mean that the church in Ireland was less religious or effective. On the contrary, localised forms of organisation were resilient, adaptable and efficient in providing spiritual care.

The growing wealth of the larger Irish churches in the Viking Age did not cause an inevitable decline in moral standards. Payments to the churches according to texts written by churchmen created a reciprocal obligation for spiritual services. Over time, systems of tithe collection and pastoral provision became more comprehensive. It was important to secular patrons that the clergy who offered prayers on their behalf maintained spiritual moral standards. This is illustrated by an episode in the 'Life of St Cainnech'. The worthy saint is praised in contrast to a gluttonous church leader who liked to travel ostentatiously by chariot.[102] Cainnech's piety is shown to be more effective in winning divine favour for his lay supporters. Ninth- and tenth-century Saints' Lives continued to show a concern with maintaining high religious standards among conventional monks. The Céli Dé ('clients of God') who emerged at the end of the eighth century espoused a rigorous ascetic regime. By the tenth century Céli Dé had settled in some of Ireland's largest ecclesiastical communities, and they were particularly associated with attendance on the sick and the poor.[103] Irish churchmen also maintained their high spiritual reputation abroad during the Viking Age. They attracted aristocratic and royal patronage, giving rise to new church foundations in Ottonian Germany.[104] In general the Church did not appear to suffer a general depletion in its wealth or spiritual standards as a result of the vikings, nor did it stagnate, despite the claims of later reformers.

[102] Charles-Edwards, *Early Christian Ireland*, pp. 262–3.
[103] Etchingham, *Church organisation*, pp. 340–60.
[104] Gwynn, 'Irish monks'; Picard, 'The cult of Columba'.

ELEVENTH-CENTURY DEVELOPMENTS

In the eleventh century Ireland's contacts with churches overseas increased. Travel to Rome was especially popular. No less than nine Irish kings set out for Rome in the years from 1026 to 1064. Many clerics also undertook this pilgrimage. This gave renewed vigour to earlier Irish church foundations along the route through Belgium, the Rhineland and southern Germany. Máel Brigte (also known as Marianus Scotus) set out from Moville (Co. Down) for the Continent in the 1050s, and he dwelt at three monasteries at Cologne, Fulda and Mainz where he died as a recluse in 1082. Máel Brigte is famed for a highly reputed universal chronicle that he wrote on the Continent. A series of new foundations were also made for Irish monks in southern Germany in the late eleventh and twelfth centuries. Foremost among these was the church of St James at Regensburg that was founded in 1076 by Muiredach mac Robartaig (also called Marianus), who had travelled to the Continent with two companions.[105]

Despite the continued activities of Irish scholars and holy men abroad, the moral reputation of the Irish came under increasing criticism from Norman and Anglo-Norman writers in the late eleventh century. An early example can be found in the poem 'Moriuht', composed by Warner of Rouen in the early eleventh century. Warner wrote a satirical account of a rival Irish poet who had been captured from his homeland by vikings and who eventually made his way to Rouen. Within the poem Warner denigrates the Irish as promiscuous and bestial, claiming that the men did not wear trousers because they were so frequently engaged in sexual activity.[106] As the influence of the Church on social mores increased in much of Europe, Ireland's secular marriage laws were seen to be increasingly out of step with canonical rulings. Ireland also lagged behind in economic development compared to the lands where the criticism originated. The Irish began to be seen as backwards and aberrant in some circles. The representation of the Irish as 'Other' drew on images of barbarity from Classical antiquity.[107] Pope Gregory VII wrote to Lanfranc, the archbishop of Canterbury, in the 1070s, mentioning rumours of the sinful marriage practices of the *Scotti* and vested him with the authority to punish these crimes.[108] The anti-Irish propaganda had a

[105] Ó Cróinín, *Early medieval Ireland*, p. 230.   [106] McDonough, trans., *Moriuht.*
[107] Freeman, *Ireland and the classical world*, pp. 44–50.
[108] Downham, 'England', p. 70.

political edge for it was used to justify the intervention of the English Church in Irish affairs. Lanfranc was consecrated archbishop of Canterbury in 1070 at the behest of William the Conqueror. Two years later, Lanfranc outlined a claim to metropolitan authority over Britain and Ireland in a letter to the Pope.

By the eleventh century, Armagh's claims to ecclesiastical primacy in Ireland had been well established. Armagh had developed its prestige through association with St Patrick and alliance with Ireland's most powerful kings. Some other churches that had formerly held great power became increasingly marginalised in the eleventh century. These included Bangor (Co. Down) and Iona (Argyll). As power in Ireland shifted south into the hands of Uí Briain kings in the late eleventh century, even the precedence of Armagh was called into question. Lanfranc was able to cultivate links with Toirdelbach Ua Briain, over-king of Munster, and appears to have won his support for two successive bishops of Dublin to be consecrated in England in 1074 and 1085. This may reflect a bid by Toirdelbach to establish Dublin, a city that lay within his sphere of influence, as a rival to the ecclesiastical preeminence of Armagh.[109] Lanfranc's successor Anselm also consecrated a bishop of Waterford in 1096. These arrangements helped support the claims of the see of Canterbury over the Irish church, which would have important political ramifications in the twelfth century.

CONCLUSION

The adoption of Christianity entailed social and cultural changes as well as 'the reorientation of the soul'.[110] Older beliefs systems had a lingering influence for centuries after the mission of St Patrick. In the Irish landscape Christian and pagan place names might stand in close proximity. There was a gradual shift in the locations of ritual activities towards the enclosed spaces of church settlements, and these places were sanctified by their association with the cults of saints. The Church espoused the virtues of unworldliness as reflected in practices of penitence, asceticism and exile. On the other hand, churches came into unedifying conflict over doctrine and jurisdiction, and its institutions became deeply enmeshed with local politics and dynasties. This uneasy coexistence of sacred aspiration and mundane reality may be

---

[109] Holland, 'Dublin', pp. 114, 118.   [110] Nock, *Conversion*, p. 7.

illustrated by legal promulgations or *cána*. These upheld moral tenets but they also profited from the perceived sins of the laity and served to assert the power of a particular church. Successful churches accumulated wealth and competed with each other. They became embroiled in violence, particularly during the Viking Age. However, the claim that vikings had a catastrophic effect on the material and spiritual wealth of the Church can be called into question. The ideals of the Church were never cast aside and its institutions proved to be resilient in the face of many challenges. A narrative of decline and immorality was nevertheless adopted by reformers in the late eleventh century to suit their own political ends.

6

THE ARTS AD 500–1100

•

The claim that the Irish saved medieval civilisation is highly exaggerated; however, the Irish made an impressive contribution to European literature and art in the early Middle Ages.[1] Literacy came to Ireland through contact with the Roman world, as illustrated by the development of ogam. Christianity introduced the Bible and a vast store of written knowledge (both contemporary and historical) from across Latin Europe. These influences combined with native learning to create a vibrant written culture in Ireland both in Latin and in the vernacular. Many works written by Irish authors circulated in Britain and on the Continent. Similarly, artistic production in the early Middle Ages represented a fusion of indigenous and imported styles, creating objects and buildings that still inspire awe and attract visitors from across the globe.

LEARNING AND LITERATURE

The Church was the main provider of literate education in the early Middle Ages. It taught clerics and secular literate elites. This situation is effectively illustrated in the preface added to the Old Irish text *Auraicept na nÉces* ('The Scholars' Primer'). It describes the church of Tuaim Drecain (Tomregan, Co. Cavan) as possessing a school of Latin learning, a school for vernacular studies including law, and a school of poetry.[2] Schools were costly institutions to organise and run, so it

[1] Cahill, *How the Irish saved civilisation.* [2] Johnston, *Literacy*, p. 57.

might be envisaged that there was a hierarchy within Irish education. With exceptions, smaller churches might provide pastoral care and basic religious instruction, middling churches might provide foundational literacy to local elites, and the biggest or most prestigious institutions might draw in students from a wide area for advanced training, as did Armagh (Co. Armagh) and Clonmacnoise (Co. Offaly). From the eighth century, teaching seems to have become more centralised within the larger ecclesiastical centres.[3]

The learned minority in Ireland coexisted and moved in similar circles. The poet and the cleric might train in one place and be the same person, but equally they might not. The Church did not have a monopoly on learning, as education was also provided through apprenticeships and private schools. However, the sharp distinction drawn in the modern popular imagination between pre-Christian and Christian learning or between literate and non-literate education, or Latin and vernacular, does not seem justified. The influence of biblical and Classical learning can be seen in Irish sagas, while native tales influenced Latin hagiography. Thus, the creative worlds of medieval learning overlapped and offered inspiration to one another.

The costs of literate education included the collection of books, writing tools and wax tablets or slates to write on. The production of manuscripts involved the careful preparation of vellum (calfskins), quills and ink. The skill of formal calligraphy also took years of practice. One of the many cultural inheritances from early medieval Ireland is the use of Insular script.[4] A stately script, Insular half-uncial, was developed for important manuscripts, while minuscule forms that could be written more quickly were employed for other types of text. Within two centuries, forms of script used in Ireland had developed distinctive features. These include flat-headed forms of the letters G and T, wedge-shaped serifs on ascenders on letters such as b, d, h, l, and wide bows of rounded letters. Insular script was also characterised by the use of many abbreviations and ligatures (running together two or more letters). This style of script was shared by the Britons and spread to many Continental religious centres under Irish influence from the late sixth century. In the early Middle Ages, a lively network of Irish scholars exchanged manuscripts and ideas and travelled through Christian Europe.[5] By the late seventh century Irish

---

[3] Ibid., pp. 128, 168.   [4] O'Sullivan, 'Manuscripts', p. 511.
[5] Johnston, *Literacy*, p. 41.

influence had been established at a string of monasteries in Britain, Italy, France, Belgium, Germany and Switzerland. Insular script was widely used in England until the end of the tenth century. Elements of Insular script can be seen in the development of Carolingian minuscule, which was used in Latin Europe from the ninth to the twelfth century. In Ireland and Gaelic Scotland, the tradition of using Insular script forms continued beyond the Middle Ages. A Gaelic typeface was developed from Insular script in the late sixteenth century and continues to be used to evoke Irish identity on a range of objects from pub signs to greeting cards.

As the language of scholarship and the Church, Latin was used for a great deal of literary composition. Because Ireland stood outside the Roman Empire, Latin had not been an everyday language in antiquity. To help students master the language, various Latin grammatical texts were composed.[6] Some of the earliest writings, including glosses and biblical commentaries, might contain a mix of Latin and Irish. This suggests that scholars moved comfortably between the two languages. To help communication across the scholarly community of Gaeldom, a common register of written Gaelic was practised from about AD 700 to AD 900, which scholars have called 'Old Irish'.[7] As literacy and composition in the vernacular became more common in the ninth century, the old conventions of written Irish gave way to more varied forms. 'Middle Irish' may have mirrored adaptations in the language as it was spoken in different parts of Ireland and Gaelic Scotland. Artificial forms of the language were nevertheless maintained, especially for poetic expression, which represented the authors' craft and signalled to the audience the elevated purpose of the composition.

The high linguistic standards attained by Irish scholars are illustrated by glossaries.[8] *Sanas Chormaic* ('Cormac's Glossary') was written in Irish around AD 900 and comprises a compendium of etymologies not just in Irish but also in Latin, Greek, Hebrew, Brittonic, Pictish, English, and Old Norse and drawing from a wide range of sources.[9] The impressive range and linguistic competence of Irish scholars encouraged students to come from abroad, a phenomenon mentioned by the Anglo-Saxon writers Aldhelm and Bede. The sophisticated understanding of Latin that was fostered in the best

---

[6] Ó Cróinín, 'Hiberno-Latin', p. 376.   [7] Johnston, *Literacy*, pp. 20–1.
[8] Russell *et al.*, 'Early Irish Glossaries Database'.
[9] Carney, 'Language and literature', p. 486.

Irish schools encouraged creative wordplay. *Hisperica Famina* ('Western Sayings') seems to have been developed by a group of students competing to outdo each other in the composition of bizarre and complex Latin statements drawing on a range of exotic words from Greek and Hebrew.[10]

Language skills facilitated travel, and throughout the early Middle Ages a stream of Irish scholars set sail from home for the sake of piety, out of curiosity, or in search of patronage. Perhaps the most famous gatherings of Irish scholars were at the courts of the Carolingian kings in the mid-ninth century. The names of two prominent intellectuals, Sedulius Scottus and John Scottus (also called Eriugena), suggest that their Gaelic origins were an important part of their identity. A range of works has survived from these two authors. Sedulius's writings included a Latin grammar, a commentary on the Gospel of Matthew, nature poetry, religious poetry, royal panegyric, and a guide to the morals and behaviour appropriate for princes. Eriugena's writings include a commentary on the Gospel of St John, translations of Greek works attributed to Dionysius the Areopagite, a commentary on the Late Antique author Martianus Capella, and poems in Greek and Latin. He also wrote a theological treatise *De diuina praedestinatione* ('On Divine Predestination'), which stirred up a scholarly controversy. Eriugena's best-known work is *Periphyseon* ('The Division of Nature') in which he discussed the concept of creation in a way that has influenced Western philosophy for centuries.[11]

The works of these scholars show that sharp lines were not drawn between different disciplines of study in the early Middle Ages, and curious minds often ranged across different fields. Many texts defy simple categorisation. Nevertheless, to provide some overarching structure for such a broad topic, discussion is divided here into 'rules and regulations', 'religious literature', 'praise poetry' and 'heritage'. With the space available, no attempt has been made to give a comprehensive overview of early medieval literature from Ireland. This is just a taste of the range of texts that are available.

RULES AND REGULATIONS

Some of the earliest writings in Ireland were guidelines for clerics and Christian communities. These give insight into processes of

---

[10] Jenkinson, ed., *Hisperica famina*; Ó Cróinín, 'Hiberno-Latin literature', p. 383.

[11] Ó Cróinín, 'Hiberno-Latin literature', pp. 399–400; Moran, *Philosophy*.

conversion. They demonstrate that Christianity did not win an easy victory over old belief systems and that Christians and heathens lived side by side for some time. 'The First Synod of St Patrick', which (despite its name) belongs to the sixth or seventh century, shows matters that could arise, such as a heathen offering alms to Christians, or a cleric standing as a legal surety for a heathen.[12] While some rules may have been developed in Ireland *ad hoc*, many looked to authorities outside Ireland for guidance. In the early eighth century, a great compilation of citations from Scripture and Church Fathers, canon law and synodal decrees was gathered by Ruben of Dairinis and Cú Chuimne of Iona. The resulting *Collectio Canonum Hibernensis* ('Irish Collection of Canons') provided guidance through a 'great forest of writings' concerning the proper conduct of Christian life.[13]

Rules were also necessary for communal religious life. In Ireland, these rules were often associated with a particular saint, and they may have been observed, with some local variations, across their *familia*. The earliest surviving monastic rules by an Irishman are probably those attributed to St Columbanus (who died in AD 615) for a Continental audience.[14] Columbanus's rule was at pains to lay out the principles of monastic life as well as guiding its practices. Particular emphasis is laid on the monks' obedience, silence and self-control. To accompany the rule, there is a list of punishments for breaches of monastic decorum, such as laughing during services or talking while eating.[15] A later example of an Irish monastic rule is that of the *Céli Dé* written in the ninth century, which is notable for its strict dietary regulations and concern for devotional and pastoral duties.[16]

The Christian principle that sins must be atoned for led to the prodigious development of penitential literature in Ireland. These comprise tariffs of punishments, self-denying or devotional acts proportionate to sins that might be committed by clerics or lay people. Irish writers developed a sophisticated system of private penance and categorised a dizzying range of malpractices (which sometimes took some thought and imagination) from premeditated murder to getting drunk. In the seventh-century 'Penitential of Cumméne', the penitence for the former act must last a lifetime, while for the latter a

---

[12] Dumville, *Councils*.   [13] Hughes, *Early Christian Ireland*, p. 68
[14] Charles-Edwards, 'Penitential'.
[15] Walker, ed. and trans., *Sancti Columbani Opera*, pp. 123–68.
[16] Gwynn, ed. and trans., 'Rule of the Céli Dé'.

layman must live on bread and water for seven days. The penitentials often show authorial familiarity with secular law. For example, Cummène states that someone who causes an injury must cover medical expenses and provide compensation and labour, just as secular laws do, but in addition the perpetrator performs penance. Thus, while secular laws sought to compensate victims of crime, penitentials sought restitution for the soul of the sinner.[17]

Christian writers were also concerned with rules and proper conduct within secular society. Particular emphasis was placed upon the duties of rulers. The seventh-century tract *Audacht Morainn* ('The Testament of Morann') is one of seven early medieval 'wisdom texts' dispensing advice to kings.[18] Their contents are linked with the large corpus of secular laws that have survived from the seventh and eighth centuries, albeit preserved in late medieval and early modern manuscripts.[19] The system of law was inherited from pre-literate Ireland; however, the outlook of the written texts is Christian as well as aristocratic. The laws may have been written down to establish and codify principles resulting from the negotiation between old traditions and new influences. The attempt to establish a cohesive body of written law that could be observed across Ireland may also reflect the political ambitions of Uí Néill rulers and their allies to bring a degree of unity to Irish institutions.[20] Once laws were written, they were made less flexible, and religious and political ideologies were embedded within them. From the late eighth century, the focus of legal composition was on glosses and commentaries on existing tracts. This may reflect the exegetical tradition of church schools being applied to the laws.

Early Irish laws detailed social relationships and obligations according to inheritance, status and individual contracts. Underlying the law was the desire to avoid violent conflict by setting out the duties and entitlements of each social rank and providing a system of arbitration for parties who were in disagreement. As one might expect, law tracts were replete with technical language that required a class of specialists to help interpret. However, this does not mean that laws were devoid of literary merit. Legal material might be presented in verse, in rhetorical prose or in mnemonic patterns. The laws had to be

---

[17] Hughes, *Early Christian Ireland*, p. 87.   [18] Kelly, *Guide*, pp. 284–6.
[19] Binchy, ed., *Corpus*; Breatnach, *Companion*.
[20] Charles-Edwards, 'Early Irish law', p. 370.

communicated well because their effectiveness depended on communities listening to and memorising proclamations of regulations and agreements. In their public utterances and composition, the skills of the jurist might therefore overlap with those of the poet.[21] The vast body of legal material that has survived from early medieval Ireland is remarkable, and it offers much potential for further study.

RELIGIOUS LITERATURE

In addition to linguistic and legal studies, the main preoccupations of schools in early medieval Ireland were biblical exegesis and the calculation of the date of Easter (*computus*). Early medieval computistical tracts illustrate the significance of links between Ireland and the Mediterranean. Some texts from North Africa concerning the calculation of Easter seem to have come to Ireland via Spain.[22] In the seventh century the debate raged as to which method of calculating Easter was the best. The letters of Columbanus and Cumméne show how major Irish scholars could offer contrary opinions on this topic. Columbanus addressed the pope on this matter, defending the eighty-four-year cycle.[23] Cumméne wrote some years later, around AD 632, to Ségéne, abbot of Iona, and Béccán, a hermit, defending the Alexandrine calculation of Easter favoured by Rome and widely adopted in the south of Ireland at this date. Both letters reveal an extensive knowledge of biblical texts and Late Antique scholarship.[24]

The skills developed by Irish scholars in biblical exegesis are exemplified in manuscript copies that have survived on the Continent as well as in Ireland. To help summarise knowledge in this field, a massive Reference Bible was put together around AD 800, comprising commentaries on every biblical book. It drew on a wide range of Late Antique authors and also non-canonical texts or apocrypha, some of which are not recorded outside Ireland.[25] An interesting category of noncanonical literature dealt with otherworldly themes. These drew from a well of Christian learning, but were also inspired by indigenous myths of otherworldly islands and subterranean fairy folk. Perhaps the most famous example is *Navigatio Sancti Brendani* ('Voyage

[21] Stacey, *Dark speech*, pp. 53–94.   [22] Ó Cróinín, 'Hiberno-Latin literature', p. 390.
[23] See the earlier discussion.
[24] Walsh and Ó Cróinín, eds. and trans., *Cummian's letter*; Walker, ed. and trans., *Sancti Columbani Opera*, pp. 3–13.
[25] Ó Cróinín, 'Hiberno-Latin literature', p. 394.

of St Brendan'). This story of Brendan and his monks setting out to discover otherworldly islands was very popular in medieval Europe. It has survived in more than one hundred manuscripts and in numerous vernacular retellings. The tale was allegorical: for example, the monks travel for seven successive years, but always celebrate Easter on what they first thought was an island but that turns out to be a whale. This is appropriate as Easter is a movable feast. The story may be read as a quest for spiritual perfection in monastic life.

Otherworldly tales might also take the form of a romantic quest. *Echtra Chondla* ('Adventure of Connla') is an early tale that tells of a prince torn between the love of his people and his love of an immortal woman who lives in an Otherworld. However, this tale can also be read allegorically, with the woman representing the life of the Church.[26] More overt heathen themes appear in the eleventh-century story *Baile in Scáil* ('The Phantom's Frenzy'). In this tale, the Uí Néill dynast Conn Cétchathach ('Conn of a Hundred Battles') enters an unearthly plain through thick fog. There he encounters the deity Lug and a woman with a golden crown who represents the sovereignty of Ireland. She offers food and drink to Conn, and Lug prophesies kings of Ireland who will succeed him.[27] The tale should not be read as a heathen throwback, but as an endorsement of Uí Néill kingship. In a comparable way, Italian Renaissance writers celebrated Roman gods, adapting their stories to suit their own ends.

Native folktales and Christian scholarship also combined in medieval Saints' Lives. Around fifty Irish Lives and more than one hundred Latin Lives have survived from medieval Ireland.[28] Precise dating, especially for the Latin Lives, is fraught with difficulty. Nevertheless, a significant number have been attributed to the years before 1100. The writing of Saints' Lives seems to have developed in the seventh century, perhaps at a time when wealthier churches could commission writings to help win patronage and influence. They emphasise the miraculous powers of the saints. Scholarship has tended to focus on the earliest Lives of the three most famous saints: Patrick, Brigit and Columba. The 'Life of St Brigit' by Cogitosus is regarded as one of the first Lives composed in Ireland, around the mid-seventh century. This was soon followed by Muirchú's 'Life of St Patrick',

[26] Oskamp, ed. and trans., 'Echtra Condla'.
[27] Dillon, *Early Irish literature*, pp. 107–9.
[28] Sharpe, *Medieval Irish Saints' Lives*, pp. 5–6.

which presents a much more confident version of the saint than that found in his 'Confessio'. At the end of the seventh century, Adomnán wrote his biography of St Columba. These Lives were influenced by Scripture and the works of Late Antique hagiographers. This influence can be exemplified in Adomnán's 'Life of St Columba', which drew from the 'Life of St Martin of Tours' by Sulpicius Severus, the 'Life of St Benedict' by Gregory the Great, and the 'Life of St Anthony' by Athanasius. Adomnán also drew from the works of Jerome, Vergil and Juvencus.[29] The Lives, like the Gospels, were open to interpretations on an allegorical, as well as on a literal, level. Perhaps the most famous episode in Adomnán's Life is St Columba's encounter with the Loch Ness monster. As the hungry beast pursues a swimming monk, the saint uses the sign of the cross to banish it into the depths. While this is an entertaining and highly visual tale, it may also allegorise the saint's ability to overcome the monstrous paganism of the local Picts.[30] The Bible was the most prolific model for miracles, although some were adapted to local mores.

Saints not only imitated Christ in acts of charity and healing. They are also shown vigorously defending the Faith and the property of their communities. The bilingual 'Tripartite Life of St Patrick', which may date to the ninth century, presents the saint as a powerful ruler. St Patrick wields authority over angels, scatters curses on those who oppose his will and passes harsh judgement on sinners (including his niece whom he orders to be run over by a chariot for breaking her vow of chastity). The terrifying characteristics attributed to many Irish saints drew from scriptural precedents.[31] They were intended to inspire fear and devotion, but quick-tempered characters also made for good drama. The eleventh-century 'Life of St Findchú of Brigown' presents a warrior turned holy man who wields a crozier with the name of 'head-battler' and who can destroy a band of vikings with the fiery sparks that fly from his teeth.[32] The remarkable episodes in Irish hagiography must have helped stories of saints to circulate orally among the laity.

POETRY

The artistry of early medieval poetry lay not just in the power of the words but also in the author's ability to follow metrical and stylistic

---

[29] Hughes, *Early Christian Ireland*, p. 223; Charles-Edwards, 'Structure and purpose'.
[30] Borsje, 'Monster'.   [31] Johnson, 'Vengeance is mine', pp. 21–3.
[32] Hughes, *Early Christian Ireland*, p. 243.

conventions that might dictate the number of syllables or stresses in each line or the patterns of rhyme or alliteration. These attributes were best appreciated when verses were heard: poetry was meant to be declaimed in company, rather than read in silence. Most poems may never have been committed to parchment and so passed from memory with their last reciters.[33]

Many of the poems that have survived from the early Middle Ages were devotional in character. An early example is *Amra Choluim Chille*, an elegy for St Columba of Iona, possibly composed soon after his death in 597.[34] The saint is lauded for his scholarship and piety, but in heroic terms that echo secular eulogies. These terms may have seemed appropriate for the honorand's Uí Néill heritage. The praise of saints was a popular theme, as may be seen in the range of hymns of 'The Antiphonary of Bangor' that was put together in the late seventh century, and the *Liber Hymnorum* of the eleventh century.[35] Longer poetic works include *Félire Óengusso* ('Calendar of Oengus'), written at the turn of the ninth century. Between its lengthy prologue and epilogue, it has 365 quatrains, each commem-orating the feast days of saints.[36] Sacred history and eschatological themes were also explored in verse for the glory of God. The Middle Irish *Saltair na Rann* ('The Psalter of the Quatrains') comprises 150 cantos providing a sacred history of the world from creation until Doomsday.[37] This text drew heavily upon biblical apocryphal texts, as did *In Tenga Bithnua* ('The Evernew Tongue') in which the spirit of Philip the Apostle described the universe, including heaven and hell.[38]

Much of the poetry composed for secular patrons often related to a particular event.[39] These poems are often chance survivals in single manuscript copies; others have been saved through incorpo-ration within another text, such as a chronicle or a metrical tract. Examples of this genre include the eight stanzas addressed to a royal dynast of Leinster, Áed son of Diarmait, in the late eighth or early ninth century. As well as highlighting Áed's ancestry and personal brilliance, the verse gives insight into the working conditions of pro-fessional poets: 'At the ale-drinking, odes are chanted . . . over pools

[33] Carney, 'Language and literature', p. 458.
[34] Clancy *et al.*, trans., *Triumph Tree*, pp. 102–7.   [35] Curran, *Antiphonary*, p. 19.
[36] Stokes, ed. and trans., *Martyrology of Oengus*.   [37] Stokes, ed., *Saltair*.
[38] Herbert and McNamara, eds. and trans., *Irish biblical apocrypha*, pp. xxi, 44–7, 109–18.
[39] Carney, 'Language and literature', pp. 459–60.

of liquor'.[40] Verses were composed immediately after the death of
Máel Sechnaill , the Southern Uí Néill over-king, in 1022. The poet
praised Máel Sechnaill's great victory over the men of Dublin at Tara
in 980, celebrated his realm and his ancestry and lamented the loss of
the poet's generous patron.[41] Longer poems were commissioned that
eulogised lines of kings. These historical works drew on the glories of
the past to endorse the rulers of the present. A poem on the Christian
kings of Leinster was originally composed in the early tenth century
and then updated a century later, presumably to bolster the reputation
of the last-named leader.[42]

Some of the best-known poems from early medieval Ireland
were not obviously written to praise an aristocratic or religious
patron. These include the ninth- or tenth-century poem 'Líadan and
Cuirither' in which the poetess Líadan rejects her lover Cuirither out
of piety, but laments the heartbreak that resulted. A female narrative
voice is adopted in the eighth-century 'Nun of Beare', which is a
poignant reflection on ageing. On a lighter theme is a ninth-century
poem 'Pangur Bán', where the author compares his scholarly endeavours with his cat's efforts to catch mice. The enduring popularity of
these particular poems relates to their timeless sentiments of romantic
love, nostalgia and companionship, and the skill in their expression.[43]
A body of Old and Middle Irish poetry praising the beauty of nature
has also survived: its continued appeal is reflected in a number of
modern translations.

Reverence for the Irish landscape was expressed in a genre of
poems that explained how particular places obtained their names.
The *dinnshenchas* ('Lore of Places') in prose and verse reveal former
communities' imaginative engagement with the places in which they
lived and worked. The poems suggest an environment filled with
legends, some of which may have been passed down through generations. These stories about places tend to cluster around symbolic
centres of power and prominent landscape features, such as the prehistoric earthworks at Tara. This connection between legends and places
also found expression in Irish saga literature, and it still finds an echo
in modern folklore. A great gathering of *dinnshenchas* from across

[40] Stokes and Strachan, eds. *Thesaurus Palaeohibernicus*, II: 295; Knott, trans., *Irish classical poetry*, pp. 53–4.

[41] Carney, ed. and trans., 'Ó Cianáin miscellany', pp. 142–7.

[42] 'O'Brien, ed. and trans., 'A Middle-Irish poem'.

[43] Crotty *et al.*, trans., *Penguin book of Irish poetry*, pp. 16–17, 62–7.

Ireland was made in the eleventh century, accompanied by prose commentaries and tales.[44] The resulting compilation gave an overview of stories of Irish places, which overlapped with other accounts of the history and heritage of Ireland.

Historical works were perhaps only second in significance to religious writings in early medieval Irish literary production, but what counted as 'historical' writing was broader than what a modern audience might expect. It included poems, some of which are already mentioned, origin legends, genealogy, annals and sagas. These works often combined prose and poetry in a single narrative. The need to reconcile inherited stories of the Irish past with universal and biblical history led to the development of stories about the origins of the Irish.[45] Systematic accounts of Irish origins were developed in ninth-century texts in Ireland and Britain, including the poem *Can a mbunadas na nGael* ('What is the Origin of the Irish?') and *Historia Britonum* ('History of the Britons'), which identify prehistoric migrations of people to Ireland. These stories evolved to describe a more complex sequence of migrations in *Lebor Gabála Érenn* ('The Book of Invasions of Ireland'). It survives in several versions that depend on an eleventh-century verse archetype. These narratives combine indigenous legends with biblical and learned accounts of Continental scholars, including Jerome, Orosius and Isidore of Seville.

The first inhabitants of Ireland were said to have accompanied a woman called Banba or Cessair, who was identified in *Lebor Gabála* as the granddaughter of Noah. After the biblical flood, Partholón was identified as the first settler in Ireland. His name is derived from Hebrew, Bartholemew, and his people were said to have been wiped out by plague. Nemed, who follows, has a name that looks back to indigenous mythological tradition. It means 'sacred' or 'sanctuary'. Nemed and his people are said to have battled against malevolent and oppressive giant folk called Fomorians, and they eventually abandon Ireland. According to *Lebor Gabála* the descendants of Nemed comprise two groups who return to Ireland, called Fir Bolg ('Men of Bags') and Tuatha Dé Danann ('People of the Goddess Danu'). The latter, whose name reveals them to represent the heathen deities of

---

[44] Gwynn, ed. and trans., *Metrical Dindshenchas.*   [45] Carey, *Irish national origin.*

pre-Christian Ireland, win the upper hand. Finally, the Gaels arrived in Ireland under the leadership of Míl Espáine. Míl's name derives from Latin 'Miles Hispaniae' ('soldier of Spain'), and his story seems to have been a scholarly invention derived from Isidore of Seville's description of Spain as the mother of nations and his attempt to derive the Latin name *Hibernia* (Ireland) from *(H)Iberia* (Spain). According to *Lebor Gabála*, the followers of Míl fought against the Tuatha Dé, and the resulting treaty held that the Gaels took Ireland above the ground and the Tuatha Dé took Ireland below the ground. This tale provides an explanation for other Irish legends that identify burial mounds, caves and lakes as entry points to an otherworld inhabited by little people. The tales of the origins of the Irish that come down from the early Middle Ages represent a creative mixture of inherited legends, imported texts and a significant dose of imaginative scholarship.

Lebor Gabála asserted that Irish dynasties were descended from the Milesians. In the early Middle Ages, Irishness was defined by descent. Lineages who came from outside, such as Scandinavians in the ninth century, continued to be regarded as *Gaill* (foreigners) even after centuries of settlement, acculturation and intermarriage. Ancestry underpinned claims to status and political legitimacy. Its importance can be seen in the large volume of genealogies that have survived from the Middle Ages. These identify more than twenty thousand individuals. These texts promoted fictions of unbroken bloodlines reaching back into prehistory, laying out ancient claims to power and asserting links between contemporary dynasties. Such connections were sometimes forged to suit political conditions, and parts of a genealogy were often expanded or diminished to suit changing circumstances.[46] The genealogies emphasise a view of history dominated by a succession of male royal dynasts.

The genealogies are useful for historians, but still grievously underresearched. The focus of scholarship has tended to be on the abundant annalistic material surviving from the early Middle Ages. These records tend to be brief. They are predominantly focused on conflicts and the obits of important political and religious figures. Some attention is also given to crops, weather, unusual events and acts of patronage. For the main part annals were written in prose, but verses related to crucial events, such as a battle or the death of a king, are sometimes included. Chronicles may have been kept in Ireland as

[46] Johnston, *Literacy*, p. 86.

early as the sixth century. The earliest layer of surviving annalistic records has been dubbed 'The Chronicle of Iona' as it seems likely to have been kept at that church until about 740. Thereafter the records were continued somewhere in the Irish midlands. The main centres of record until 911 include Clonard (Co. Meath) and Armagh. The foundational text that underpins Irish chronicles from c. 660 to 911 is often called 'The Chronicle of Ireland'. The name does not mean that foreign events were entirely excluded from the text. The period from 731 to 911 was a time when non-Irish sources were incorporated into earlier chronicle accounts to present Irish events in a wider context.[47]

After about 911, 'The Chronicle of Ireland' was expanded and continued at different centres. One version seems to have been kept in the northeast midlands and then at Armagh until the late twelfth century. This text is known as the 'Annals of Ulster', which survives in manuscripts dating from the fifteenth century. It is particularly important because the scribes of this chronicle faithfully transcribed their sources over a long period. This allows the development of the Irish language to be traced over time, and it also provides a record of the shift from Latin to vernacular composition during the eighth and ninth centuries. The linguistic changes apparent in the 'Annals of Ulster' add to the impression that it preserves contemporary records, even though its manuscripts are late. After 911, another important set of annals was kept in Meath; this underpins a series of extant Irish chronicles including the 'Annals of Tigernach', *Chronicon Scotorum*, and the Hiberno-English 'Annals of Clonmacnoise'. These are collectively dubbed 'The Clonmacnoise group', as they share a common core of material that was linked to that major midland church. The 'Annals of Inisfallen' are also related to this group, but this chronicle also contains unique Munster sources. Another text, known as 'Fragmentary Annals of Ireland', also drew in part from the Clonmacnoise group of chronicles and combined its contents with a saga-like narrative. In the seventeenth century, a project led by the Franciscan friars to record and preserve medieval Irish records resulted in the great compilation known in English as the 'Annals of the Four Masters'. It included entries from the 'Annals of Ulster', 'The Clonmacnoise group' of chronicles and some other sources. The surviving annals of medieval Ireland are an invaluable guide to

---

[47] Charles-Edwards, trans., *Chronicle of Ireland*.

political events, but they also say much about social issues and a culture of commemoration.[48]

Another window on social concerns and perceptions of the past is provided by sagas. From the ninth to the twelfth century there was a blossoming in this genre of literature. Some of the literary heroes, including Cú Chulainn and Deirdre, inspired modern writers, notably Yeats, Synge and Patrick Pearse, and consequently they maintain a place in contemporary Irish culture. Irish sagas tend to be reworkings of earlier oral or written tales, drawing on a cast of characters that may already have been familiar to their audiences. This resulted in an interrelated web of narratives, perhaps akin to episodes in soap operas or the crossovers of modern fan fiction. As well as referring to earlier tales, sagas often embedded influences and echoes from other sources, including biblical, Classical and law texts. These tales were often intended to instruct as well as to entertain their audiences with moral or political messages. The result was a voluminous and sophisticated body of work that could engage those who read or heard them on several different levels.

Perhaps the best-known (and longest) medieval Irish saga is *Táin bó Cúailnge* ('The Cattle Raid of Cooley'). The story is dominated by two characters: Queen Medb (Maeve) of Connacht who attacks Ulster to seize a prize bull, and the Ulster warrior Cú Chulainn who leads the defence against her. Ultimately the bull dies and the war is shown to be futile. The fame of the *Táin* led to different versions of the saga circulating, making for a complex textual history, and a number of subordinate tales were associated with it.[49] Other sagas that had enduring popularity include *Longes mac nUislenn* ('The Exile of the Sons of Uisliu'), which focuses on the tragic life of Deirdre, whose beauty was prophesied before her birth to bring destruction to many. The tale ends as Deirdre commits suicide rather than be handed over to the man who killed her lover. *Fingal Rónáin* ('The Kin Slaying of Rónán') is the tale of a lustful queen who attempts to seduce her stepson. After she was vigorously rejected, she provokes her husband into ordering the death of his son. This results in a blood feud. The queen takes her own life and the king dies of grief. *Togail Bruidne Da Derga* ('The Destruction of Da Derga's Hostel') is another tragic tale, which describes the fall of a great king after he makes a biased judgement that unleashes a series of mysterious and unlucky

---

[48] Evans, 'Annals'.   [49] Kinsella, trans., *Táin*.

events.[50] These and many other sagas survive in multiple versions, suggesting an interplay between oral and written culture and the further creativity of copyists and compilers. Although supernatural elements loom large in the sagas, the tales often purport to present real people from a semi-mythical past and draw real locations into the story. In this way, history, myth, genealogy and place-name lore might be intertwined within these compelling narratives.

Interest in the past is also demonstrated by the reception of non-Irish history and legend. The writing of vernacular adaptations of Classical and literary texts became popular in the eleventh and twelfth centuries. These were much more than simple translations: often these works were based on a core text, but contained other information to help contextualise the narrative or to add additional details. Early examples of this genre are *Scéla Alexandair* ('The Story of Alexander the Great') and *Togail Troí* ('The Destruction of Troy', based not on Homer but on the Latin text attributed to Dares the Phrygian). Ireland's adaptations of Classics preceded those of other European lands. There was an interest in synchronising the events of the Classical past with Ireland's own history. For example, a comment in *Cath Maige Tuired* ('The [Second] Battle of Moytura') states that the battle was fought at the same time as Troy was destroyed. This Irish saga survives as an eleventh- or twelfth-century reworking of an earlier original. A similar interest in universal history underpinned both *Lebor Gabála* and the 'Universal Chronicle' of Marianus Scotus, an Irish monk working at Mainz in the late eleventh century. Irish scholars were far from insular in their historical interests. Instead, they wished to understand the interrelationship between Classical and biblical history and their own past.

MUSIC

It is likely that some forms of literature were performed to music, including hymns and poems. Saga narratives may have also provided inspiration for tunes and lyrics. Indeed, sagas show the importance of music in life at royal courts. In *Cath Maige Tuired* ('The Battle of Moytura') the Túatha Dé rise against King Bres because of his lack of hospitality: 'however frequently they might come, their breaths

---

[50] Gantz, trans., *Early Irish myths*; Koch *et al.*, trans., *Celtic heroic age*, pp. 274–82; O'Connor, *Destruction*.

did not smell of ale; and they did not see their poets, nor their bards nor their satirists, nor their harpers, nor their pipers, nor their horn-blowers'. In the same tale, Lug of the Túatha Dé plays the harp at the court of Bres's successor to great effect, 'putting them to sleep from that hour to the same time the next day. He played sorrowful music so that they were crying and lamenting. He played joyful music so that they were merry and rejoicing'.[51] Written texts suggest that, in addition to the human voice, the harp, lyre, pipe and horn were popular musical instruments

Archaeological finds and sculpture indicate what early medieval instruments looked like. The most amazing discovery is a horn made from yew wood, bound together with bronze mounts, which was recovered from the River Erne. It is 58 cm in length and appears to date from the eighth or ninth century.[52] Excavations in Dublin have yielded a decorated wooden bow of eleventh-century date. Simple whistles and pipes of wood and bone have also been recovered from the city, although these tend to be twelfth century or later. High crosses, including those at Clonmacnoise, Kells and Durrow, depict King David singing psalms on his harp or lyre. A cross at Monasterboice provides an engaging depiction of musicians playing both stringed and wind instruments as they surround Christ in majesty.[53] Presumably the sculpture depicts contemporary instruments. Both texts and images suggest the significance of music in medieval secular and religious life.

STYLES OF VISUAL ART

Just as the heroes of Irish saga have a place in modern Irish culture, the achievements of craftsmen and architects also have an iconic role in representing Ireland and Irishness in the contemporary world. The dynamism of visual arts can be seen in the variety of styles and visual motifs employed in objects ranging from manuscripts to sculpture. The period from AD 500 to 1100 encompassed a series of developments in Irish art. At the beginning of the period art styles drew from an earlier repertoire of Iron Age 'La Tène' art work with its abstract organic motifs of curves, spirals and trumpet forms. From

---

[51] Gray, ed. and trans., *Cath Maige Tuired*, pp. 32–3, 42–3.
[52] Purser, 'Reconstructing the River Erne horn', pp. 17–25.
[53] Buckley, 'Music', pp. 165–90.

around AD 600 the incorporation of Germanic elements of interlace, geometric patterns and animal forms led to the emergence
of the 'Insular' art style that was dominant until the tenth century.
Ireland's links with the Scandinavian world brought new influences
to Ireland. A 'West Viking' style developed in Ireland's coastal ports
in the tenth century, which represented a vibrant mixture of cultural
influences. The 'Borre' style that evolved in ninth-century Scandinavia was characterised by animal ornament with large round eyes
and prominent ears that were presented in symmetrical patterns.
Borre-style interlace was characterised by double bands of ornament,
ring chains and plaited knots. The best example of this style in Ireland
appears on the frame of a wooden gaming board from Ballinderry
crannóg (Co. Westmeath), which dates from the tenth century.
In the eleventh century, the 'Ringerike' style was introduced to
Ireland, which was characterised by sinuous animal ornament combined with plant-like tendrils.[54] As Hiberno-Scandinavian communities were drawn within Irish ecclesiastical networks in the eleventh
and twelfth centuries, the production of artworks that fused Insular
and Scandinavian styles became more sophisticated and widespread.
Throughout the early medieval period, art forms were continuously
evolving with the conscious inclusion of conservative and innovative
motifs that reflected the creativity of Irish artists and their contacts
abroad.

MANUSCRIPT ILLUMINATION

The 'Book of Kells' is the best-known example of manuscript illumination from the Insular Middle Ages. It may have been produced
at the island monastery of Iona around the year 800. It represents
the peak of developments in manuscript art in the Gaelic world. As
Christianity was a religion of the book, copies of the bible and liturgy
were necessary for the new religion. The decoration of these books
was a natural adjunct to their perceived importance. Some came to
be venerated as relics in their own right. While the principal purpose
of illumination was to glorify a text, it could also serve a functional
role in highlighting the beginning and end of sections or providing
a focus for the meditations of the reader.

[54] Moss, ed. *Art*, pp. 41–4.

One of the earliest surviving manuscripts produced in Ireland is the *Cathach* ('Battler') of St Columba. This is a fragmentary book of psalms that dates from the late sixth or early seventh century. Each psalm begins with a simple decorated initial: this prefigures later developments in Insular manuscript art. The use of colour is minimal, with the initials coloured in black, but often outlined with orange dots. Decorations include La Tène-style spirals and trumpets added to the terminals of letters; sometimes these flourish into the forms of simple line-drawn animals, as if to represent the energy of the living word. Late Antique influences include the addition of Greek-style crosses to some letters.[55] The letters following the larger initials decrease in size to integrate them visually into the rest of the text. The *Cathach* is one of a handful of remaining psalters of Irish origin that date before 1100. The most lavish decoration was reserved for gospel books. As canonical accounts of Christ's life, these were central to Christian worship. Less than twenty survive wholly or in part from the early Middle Ages, and they can be divided into two groups. The most ornate are large volumes intended for display. These include the 'Book of Kells', the 'Book of Durrow', the 'Lichfield Gospels' and the 'Echternach Gospels'. Smaller, more humbly decorated, gospels were more portable and seem intended for personal use (these are often called 'pocket gospels').[56] These include the 'Book of Mulling' and 'The Book of Dimma'.

The development of manuscript art between the *Cathach* of St Columba and the 'Book of Kells' can be demonstrated by an analysis of the 'Book of Durrow', which was produced in the eighth century. This is an elaborately decorated manuscript with each gospel being preceded by a full-page depiction of the relevant evangelist symbol (which is based on the Old Latin Bible rather than the more familiar Vulgate: a lion represents St John, and an eagle represents St Mark). There is also a page of abstract ornament before each gospel, and the opening words of the text are decorated. The manuscript may have been produced at Durrow (Co. Offaly), for the manuscript is recorded there from the ninth century. This church belonged to the powerful Columban *familia*, which also included the church of Iona. Pictish as well as Anglo-Saxon influence can be seen in the artwork. For example, the lion of St John (folio 191v) – with its simplified

[55] Edwards, *Archaeology*, p. 150.   [56] Moss, ed. *Art*, p. 225.

form and scrolled bands of ornament above the legs and framing the neck – bears close comparison to the wolf on the Pictish symbol stone from Stittenham, Invernessshire. The page of abstract ornament before St Luke's gospel (fol. 125v) has rectangular panels of geometric ornament that compare with those on seventh-century sword fittings from the Anglo-Saxon royal burial at Sutton Hoo (Suffolk).[57]

The 'Book of Kells' represents the pinnacle of Insular manuscript art. It was made around AD 800, probably within the Columban *familia* of churches, and like the earlier 'Book of Durrow' it combines elements of Gaelic, Pictish, Anglo-Saxon and Mediterranean art styles in its decoration. The extent and detail of the illumination are, however, incomparable. Each page contains skilfully decorated letters and animal ornament, and Eucharistic images of vines and hosts commonly recur. The canon tables that appear at the start of the book contain arches and columns variously filled with spiral ornament, knotwork, animal interlace and evangelist symbols. Full pages of ornament appear at the beginning and end of each gospel, as well as a full-page decoration of the opening words. The best-known pages include portraits of the Virgin and Child, Christ being tempted by the devil, St Matthew, and St John. The full-page decorations are characterised by frames outlined by bands of gold, echoing the designs of precious metalwork. These contain lavishly coloured illustrations, including depictions of angels, evangelists and monks, as well as patterns of spirals and interlace that sometimes require magnification before their intricacy can be fully appreciated. In addition to the technical excellence of these designs, there is a certain playfulness and charm to the many animal depictions in the text. The complex designs hint at visual riddles that the reader is encouraged to spend much time contemplating. The 'Book of Kells' is more or less contemporary with the 'Gospels of Macregol', which is a larger manuscript that is also decorated but not to such high standards. The author of the 'Gospels' has been identified as Mac Ríagoil, a scribe, bishop and abbot of Birr who died in 822.[58]

It may be that the political instability of the ninth century heralded the end of the production of large-format gospel books. Artistic patronage was then funnelled into other works that were less exposed to theft and damage. The vulnerability of large manuscripts is exemplified in the history and remarkable survival of the 'Book

[57] Ibid., p. 230.   [58] Farr, 'Incipit', p. 275.

of Kells'. In 1007, the 'Annals of Ulster' record that 'the great gospel
of Columba,... the most precious object of the Western world' was
stolen. It was found nearly three months later with the gold removed
from its cover. The churches of Kells were attacked and burned several
times during the Middle Ages, yet it survived. The book also avoided
the ravages of the Reformation. When Cromwell's troops were stationed in Kells, the government decided to remove the manuscript to
Dublin where it has remained. Around thirty folios of the book have
been lost over the years, which may be due to one of these events or
other causes.[59] Such vagaries of fortune illustrate why many medieval
manuscripts must have been lost. Those that remain attest to the technical and artistic skills of Ireland's early scribes and illustrators.

METALWORK

The treasures of early Irish metalwork, including 'Ardagh Chalice'
and 'Tara Brooch', are famous within Ireland and familiar to many
beyond its shores. While similar techniques were employed in secular
and ecclesiastical metalwork, different types of objects were produced
for different patrons. The growing wealth and status of the Church
in the seventh and eighth centuries encouraged the creation of great
artworks to adorn the interiors of churches and shrines. While many
of these adornments may have been of perishable materials including wood and cloth, an array of fine metalwork has survived. Some
of the metalwork involved liturgical practice, including chalices used
for Mass. The most famous examples are the 'Ardagh Chalice' and
the 'Derrynaflan Chalice'. Both are silver bowls with handles, gilt
cylindrical stems, and large domed feet. The rims and stem of each
are decorated with applied gold filigree and coloured studs (made
of amber on the 'Derrynaflan Chalice' and glass and rock crystal on
the 'Ardagh Chalice'). Decorative escutcheons of similar ornament
were placed on the sides of these cups.[60] Both objects were found
in hoards of other precious objects (including church plate) that may
have been buried in the ninth century (perhaps to protect them from
viking attacks). The 'Ardagh Chalice' is probably eighth century in
date, and the Derrynaflan example is probably from the ninth century. The more muted colour scheme of the 'Derrynaflan Chalice' of
amber, silver and gold (contrasting with the red and blue glass studs of

[59] Gwynn, 'Some notes'.   [60] Moss, ed. *Art*, pp. 259–64.

the 'Ardagh Chalice') and its employment of diamond-shaped frames of relatively simple filigree show changes in fashion between the production of both cups.[61]

Shrines and reliquaries represent another significant category of ecclesiastical artwork. Perhaps the most distinctive are house-shaped shrines used for carrying portable relics. These take the form of a small box of wood or metal (or both) with a hinged roof and exterior decoration. Three complete examples and numerous fragments have been found in Ireland. Shrines of this type of Gaelic manufacture or style have also survived in Scandinavia, Italy and Scotland.[62] They may once have held human remains. Other shrines were made for sacred books or associative relics. A fine example of the latter is the 'Moylough Belt Shrine'. It is made from four copper alloy sections with an imitation buckle. The sections were tinned to give a silvery appearance and were decorated with cast bronze frames with geometrical, dragon and bird-head designs. These frames contain silver foils stamped with spiral motifs and interlace, and studs of colourful glass and enamel. It is a unique object probably dating from the eighth century.[63] Scandinavian influence began to affect Irish ecclesiastical art from the eleventh century. For example, the 'Shrine of the Cathach' was originally made to hold the 'Cathach of St Columba' in the late eleventh century by a craftsman bearing the Scandinavian name Sitric. The short ends of this reliquary include cast metal panels of interlacing snakes and tendrils that belong to the Ringerike style.[64]

Jewellery represented the greatest investment in fine metalwork outside an ecclesiastical milieu. It was valued not merely in terms of aesthetic and financial worth: these objects were symbols of status. They reminded others where the bearer stood in the social hierarchy. In the sixth century, different types of dress fasteners, including brooches and pins, were produced in Ireland under the influence of styles used in post-Roman Britain. These tended to be small items cast in silver or (more commonly) in copper alloy.[65] The penannular brooch became the most common brooch style during the early Middle Ages. It was made from two components: a nearly circular ring and a pin with a flattened head that was either pierced by the ring or looped around it. From the seventh to the ninth century the

[61] Ó Floinn 'Beginnings', pp. 185–6, 205–9.   [62] Edwards, *Archaeology*, pp. 137–8.
[63] Moss, ed. *Art*, p. 296.   [64] Wallace, 'Viking Age Ireland', p. 233.
[65] Edwards, *Archaeology*, p. 133.

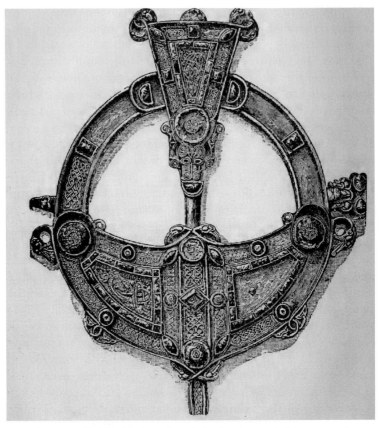

Figure 6.1 Sketch of the Tara Brooch (by William Frederick Wakeman)

average size of these brooches grew, and the terminals were widened to allow more space for decoration. This suggests a social demand for larger and more ornate status symbols, and it shows that those at the top of the hierarchy commanded greater wealth to commission them.

The best-known example is the 'Tara Brooch' (see Figure 6.1). Given the extravagance of its decoration, it is surprisingly small, only 8.7 cm in diameter with a 32 cm pin. To provide more space for decoration, the terminals of the ring are closed, and an attachment made of silver wires in the form of a snake was added. The brooch was cast in silver, with recessed panels, and the edge of the hoop is ornamented with dragons and birds in high relief. Sections of the brooch and the layout of the design were carefully planned and measured. The panels on the front are filled with beaded and twisted gold wire and gold granules, separated with studs of glass, enamel and amber – creating spirals, interlace and zoomorphic motifs. The patterns are so intricate that a magnifying glass is necessary to see all the details, and it is possible that much symbolic meaning was invested in the design. The back is ornamented with gilded panels of cast and engraved spirals and polychrome glass studs. The brooch was probably produced in the eighth century. It was found around AD 1850 at Bettystown (Co. Meath) and takes its name from an imaginative link with the royal site at Tara.[66]

Viking trade brought an increased flow of silver into Ireland, which promoted the craft of silversmiths. Pre-Viking Age jewellery tended to make a virtue of maximising the decorative effect of items while using small amounts of precious metals. From the ninth century, more brooches were cast from solid silver, and they became bigger. Imported amber also came to be used instead of glass to ornament metalwork. New ornament forms emerged, including the bossed pennanular brooch that had plate terminals decorated with round studs, and the thistle brooch that had brambled ball-shaped terminals. These innovations developed the penannular form in various ways. Pin forms also diversified. One innovation was the kite-brooch that developed from a hinged pin and the evolution of the pinhead into a flat lozenge or almond shape for decoration. These were produced in Hiberno-Scandinavian towns in both silver and copper alloy from the late tenth century. Ring headed pins and stick pins were also produced in great quantities. These were exported around the viking world.[67] The Viking Age witnessed a trend towards mass production of copper alloy jewellery and the centralisation of craft activities within larger settlements. The Hiberno-Scandinavian towns became centres of excellence in metalwork that combined different cultural traditions.

WOOD AND BONE

Excavations from waterlogged sites including Dublin and Lagore crannóg (Co. Meath) also reveal artistic production in wood and bone,

---

[66] Ó Floinn 'Beginnings', p. 183; Edwards, *Archaeology*, p. 141.
[67] Wallace, 'Viking Age Ireland', p. 216.

often on functional objects. These finds are immensely important as they demonstrate that artistic production was not the exclusive preserve of the elite. The wooden and bone finds of Dublin have generated the greatest interest due to their abundance and their fusion of Irish, Scandinavian and Anglo-Saxon art styles. Some of the finds reflect Insular adaptations of Scandinavian designs, which created a common 'West Viking Style' around the Irish Sea region and in Northumbria, highlighting political and cultural links between these regions. This style is nicely exemplified in a small wooden box with a sliding lid recovered from Christchurch Place, which can be dated to the mid-tenth century. It combines geometric interlace and fret patterns, which are familiar in Irish sculpture, with a ringed knot pattern of Borre style.[68] Other ornamented pieces of wood and bone include handles, combs, toys, gaming pieces and pieces of furniture.

The trial pieces of Dublin are commemorated in the poetry of Seamus Heaney, and more than two hundred have been recovered during fifty years of excavation. The majority are pieces of bone waste on which artists and pupils were trying out incised designs intended for metalwork or other media. Some of these pieces are highly ornate and accomplished. This suggests the emergence of Dublin as a centre for artistic training and production from the late tenth century. Similar trial pieces have been recovered not only from York and London but also from sites within Ireland, including Killaloe (Co. Clare) and Clonmacnoise (Co. Offaly). This shows that the fusion of Scandinavian and Insular art styles in Ireland was not limited to coastal towns.[69] The corpus of artworks in wood and bone come from a limited range of archaeological sites with good organic preservation. They help to demonstrate that creative expression was part and parcel of the lives of our medieval forebears.

SCULPTURE

Most of the sculpture from early medieval Ireland is linked to ecclesiastical sites. The earliest comprise ogam stones, a number of which bear incised crosses, and cross-carved stones and pillars found along the western seaboard of Ireland. These monuments may range in date from the fifth to the seventh century. In this early period, stone monuments may have been less fashionable in the east or wood was

[68] Wallace, *Viking Dublin*, p. 388.   [69] Ibid. pp. 393–5.

used instead.[70] Carved stones may have been used to provide a focus for religious rituals to mark out the sacred landscape, representing holy spaces, boundaries or routeways. They are found within early church sites and also on pilgrimage routes, including the 'Saint's Road' around Mount Brandon in the Dingle peninsula (Co. Kerry) and the valley of Glencolmchille (Co. Donegal).[71] The decoration of these upright stones is often simple, comprising a variety of cross forms, usually ringed, sometimes with the addition of abstract geometric patterns or knotwork.

The recumbent grave slab is another form of medieval monument. Hundreds of these have survived of varied shapes and sizes. They are inscribed with one or more crosses and often a name, which may be accompanied by a formula invoking a prayer or blessing for the deceased. The forms of the crosses on these monuments range from very simple to highly sophisticated and ornate compositions. Further typological work is necessary to determine their dates of production, but they may range from the seventh to the eleventh century.[72] Some styles may be linked with particular workshops. The largest of these was at Clonmacnoise (Co. Offaly) where more than four hundred complete or fragmentary early medieval slabs have been recorded since the nineteenth century.[73] The influence of Clonmacnoise designs can be seen in the impressive collection of slabs at Gallen (Co. Offaly), seven miles away, and at Iniscealtra (Co. Clare), which was linked to Clonmacnoise by the River Shannon. However, early medieval recumbent grave slabs are found in smaller numbers at sites across Ireland, including Glendalough (Co. Wicklow), Nendrum (Co. Down) and Inishmurray (Co. Sligo).[74]

The high cross is perhaps the best-known early medieval sculptural form. They seem to have developed in the late eighth century at Iona, based on earlier wooden forms, and they became popular across Ireland in the ninth century. The popularity of stone high crosses continued into the twelfth century, and more than 200 of these monuments survive. High crosses have a distinct ringed head profile, often with a hollowed ring and carved decoration. There are regional trends in their form and style, but most often the head and shaft were carved in a single block (although in a group of sculptures from the province

[70] Edwards, *Archaeology*, p. 161.   [71] Harbison, 'Early Irish pilgrim'.
[72] Swift, 'Dating Irish grave-slabs'.
[73] Lionard and Henry, 'Early Irish grave-slabs', pp. 144–6.   [74] Ibid., pp. 146–51.

of Ulster they are separate). The base of the cross is commonly in the form of a truncated pyramid. The decoration is often carved within mounded frames and may comprise abstract designs (common on the shafts of Ossory crosses) and figurative scenes from the Bible or relating to war and kingship. Regional styles were influenced by local geology. For example, the hard granite of the Barrow Valley crosses of Leinster favoured flat, symmetrical, chunky, minimalist representation of figures, while the softer sandstone used in the Midlands crosses lent itself to lively and naturalistic figurative scenes.[75]

The popularity of high crosses may be linked to European associations between the cross, the Church and the power of kings and emperors. A number of them were set up at important ecclesiastical settlements under royal patronage. The ninth-century crosses in Mide tend to be associated with the patronage of Clann Cholmáin, and those in Ossory are linked with the reign of Cerball mac Dúnlainge.[76] At Clonmacnoise, the 'Cross of the Scriptures' was erected with the support of King Flann Sinna of the Southern Uí Néill in the early tenth century, and he is thought to be represented on a scene on the cross shaft. Flann also oversaw the construction of a stone cathedral at Clonmacnoise. The popularity of stone crosses can be linked to the increasing power of major over-kings, and ninth-century examples are rare in Connacht and Munster, which lay outside Uí Néill control. This defiant symbol of Christianity and Irish kingship also developed during a period of political turmoil and viking raids. They are more common in the midland and eastern areas of Ireland in the ninth century, where attacks on churches (by Irish or vikings) are more often recorded. Wood could be burnt and precious ornaments could be carried away, but high crosses could not be easily stolen or destroyed. The monuments seem to have been most popular during the ninth and twelfth centuries, which were significant periods in the development of hierarchies in Church and kingship in Ireland. These centuries may also be characterised as times when Irish national and regional identities were reevaluated in response to foreign threats and internal competition.

ECCLESIASTICAL ARCHITECTURE

As a result of the patronage given to early medieval Irish churches, their architecture is often more elaborate and enduring than the

---

[75] Moss, ed. *Art*, pp. 143–6.   [76] Ibid., p. 479.

dwelling places of the people. Ecclesiastical architecture is represented at a wide range of sites from tiny enclosures in remote locations to large complexes commanding major routes through the Irish landscape. The majority of early medieval Irish churches were established in the sixth and seventh centuries, with additional foundations recorded in the eighth and early ninth centuries. After that time, patronage was invested in adorning older sites rather than founding new ones. These changes may reflect developing settlement hierarchies and a tendency for provincial over-kings to associate themselves with older and more prestigious religious sites.

Early medieval Irish churches were most commonly single-cell rectangular structures with a single doorway at the western end. Before 900, most were constructed of timber, turf and wattle. The term *dairthech* ('oak house') described churches built with hewn oak walls and roofs of thatch or wooden shingles. Archaeological evidence suggests that many were built using wooden sill beams attached to earth-fast posts or sill beams and structural posts jointed together without the need for postholes.[77] These carpentry techniques probably developed in the sixth century through contact with Britain and the Continent. The best description of a wooden Irish church in the seventh century was provided by Cogitosus in his 'Life of St Brigit'. He described Kildare as being 'of awesome height . . . adorned with painted pictures, and inside there are three chapels . . . divided by board walls under the single roof . . . this church contains many windows and one finely wrought portal' and 'an ornate altar and . . . tombs adorned with . . . gold, silver, gems and precious stones with gold and silver chandeliers . . . presenting a variety of carvings and colours'. The account indicates that, while the ground plan and materials of early medieval Irish churches tended to be modest, the greater churches could have had lavish interiors.

According to Bede, writing in eighth-century Northumbria, building in stone represented *Romanitas*. For this reason, construction in stone may have become more familiar in seventh-century Ireland when tensions between local and international practices of when to observe Easter and what tonsure to adopt were being resolved. An early example of a stone church was at Duleek (Co. Meath), mentioned by the seventh-century writer Tírechán. A stone church was mentioned at Armagh in 789.[78] From 900 there was a more significant shift towards construction of important churches in stone. Some

77 Ó Carragáin, *Churches*, pp. 15, 19.   78 *AU, s.a.* 789.

of these edifices are linked with the patronage of Clann Cholmáin in the Midlands (as at Clonmacnoise, Co. Offaly) and of Dál Cais in Munster (as at Killaloe, Co. Clare). Stone buildings could therefore represent the power of patrons, as well as affiliation to wider ecclesiastical practices. Stone churches were also more common in more rocky environments. In western Kerry, corbelled structures of tightly fitting stones are a feature of the ecclesiastical landscape. The most famous is Gallarus's oratory (Co. Kerry), which has a form akin to an upturned boat. Farther north at Temple Mac Dara (Co. Galway), the form mirrors earlier wooden churches. Its skeuomorphic features include carved finials at the apex of a steep, pitched stone roof and antae (side walls that project a short distance beyond the end of the church). During the eleventh century, there was greater investment in building in stone, and architectural innovations that reflect links abroad can be noted towards the end of the century. These include the addition of a chancel at some sites, including Glendalough (Co. Wicklow). This segregation of space between the clergy and the laity may reflect the influence of Gregorian reform in Ireland.[79]

Larger ecclesiastical sites did not have just one church: they hosted a range of other buildings and monuments. In the seventh century, Armagh already had three churches, and by the twelfth century, Armagh, Glendalough (Co. Wicklow) and Clonmacnoise (Co. Offaly) had ten or more churches. Middle-ranking ecclesiastical sites might have a principal church and one or two subsidiary ones. The term *airdam* described free-standing buildings that were associated with principal churches.[80] The structures on an ecclesiastical site reflected a range of devotional, liturgical and ascetic practices. Separate chapels might serve different functions, such as the veneration of shrines or relics or for baptism. From the eighth century, shrine chapels were more commonly built in stone. This may have resulted from a practical concern to protect relics by making the building more fireproof. Some sites also have *leachta*, which are open-air drystone structures. Stone hermitages were also constructed at some churches and stood a little way from the main settlement. Perhaps the most striking is at the twin-peaked island of Skellig Michael, off the Kerry coast. Here the lower peak hosted the main monastic site, reached by dizzying flights of stone stairs, while the hermitage was

[79] Ó Carragáin, *Churches*, pp. 118–28, 149–51, 242–4; Moss, ed. *Art*, pp. 138–9.
[80] Ó Carragáin, *Churches*, pp. 34–5.

perched on a confined space on the upper peak, 218 metres above sea level.[81]

Perhaps the most iconic form of Irish ecclesiastical building is the round tower. Just over sixty of them survive, but their great height (typically around 30 metres) and slender tapering form make them some of the most memorable monuments in the Irish landscape. These are often free-standing buildings, although a few (as at the Rock of Cashel, Co. Tipperary) adjoin a church. They have a narrow circumference (typically 15 metres at base) and shallow foundations. Their doorways are often raised up to 3 metres above ground to give greater stability to the base of the building. The elevated doorways have also been linked to records of towers being used as refuges when a settlement was under attack. Round towers had internal wooden staircases and were divided into different storeys lit by single narrow windows. At the top of the round tower, beneath a typically conical roof, there would be more windows. Their presence relates to the primary function of these buildings as a *cloictheach* or 'bell tower', to let the sound ring out. As expressions of status and authority, the origins of round towers may be comparable with those of the *campanile* in Italy or the minarets of a mosque used to call the faithful to prayer. The earliest reference to a round tower in Ireland is in 950 when the one at Slane (Co. Meath) was burnt in an attack by vikings from Dublin. The last recorded tower to be built was at Annaghdown (Co. Galway) in 1238. Within the same time frame a small number of round towers were built in eastern Scotland, and one was erected on the Isle of Man: both of these developments suggest links with Ireland.[82]

DOMESTIC ARCHITECTURE

Early medieval house building was often done with perishable materials, including timber, wickerwork and turf. Building with stone was more common in the west, where stone was plentiful but wood was scarce. As a result, the remains of early medieval houses are often invisible above ground or consist only of traces of the lower walls, providing limited information available about domestic architecture. The exception is where waterlogged conditions have allowed better preservation of organic materials, as at Dublin and at Deer Park

---

[81] Edwards, *Archaeology*, p. 118.   [82] Stalley, 'Ecclesiastical architecture', p. 733.

Farms (Co. Antrim). House styles changed during the early Middle Ages, with roundhouses being most the most common form until the ninth century. These structures were continuations of late Iron Age types with post-and-wattle or stone walls; wooden joists; straw, reeds or turf thatch; and a central hearth. They were typically quite small (4 to 10 m in diameter).[83] From the ninth century there was a shift towards the use of rectilinear houses. These were built of stone, earth or turf, with an average length of 6–8 metres. Rectangular buildings required greater investment in their construction. Their use may reflect wider architectural trends in North Europe and more individualistic social practices, as rectilinear buildings are more easily divided into private spaces.[84]

Rectangular houses were the dominant form in urban settlements. The best evidence for ninth-, tenth- and eleventh-century housing comes from Dublin in a series of excavations conducted from the 1960s onwards.[85] Overwhelmingly the most common domestic structure used in Dublin was the so-called Type 1 house, which was typically about 7.5 m × 5.5 m. This house type is also attested in Waterford, Cork and Wexford. These homes were constructed with low post-and-wattle walls with rounded corners. Two pairs of large internal posts were used to support the roof. The central space was dominated by a stone-lined hearth with raised areas of bedding on either side for sitting and sleeping. Entry to the building was through a door in each of the end walls (one usually leading to a street and the door at the back leading to a private enclosure). Variations of these houses and sunken-floored buildings have been found in early medieval urban contexts, but there was surprisingly little variation in urban architecture until the twelfth century.[86]

In both urban and rural contexts, there does not appear to be a significant difference in the architecture of houses used by different ranks of society, save that the houses of the more powerful were slightly bigger. Social conventions meant that status was not displayed through the size of the home, but more often through the level of fortification. While the standard settlement enclosure had one circuit of earth or stone, more elaborate settlements had two or three rings of banks. Higher-status enclosures might also have complex

[83] O'Sullivan *et al.*, *Early medieval dwellings*, p. 10.   [84] Ibid., pp. 11–12.
[85] Wallace, *Viking Dublin*, pp. 76–121.
[86] O'Sullivan *et al.*, *Early medieval dwellings*, pp. 22–4.

entryways. At Garranes (Co. Cork) the early medieval fort had a set of four gates that may have been in use contemporaneously.[87] Defence, exclusivity and greater investment in construction are also displayed in crannógs, which were made by laying boulders, cobblestones, peat and wood in layers on the bed of a lake or on an existing island. Domestic architecture was one of several means by which high social status could be expressed; other ways were the size of one's retinue, generous hospitality, sumptuous dress and generous patronage.

CONCLUSION

In the nineteenth and early twentieth centuries, scholars tended to regard the years AD 400–800 as the 'Golden Age' of the Irish Church and Irish art, which came to an abrupt end due to viking attacks. However, many of the greatest written works, including the sagas, and some of the most iconic features of the Irish landscape, including the round tower and the high cross, flourished from the ninth to twelfth centuries. While the production of large-scale gospel books and the composition of legal tracts may have ended around AD 800, creativity continued unabated. However, it was expressed in different media and literary forms.

[87] O'Sullivan *et al.*, *Early medieval Ireland*, pp. 85–6.

EPILOGUE TO PART I

——————————— • ———————————

The early Middle Ages was a dynamic phase in the history of Ireland. The fifth and sixth centuries witnessed the spread of a new religion, improved agricultural techniques and the emergence of new political dynasties. By the seventh and eighth centuries a highly stratified Christian society is in evidence. Uí Néill would emerge as the dominant political dynasty in Ireland, and the church of Armagh sought to establish ecclesiastical primacy. The centralisation of authority heightened inequalities between smaller and larger institutions. The elites maintained their position through the ownership of resources, clientship and patronage of literature and art. Economic growth proceeded apace from the ninth century. This fostered the development of towns and viking settlement and the growth of overseas trade. The failure of Uí Néill to establish their rule over viking ports and regional kings in the tenth and eleventh centuries allowed the rise of other contenders for the over-kingship of Ireland. The first of these was Brian Boru, over-king of Munster. In the eleventh and twelfth centuries, the struggle to dominate Ireland would continue, but the English crown and Church also began to intervene.

Part II

LATE MEDIEVAL IRELAND AD 1100–1500

7

LANDSCAPE AND ECONOMY AD 1100–1500

•

There was a general trend in Europe from the tenth to the thirteenth centuries towards increased agricultural productivity and population growth. This promoted a shift towards arable farming, more international trade, the colonisation of new lands, and greater of concentration of wealth and power into the hands of elites who reaped the profits from a buoyant economy. Across Europe, these economic changes are linked to urbanisation and the development of more nucleated settlements. This phenomenon in Ireland varied greatly from region to region. It was most evident in the richer agricultural lands in the south and midlands that would be conquered and colonised by the English in the years AD 1170–1250. By the late thirteenth century, the boom years of economic growth were ending. A series of demographic crises in the fourteenth century led to the abandonment of intensive cash crop production in marginal areas and the decline of the English colony. In Gaelic-held areas of western and northern Ireland, changes in land ownership and production had been less radical. These areas, which had less economic strength in the late twelfth and thirteenth centuries, seemed to possess greater resilience during the famines, plagues and wars of the fourteenth and fifteenth centuries.

CLIMATE

The late thirteenth and early fourteenth centuries witnessed a crisis. The fertility of agricultural land was in decline due to overuse, more land was cleared to compensate, and the loss of forest cover may have contributed to declining climatic and environmental conditions.[1] A series of wet summers damaged crops and aggravated the spread of disease in livestock. In the years 1315–17 a 'Great Famine' raged across swathes of northern Europe.[2] Its impact in Ireland is recorded in chronicles including the 'Annals of Connacht', which records in 1315 'Many afflictions in all parts of Ireland: very many deaths, famine and many strange diseases, murders and intolerable storms as well'.[3] Storms and floods in 1328 and 1330 may have contributed to a famine in the Dublin region in 1331 and 1332. Wet weather and flooding accompanied the first outbreak of the Black Death in the mid-fourteenth century.[4] The early to mid-fourteenth century was a period of climatic flux when the Northern Hemisphere experienced a decade of severe average temperature reduction.[5] After the mid-fourteenth century, mean annual temperatures appeared to rise in northern Europe until the 1380s, when a decrease followed. The period of cooler mean temperatures lasted during the fifteenth century and made the practice of growing corn less profitable in Ireland. It was one of the factors that contributed to the decline of the English colony in Ireland and a shift towards pastoral farming.

SETTLEMENT PATTERNS

The towns of Ireland boomed in the twelfth century. Prominent among these were the old viking ports. Limerick and Waterford were important sources of profit for the over-kings of Munster and Leinster, respectively. Dublin was the biggest settlement in Ireland, and control of the port was key to the ambitions of any leader who sought to dominate all Ireland. This control was hotly contested by Irish over-kings in the twelfth century, although rulers often delegated authority to a local king of Gaelic-Scandinavian culture who would be more acceptable to the inhabitants of the port. Economic development was not confined to the coast. Important ecclesiastical and regional centres continued to grow and develop an urban character. Records are sufficient to indicate that Armagh, Downpatrick, Kells, Kildare, Cashel, and Clonmacnoise functioned as towns in the early twelfth century.

---

[1] Ruhaak, in press.   [2] Jordan, *Great Famine*.   [3] *AConn, s.a.* 1315.
[4] Lyons, 'Weather', pp. 64–6.   [5] Stothers, 'Volcanic'.

Towns increasingly became centres of power and the residences of provincial rulers. Over-kings invested patronage in political and ecclesiastical centres and sought to impose greater control over route-ways across the landscape. A good case study of this phenomenon is Athlone, a strategically significant fording point on the River Shannon between Meath and Connacht. A wooden bridge was built here in 1120, followed by a castle or *caistél* in 1129 under the patronage of Toirdelbach Ua Conchobuir, king of Connacht; a new bridge was built in 1140.[6] To secure the spiritual as well as temporal influence of Connacht over-kings at this important river crossing, the Cluniac priory of Saints Peter and Paul was founded in the decades that followed. The term *caistél* or *caislén* was first used to describe a small number of fortresses in the early twelfth century, mainly in Connacht. These may have been earth and timber castles (mottes) in the European style. Motte-like structures dating from the early twelfth century have been studied at Ballinasloe (Co. Galway) and Duneight (Co. Down).[7]

Centralisation of power was fostered through the development of nucleated settlements and through the spatial organisation of land into units of taxation, local government and military levies. Before the English invasion, Ireland had been divided into a uniform system of *trícait cét*, of which around 185 have been identified.[8] These units were then utilised by the English, who renamed them cantreds (following the Welsh name cantref). Smaller units that were established in pre-conquest Ireland were called *baile* (*biataig*), which usually indicated an estate belonging to a kin group whose average size was above 2000 acres, but their extent varied greatly. These units often coincided with later parochial and manorial divisions.[9] The Church also promoted a system of more centralised territorial organisation. A new diocesan framework was established in 1152 at the Synod of Kells-Mellifont that divided Ireland into four archdiocese and thirty-eight dioceses. A system of parochial organisation gradually developed thereafter. At the eve of the English invasion, Ireland possessed a system of territorial organisation similar to its European neighbours. Power was less unified than in the neighbouring kingdom of England, but England was unusual in its degree of centralisation.

---

[6] *AFM, s.aa.* 1120, 1140; *AU, s.a.* 1129.5; *AClon, s.aa.* 1131, 1132.
[7] O'Keeffe, *Medieval Ireland*, p. 27.   [8] MacCotter, *Medieval Ireland*, pp. 125–254.
[9] Toner, '*Baile*', pp. 32–43; MacCotter, *Medieval Ireland*, pp. 23–4.

The economic expansion of Europe may provide something of a *long durée* explanation for Ireland's partial conquest and settlement by a more populous and powerful neighbour after 1169. However, English intervention was motivated by short-term political goals as much as any long-term economic cause. The fiscal potential of Ireland was a key factor in drawing colonists to Ireland. In 1171 Henry II confiscated the main centres of wealth in Ireland (Dublin, Wexford and Waterford). The richest agricultural lands in eastern and southern Ireland were then seized by colonists in the last decades of the twelfth century. English conquest and settlement proceeded more gradually into more fertile areas of the north and west. The settlers prompted population growth and the development of old and new centres of lordship that would leave a long-term imprint on the Irish landscape.

Dublin became the centre of English power in Ireland, and it grew rapidly as a political centre and a hub of international trade. In the mid-thirteenth century, realistic estimates of its population range between 10,000 and 35,000.[10] Other Viking Age port towns along the south and east coast continued to flourish in the twelfth and thirteenth centuries. New ports were also founded. These included Drogheda in the east, established by Hugh de Lacy in the 1180s, and New Ross in the south, founded by William Marshal about 1200. Carrickfergus, Coleraine, Dungarvan, Dundalk, Galway, Sligo and Youghal also owe their development as towns to English settlers. Along the major rivers that led inland from these ports a network of inland towns was established for the acquisition and distribution of goods transhipped to and from the coast. These local centres of administration provided goods and services through craftsmen, clerics, merchants and other workers to their regions. Like their contemporary European counterparts, the new towns were often endowed with charters, defended by castles and demarcated by ditches and banks or walls. Their sites were often determined by pre-existing pre-existing Gaelic patterns of settlement. For example, Kilkenny became one of the most important medieval inland towns of Ireland, but its origins lay in the sixth-century ecclesiastical settlement of St Cainnech. Kilkenny became an important seat for the Mac Giolla Phádraig kings of Ossory. The Anglo-Welsh adventurer Strongbow took over the settlement, and the town was developed by William Marshal who granted its charter in 1207.

---

[10] Glasscock, 'Land', p. 234; Kelly, *Great dying*, pp. 26–7.

In addition to developing towns of regional significance, many small boroughs were created by English lords in a bid to generate wealth and attract settlers. Burgess status offered freedom from some burdens of lordship, providing an incentive for English and Welsh migrants to relocate to Ireland. There were 250 or more medieval boroughs in Ireland, but many lacked sufficient population to be classified as towns by modern geographers.[11] Nor were they purely colonial enclaves: Gaelic Irish remained in the majority on most English estates, especially beyond the intensely colonised areas of the south and east coast. To take an example, an extent survives for the manor of Cloncurry (Co. Kildare) in 1304, which lists 191 tenants of non-Gaelic identity (112 burgesses and 79 others) and 111 Gaelic Irish tenants, most of whom were of lower ranks (betaghs or cottars).[12] These numbers represent heads of households, and so the total population can be calculated to be more than a thousand people. The extent provides a snapshot of a community in decline, describing an abandoned motte and dilapidated estate buildings. The boom years of manorial settlement between 1170 and 1250 were over.

By the late thirteenth century, economic stagnation and warfare were taking their toll on many boroughs. In 1238, David mac Cellaig Ua Gilla Pátraic, bishop of Cloyne, founded a borough at Kilmaclenine (Co. Cork). In 1341 it boasted thirty burgesses, mostly of English origin, but it was abandoned after the 1380s. Some boroughs never attracted enough settlers to have long-term viability, while those on marginal lands were more vulnerable to the effects of climatic decline or soil exhaustion. In the thirteenth century, more isolated moated farm sites were built in English-held areas (except in the northeast), which may hint at a departure from nucleated rural settlements.[13] The burdens of royal English taxation had encouraged exploitation of the resources of Ireland, but with little reinvestment of wealth into the colony. With this economic drain, the smaller boroughs of the colony were ill equipped to weather the ravages of famine, plague and warfare of the fourteenth century.

The Great Famine and the Black Death of the fourteenth century caused a significant drop in population, particularly in the south

[11] Barry, 'Rural settlement', pp. 134–5.   [12] Glassock, 'Land', p. 222.
[13] Barry, *Archaeology*, pp. 87–93; O'Keeffe, *Medieval Ireland*, pp. 73–80.

and east of the country. These crises prompted significant levels of migration from the English colony to western England.[14]

Up to 40 per cent of the population of the English colony was lost.[15] This corresponded with the Gaelic takeover of areas of land in Munster, Connacht and Ulster, which had previously been under English lordship. References to untilled lands within the English lordship became more common in the fourteenth century. An example is the manor of Callan (Co. Kilkenny), which in 1348–9 had 95 out of 548 acres lying tenantless. In the following year the area of vacant lands had risen to 302 acres. Rapid readjustment in landholding followed, for in 1352 the area of vacant holdings in Callan had declined to twenty-six acres, but the manorial revenues continued to fall. This either suggests that rents dropped significantly to attract tenants or that holdings were enlarged to prevent lands going to waste.[16] The loss of English tenants improved the position of the Gaelic Irish in English-held areas as the labour shortages meant they could hold land on better terms. As the English colony lost ground, power became decentralised. Some of the great castles built to symbolise English power, including Trim, fell into disuse, and more modest tower houses were built.

Roughly one-third of the landmass of Ireland had never been conquered by the English. Most of these areas in western Ulster, Connacht and southwest Munster comprised poorer lands where the limited potential for economic gain through conquest was outweighed by the difficulty of wresting the lands from Gaelic control. Differences emerged between the cultural landscapes of the English lordships and the Gaelic areas, as the former were characterised by more nucleated settlement than the latter. These distinctions were driven in part by economic variance, as poorer lands necessitated a more dispersed settlement pattern that provided access to a range of resources. Political and social differences also played their part. English lords promoted nucleation in areas under their control but similar developments in Gaelic-held areas were initially stunted or reversed by English colonisation. It did not serve the interests of Gaelic lords to have a fixed centre of lordship that would be vulnerable to attack. Only ecclesiastical centres bucked this trend as centres for collecting tithes, for trade and craftsmen, and as providers of goods and services for clerics,

[14] Down, 'Colonial society', p. 449.   [15] Kelly, *History of the Black Death*, p. 99.
[16] Ibid., p. 103.

high-status visitors and pilgrims. One of the more successful Gaelic episcopal seats on the south coast was Rosscarbery (Co. Cork), which by 1517 had a walled town with two gates and nearly two hundred houses.[17] As more land in Ireland fell into Gaelic control in the fourteenth century there was a modest shift towards more nucleated settlement. Cavan, Longford and Granard (Co. Longford) were among the sites developed as markets in the fifteenth century. There was also significant Gaelic migration to English-held towns in the fifteenth century as witnessed by the surnames of burgesses.

Much of the population in Gaelic-held areas lived in scattered farmsteads or small house clusters. These dwellings often had a temporary character. Permanent dwellings may have been eschewed for the political and economic reasons mentioned earlier, but also as a consequence of Gaelic landholding practices. Clan lands were divided into shares among male heirs and frequently redistributed (on the death of an heir or more often according to local customs), giving little reason to invest labour in substantial buildings. Transhumance (or 'boolyeing') was also a feature of rural life in many areas that promoted the construction of seasonal dwellings.

In the early thirteenth century, the temporary dwellings of the Gaelic elite were scorned by the English Cistercian abbot Stephen of Lexington as 'little huts of wattle such as birds are accustomed to build'.[18] These wattle structures might nevertheless be placed in grand settings. During the later Middle Ages older sites of lordship, large ringforts and crannógs were occupied or reoccupied. This had a symbolic as well as defensive function, for those sites represented the historic legitimacy of local Gaelic rule. The buildings of the elite also developed a more permanent character towards the end of the Middle Ages. From around 1300 a poetic eulogy survives describing the large hall of Áed Ua Conchobuir at Cloonfree (Co. Roscommon). Its English-style roof supports (crucks?) are singled out for praise.[19] In the late fourteenth century stone-built tower houses became popular among both the Gaelic and English elite. Around 7000 of these were constructed in Ireland, although most may date to the sixteenth century.[20] They cluster in the south of Ireland and in coastal regions,

---

[17] Nicholls, *Gaelic and Gaelicised Ireland*, p. 122.
[18] O'Dwyer, trans, *Stephen of Lexington*, p. 112; Andrews, 'Mapping', pp. 166–7.
[19] McKenna, ed. and trans., 'Poem to Cloonfree', p. 643 §33; O'Conor, 'Housing', p. 206.
[20] Barry, 'Rural settlement', p. 140.

but are sparse in central Ulster and the North Midlands. While tower houses often stand as isolated structures in the Irish landscape today, most were accompanied by bawns or enclosures and a group of buildings that might include a hall for feasting, homes of retainers, stables and workshops.[21] The tower houses of Ireland represent a fusion of Gaelic and English culture that resulted from two centuries of close contact and a shift in power and wealth out of English governmental control.[22]

FARMING AND NATURAL RESOURCES

Farming and the exploitation of natural resources remained the mainstay of the Irish economy throughout the Middle Ages. What was not immediately consumed by producers was used to pay taxes and tributes, traded for goods or services, invested in supporting the family, or stored. In the poem the 'Circuit of Ireland by Muirchertach mac Néill' that has been dated to between 1157–66, the stores of Dublin are said to comprise 'bacon, of fine wheat . . . joints of meat and fine cheese'.[23] In the period from the eleventh century to the mid-thirteenth century there is evidence of agricultural intensification in the fertile lands of Ireland, particularly in the east and the south where denser populations and access to overseas trading routes provided a ready market for surplus crops. The more widespread cultivation of bread wheat and pulses probably reflects not only the demands of a growing population but also the desire of landowners to maximise profit or meet the growing tax burdens imposed by centralising governments.[24]

At the end of the twelfth century English colonisation led to a wholesale redistribution of land between the crown, the church, and tenants-in-chief while more than one-third of the island remained in the possession of the Gaelic Irish. Ireland's richest lands were seized by colonists with the desire to generate a large surplus of cash crops for export. To achieve this surplus, additional land was brought under the plough and improved agricultural methods were introduced. New technologies included using the coulter to plough with

---

[21] O'Keeffe, *Medieval Ireland*, p. 46.
[22] Barry, 'Rural settlement', p. 140; O'Conor, *Archaeology of medieval rural settlement*, p. 104.
[23] Ó Corráin, 'Muirchertach', p. 240; O'Donovan, ed. and trans., *Circuit*, pp. 32–5.
[24] Bartlett, *Making of Europe*, pp. 269–70.

a team of oxen and the scythe for haymaking on a large scale. There was also greater use of corn-drying kilns and watermills. Wheat, barley and rye had a bigger role in the English diet (in bread, stews, pottages) and ale compared to the greater dependence on oats and dairy products in the Gaelic economy. Large quantities of grains were also grown for export in the thirteenth century, which lined the pockets of landowners and government. For example, in 1224–5, the mayor of London imported one thousand crannocks (quarters) of wheat from Ireland.[25] The colonisation of Ireland proved to be a profitable enterprise in the first century after its inception. While these changes have been dubbed an 'agricultural revolution' it could be argued that the English capitalised upon and developed existing trends in Irish farming.[26] Economically the land in Gaelic lands was usually less suited to cash crop cultivation, but where soil fertility and access to markets allowed, similar practices were adopted.[27] In the classic model of an Anglo-Norman manor demesne, lands were farmed for the lord and remaining portions of land were let to tenants. An open field system was operated whereby farmland was divided into two or three sectors in which there was a rotation of arable crops (usually wheat or rye and oats) and a fallow period. In this system, individual farmers held their land in strips scattered across these sectors.[28] The model of interpretation used in Gaelic areas is that of infield and outfield cultivation, whereby lands closer to dwelling places were intensively farmed and regularly manured with less intensive use of the outfield. This model was better suited to wetter areas.[29] However, like all models there was plenty of divergence from stereotypes. For example, open field cultivation was practised in parts of Ireland as early as the eighth century, while the use of small enclosed fields is witnessed in both Gaelic and Anglo-Irish areas.[30] Different practices could operate side by side on a single estate.

For those at the top of the social scale, beef, pork and imported luxuries would have been part of an elite pattern of consumption regardless of ethnicity. Some changes were wrought through English settlement. Rabbit warrens, deer parks and fishponds were a feature of the English manorial economy transplanted to Ireland. Fowl (which

---

[25] Kelly, *Early Irish farming*, p. 21.   [26] Down, 'Colonial society', pp. 480–1.

[27] Nicholls, *Gaelic and Gaelicised Ireland*, p. 114.

[28] O'Keeffe, *Medieval Ireland*, pp. 58–66.

[29] Kelly, *Early Irish farming*, pp. 368–70; Christiansen, 'Infield-outfield'.

[30] Kelly, *Early Irish farming*, pp. 370–2; Down, 'Colonial society', p. 477.

already featured in the Irish diet) were also consumed in greater quantities and references to dovecotes occur on English estates.[31] Gaelic farming practices placed much emphasis on cattle rearing; however, Anglo-Irish areas were also often heavily dependent on cattle, which may hint at some adaptation to native practices. Bovine remains dominate the bone assemblages recovered from Dublin and its hinterland throughout the Middle Ages.[32]

Dairying continued to be significant in late medieval Ireland. Gerald of Wales commented that the weather in Ireland was so mild that grass grew all year. Characteristically Gerald got his facts muddled, but cattle were kept alive through the winter months in Ireland through stocks of preserved grass, and evergreens including holly and ivy. Areas of winter grassland were reserved through the practice of booleying, whereby livestock moved to upland pastures in the summer months and returned to the lowlands in winter. This practice was suited to areas where land was insufficient for agriculture, and the mobility of cattle herding also suited social conditions of instability and warfare.[33] While agricultural expansion in the more fertile lands of Ireland sustained population growth in the thirteenth century, it also made sections of the population (predominantly in English territories) more vulnerable to changing climatic conditions and warfare that could destroy crops.

The Great Famine and the Black Death of the fourteenth century caused a significant drop in the population of Ireland. The twin forces of economic and political change led to the abandonment of cereal cultivation in marginal areas and a corresponding growth of pastoralism.[34] Increased emphasis on pastoral farming is reflected in references to nomadic herds or creaght (Irish *caoraigheacht*) from the late fourteenth century, whose 'wild and transitory' nature caused consternation to the English authorities.[35] A statute of 1430 sought to limit those 'Irish rymers, outlaws and felons' who grazed their animals on the borders of land under English control.[36]

Sheep farming also increased at that time, although with greater significance in English areas for providing cheese, sheepskin and wool for export and consumption. During the later Middle Ages more

[31] Murphy and O'Conor, 'Castles'.
[32] Murphy and Potterton, *Dublin region*, p. 333.
[33] Nicholls, 'Gaelic society', pp. 413–15.   [34] Hall, *Making*, p. 127.
[35] Simms, 'Nomadry'; Prendergast, 'Ulster creaghts', p. 422.
[36] Nicholls, 'Gaelic society', p. 414.

white-wooled sheep were introduced to Ireland for cloth production. The economic, demographic and environmental changes of the
fourteenth century encouraged a shift towards livestock rearing and
also saw Ireland switch from a prodigious exporter of corn in the
thirteenth century to importing corn for the maintenance of urban
populations in the fifteenth century.[37]

The diet of grains, dairy products and meat was supplemented by
cultivation of fruit and vegetables in gardens and through gathering food from the wild. Woodlands provided nuts, berries, herbs and
fungi for human consumption. They also provided mast crops for
pigs as well as evergreen for cattle. Woodlands were also exploited for
timber and fuel. 'The Pipe roll of Cloyne' (mostly compiled in the
fourteenth century but with some fifteenth-century records) indicates that a distinction was made between *silva* (timber woodland),
boscus (underwood) and *bruaria* (scrub). Timber was mainly used for
large-scale construction; underwood and coppice were used for post-
and-wattle construction, while scrublands provided a source of fuel.
While large areas of Ireland were deforested before the twelfth century, there is evidence for an abundant supply of oak in the Dublin
region until the thirteenth century.[38] A trend towards more substantial housing in the twelfth century meant greater use of timber for
construction.

The English invasion led to rapid population growth in urban centres, and the sale of wood for export corresponded with a decline in
woodlands. After the Black Death the pressure on woodland management decreased, some marginal lands were abandoned, and there
is evidence of woodland regeneration in the late fourteenth and early
fifteenth centuries.[39] Woodland coverage was nevertheless very variable across Ireland; it was probably less than 10 per cent around Dublin
and in the fertile midland zone, but was extensive in some other areas,
including south Wicklow and the Erne basin.[40] In addition to foodstuffs, fuel and building material, woodlands provided other products such as moss (used as an absorbent material and often found in
latrines), dyestuffs and animal skins. The 'Libelle of Englyshe Polycye'
composed around AD 1436 lists goods from Ireland including 'hertys

[37] Childs and O'Neill, 'Overseas trade', p. 503.
[38] Murphy and Potterton, *Dublin region*, p. 357.
[39] Baillie, *New Light*, pp. 15–25.   [40] Kelly, 'Agriculture', pp. 7–9.

hydes and other hydes or venerye, skynnes of oter, squerel and Irysh hare'.[41]

The rivers and coasts of Ireland were a welcome source of fish and shellfish. Rivers also provided watercress, rushes and fowl. The main river estuaries had salmon fisheries, while eels from the Gaelic interior were purchased by Anglo-Irish merchants. An Irish marine fishing fleet is mentioned in 1217 that helped supply the growing demand for herring and cod. Coastal areas also provided fertiliser in the form of seaweed and sand. Other natural resources of Ireland included peat, which could be dug from the extensive tracts of bog-land as a source of fuel. There is also increased evidence for quarrying stone and slate in the later Middle Ages to build new styles of houses, churches and bridges. The exploitation of natural resources was influenced by changes in technology and trade.

CRAFT AND INDUSTRY

The processing of natural resources was a source of much rural employment. In areas of large-scale grain production, corn-drying kilns are attested long before the English invasion, while late medieval examples have been found in both rural and urban contexts.[42] In addition to being kept dry, grain has to be milled (although in some Gaelic areas it was burnt from the straw before grinding). Milling was often done laboriously by the use of a rotary quern, and many examples have been found on medieval sites. Watermills nevertheless became common on secular manors and monastic estates.[43] From the thirteenth century windmills and horse mills were also in use in Ireland.[44] The evidence points to the intensification of agricultural production during the twelfth century, a process that English colonists developed further.

In rural areas brewing, baking, and making butter and cheese were household tasks. The work was often undertaken by women as it was compatible with child-rearing. However large-scale production, as witnessed in or near urban centres, led to a degree of professionalism. In 1282 the estates of the earl marshal in Ballysax (Co. Kildare) and Old Ross (Co. Wexford) provided thirty stone of cheese to be sent to

[41] Wright, ed., *Political poems*, II: 185–9.
[42] Murphy and Potterton, *Dublin region*, p. 409.   [43] Ibid., p. 417.
[44] O 'Keeffe, *Medieval Ireland*, p. 67.

Dublin.[45] Urban brewing and baking served the essential day-to-day needs of town dwellers. This activity was undertaken not only at a micro-scale but also in specialised breweries and bake houses. The protection of supplies, measurements and quality assurance of bread and ale was a frequent topic of municipal regulation that illustrates its importance.[46]

Cloth and leather production was also essential in serving the basic needs of the population. Flax was an important crop for linen production in the west of Ireland as it flourishes in cool, damp environments. Harvested flax was threshed to remove seeds and then soaked in ponds or bogs to separate the fibres from the stalk before it could be spun into yarn. The wearing of fine linen was a symbol of status, while wool was the staple fibre of cloth production. Spinning was considered to be women's work. In medieval Europe, the distaff was a gender icon. Its images appear variously in medieval manuscript illuminations in the hands of Eve as the world's first woman, as flying vehicles for witches, or as husband beaters. According to Ramón de Perilhos who visited Ireland in 1397, coarse woollen cloaks were the main attire of the Gaelic Irish, even if little else was worn.[47] In the thirteenth century there is evidence that cloth production was increasing, aided by the introduction of new breeds of sheep and water-powered fulling mills in the east of Ireland. Weavers, dyers, tailors and mercers were among the most common professions listed in the 'Dublin Guild Merchant Roll' that covers the years from around 1190–1265. Tanners and skinners are also frequently mentioned in the 'Dublin Guild Merchant Roll'. Tanning, like cloth production, could be carried out as a part-time activity by country dwellers or as a full-time profession in the towns. It principally required access to water and woodlands resources. Tanning was often a suburban industry. It was too space consuming and smelly to be practised in town centres, but it was ideally situated close to major markets. The abundance of hides produced in Ireland encouraged diversification in the types and qualities of leather produced, and tanners from overseas came to practise their craft in Ireland.[48]

Other industries common to both rural and urban areas included ironwork and pottery. Charcoal was needed to generate the heat to

[45] Murphy and Potterton, *Dublin region*, pp. 433–4.
[46] Gilbert and Mulholland, eds., *Calendar of ancient documents*, I: 219, 313.
[47] Mahaffy, ed., 'Early tours', p. 7.
[48] Murphy and Potterton, *Dublin region*, pp. 439, 441.

smelt iron or fire pottery, which fostered a minor industry in woodland areas through to the twentieth century. Iron slag and related
metalworking debris appear regularly on medieval rural sites, while
furnaces and workshops for metalworking have been excavated in
major towns.[49] As smithing became more common in Ireland there
may have been a corresponding decline in the social status of blacksmiths compared to the law tracts of the eighth century. More than
forty smiths are listed in the 'Dublin Guild Merchant Roll' c. 1190–
1265. Pottery production was fairly limited in Ireland before the
English invasion. Functional coarse pottery dubbed 'Souterrain ware'
was produced in northeast Ireland from the eighth to the thirteenth
centuries.[50] Hand-built cooking wares were also used throughout
Leinster in the twelfth century, which may reveal foreign cultural
influences in practices of food preparation.[51] The last decades of the
twelfth century witnessed a rapid increase in pottery production. A
street of potters (*vicus pottorum*) is witnessed in Dublin by 1190, while
excavations in Wexford and Waterford have yielded sherds of locally
made glazed ware from the early thirteenth century.[52]

The larger boroughs of Ireland were home to a plethora of craftsmen, including masons, carpenters, shoemakers, tailors, comb makers,
butchers, bakers and cooks. An insight into Dublin's economy can be
found in the late twelfth-century 'Life of St Patrick' by Jocelin of
Furness. In listing the tribute that Dubliners promised to give to the
saint, he reports 'for every merchant ship a cloak suitable for the primate of Armagh, or a cask of honey or wine, or a load of iron or a
measure of salt; for every tavern a jar of mead or beer; for all workshops, courtyards, and virgates, presents and an appropriate gift of
shoes, gloves, knives, combs, and other things of this kind'.[53] Archaeology also reveals how the premises of craftsmen and merchants vied
for space among the main urban thoroughfares with their houses,
sheds and outhouses crammed within narrow burgage plots.

COMMERCE AND COMMUNICATIONS

An impression of the goods that could be bought in a medieval
Irish town is provided by the murage grant of Fethard in Tipperary,
which survives from 1292 (see Figure 7.1). It lists the commodities

---

[49] Ibid., p. 446.   [50] Edwards, *Archaeology*, pp. 74–5.   [51] Ó Floinn, 'Handmade'.
[52] Brooks, ed., *Register of the Hospital of S John*, p. 22.
[53] Sperber *et al.*, ed. and trans., *Life of St Patrick* (in press).

Figure 7.1 Town wall and Holy Trinity Church, Fethard, Co. Tipperary

upon which a toll could be taken to pay for the building of the town walls. These included horses, oxen, cows, sheep, goats and hogs; hides, salt, meat, butter, cheese, onions and garlic; sea fish, salmon, lampreys and herring; skins, wool, hides, linen and other cloth; salt, wine, honey, soap, alum and wood; and coal, firewood, lead, iron, nails and horseshoes.[54] The buying and selling of goods and services in medieval Ireland were undertaken directly by providers or indirectly through middlemen. The significance of the service sector in the Irish urban economy is indicated by references in the Dublin guild merchant rolls to vendors, merchants, taverners, servants, stewards, clerks, barbers, painters, water bearers, carriers and carters.

The distribution of the main urban settlements in Ireland was dictated by the transport routes that made trade possible. The larger boroughs were situated along rivers where goods could be shipped to and from wharves and quays. Land communication was also important, and developments in infrastructure are witnessed in the eleventh and twelfth centuries. Within the English colony, the pre-existing network of roads was developed into royal highways, and new routeways were constructed in the thirteenth century, laying the foundations of the modern road map of Ireland. The maintenance of routes and

[54] Glasscock, 'Land', p. 238.

bridges was a concern of government, touched upon by parliamentary enactment in the English colony.[55] Routeways in Gaelic areas require further study, but as in the English colony, the pre-existing road network was developed. The earliest surviving map of all of Ireland that shows medieval roads was drawn in the reign of Henry VIII. Although it is biased towards eastern Ireland and Dublin, the map is instructive in illustrating some of the major routeways that radiated out from Dublin.[56] The economic growth of western Irish ports in the fifteenth century probably stimulated the construction of roads and tracks. Travel had its perils. The Kilkenny parliament of 1310 heard a report of 'those of great lineage' who regularly robbed or held to ransom travelling merchants.[57] In 1452 a convoy transporting fish from Athlone (on the borders of counties Roscommon and Westmeath) to Trim (Co. Meath) was attacked by one Fergal Óg Mac Eochagáin, and a number of the merchants and their guards were killed.[58]

The extent to which Anglo-Irish towns depended on trade with the Gaelic Irish has sometimes been under-represented in the historiography. The trade across cultural boundaries became more significant in the fourteenth and fifteenth centuries as the colonial population and landholdings shrank. Attempts by the English government to restrict interaction between the Anglo-Irish and Gaels were met with complaints and noncompliance. In 1463, parliament pragmatically granted an allowance to Cork, Limerick and Youghal to sell every kind of goods, apart from artillery, to the Gaelic Irish because 'the profit of every market, city and town in this land, depends principally on the resort of Irish people bringing their merchandise to the said cities and towns'.[59] Seaports in the east of the colony appeared to be struggling economically from the late fourteenth century, but those in the west experienced new growth.[60] In the fifteenth century the wills and inventories of Galway and Limerick merchants reveal extensive dealings with Gaelic peoples. Gaelic merchant families were also able to establish themselves in prominent positions within chartered towns, as for example the Sextons (Uí Seasnáin) in Limerick and the Ronaynes (Uí Ronáin) in Cork and Kinsale.[61]

[55] Connolly, 'Enactments', p. 159.   [56] Andrews, *Shapes*, p. 12.
[57] Lydon, 'Impact', p. 278.   [58] Nicholls, 'Gaelic society', p. 416.
[59] O'Brien, 'Politics, economy and society', p. 134.
[60] Smith, 'Late medieval Ireland', pp. 553–4.
[61] Maginn, 'Gaelic Ireland's English frontiers', p. 184.

COINAGE

The use of coin in Ireland predated the English invasion. The
Hiberno-Scandinavian mint at Dublin was active from the reign of
Sitric Silkenbeard until the English arrived. Its last twelfth-century
issues were low-quality bracteates – thin discs of silver that could
only be struck on one side. There is slight evidence that one or two
mints in operated outside Dublin in the twelfth century, which would
indicate a level of monetization in Gaelic society outside the major
port towns.[62] From the 1180s new Anglo-Irish coins were minted
under Prince John, lord of Ireland. The first issues of halfpennies
and farthings promoted the expansion of trade in a developing colonial economy. Coin production was centred on Dublin, with mints
operating intermittently at Kilkenny, Waterford, Cork and Limerick.
The lord of Ulster, John de Courcy, briefly issued coinage at Downpatrick and Carrickfergus. After Prince John became John, king of
England, in 1199, pennies were minted to the full English standard,
which enabled them to circulate outside Ireland. One major motive
for English kings to mint Irish pennies was to create a convenient
medium to export wealth from Ireland. The island's resources were
drawn upon extensively in the thirteenth century. Unofficial tokens
also circulated (e.g. more than 2000 pewter tokens were recovered
from a thirteenth-century pit in Winetavern Street).[63] Coin production increased further during the reign of Edward I, but declined
during the economic depression of the fourteenth century (see
Figure 7.2). Unlawful and foreign coinage, including English and
Scottish forgeries, circulated widely in the late fifteenth century,
which prompted the Anglo-Irish parliament to request the production of Irish coins. These were issued with a lower silver component
than their English counterparts to serve the internal economy rather
than being used for foreign trade. Coins were used more in towns,
but a mixed economy operated through all sections of Irish society.
Alternatives to coin transactions included barter (swapping goods or
services) and use of commodity money (lengths of cloth, cows, metal
or other items as units of payment).[64]

[62] Woods, 'Economy and authority', I: 107–13; Dolley, 'Coinage to 1534', p. 818;
AClon, p. 214; Ware, *Antiquities*, III: 28.
[63] Halpin, 'Coinage', pp. 96–8.
[64] Nicholls, 'Gaelic society', p. 417. Cf. Skre, 'Commodity', pp. 74–80.

Figure 7.2 Silver penny of Edward I, minted in Dublin

OVERSEAS TRADE

By 1100 overseas trade was flourishing in Ireland. Much of this was channelled through the Hiberno-Scandinavian towns of the south and east coasts. Evidence of overseas trading links is also witnessed at large monastic centres and Gaelic royal sites. The growing economy of the eleventh century is reflected in the frustrated interest of Jewish entrepreneurs to invest in Ireland. In 1079 the 'Annals of Inisfallen' reports that 'Five Jews came from over sea with gifts to Toirdelbach', king of Munster, but 'they were sent back again over sea'.[65] In the twelfth century Ireland's main trading partners were England, Normandy, and southern France, as witnessed by numismatic and archaeological evidence. Bristol had risen to become Dublin's main trading partner, and as a result Diarmait Mac Murchada came to know Bristol merchants, particularly Robert fitz Harding who acted as an intermediary in his negotiations with Henry II.[66]

One of Henry II's first concerns on invading Ireland was to secure control of the principal ports. He issued a charter in 1171–2 placing the port of Dublin in the care of the loyal men of Bristol who were given the right to dwell there. Naturally enough, Ireland's principal trading partner continued to be England through the later Middle Ages. Dublin and the south and west coast ports traded mainly with Bristol, while Chester continued to be a significant trading partner

[65] *AI, s.a.* 1079.　　[66] Mullaly, ed. and trans., *Deeds.*

not only with Dublin but also Drogheda and the more northerly ports. Some Irish trade went to Wales, the southwestern counties, and the southeast of England. The principal Irish exports were of basic commodities, especially grain (oats and wheat), fish, hides, wool, linen and timber. Oak exported from southeast Ireland in the early thirteenth century has been traced archaeologically at sites in Salisbury, Exeter and Shetland.[67] This may attest to large-scale woodland exploitation by English colonists in Leinster.

In the early years of the thirteenth century, grain was one of the main Irish exports. From the 1240s until 1324 a major market for grain was English royal armies. The use of Irish resources radically increased under Edward I due to his ambitious foreign policy. In 1297 alone, well in excess of 11,600 quarters of wheat and 1,850 quarters of oats were shipped to the army in Gascony.[68] The profit to the Irish economy was limited due to fixed prices, delayed payment and corruption. The over-exploitation of grain resources by the English crown exacerbated the decline in agricultural productivity in Ireland during the fourteenth century. Grain production was also disrupted during the fourteenth century by increasing warfare against the Gaelic Irish and by the Black Death. As a result, Ireland ceased to export large quantities of grain. By 1437 Bristol was shipping grain to Ireland, and in 1475 there was a ban on the export of Irish corn.

The decline in grain exports was partly compensated by a burgeoning export trade in fish and hides. In the late fifteenth century, fish worth from £1,001 to £2,843 a year made up on average 80 per cent of Bristol's Irish imports by value.[69] Herring was the most important, followed by hake and salmon. The main centre of the fish trade in Ireland was Waterford, a large port opposite Bristol, with a wealth of herring off its coast; yet boats from many other ports from Wexford to Dingle (Co. Kerry) were prominent in the trade. Estuarine fisheries provided the highly prized salmon of Ireland. During the fifteenth and sixteenth centuries, French and Spanish fishing fleets operated off the Irish coast, which brought some profit to Gaelic and Anglo-Irish ports where they landed for supplies.

Animal products were another major export. Regular shipments of hides were sent to Bristol, Normandy, Calais, Flanders, Brittany,

---

[67] Bridge, 'Locating the origins', p. 2830; Hillam, 'Medieval oak'; Moss, ed., *Art*, p. 86.
[68] Down, 'Colonial society', p. 485.
[69] Childs and O'Neill, 'Overseas trade', p. 505.

Bordeaux and Lisbon from the early thirteenth century. Italy was one of the biggest markets, and the leather industries of Pisa alone took 34,000 hides in one half-year (1466–7). Wool and woolfells were exported in large quantities to England, France, Flanders and farther afield. Italian merchants were in charge of the customs on wool from 1275 until 1311, and they provided banking services to Anglo-Irish magnates.[70] Wool for export was secured in repayment of debts, and the merchants employed policy of forward buying from the Cistercians. Such foreign interest declined in the fourteenth century. Edward III's wool taxes in the fourteenth century also hit the Irish harder than the English, because Irish wool tended to be of lower quality.

From the late thirteenth century, it became more profitable to produce cheap woollen cloth rather than to export wool. Cloth became an important part of Ireland's export trade by the end of the fifteenth century. A shift in the cloth trade from towns and guilds to cottage weavers doing piecework for merchants brought greater wealth to rural areas, both Gaelic and Anglo-Irish, in the fifteenth century. Large amounts of linen often made in Gaelic areas were exported in the fifteenth century. In 1477–8 twenty thousand yards of linen worth £100 were sent to Bristol, representing a peak in linen exports, which declined thereafter.[71]

Throughout the later Middle Ages, one of Ireland's largest imports was wine. During the twelfth century, most of the wine shipped to Ireland came directly from La Rochelle and Rouen, but some also came via England. In 1275 Edward I granted a charter of privileges to Gascon merchants, which made the wines of southwestern France a principal import to the English colony. In the fourteenth century, wines from Spain and Portugal were shipped along Ireland's west coast and aided the rise of the port of Galway. Other commodities needed in Ireland included salt, which was essential for preserving meat and fish, and was also used in tanning. It was principally obtained through Chester, which had ready access to the brine pans of the Cheshire plain. Metals were also imported, of which iron came in the biggest quantities either through Bristol or from the Continent. In addition to these bulk commodities, Ireland imported a variety of manufactured goods and luxuries. Fine cloths were imported

[70] Down, 'Colonial society', p. 486.
[71] Childs and O'Neill, 'Overseas trade', p. 503.

principally from England. From the fourteenth century, Anglo-Irish and Gaelic Irish elites followed the contemporary fashions, including the doublet. In the early fifteenth century, fine cloth was Bristol's chief export to Ireland. Other wares that came to Ireland included Mediterranean spices, dried fruits, drugs and perfumes, which were either imported directly or came via England.

One of the challenges facing overseas trade in Ireland was the attacks made on towns and traders by the king's enemies and by pirates. Depredations by Anglo-Irish and Gaelic 'rebels' are recorded in complaints to the English king made by the principal ports of Ireland during the fourteenth and fifteenth centuries. Foreign rivalries also brought trouble, as witnessed in the petition of Drogheda and Waterford in 1442 for help in repairing fortifications damaged by Scots, Bretons and Spaniards.[72] English pirates also frequented the Irish seaways. The records of the Court of Admiralty suggest that in a number of cases local lords and port authorities were complicit in the profits of their trade, so that the presence of pirates was not always a drain to the Irish economy.[73]

In general, Irish overseas trade from its southern and eastern coasts flourished in the thirteenth century, but declined during the fourteenth century, even before the Black Death devastated the population. English purveyance, taxes and foreign policy (for example the Hundred Years' War) had a negative impact. Irish exports were also hit by the mid-fourteenth-century demographic catastrophe. Despite these setbacks, the Irish economy adapted. In the fourteenth and fifteenth centuries, political and economic changes promoted a shift in wealth towards the western regions of Ireland. This was reflected in the growth of western ports including Galway and Sligo. Wealth that accrued through overseas trade in the later Middle Ages supported the construction of town walls, churches and stone merchant houses, which still grace a number of Ireland's towns.

TAX, TRIBUTE AND RENDERS

The sources for Gaelic and English governmental exactions differ in their character and detail. English records provide comparatively good data concerning, tax, tribute and renders. This has led to a much greater emphasis in scholarship on the revenues of the English crown

---

[72] Childs and O'Neill, 'Overseas trade', p. 523.   [73] Manning, 'Piracy'.

in Ireland for the late Middle Ages. However, since the 1970s, there has been more research on lordship in Gaelic society and greater study of its social and economic underpinnings. It highlights similarities as well as differences in sources of seigneurial revenue between the Gaels and Anglo-Irish during the later Middle Ages.

The economic concerns of lords are well evidenced during the reign of Muirchertach Ua Briain, over-king of Munster. He was the most powerful man in Ireland at the turn of the twelfth century. In 1101 Muirchertach undertook a circuit of all of Ireland. It was around this time that the bulk of *Lebor na Cert* ('Book of Rights') was composed, which laid down the rights of the king of Munster as over-king of Ireland within each province and the entitlements of lesser kings.[74] In this text, authority was defined by a system of stipends granted by a lord to his clients in return for tribute and tax. The system was presented as if sanctioned by antiquity, and ordained by Benén, a disciple of St Patrick. Although *Lebor na Cert* developed its format from pre-existing texts on clientship, the reference to *túarastla* (stipends paid from an over-king to an under-king) reflects political developments in the eleventh century. Innovation was therefore cloaked in tradition in this text.[75]

Lebor na Cert provides a snapshot of a perceived relationship between the over-king of Ireland and the provincial rulers, and between provincial rulers and their sub-kings, presented from a Munster perspective. Apart from the contextual biases of the text, its underlying principles reveal mechanisms of power in pre-Norman Ireland, elements of which continued for the rest of the Middle Ages. According to *Lebor na Cert*, the stipends granted by over-kings to lesser kings comprise high-status gifts including horses, slaves, fine clothes, horns, military equipment, ships and bracelets.[76] In return most of the kings who receive a stipend provide food, tribute and military service to their overlord as well as hostages. The tributes and services are rendered annually (or triennially) and consist of livestock (cows, swine, oxen, sheep) and mantles. Certain groups were exempt from giving tribute either due to a perceived kinship between their people and that of the overlord, or occasionally on account of an

[74] Charles-Edwards, '*Lebor na Cert*', pp. 16–18.   [75] Ibid., p. 21.
[76] In practice however, cattle may have been more commonly exchanged; see *AT*,
     s.a. 1166.

agreement. These groups might also be exempt from military service unless for pay. One tax that is mentioned in *Lebor na Cert* may have been introduced to Ireland based on Scandinavian models; it was a ship levy or *leiðangr* in Old Norse. This word gave rise to the Irish term *láideng*, which is also found in other twelfth-century texts. In essence, the system of taxation and military service presented in *Lebor na Cert* does not differ substantially from other polities in western Europe at that time.[77]

Cogad Gáedel re Gallaib ('The War of the Gaels and the Foreigners') is another text thought to have been written during the reign of Muirchertach. In detailing the oppression wrought by vikings on Munster, it describes royal agents being appointed to high office in every territory and a soldier being sent to every house to obtain supplies. Furthermore, it is claimed that a man from each household was obliged to provide military service in return for a stipend (*túarastal*), and his family was required to maintain him. A poll tax of an ounce of *findruine* (electrum?) on each nose was also levied every year.[78] In this portrayal of a nightmarish world of excessive taxation, we may get a glimpse, albeit an exaggerated one, of the systems of exaction that were in place in Munster during the time when Muirchertach Ua Briain was king.

References to a poll tax or 'nose tax' are also found in hagiographic texts where a king grants tributes to the successors of a saint. In the eleventh- or twelfth-century 'Life of St Findchú of Brigown', the king of Munster grants the first fruits of livestock, protection and 'alms from every nose in Fermoy'.[79] In the late medieval 'Life of St Maignenn of Kilmainham' a king assigns the alms of 'a screpal on every nose, for every chieftain's daughter that should take a husband, an ounce of gold or, should his stewards choose it rather, such raiment as they should have had on them. Of the gold which he had in tribute of the men from overseas the king conferred on him the making of a pastoral staff likewise and of a crozier.[80] While the 'nose tax' may have come from the levying of tax in coastal towns with links to Scandinavia, it seems to have been adopted by Church and state in Ireland. A variety of texts indicate the substantial income churches drew from tithes, alms, gifts and one-off payments for ecclesiastical

[77] Swift, 'Taxes', p. 60.   [78] Todd, ed. and trans., *Cogadh*, §40, pp. 49–51.
[79] Stokes, ed. and trans., *Lives of Saints*, p. 245.
[80] O'Grady, ed. and trans., *Silva Gadelica*, I: 38; II: 36.

services.[81] This was in addition to the profits of landholdings, which were extensive in twelfth-century Ireland. The reform movement of the twelfth and thirteenth centuries encouraged bequests of land to new and established monasteries, a matter that is discussed in more detail later.[82]

The English conquest brought a new land-owning elite to Ireland. Notionally lands were held by greater lords as gifts from the crown in exchange for military service or other dues. Greater lords in turn made a series of land grants to their followers for service and revenues. For Anglo-Irish lords, land would be a key source of revenue, with the profits and labour services of demesne land being received directly, in addition to the rents received from rural and urban tenants. From time to time, the crown was able to regain landholdings through escheat (when a suitable heir to an estate was lacking) and forfeiture (in punishment for disloyalty). Most Gaelic lords had lands attached to their office; however, this was not always the case, nor was demesne always distinguished from lands inherited from the family.[83] Gaelic lords could also extend their landholdings through the exercise of seigneurial rights in lieu of dues and exactions, or in pledge for a fine or in the absence of rightful owners.[84] Both Anglo-Irish and Gaelic lords might opt to farm their lands directly or grant them to tenants in exchange for renders, labour obligations and military dues.[85]

In addition to land and labour, tributes and taxes were collected. Gaelic lords received money, cattle or foodstuffs from the territories under their control in amounts that were often fixed according to the units of land assessment established in the eleventh century of *trícha cét* and *baile*.[86] The majority of Anglo-Irish land divisions were also based on this pre-existing Gaelic system.[87] The profits of justice from seigneurial and royal courts were of greater significance to English lords than in Gaelic areas, where an independent judiciary continued to practise its craft. However, a proportion of the legal fines paid to a victim's family might also be claimed by a Gaelic lord. The English

---

[81] Russell, ed. and trans., 'Nósa Ua Maine', pp. 536–9; Stokes, ed. and trans., *Lives of Saints*, pp. 232, 278.

[82] Britnell, *Britain and Ireland*, pp. 223–4.

[83] Simms, *From kings to warlords*, pp. 129–30.

[84] Nicholls, *Gaelic and Gaelicised Ireland*, pp. 37–9; Butler, *Gleanings*, pp. 15–16.

[85] See Chapter 8.   [86] See the earlier discussion.

[87] MacCotter, *Medieval Ireland*, p. 16.

crown claimed the rights of knight service, feudal aids and wardship from the lands under its control. There was a tendency for knight service from military tenants and rents from communities to be converted over time into cash payments as scutage (a tax levied in lieu of military service) and revenue farms. References to scutage in Ireland first appear in 1222, and it became a regular part of crown revenue by the late thirteenth century.[88] Scutage was abandoned in England in 1340, but continued in Ireland, albeit with waning significance. Attempts to revive the importance of this military levy for the Irish exchequer in the fifteenth century provoked resistance, leading to its eventual abandonment in 1531.[89]

Urban taxation developed in the late Viking Age. A twelfth century poem in the 'Book of Uí Maine' states that a tenth of the trading goods which arrived in Dublin were owed to Armagh as well as a scruple of gold for each man, while the kings of the town claimed a tax upon the wares of craftsmen and merchants.[90] The major urban centres of Ireland fell under English royal control from the late twelfth century and were taxed by their new overlords. King John collected one-fifteenth of the value of imports on a few occasions after 1203, and Henry III followed suit from 1266. In 1275 a heavy tax of 6s 8d per sack of wool, per 300 woolfells and every 100 hides was introduced. The wool tax would be a main component of English customs duties for the rest of the Middle Ages. Foreign merchants also paid customs on cloth, wax, wine and other merchandise.[91] As Gaelic society become more urbanised in the fifteenth century, local lords claimed burgage rents and custom duties in the manner of their English neighbours.[92]

The English royal right to purveyance (the compulsory purchase of supplies for war) was exercised with increasing frequency in late thirteenth-century Ireland. In principle, goods taken were meant to be paid for at market prices, but in reality, payments were in arrears, often fixed low, or never forthcoming. Wealthier landlords could avoid this exaction by purchasing exemption or by bribing officials. The burden of taxation therefore fell heavier on those with less political influence. Proportionate to its size and wealth, Ireland

---

[88] Ellis, 'Taxation and defence', p. 5.   [89] Ibid., p. 17.
[90] Dillon, ed. and trans. *Lebor na Cert*, pp. 116–19; Valante, 'Taxation', pp. 249–53.
[91] Britnell, *Britain and Ireland*, p. 257; Dryburgh and Smith, eds., *Handbook*, pp. 277–8.
[92] Simms, *From kings to warlords*, p. 136.

was burdened more heavily with purveyance than England during the ambitious military campaigns of Edward I.[93] For example, in December 1298 the king requested from Ireland 8,000 quarters of wheat, 10,000 quarters of oats, 2,000 quarters of crushed malt, 1,000 tuns of wine, 500 carcasses of beef, 1,000 fattened pigs and 20,000 dried fish export to support his military campaign in Scotland.[94] The hardships imposed on merchants and landowners led to numerous complaints and incidences of resistance.[95]

Direct taxation was levied in areas under the control of the English crown, initially as an occasional levy to fund war efforts.[96] The yield from subsidies on land and moveable goods varied. During the thirteenth century, direct taxation became increasingly frequent in a system that was open to abuse and corruption.[97] In the closing years of the thirteenth century the economy of Anglo-Irish areas was under exceptional pressure. Figures for the last years of the reign of Edward I show a decrease in revenues from £6,112 in 1301–2 to as little as £2,865 in the early years of Edward II's reign in 1311–12 as the English colony fell into financial crisis. The Irish council took the decision in August 1311 that all revenue from customs should be paid into the Dublin exchequer, rather than be granted to revenue collectors for the crown. Nevertheless, money and supplies continued to be sent from Ireland to support Edward II's war in Scotland. By the end of Edward's reign in 1327, the finances of the English administration in Ireland were so enervated that support was sought from England.[98] What had been a profitable colony for English kings became an increasing drain on their finances in the fourteenth and fifteenth centuries.

During the reign of Edward III, general subsidies were authorised by the Irish Parliament to maintain the government. For example, in 1346 the tax granted was two shillings a ploughland or per £6 worth of moveable goods and one-tenth on the spiritualities of the clergy.[99] Over the course of the fourteenth century, the taxable area that was effectively governed by parliament declined, and the yields from taxation were largely disbursed on local defensive and other

---

[93] Britnell, *Britain and Ireland*, pp. 258–9.
[94] Lydon, 'Years of crisis', p. 199. A tun is a measure of liquid equivalent to eight barrels.
[95] Smith, *English in Louth*, p. 15.   [96] Britnell, *Britain and Ireland*, p. 454.
[97] Britnell, *Britain and Ireland*, pp. 258, 461; Lydon, *Lordship*, pp. 127–36.
[98] Lydon, 'Edward II', p. 49.   [99] Lydon, *Ireland*, p. 37.

needs.[100] Economic depression led to the lowering of a number of tax assessments in the fifteenth century, and by the early 1470s subventions from England to bolster the Anglo-Irish government became a necessity.[101]

Provincial and county assemblies continued to grant sectional subsidies locally. This was based on the historic principle that a local community should be responsible for the cost of its own defence. Rights to levy taxes were granted to lords and burgesses for building and maintaining town walls, bridges, castles and quays. The tributes or 'black rents' paid by many Anglo-Irish communities to Gaelic lords as protection money in the later Middle Ages were often raised by local subsidy assessments.[102] The Irish system of local taxation was alien to England and reflected both unsettled conditions in Ireland and the decentralised exercise of power. In the fifteenth century, parliament sought to impose control over local taxation by mandating that its approval was necessary for any such exactions.[103]

Hospitality appears to have had increasing economic significance in relation to taxes and tributes for Gaelic lords as the Middle Ages wore on.[104] In return for land or stipend a lord might demand hospitality and refection for himself, his servants and retinues. The practice of free board and lodging was dubbed *coinnmed* or *cóisir* and Anglicised as 'coyne' and 'coshering', although it was also practised under a variety of other names. It was an effective method of fiscal exploitation utilised by both secular lords and bishops. It relieved lords of household expenses and provided for their retinues or troops, as well as reinforcing the bonds between lord and subject.[105] These perceived merits led to the practice being widely adopted in Anglo-Irish areas by the fifteenth century.[106]

Although the seigneurial exactions of Gaelic and English lords and kings in Ireland are often analysed separately, there were in fact numerous similarities between them. Towards the end of the Middle Ages, practices of gathering revenue were increasingly shared by the Anglo-Irish and Gaelic elites. Economic strength had political ramifications. The revenues of the English colony showed a healthy return in the thirteenth century, but decreased through economic decline,

---

[100] Ibid., p. 38.
[101] Britnell, *Britain and Ireland*, p. 460; Ellis, *Reform and revival*, pp. 67–8.
[102] Quinn, 'Irish parliamentary subsidy', p. 220.   [103] Lydon, *Ireland*, p. 37.
[104] Simms, 'Guesting', p. 80.   [105] Nicholls, 'Gaelic society', pp. 425–6.
[106] Smith, 'Concept of the march', p. 267; Hore and Graves, eds., *Social state*, p. 161.

over-exploitation, corruption and spiralling defence costs. The dwindling profit to the English royal government was a contributory factor in a policy of retrenchment adopted towards the end of the Middle Ages and the resultant 'making of the Pale'. This left much of Ireland in the hands of Gaelic and Anglo-Irish lords who operated with a high level of independence from the English crown.

CONCLUSION

The economic history of Ireland from AD 1100 to 1500 is characterised by economic growth in the twelfth and thirteenth centuries. This was followed by decline in the fourteenth century as a consequence of famines, epidemics and warfare. There was a shift in farming practices from intensive arable production to the more traditional and sustainable practices of dairying and cattle rearing from the fourteenth century. In the fifteenth century, signs of economic recovery are more apparent in Gaelic-held areas that were less severely affected by the catastrophes of the preceding century. Meanwhile the economic problems of the English colony were exacerbated by territorial shrinkage and political infighting.

8

SOCIETY AD 1100–1500

•

Society in Ireland would be changed irrecoverably by the English conquests of the late twelfth century. Nevertheless, changes were already in train from the late eleventh century due to increasing contacts between Ireland, Britain and the Continent and the movement for ecclesiastical reform. In 1171 these external influences combined in the invasion of Henry II of England, which was undertaken with the prior assent of Pope Hadrian. Thereafter, medieval Irish society would be characterised by a division between Gaels and 'the English born in Ireland', as the descendants of English settlers would come to style themselves.[1] While the division between the two groups was rarely clear-cut, it remained politically significant. The perceived need to reinforce boundaries between English and Gaelic identities was continually upheld by the elites who had a vested interest in maintaining segregation.[2] To place the relations of Gaels and the English in context, it is worth considering Ireland's external contacts and identity before the invasion of Henry II.

The takeover of England in 1066 by William 'the Bastard' (later known as 'the Conqueror') seems to have coloured Ireland's relationship with the Continent. It has been noted that the number of Irish kings and clerics going on pilgrimage abroad appears to decline significantly after 1064, which may reflect some reluctance by high-status figures to travel through territory under Norman control.[3]

---

[1] Frame, "'Les Engleys'", p. 83.   [2] Morrissey, 'Cultural geographies', p. 553.
[3] Richter, 'European dimension', p. 332.

Contact was soon made between the Norman Church in England
and Ireland as successive archbishops of Canterbury sought to claim
authority over the Irish Church. Dublin was used as a foothold for
these ambitions. Its bishops were consecrated by successive archbishops of Canterbury in 1074 and 1085, 1096, and 1121. King Stephen
(1135–54) tried and failed to obstruct Irish efforts to gain papal recognition for an ecclesiastical hierarchy that made Dublin free from
English control. Thereafter the English Church sought papal sanction for military intervention in Ireland on the basis that the Gaels
were in need of externally imposed ecclesiastical and moral reform.[4]

Ecclesiastical matters alone cannot explain the growing tension
in relations between the English and the Irish in the twelfth century. The participation of Muirchertach Ua Briain, king of Munster
(d. 1119) in Irish Sea politics conflicted with the interests of Henry I,
who used economic sanctions to bring him to heel.[5] Techniques of
intimidation were also used by Henry II. In 1154 the Irish over-king
Muirchertach Mac Lochlainn imposed his authority over Dublin,
seizing it from the control of Henry's ally, Diarmait Mac Murchada,
king of Leinster. In the following years the king's council discussed
the invasion of Ireland, and the papal bull *Laudabiliter* was acquired
to support Henry's invasion 'to proclaim the truths of the Christian religion to a rude and ignorant people' in return for an annual
tribute to Rome.[6] Once Muirchertach's threat to Dublin receded,
Henry shelved plans to invade until Diarmait Mac Murchada's death.
The invasion of Ireland in 1171 was the culmination of a century
of changing Anglo-Irish relations, whereby English lay and spiritual
leaders sought to impose their will on a people increasingly regarded
as 'rude and ignorant'.

Negative stereotyping became a common feature of Anglo-
Norman writings concerning their Celtic-speaking neighbours from
the 1120s.[7] This discourse had colonial connotations, depicting the
neighbours of the English as inferior and in need of domination.[8]
However, Celtic-speakers were not uniquely denigrated in European

[4] Duffy, *Ireland*, p. 25.
[5] Mynors *et al.*, eds. and trans., *William of Malmesbury*, V: 409, I: 738–9.
[6] Scott and Martin, eds., *Expugnatio*, II: 5, pp. 144–6; Curtis and Dowell, trans., *Irish
     historical documents 1172–1922*, p. 17.
[7] Gillingham, 'Context and purpose', p. 108.
[8] Mitchell, 'Gender(ed) identities', p. 13.

literature. 'Othering' was not unusual in twelfth-century texts commenting on minorities and those who belonged to different cultures. It was a tactic used to present a writer's ethnic, political or linguistic community as superior in relation to another, towards which the writer, and his audiences, harboured animosity.[9] For example, in the 'Pilgrim's Guide to Santiago de Compostella', the Poitevan author describes the people of Navarre as 'a barbarous nation . . . debauched, perverse, perfidious, disloyal and corrupt, libidinous, drunkard, given to all kinds of violence'.[10] English stereotypes of the Irish reached advanced and notorious development in the writings of Gerald of Wales at the end of the twelfth century. Gerald's family had taken part in the invasion of Ireland, and he had a vested interest in portraying the Gaels as lesser people. While Gerald was favourable towards Irish music and clerical piety, he was overwhelmingly negative in presenting the Irish as sexually deviant, barbaric, faithless, treacherous and licentious. The words of Gerald would echo through the centuries in later English representations of the Irish.[11] A counterbalance to a few of the judgements made by Gerald of Wales can be seen in the writings of his contemporary Jocelin of Furness (1180–1214), who defended some differences in custom and the faith of the Irish people.[12] Another hagiographer, William of Canterbury, was critical of Henry II's expedition to Ireland and the growth of anti-Irish prejudice.[13] Nevertheless there was an overwhelming political incentive for English leaders to portray the Gaels as deviant and inferior.

In return, sections of Gaelic society held a less than flattering attitude towards the foreigners in their midst. The word *Gall*, used by the Irish for the vikings, carried connotations of impiety, oppression and savagery in twelfth-century literature. This label was soon transferred to the English in Ireland.[14] The invasion of 1171 was accompanied by losses of territory, bloodshed, trauma and displacement. No wonder that some Irish poets wrote negatively of the invaders' arrival and hoped their royal patrons would overwhelm them. The poet Muiredach Albanach Ua Dálaig likened the Brittonic, English

[9] See for example Moore, *Formation*, p. 62.
[10] Melczer, ed. and trans., *Pilgrim's guide*, p. 94.   [11] Martin, 'DIarmait', pp. 60–1.
[12] Sperber *et al.*, eds. and trans., *Life of St Patrick*, Introduction.
[13] Bull, 'Criticism of Henry II's expedition'.
[14] Goedheer, *Irish and Norse traditions*, pp. 50, 55.

and French invaders to 'shoals of coarse fish, ugly shapes with the
repulsiveness of serpents' invading a pool of noble salmon.'[15]

The conquest of Ireland was largely undertaken by land-hungry
magnates rather than through the direct intervention of the English
crown. As a result, English rule remained decentralised and incomplete during the later Middle Ages.[16] Henry II had given permission for Diarmait Mac Murchada to recruit his subjects in a military bid to regain control of Leinster in 1169. One of these, Richard
de Clare (better known as Strongbow), brokered a marriage alliance
with Diarmait's daughter Aífe. Strongbow's succession to the throne
of Leinster in 1171 prompted Henry II to invade Ireland to secure
Strongbow's submission, by granting Leinster to him as a fief and
seizing direct control over the coastal ports of the province. Henry
also received submissions from many Irish kings whom he entertained in Dublin during the winter of 1171. Before leaving Ireland
in 1172, Henry granted the rich lands of Meath to Hugh de Lacy to
hold by the service of fifty knights. The Treaty of Windsor, which
was drawn up with Ruaidrí Ua Conchobuir, high-king of Ireland in
1175, indicates that Henry was not intending to subdue all Ireland,
but envisaged an island divided between a subject king of the Gaels
and the English lordship. However, the terms of the treaty were soon
dishonoured, and the Irish colony continued to expand until 1235
when Connacht was seized by Richard de Burgh. This brought the
majority of Ireland under English rule.[17]

The land grants introduced a new elite to large parts of Ireland,
but tenants and serfs were needed to farm the lands for them. The
Treaty of Windsor hints that many people fled in the wake of invasion. Ruaidrí Ua Conchobuir was obliged, if asked, to force Gaels
from areas of English control to return to them. The Gaelic Irish
were treated as an underclass in areas of English control. The majority
were assigned servile status, but a small number of free Gaelic tenants are recorded. In lands of lesser agricultural potential, Gaelic lords
could retain lands as vassals under English lordship and might possess a high degree of autonomy. Thus, in Leinster, the Gaelic relatives

---

[15] Ó Cuív, ed. and trans., 'A poem', pp. 167, 171.
[16] Otway-Ruthven, 'The native Irish', p. 2.   [17] Down, 'Colonial society', p. 442.

of Diarmait Mac Murchada controlled lands in Uí Felmeda and Uí Chennselaig.[18]

By the reign of Edward I, a new class of small free tenants bearing non-Gaelic names can be seen in the records of English-ruled areas. Judging by their surnames, the bulk of these came from England and Wales (although a few Gaelic Irish also bore English names). In addition to English and Welsh colonists, Flemings and Continental craftsmen and traders arrived after the invasion, while Ostmen (Hiberno-Scandinavians) remained as a distinct group until the thirteenth century. Little is known of the numbers who migrated to Ireland and how they were recruited. Nevertheless, what is clearly documented is a perceived distinction between those of Gaelic and non-Gaelic ancestry.

LEGAL DISTINCTIONS

A remarkable form of judicial dualism came to exist in late medieval Ireland due to the differences between the English and Irish legal systems and the imposition of legal apartheid by the English colonial government.[19] England had by 1171 a distinctive common law system, centrally directed and administered by royal judges. This was different from Gaelic society where crimes were commonly resolved by payment of compensation under arbitration. At the council that met before King John in Dublin in 1210, the magnates of Ireland swore to observe the laws and customs of England.[20] English common law was extended to colonists and Ostmen, but not to the Gaelic Irish in general, except (perhaps from the reign of Henry III) to those who belonged to five of the leading royal dynasties of pre-conquest Ireland (the Uí Néill of Ulster, Uí Maíl Sechnaill of Meath, Uí Chonchobuir of Connacht, Uí Briain of Munster and Meic Murchada of Leinster).[21]

The majority of the Gaelic Irish were excluded from common law, which gave them the status of villeins in England. They were unable to access the king's courts, regardless of their status within Gaelic society. Consequently, the Gaelic Irish were at the mercy of English lords on legal matters. Technically they might be held incapable of holding land in inheritance or even bequeathing their chattels. They lacked legal redress against injustice. These were obvious

[18] Down, 'Colonial society', p. 445.   [19] Bartlett, *Making of Europe*, pp. 214–17.
[20] Lydon, *Ireland*, p. 43.   [21] Hand, *English law*, p. 206.

sources of grievance.[22] This system of apartheid could only be ameliorated through individuals being granted the right, acquired by
payment or through personal connections, to have their cases heard
according to English law, or by obtaining burgess status, which could
entitle them to English law. Some attempts were made to remedy
these inequalities. In the 1270s the Archbishop of Cashel led a bid for
the extension of English law to the Irish of Munster in return for the
sum of 10,000 marks. However, a lasting agreement was not put in
place. In the 1290s, Edward I declared in his great council at London
that English law should be granted to all who seek it. In 1331 one law
was ordained for the Irish and English of free status.[23]

Throughout the later Middle Ages, Brehon Law continued to
flourish in lands under Gaelic lordship. Its penetration into areas of
English control was seen to challenge and undermine the power
of the royal courts.[24] The problems of lawlessness that plagued the
English colony from the end of the thirteenth century led to the
expedient adoption of some principles of Gaelic law. These included
cin comhfhocuis – the principle that leaders of kin groups were responsible for the misdeeds of their members.[25] Legal divisions between
the Gaels and the English of Ireland reinforced other cultural differences witnessed in language, dress and custom. However, a degree of
pragmatic acculturation between the two groups occurred.

Many first-generation settlers helped to establish themselves in
Irish society by marrying daughters of the Gaelic elite. More generally contact across cultural boundaries was a feature of daily life
in Ireland. From the mid-thirteenth century, a more self-confident
assertion of Gaelic culture and traditions can be observed. As the
strength of English lordship in Ireland started to wane, there were
fears that the English of Ireland would unite culturally and politically
with their Gaelic neighbours. A raft of parliamentary legislation was
passed to try and prohibit 'degeneracy' (from Latin *degenere*to depart
from one's 'genus' by adopting alien traits) and the absenteeism of
English landlords from Ireland in 1297, 1310 and 1320.[26] English fears

---

[22] Curtis and McDowell, trans., *Irish historical documents*, p. 41; Otway-Ruthven,
'Native Irish', p. 12.

[23] Otway-Ruthven, 'Native Irish', p. 14–16; Lydon, *Ireland*, p. 44; Curtis and McDowell, trans., *Irish historical documents*, pp. 46–7.

[24] Otway-Ruthven, 'Native Irish', pp. 13–14; Lydon, *Ireland*, p. 46; Curtis and
McDowell, trans., *Irish historical documents*, p. 37.

[25] Lydon, *Ireland*, pp. 45, 50–1.   [26] Watt, 'Approaches', p. 310.

of degeneracy in Ireland might usefully be compared to those of the French in Outremer, and reflect wider European insecurities about identity and political allegiance.[27]

In unsettled conditions English magnates might, for their own security, reach a *modus vivendi* with Gaelic communities. The fourteenth century saw an increase in licenses to parley, that is, negotiations between English and Gaelic leaders to secure peace. Undoubtedly many negotiations took place without official consent. The severe impact of the Black Death on the English community and the increasing Gaelicisation of the English in Ireland may have heightened fears that the colony was heading towards oblivion. The 'Statutes of Kilkenny' were drawn up in 1366 in a bid to reassert English royal control and limit the growing vigour of Gaelic culture.

The statutes are remarkable for the power that government attempted to wield over society.[28] Not merely were English laws and peace between English subjects to be maintained but the English were also prohibited from sex, alliance or trade with the native Irish. The Irish language was banned in areas of English control. Gaels were also prohibited from ecclesiastical professions or working as minstrels in English-held areas. Even name calling between the English born in Ireland and the English born in England was banned. The statutes indicate that the identity of English in Ireland was becoming more unfamiliar to other English subjects. However, English government lacked the power to enforce the statutes and many were ignored. Yet, the mistaken assumption that cultural difference could be equated with political disloyalty would continually resurface.

ACCULTURATION

According to the 'Statutes of Kilkenny', 'many English of the said land . . . live and govern themselves according to the manners, fashion and language of the Irish enemies and have also made divers marriages and alliances between themselves and the Irish enemies foresaid'. How the English in Ireland saw themselves has been a matter of heated debate. One question has been whether the English in Ireland had become by the late fourteenth century a 'middle nation'[29] –

---

[27] Stewart, trans., *History of Jerusalem*, pp. 64–6.
[28] Curtis and McDowell, trans., *Irish historical documents*, pp. 52–9.
[29] Watt, 'Approaches', pp. 304–5; Lydon, 'Middle nation'.

neither fully English nor fully Irish – or whether their distinctiveness
was more of a regional trait akin to the 'northerners' living on the
march near Scotland.[30]

There are numerous examples of English people in Ireland who
embraced aspects of Gaelic identity. One oft-cited individual is Gerald Fitzgerald, third earl of Desmond (d. 1398). He was born to one of
the most distinguished English families in Ireland and served as justiciar from 1367 to 1369. Gerald was also a patron and author of Gaelic
poetry. Thirty short Irish poems attributed to him survive. Although
somewhat lacking in technical skill, Gerald's poems reveal his knowledge of Irish legends and social ties with the Gaelic world. Gerald
sent one of his sons, James, to be fostered with the Gaelic magnate
Conchobar Ua Briain of Thomond in 1388.[31]

However, the 'English born in Ireland' were a diverse group, and
evidence can be found to support opposing views of Hiberno-
English identity.[32] The 'English of Ireland' frequently protested their
Englishness and loyalty to the crown in official documents. Their
links with England were continually rejuvenated by marriage, military service, rewards and favour.[33] However, it should be noted that
expressions of identity are situational and more complex than individual pronouncements may suggest.[34] Arnold le Poer, seneschal
of Kilkenny (d. 1328), provides one example. His loyalty to the
English crown was demonstrated in 1316 in warfare against the Bruce
invasion.[35] In 1324 le Poer spoke out against the English-born bishop
of Ossory, Richard Ledrede, who was accusing his townspeople of
heresy. Le Poer called Ledrede 'a foreigner' and stated that the people of Ireland (encompassing both Gaelic and English people) were
never known as heretics. In the same speech, le Poer refers to the
Magna Carta, positioning himself as an English subject in Ireland.[36]
Le Poer displays a multilayered identity: he is Irish in conflict with
his English-born rival, Anglo-Irish in his personal connections, and
English in his loyalty to the crown. In this respect, the English colony
in Ireland can be regarded not as a land of fixed identities and frontiers

[30] Ellis, *Pale*, pp. 32–3.   [31] Mac Niocaill, 'Fitzgerald, Gerald'.
[32] Maginn, 'Gaelic Ireland's English frontiers', p. 176.
[33] Frame, 'Exporting state', pp. 146–7, 151; Crooks, 'Constructing a laboratory', p. 18.
[34] Scott and Martin, eds., *Expugnatio*, I: 23, pp. 80–1.
[35] See the later discussion.
[36] Frame, 'Exporting state', p. 155; Crooks, 'Constructing a laboratory', p. 19; Davidson
and Ward, eds. and trans., *The sorcery trial*, p. 48.

but as a contact zone between cultures.[37] Identities may be situational and multifaceted.

The possession of a Gaelic identity in Gaelic society differed from English identity in that it was based on agnatic descent, rather than status or law. It was theoretically not possible for those of English paternal descent to adopt Gaelic identity unless they faked their genealogy.[38] Gaelic writers did at times distinguish between the English born in Ireland, known as 'Gaill', and those who came from England, whom they called 'Saxain', demonstrating a perception of difference between the two groups.[39] While Gaelicisation was a feature of English society in Ireland, Anglicisation was also observed. Gaels within areas of English lordship occasionally surmounted the ethnic obstacles to their advancement. For example, Robert de Bray, a mayor of Dublin in the 1290s, possessed an English name, but had to petition Edward I to gain English legal status.[40] Throughout areas of English lordship it is possible to find Gaels who assumed an English persona.[41] Partial acculturation was also common. Gaelic dynasties intermarried with the English and adopted English customs without surrendering their adherence to local society. Individuals' principal allegiances were often familial and regional rather than ethnic, so that 'foreign' cultural traits could be adopted without compromising self-identity.

The whole of Ireland might be deemed a 'contact zone' where cultural exchange went in both directions. No corner of Ireland was sealed from English influence, and even in the heart of the English lordship there was a significant Gaelic population, often relegated to lower social status. Generally speaking, one might identify an 'Anglocentric zone' focused on the midlands and southeast, where the trend might be to draw Gaels who dwelt there into a more Anglicised existence. In the 'Hiberno-centric' zone that made up other parts of the island, the trend would be towards Gaelicisation of English settlers. These zones were, however, unstable and influenced by shifts in political power.

The unequal social distribution of English settlers in Ireland would also be a factor in processes of assimilation. Examples abound of Gaelic and English lords selectively adopting elements of each other's

---

[37] Morrissey, 'Cultural geographies', p. 552.   [38] Nicholls, 'Gaelic society', p. 422.
[39] Maginn, 'Gaelic Ireland's English frontiers', pp. 178, 183.
[40] Watt, 'Approaches', p. 308.   [41] Verstraten Veach, 'Anglicisation', p. 134.

culture within political border zones. These might be dubbed as
top-down processes or peer emulation prompted by physical adja-
cency. Throughout the English lordship, a substantial Gaelic peas-
antry remained, but there was no significant English underclass in
Gaelic-held areas. Thus, in English-held areas cultural hybridisation
also occurred as a bottom-up process. The cultural practices of a
Gaelic underclass became woven into colonial society through day-
to-day contact.[42] Gaelic influence filtered through all levels of English
society in Ireland. This generated anxiety within English colonial
society and the conscious desire to enforce cultural separation that
was reflected in legislation from the end of the thirteenth century.
As Anglicisation was more a matter of selective adaptation in Gaelic
areas, it may have been deemed less of a threat.

From the late thirteenth century until the late fifteenth century,
many lands that had fallen under English control were taken by Gaelic
rulers. The label 'Gaelic revival' is often used to describe this process,
but this term obscures the subtleties of highly localised and variable
shifts in political power. These changes helped revitalise expressions
of Gaelic culture in literature and political ritual during the fourteenth and fifteenth centuries.[43] The overlap of areas of English and
Gaelic control also encouraged greater assimilation between English
and Irish cultures.[44] Studies of later medieval Ireland have tended to
analyse divisions and boundaries between Gaelic and English politics and culture. However, the fluidity of relations in a contact zone
undermines attempts to gather much more than individual snapshots
of identity and acculturation over time. Nor were there only two
cultures in contact in Ireland: the coasts of Ulster were a gateway
to Scottish influences, and farther south, regular contacts with Continental Europe and Wales added to the cultural mix in medieval
Ireland.

PLAGUE AND FAMINE

Plague and famine had a significant impact on society in the later
Middle Ages. In the twelfth century harvests had generally been
profitable and the population grew. However, even in those times
famine and pestilence visited Ireland each generation. A series of poor

[42] Cf. Webster, 'Creolizing'.   [43] See the later discussion.
[44] Verstraten Veach, 'Anglicisation', pp. 129–30.

harvests led to famine and epidemics in the late 1220s, particularly in Connacht where warfare aggravated the misery. Population growth continued until the 1270s, when the deteriorating climate and over-exploitation of resources led to increased incidences of famine. In 1295 the great scarcity of food was exacerbated in English areas by purveyance for the wars in Scotland. In the margins of the *Liber Niger* of Christ Church, Dublin, it was noted that 'so great was the famine in Ireland that the poor were eating those hanged from the gallows'.[45] Worse times followed. The great northern European famine of 1315–18 followed the destruction of harvests by wet, stormy weather and a livestock pestilence of cattle and sheep.[46] The problems in eastern Ireland were exacerbated by the military campaigns of the Scottish magnate Edward Bruce.[47] The devastations of the early fourteenth century weakened the population's resistance to later outbreaks of disease in 1327 and 1328. The populations that had survived these crises in their youth had compromised immunity and so were vulnerable to the Black Death of the mid-fourteenth century.[48]

The Black Death was the greatest disaster to befall medieval Europe. Across the Continent the estimated mortality rates from the mid-fourteenth century plague vary from 25 to 65 per cent of the population, with high levels of regional differentiation. Episodic recurrence led to further loss of life in the late fourteenth and fifteenth centuries. The pathogen *Yersinia Pestis* was identified at the end of the nineteenth century as the cause, although some scholars have suggested that more than one disease was responsible. Recent DNA studies have strengthened the case that *Yersinia Pestis* in both pneumonic and bubonic form led to widespread mortality.[49]

The plague arrived in Ireland in 1348. One of the most vivid contemporary accounts was penned by Friar John Clyn of Kilkenny. It illustrates the grievous impact of plague and describes both forms of infection (one causing buboes [swollen lymph nodes] and the other characterised by bloody discharge from the lungs): 'That disease entirely stripped vills, cities, castles and towns of inhabitants of men, so that scarcely anyone would be able to live in them. The plague was so contagious that those touching the dead or even the sick were immediately infected and died, and the one confessing and the confessor

---

[45] Gwynn, ed., 'Some unpublished texts', p. 337; Lyons, 'Weather', pp. 39–40.
[46] Jordan, *Great Famine*, pp. 48–59.   [47] See the later discussion.
[48] *AFM, s.aa.* 1327, 1328, 1349.   [49] Kelly, *History of the Black Death*, p. 10.

were together led to the grave . . . For many died from carbuncles and from ulcers and pustules that could be seen on shins and under the armpits; some died, as if in a frenzy, from pain of the head, others from spitting blood.'[50] The pneumonic form of the plague is more aggressive, and it flourished in the cold and wet weather conditions of the mid-fourteenth century.

Contemporary sources comment on the disproportionate impact of Black Death on the English population in Ireland. They include the chronicler Geoffrey le Baker, who wrote that the plague 'killed the English inhabitants there in great numbers, but the native Irish . . . were scarcely touched'.[51] While this is probably an exaggeration, the brevity of records of plague in Irish annals provides some support for this view. The effects of the plague varied from region to region. Records from English manors suggest that the disease hit heaviest in Leinster and was less virulent in Ulster.[52] Population density and trade, often regarded as key factors in determining the impact of the Black Death, could explain these disparities. Nevertheless, recent studies have shown that 'marginal' regions, including Iceland and the Scottish highlands, suffered high mortality rates, while some 'central' areas of Europe including Flanders escaped relatively lightly.[53] A host of factors might affect the virulence and frequency of pathogens as well as a population's resistance, including levels of nutrition and adaptability in the face of crisis. The Black Death exacerbated the problems of the English colony that had already suffered from subsistence crises and warfare.

Four further episodes of plague were witnessed in the late fourteenth century, with five further occurrences in the fifteenth, the most severe of which was a major outbreak in 1446–8. In 1404, it was reported that 'many fevers raged throughout Ireland'.[54] The population crash may have temporarily abated the risk of famine, although famines continued to be recorded periodically in the later Middle Ages. There seems to be some correlation between food scarcity and epidemics. While some demographic recovery may be posited for the fifteenth century, recurrent wars, famines and outbreaks of disease prevented any rapid return to pre-plague population levels.

[50] Willliams, ed. and trans., *Annals of Ireland by Friar John Clyn, s.a.* 1349.
[51] Kelly, *History of the Black Death*, p. 45.   [52] Lyons, 'Weather', p. 45.
[53] Kelly, *History of the Black Death*, pp. 20–1.   [54] Lyons, 'Weather', pp. 46–7, 67.

RANKS AND ROLES IN SECULAR SOCIETY

Slaves

A number of changes in the social hierarchy can be identified in Ireland after AD 1100. Slavery was widespread in Ireland during the early Middle Ages, but it had long ceased by 1500. The vitality of the slave trade in 1100 is reflected in *Lebor na Cert*, which lists slaves among the high-status gifts given as stipends by Irish over-kings to their under-kings.[55] Nevertheless, slavery was in decline elsewhere in Europe. Population growth and the centralisation of authority forced lower classes of freemen into worse conditions of landholding, and slavery was becoming economically unnecessary. At the same time, the slave trade was targeted by religious reformers as synonymous with sexual sin and barbarism.[56] In 1102 the Council of London prohibited the slave trade as practised by the pre-Norman English, as a 'nefarious business'. Similarly, the ecclesiastical Council of Armagh in 1171 ordered that English slaves in Ireland should be freed.[57] The English occupation of coastal ports brought large-scale slave trading to an end. The conquest may have ended slavery, but it supported in a system that saw people of low rank partially enslaved as serfs.

UNFREE TENANTS

In the early twelfth century, a *biattach*, literally 'one who gives food', was a free commoner who owed services to a lord. In Ulster and Connacht they maintained their pre-invasion status as minor landowners throughout the Middle Ages. However, in areas that fell to English rule most of the conquered Irish were gathered into one class who were bound to the land. *Biattach* or betagh (as their name was Anglicised) became unfree, customary tenants. On the manor of Cloncurry (Co. Kildare) in 1311, sixty-three betaghs shared 341.5 acres of land, just under 5.5 acres each on average.[58] As the equivalent of English villeins, betaghs could be sold or given away with their holdings. The typical unfree tenant might be obliged annually to plough two acres; to reap one or two days; perhaps to cart hay, corn, or fuel; and sometimes to dig turf, and pay rents and burdensome customary payments

---

[55] Swift, 'Taxes', p. 50. [56] Wyatt, *Slaves*, p. 388.
[57] Cave and Coulson, eds. and trans., *A source book*, pp. 285–6.
[58] Down, 'Colonial society', p. 458.

in cash or kind.[59] From the end of the fourteenth century, labour shortages led betaghs to occupy larger holdings and work on better terms, and the label gradually fell out of use in English areas.[60]

In Gaelic society, individuals of semi-free status continued to exist throughout the Middle Ages. There seem to be many variations on their level of legal dependency and status. It has been suggested that much agricultural labour was undertaken by sharecroppers, dependent on their lords for legal status and a supply of livestock. A perennial workforce shortage led Irish lords to claim that even their higher-status subjects owed labour services, among other impositions, for their lands. This has created a difficulty for historians trying to establish a clear division between those of free and unfree status.[61] In reality, these distinctions became blurred in both English and Gaelic areas as tenants often held land by more than one form of tenure.

FREE TENANTS AND FARMERS

In both Gaelic and English society, free tenants and farmers varied greatly in status and wealth and could include lords with subjects or tenants of their own. During the twelfth century, the position of landowning commoners in Gaelic society came under duress. Lords sought to extend their rights, seeking tribute and labour services.[62] The townland persisted as the basic estate-unit of freemen, held in common by kin groups or clans, with varying degrees of complexity in their organisation and assessment.[63] Partible inheritance was generally practised, and lands were periodically redistributed within a kin group (including to legitimate and illegitimate heirs). However, divisions of the patrimony could also be problematic or challenged. Partible inheritance might give rise to family discord or could lead to the creation of unviable holdings, pushing individuals into a landless state. Lands might also be acquired through pledge, purpose or force, as well as inheritance, causing dynasties and clans to rise and fall over time. Land and cattle could also be acquired as 'fiefs' by free tenants in a temporary alliance with a patron in return for produce and services of escort and hospitality rather than manual labour.[64]

[59] Foley, 'Chieftains', pp. 208–10; White, ed., *Red Book*, pp. 49–50, 66, 123.
[60] Down, 'Colonial society', p. 459.   [61] Simms, *From kings to warlords*, p. 96.
[62] Kelly, *Early Irish farming*, p. 428.   [63] Nicholls. 'Gaelic society', p. 407.
[64] Simms, *From kings to warlords*, p. 96.

In areas of English lordship, free tenants tended to be of English or Welsh origin, although more Gaelic Irish were admitted to their ranks in the fourteenth and fifteenth centuries. Free tenants might hold land for rent, customary dues, and services including suit to the lord's court. At the bottom of this scale were cottagers who held a dwelling and a small piece of land in return for rent and labour services. Cottagers often undertook other employment including paid labour to make ends meet. 'Gavillers' had better terms, owing fewer or no labour services.[65] From the fourteenth century, English lords tended to lease lands to farmers on set terms for payment because of a shortage of tenants.

BURGESSES AND GUILD MEMBERS

Many boroughs were founded in the wake of English colonisation to encourage settlement nucleation and economic growth. British immigrants were also attracted by offers of burgage tenure.[66] Burgesses paid an annual rent, generally without labour obligations, had access to common law and were free from seigneurial rights over wardship and marriage. While many rural and minor boroughs failed in the crises of the fourteenth century, larger towns and cities played an important part in Irish society. Cities enjoyed a degree of autonomy and their citizens received trading privileges and the right to vote in parliamentary and municipal elections. Their social elites were bound through fraternities or guilds.[67] The guild system of Dublin, which existed for merchants, traders or craftsmen, was formally licensed by Prince John in 1192, but probably flourished before the English invasion.[68] Membership did not require residency, but could be obtained through apprenticeship, birth or invitation and was confirmed by oaths and payments. Within the major Irish towns, guilds organised charitable, religious and social activities including plays and pageants, which made them a central part of urban life. While Gaels were largely excluded from the benefits of burgess status or guild membership, a significant number had gained entry by AD 1500.[69]

---

[65] Down, 'Colonial society', p. 468.   [66] See the earlier discussion.
[67] For religious fraternities see the following discussion.
[68] Gilbert and Mulholland, eds., *Calendar of the ancient records*, I: 1–13; Connolly and Martin, eds., *Dublin Guild*, p. xvi.
[69] Watt, 'Anglo-Irish colony', p. 396.

On the fringes of urban life were a large number of individuals without burgess or guild status who were minor craftsmen, hawkers, carters, servants and labourers. The wealth of towns also attracted individuals with no formal role in society, including beggars (whose numbers swelled during times of famine) and prostitutes, who tend to be regarded with either contempt or pity in the written sources.[70]

CRAFTSPEOPLE AND TRADERS

Craftspeople and merchants were mainstays of the urban economy, but were also a feature of rural areas, sometimes supplementing their income through agriculture. Some craftworkers, including comb makers and brewsters, were of relatively low status, producing items for everyday consumption. Other crafts including silversmithing were endowed with wealth and prestige. Craftworkers often sold their own produce, but traders served an important economic role and ranged in status from itinerant peddlars to international merchants.

The incomes of craftsmen and traders were vulnerable to economic fluctuations. These uncertainties could be mitigated by entering a long-term relationship with a patron. For example, in 1479, Matthew Ua Maíl Ruanaig was identified as a master and goldsmith to the Meic Uidhir of Fermanagh. Economic security might also be sought through social and familial bonds. Examination of guild records demonstrates the patterns of intermarriage among goldsmiths in late medieval Dublin.[71] Many women were involved in crafts and sales, often as part of a family business fulfilling less prestigious tasks, or selling products such as homemade ale.[72] On occasion, prominent female entrepreneurs come to light. These were often widows such as Dame Alice Kyteler of Kilkenny. The accusations of witchcraft made against Alice in 1324 suggest that successful businesswomen might become targets for the jealousy and suspicion of others.[73] Training in crafts and trades was often provided within families, which perpetuated lineages of craftsmen and traders. Others might learn their skills as apprentices and assistants.

Information concerning craft production and trade in rural areas is slim. Cloth production of wool and linen was time consuming and often involved women's work. Smiths and shoemakers were also common in rural areas, sometimes paying their rent in shoes

[70] Moylan, 'Vagabonds'; Dyer, *Making a living*, p. 201.   [71] Moss ed., *Art*, p. 504.
[72] Kenny, *Anglo-Irish and Gaelic women*, pp. 64–6.   [73] Williams, 'Sorcery trial'.

and horseshoes. The craft elite, including skilled carpenters and metalsmiths, who worked for aristocratic patrons, sometimes find mention in Irish chronicles. Monumental masons were employed by both secular and ecclesiastical patrons. Gaelic lords appear to have exercised rights of preemption and monopoly that limited the power of traders in their territories. Nevertheless, some successful Gaelic merchant families were able to extend their operations into English towns in the later Middle Ages.[74]

The municipal records of medieval Ireland provide detailed insight into the specialised crafts and salespeople operating within areas of English lordship. Production and sales of food and drink, cloth, leather, metalwork and woodwork emerge as important sectors of the urban economy, with many arcane-sounding names including coopers (barrel makers), cordwainers (shoemakers), crokers (potters) and cutlers (makers of knives and other small implements) appearing in urban records.[75] Mercantile oligarchs emerged, with the richest town dwellers often occupying municipal offices and sometimes acting as government advisors. Foreign merchants might also rise to a position of influence, exemplified by the Italian families of Riccardi and Frescobaldi who collected customs in Ireland for Edward I, although political machinations would cause both families to fall from power.[76]

SERVITORS AND PROFESSIONALS

The position of the government and the elite was bolstered by a range of skilled professionals. These had diverse roles and included clerks, judges, estate workers, poets, musicians and warriors. The centralised English government created posts within the treasury, chancery, and judiciary in Dublin and in the shires. In areas of Gaelic lordship, officers, judges and lawyers were often hereditary roles, fulfilled by generations of families maintained by fees for their services, and compensated by lands or a portion of the taxes and tributes levied in the territory where they worked.[77]

Larger landowners and lords employed officers to help run their estates. In areas of English lordship demesne, lands were usually overseen by reeves or bailiffs who rendered annual accounts. The reeve

[74] Nicholls, 'Gaelic society', p. 419.
[75] Connolly and Martin, eds., *Dublin Guild*, p. 157.
[76] Childs and O'Neill, 'Overseas trade', pp. 509–10; Hudson, 'Changing economy', p. 63.
[77] Nicholls, *Gaelic and Gaelicised Ireland*, pp. 40–1, 79–81.

was placed in charge of a single manor in return for wages and allowances, while a bailiff might oversee a group of manors. The overall direction of estates usually lay with a steward (Latin *senescallus*) who would then report to his lord. In Gaelic areas *maoir* or stewards collected rents and dues, while the *rechtaire* was a high-ranking official sometimes equated with a *senescallus*, who might fulfil a range of duties and wield power as a noble in his own right.[78]

An essential feature of the households of greater lords was entertainment. The influence that poets and musicians could wield aroused mistrust among English authorities. In 1366, the 'Statutes of Kilkenny' forbade the employment of *tympanours, fferdanes, skelaghes, bablers, rymours and clarsaghours* ('players of stringed instruments, men of learning, storytellers, babblers, poets and harp players') by the English.[79] Poets continued to have an important role in Irish society as eulogists of the elite, and their 'PR' dimension is reflected in their continuing place in the inauguration of Gaelic leaders during the late Middle Ages. Despite prohibitions, Gaelic poets and musicians were employed in the halls of Anglo-Irish lords. A substantial volume of poetry composed under Gaelic and English patronage has survived. Performing artists were sometimes credited with powers that bordered on the supernatural.[80] Bards and musicians also worked outside the corridors of power as popular entertainers, a vocation that was sometimes open to women as well as men, although women who pursued this career might face legal and social discrimination.[81]

Over the course of the late Middle Ages, there was an amalgam of Gaelic and English practices in the roles of officers, servants and retainers. This is reflected in linguistic borrowings, such as the title of *marascál* (marshal) borrowed into Irish from Old French *mareschal*. It is more broadly seen in the hybrid legal, financial and military practices employed by Gaelic and English lords in Ireland during the fifteenth century.

FIGHTING MEN

At the most basic level, power in the late Middle Ages was maintained by violence or the threat of violence. The decentralised structures of

[78] Simms, *From kings to warlords*, pp. 79–81.
[79] Curtis and McDowell, trans., *Irish historical documents*, p. 55.   [80] *AFM, s.a.* 1414.
[81] Nicholls, *Gaelic and Gaelicised Ireland*, pp. 82–4; Simms, 'Changing patterns', p. 165; Kenny, *Anglo-Irish and Gaelic women*, p. 36.

authority in Ireland made it imperative for lords to have access to a body of fighting men, as well as being trained in arms themselves. Areas under the English crown drew on quotas of military service owed by their direct tenants (later transmuted to a monetary payment called 'scutage'). Adult males were also to serve in local defence, equipped according to their status. From the thirteenth century, taxes were levied to raise paid armies. Professional soldiers were sometime recruited from abroad. For example, in 1337, the new justiciar John Charlton brought 200 Welsh archers with him, and in 1361 Lionel, duke of Clarence, brought 360 mounted archers from Lancashire.[82] From the late thirteenth century the word kerne (from Irish *ceithearn* 'troop') was used to describe Gaelic foot soldiers serving the English as mercenaries. One interesting example of a Gaelic mercenary was Philip Ua Ragallaig. In 1294–5 the crown paid him to help secure Newcastle (Co. Wicklow), but in 1302 the crown paid another body of men to detain the same Ua Ragallaig 'and other Irish felons', showing how tenuous bought allegiances could be.[83]

In Gaelic areas, there was the same obligation for adult males (excluding clergy) to serve in local defence and to supply weapons and horses if they were able. Gaelic lords also hired mercenaries. The burdening of paying and quartering these troops fell to their subjects. From the late twelfth century, the use of mercenaries increased, and some were recruited from Wales and England, perhaps to compete with the arms and techniques of the Anglo-Irish.[84] From the late thirteenth century galloglasses (*gallóclaig*) hired from the highlands and islands of Scotland were the most prominent foreign mercenaries. In addition to military service, political alliances were sought across the North Channel. For example, in 1259 Áed Ua Conchobuir of Connacht acquired a force of 160 men as a dowry for the daughter of Dubgall Mac Ruaidrí, king of the Hebrides.[85] A number of galloglass kindreds including the Meic Suibne and Meic Domnaill settled permanently in Ireland.[86] By the fifteenth century English and Gaelic lords alike maintained household retinues of armed men for protection and small-scale warfare. Some of these retainers were hereditary and gained positions of high status. These troops also became

---

[82] Dryburgh and Smith, eds., *Handbook and select calendar*, p. 315; Frame, 'Defence', p. 82.

[83] Frame, 'Defence', p. 84; Cullinan, *Thirty-Eighth Report*, pp. 68, 87.

[84] Simms, *From kings to warlords*, pp. 119–20.   [85] Ibid., p. 110; *AConn, s.a.* 1259.

[86] Nicholls, *Gaelic and Gaelicised Ireland*, pp. 87–90.

an outward symbol of prestige that excited comment from English
commentators and visitors to Ireland.

LORDSHIP AND SUCCESSION

At the apex of the secular hierarchy in Ireland were kings and greater
nobles.[87] This minority group obtained their status largely by virtue
of inheritance. Succession to the greater Gaelic lordships was determined by election within the ruling lineage. Gaelic lordship was conceived of as head of a people rather than a defined territory, reflected
in the term *airecht* 'assembly' that was often used for lordship. In
English areas, much of the land was held from the king by hereditary tenants-in-chief who succeeded by primogeniture. While the
institutions and actions of lords are discussed in the following chapter, the principles of succession and the role of kinship are important
aspects of society in late medieval Ireland and are presented here.

Succession within Gaelic lordships theoretically went to the wor-
thiest elected member of the royal lineage or *derbfhine* (a king group
defined by four generations) of a former lord.[88] As Irish law admitted inheritance rights to most illegitimate children, this could lead
to large number of candidates. For example, Toirdelbach '*in fhína*'
('of the wine') lord of Tír Chonaill who died in 1423 sired eighteen
sons by ten different women and fifty-nine grandsons in the male
line.[89] To avoid violent competition a tanist (*tánaiste*, literally 'second')
may have been chosen within the lord's lifetime as a second in command who might succeed on his death. The terms *adbar ríg* or *rígdamna* meaning 'materials of a king' defined those who were eligible
to succeed and may refer to two or more contenders. Despite the risks
of a wide pool of distant cousins stepping forward to claim power, it
was common for a son to succeed his father in the larger Irish lordships. For example, among the Meic Carthaig Mór of Munster, son
succeeded father for six generations between 1359 and 1508.[90]

When rival claimants arose, overlords, leading vassals or neighbouring lords might play a decisive role by backing one individual.
There are many incidents in the twelfth century of overlords inter-
vening in succession disputes or dividing power between contenders,
perhaps to deliberately weaken their subjects or rivals. When rival
neighbours backed opposing candidates, this could also weaken a

---

[87] Simms, 'Changing patterns'.   [88] Nicholls, *Gaelic and Gaelicised Ireland*, p. 26.
[89] Nicholls, *Gaelic and Gaelicised Ireland*, p. 11.   [90] Ibid., p. 27.

lordship through prolonged warfare. The role of leading vassals or kindreds in confirming succession was sometimes formalised in late medieval ceremonies of inauguration.[91] If a dispute between co-heirs could not be settled, a lordship could be permanently divided, but this rarely occurred without dispute.

The Gaelic system of elective succession, while potentially disruptive, tended to ensure that only capable individuals from the leading kin group took power. It also avoided the problems of minorities or the cessation of a male line, which tended to compromise the power of lordships operating under the system of primogeniture. English law distinguished between legitimate and illegitimate children, allowing legitimate daughters to succeed if there were no legitimate sons.[92] This led to something of a crisis in the 1240s when a series of leading English lords died without adult male heirs, including the de Lacys of Meath and Ulster, the Marshals of Leinster and de Burgh of Connacht.[93] Both in England and Ireland there was some reluctance to accept primogeniture when it would result in the property passing out of the male line. Thus in 1299 the Rochefords of Ikeathy (Co. Kildare) sought to disinherit daughters in order to protect their lordship.[94] Some English lords, including the Burkes, Dillons and Delameres, also adopted Gaelic succession practices from the late fourteenth century in Connacht and Westmeath.[95]

The failure of adult male succession in areas of English lordship could offer a profitable opportunity to the king who could exercise rights of escheat or wardship over a minor or unmarried female heir. This provided opportunities to reward favourites. For example, after the death of Hugh de Lacy in 1243 the earldom of Ulster was retained by Henry III and granted in 1254 to his son Lord Edward.[96] The rejection of primogeniture thereby reduced the opportunities of English royal intervention within a lordship. Nevertheless, primogeniture was maintained by the majority of English lords as an expression of their loyalty to the English crown. It offered some security that estates would remain intact as long as there was a legitimate son. It also removed a major incentive for violent disputes between kinsmen, although in this respect it was not always successful.[97]

[91] See the later discussion.   [92] Verstraten Veach, 'Anglicisation', pp. 128–9.
[93] Curtis, *History*, p. 151.   [94] Frame, *Ireland and Britain*, p. 212.
[95] Nicholls, 'Gaelic society', p. 423.   [96] Curtis, *History*, p. 152.
[97] Nicholls, 'Gaelic society', pp. 423–4.

MARRIAGE

Marriage was often treated by Gaelic and English elites as a political and fiscal transaction. However, there were significant differences between marriage laws in each society that might be exploited or cause friction as the two systems came into contact. In English society, a woman was expected to bring a dowry and any property she owned to her marriage, which then passed under the control of her husband, although he could not sell or give away her property without permission.[98] When a husband died the widow was entitled to receive one-third of her husband's estate, or if there were no children, she received half. In Gaelic society, the husband usually paid a bride price, which could be returned if the marriage broke up due to the fault of the bride. The bride's family provided a marriage portion, which could be returned on divorce or if the husband died. By the fifteenth century, the Gaelic Irish adopted the canon law principle of the dowry, which lessened the significance of the other customary payments.[99] A Gaelic Irish wife was nevertheless legally free to administer and alienate her own property.

When marriage occurred between individuals from different legal traditions, problems could arise. Both spouses could access Gaelic law, but English law was not extended to a marriage partner of an English person until the fourteenth century, and only then if it was applied for. One of the grievances reported to Pope John XXII by the Gaelic nobility in 1317 was that Gaelic women who married English husbands were denied the right to receive one-third of their husband's property on his death.[100] On the other hand, Gaelic marriage customs tended not to observe canon law. Cohabitation before marriage was not uncommon, and marriages could be entered into and terminated more freely than under English law by either partner. Towards the end of the Middle Ages, abandoned spouses increasingly used ecclesiastical courts to reach a financial settlement or oblige the return of their partner. This suggests that laws could be used selectively as matters of principle or conflict arose.[101]

Recourse was frequently made to canon law when partners were joined within prohibited degrees of kinship. From 1215 the papacy

---

[98] Kenny, 'Anglo-Irish and Gaelic marriage', p. 28.
[99] Nicholls, *Gaelic and Gaelicised Ireland*, p. 76.
[100] Curtis and McDowell, trans., *Irish historical documents*, p. 41.
[101] Kenny, 'Anglo-Irish and Gaelic marriage', p. 40

forbade marriage within four degrees of kinship, that is, to anyone related within four generations (i.e. including second cousins) by blood or affinity (i.e. the prospective partner should not have had sex with any relatives within the prohibited degrees). Prior to 1215 the rule had applied to seven degrees of kinship, but this became unworkable.[102] The elites of medieval Europe generally intermarried. In Gaelic society, where canon law was not strictly observed, marriage within the prohibited degrees was common. This was also a characteristic of English society in Ireland. When Richard Power, sheriff of Waterford, married Elena Butler, they were related according to canon law by six different criteria.[103] These prohibited degrees of kinship might later provide a convenient excuse to end an unwanted union. Nevertheless, dissolving a marriage through the church courts was a lengthy and expensive process. A formal divorce might only be pursued if either partner wished to pursue a legitimate remarriage. In Gaelic society, the need to follow these rules may have been less urgent as many illegitimate children maintained rights of inheritance. While some marriages might be dissolved due to consanguinity, couples who were related within prohibited degrees sometimes sought to legalise their union through papal dispensations. Often the basis for legalising a union was that the couple had already had children together.[104]

The relative freedom of Gaelic women in relation to property and divorce might mean they were less beholden to their spouses than were English women. However, as high-status marriage was often a matter of family agreement rather than independent volition, and expectations of gender roles were socially determined, it is questionable how much freedom Gaelic women really had. A minority of Gaelic women gained elevated status as patrons to the Church and of poets. Some women also exhibited a high degree of independence through force of personality. In 1316 Derbforgaill, wife of Áed Ua Domnaill, king of Tír Chonaill, persuaded her husband to jointly lead a military expedition into Carbury (Drumcliff, Co. Sligo). Dissatisfied with the peace that her husband made with Ruaidrí Ua Conchobuir, Derbforgaill hired a band of galloglasses to kill Ruaidrí in the following year, which violated her husband's oaths.[105] In English society,

---

[102] Schroeder, ed. and trans., *Disciplinary*, pp. 236–96 at §§50–2.
[103] Nicholls, *Gaelic and Gaelicised Ireland*, second edition, p. 85.
[104] Nicholls, *Gaelic and Gaelicised Ireland*, p. 75.
[105] *AConn, s.aa.* 1315, 1316; Kenny, 'Anglo-Irish and Gaelic marriage', p. 34.

wives may have sometimes shared in decision making or been the dominant partner, but they might only achieve economic and legal independence in widowhood.

Women in both Gaelic and English society were expected to confine sexual relations within marriage; however, outside the teachings of the church, this seems to have been less expected of men. Concubines of high-ranking men might be publicly acknowledged, especially in Gaelic society where they were entitled to legal protection for themselves and their offspring.[106] These arrangements inevitably compromised the interests of an official wife and her children. The illegitimate children of English lords were at a disadvantage in comparison to their Gaelic peers as they lacked the entitlement to paternal support.[107] Insecurities arising from potential repudiation, succession and inheritance may have been a controlling factor in any relationship. Generally speaking, in both Gaelic and English society, men of status wielded authority over their wives and dependants.

FOSTERAGE

In addition to ties of blood and marriage, fosterage generated lasting bonds between families. The outlines of medieval fosterage in Ireland are laid down in *Cáin Íarraith* at the end of the seventh century. The development of this practice over time can be compared in 'H. C.'s tract' of the sixteenth century.[108] This tract outlines five methods of fostering. One of these, 'Milk nurse fostering', compares with the earlier practice of fostering for affection. In this arrangement, the child would be reared by the family until adulthood, and the foster parents did not expect to give or receive payment and maintained the child themselves. Other forms of fosterage involved a fee. Usually children of higher rank were fostered by those of lesser status. The payments and obligations between parties depended on the duration and nature of the contract. Fosterage was regarded as important in creating vertical ties between ranks, whereas marriage was seen to be more appropriate between social equals.

Child mortality in medieval society was high, and children were considered precious, both in their own right and as a resource to help

---

[106] Simms, 'Legal position', pp. 101–2.
[107] Kenny, *Anglo-Irish and Gaelic women*, pp. 127–9.
[108] Fitzsimons, 'Fosterage', p. 138.

cement alliances between people.[109] The utility of children in forging social bonds did not imply that they were less loved by their birth or foster families. This may be exemplified in a thirteenth-century poem *Teastá Eochair Ghlais Ghaoidheal* which laments the death of Gormflaith, five-year-old daughter of Domnall Mór Ua Domnaill, king of Tír Chonaill. She was being fostered by a member of the rival Uí Néill dynasty. Gormflaith was said to be the key to peace between both families and the assets of clothing, cattle and revenues associated with her fosterage are mentioned. Aside from these references to the contractual aspects of fosterage, the grief of the mother and of the foster mother of the child is dwelt upon at length, and the personal qualities of Gormflaith in her behaviour and looks are praised.[110]

Foster parents were expected to raise, educate and maintain children in a manner appropriate to the social standing of the child's father, and children's experience in fosterage would be important for the future roles they would play in society. Fosterage was practiced in both Gaelic and Anglo-Irish communities. The bonds of fosterage aroused concern in the royal government, which sought to outlaw cross-cultural fosterage in the fourteenth century.[111] However, these laws had limited effect and exemptions to the rule were granted. According to 'The State of Ireland and Plan for its Reformation' written for Henry VIII in 1515, one of the reasons that royal power was so diminished in Ireland was that 'the Englyshe noble folke useith to deluyver therre children to the Kynges Irysshe enymes to foster'.[112]

GOSSIPRED

Gossipred was a pledge of fraternal association between individuals guaranteed by religious ritual, often between a lord and client. Its origins lie in the Old English term *godssib* meaning spiritual kin, which applied in Middle English to bonds of godparenthood and close friendship. This fictive kinship differed from marriage and fosterage as it did not require a member of one family to cohabit with another. 'H. C.'s tract' outlines four types of gossipred; the first was the sponsorship of baptism performed through public ceremony at

---

[109] Ní Chonaill, 'Child centred law', p. 24.
[110] Bourke *et al.*, eds., *Field day anthology*, IV: 308–11.
[111] Curtis and McDowell, trans., *Irish historical documents*, p. 53.
[112] Public Record Office, ed., *Calendar of state papers, foreign and domestic: Henry VIII*, II: 13.

the church font, thereby winning the support of the godparent or lord. The second type of gossipred was characterised by the symbolic breaking of bread by both parties to mark their pledge and a gift or salary from the lord to the client. The third form of gossipred was a more casual sworn allegiance between parties to serve a particular end. The last form of gossipred described by H. C. involved the parties receiving the sacrament of communion in pledge to uphold their affinity.[113]

The practices of gossipred – namely, godparenthood, sworn brotherhood and sworn allegiance – were common in late Medieval Europe.[114] Gerald of Wales describes the ritual of sworn brotherhood in Ireland. The two parties process around a church before entering it and swearing oaths followed by the celebration of mass. He also claimed the men drank each other's blood, but this may be a garbled account of consuming Christ's blood in mass.[115] Another description of gossipred is provided by the 'Annals of Connacht' for the year 1277. It recounts that Brian Ruad Ua Briain was treacherously slain by Thomas de Clare despite the men having bound themselves by oaths on the relics of Munster and mixing their blood in one vessel.[116] These accounts compare with the ritual of sworn brotherhood between the dukes of Orléans and Burgundy in November 1407. Their oaths were made before an assembly and consecrated by mass.[117] It is possible that the origins of sworn affinity overseen by the church lay with the Continental peace movement of the eleventh century. The early role of the church in peacemaking can be seen in the career of Cellach, archbishop of Armagh, who oversaw temporary truces between the warring over-kings of Munster and Northern Uí Néill in 1107, 1109 and 1113.[118]

English writers are scathing about sworn allegiances, and as with marriage and fosterage, attempts were made to ban these vows of friendship between the English and Irish. Nevertheless, fictive kinship was important in a land where power was decentralised and family identity was key to social standing and well-being. Similar circumstances prevailed elsewhere in medieval Europe.[119] The ties of fictive

---

[113] Fitzsimons, 'Fosterage', pp. 147–8.   [114] Bray, *Friend*, pp. 17, 27–8.

[115] O'Meara, ed., 'Giraldus Cambrensis in Topographia Hibernie', p. 168; O'Meara, trans., *History and topography of Ireland* p. 108. Cf. Oschema, 'Blood-brothers', pp. 279, 298.

[116] *AConn, s.a.* 1277.   [117] Bray, *Friend*, pp. 24–5.

[118] *AU, s.aa.* 1107, 1109, 1113.   [119] Wormald, *Lords*.

kinship helped avoid conflicts and aided acculturation between the Gaelic and Anglo-Irish elites.

CONCLUSION

The arrival of Henry II in Ireland was the culmination of a century of changing English attitudes towards Ireland and the emergence of a colonising mentality. The years after 1171 witnessed widespread redistribution of lands out of Gaelic control and English immigration. Society would be characterised thereafter by a division between Gaels and 'the English born in Ireland'. This dualism was enforced through legal apartheid, which restricted Gaels' access to English common law until the fourteenth century. From the late thirteenth century, English statutes sought to prevent acculturation. Based on these rules, studies of later medieval Ireland have tended to highlight the boundaries between Gaelic and English and culture. However, segregation was not strictly enforced, and the concept of a contact zone with overlapping spheres of influence may better encapsulate relations between the different populations in Ireland.

Throughout Ireland, the years from 1100 until the 1270s witnessed significant population growth. This pattern was reversed from the closing decades of the thirteenth century by climatic deterioration and the diminished fertility of land that resulted from the over-exploitation of resources. Malnourishment made communities more susceptible to plague in the fourteenth century, and the Black Death seems to have had a disproportionate impact on the English community in Ireland. The devastation wreaked by recurrent episodes of pestilence facilitated the territorial and political decline of the English colony and a corresponding rise in the territorial power of Gaelic lords. As power shifted politically and demographically, the level of acculturation between English and Irish societies increased.

9

POLITICS AD 1100–1500

•

Kingship continued to be the main political institution in Ireland in the late Middle Ages. However, no single king achieved island-wide supremacy. The twelfth century witnessed innovations in governmental structures as part of a centralising agenda. The creation of the English colony introduced new hierarchies based on foreign models. Nevertheless, English kings were often preoccupied with events in France or closer to home. They delegated leadership to an English elite, and the conquest of Ireland proceeded in a piecemeal and incomplete fashion. As the English colony declined in the fourteenth and fifteenth centuries, what had once been a profitable royal endeavour eventually became a burden on English royal finances. In northern and western Ireland, the major Gaelic dynasties that wielded power in the pre-invasion period remained as powers to be reckoned with throughout the later Middle Ages. They were able to regain a significant amount of territory that had been previously lost to the English. The Gaelic lords selectively adopted military and governmental innovations that allowed them to wield power more effectively and defend their lands. The regional histories of the late Middle Ages provide fascinating case studies of cross-cultural contact. Gaelic and Anglo-Irish lords borrowed each other's practices and often sought common ground as an alternative to open warfare. By the fifteenth century, hybrid legal, financial and military practices were employed by both English and Gaelic elites. Despite attempts within the English colony to maintain clear separation between the

English and Irish, cultural hybridisation and political interaction were facilitated by the absence of a strong central authority.

KINGS OF IRELAND WITH OPPOSITION

In the eleventh and twelfth centuries power became concentrated into fewer hands. During the twelfth century, the lower grades of Irish kingship declined in their independence as provincial over-kings battled it out for supremacy. A series of able individuals rose to the fore as kings of all Ireland 'with opposition', but their success was rarely passed to the next generation. The leading families of the Ireland were well matched in resources, regional identities were strong, tensions within families could be fatal, and a kingship over all Ireland lacked the institutional underpinnings to become an effective reality. It was in these circumstances that kings increasingly sought external support for their ambitions. One infamous example was Diarmait Mac Murchada's appeal to Henry II.

In 1100 the most powerful king in Ireland was Muirchertach Ua Briain of Munster, a great grandson of Brian Boru. Muirchertach struggled to gain recognition of his over-kingship in Ulster. In 1101 his forces destroyed the fortress of his Meic Lochlainn rivals at Grianán of Aileach on the Inishowen peninsula, which brought the kingship of all Ireland within his reach. In the same year Muirchertach presided over a synod at Cashel where he promoted the movement for Church reform that was gaining momentum in northern Europe. Muirchertach was a king with wide-ranging external connections. He corresponded with Anselm, archbishop of Canterbury; arranged two foreign marriages for his daughters; placed a nephew in charge of the kingdom of Man and the Isles; and received the diplomatic gift of a camel from King Edgar of Scotland. Muirchertach was also an enthusiastic patron of the arts and may have overseen the composition of the propaganda tracts *Cogad Gáedel re Gallaib* ('The War of the Gaels and the Foreigners') and *Lebor na Cert* ('Book of Rights'), which promoted the concept of an Uí Briain kingship of all Ireland.[1] For the remainder of his reign, Muirchertach faced continuous opposition from the Meic Lochlainn and from within his own family. When Muirchertach fell ill in 1114, power was temporarily

---

[1] Candon, 'Muirchertach Ua Briain'; Duffy, 'The career of Muirchertach'.

seized by his brother Diarmait. Toirdelbach Ua Conchobuir of Connacht took the opportunity to assert his own claim to supremacy by invading Munster in the following year. Muirchertach resigned from power in 1118 and Toirdelbach divided his kingdom between the Meic Carthaig in the south (Desmond) and the Uí, Briain in the north (Thomond).

After Toirdelbach Ua Conchobuir had quelled the power of Uí Briain, he turned against the Ua Maíl Sechnaill king of Mide, forcing him to flee to Ulster. Toirdelbach's celebration of the *Óenach Tailten* (assembly of Teltown) in Meath in 1120 was an assertion of high kingship that discomfited his former Meic Lochlainn allies. The death of Domnall Mac Lochlainn in the following year provided an opportunity for Toirdelbach to assert his claims. In 1124 a coalition of Meath, Munster, Osraige and Leinster formed against Toirdelbach, but by 1127 he had secured his supremacy over each of these rivals. Toirdelbach displayed his authority not only through military campaigns and the construction of fortresses but also through patronage of the church. Among other things he acquired a fragment of the True Cross for the church of Roscommon and commissioned the magnificent 'Cross of Cong' to enshrine it.[2]

By 1133 Toirdelbach's enemies were gaining in strength, and he was forced to make peace with the Uí Briain. A few years later Toirdelbach turned against his own family, fearing that plans to replace him were afoot. He imprisoned his son Ruaidrí and had another son, Áed, blinded. Toirdelbach held onto power until 1150 when he finally recognised the supremacy of Muirchertach Mac Lochlainn. Although he was advancing in years, Toirdelbach was not content to take a back seat in Irish politics, and in 1154 he won a naval victory over Mac Lochlainn's Hebridean mercenaries. Toirdelbach was unable to follow up with victory on land and contented himself with undermining Mac Lochlainn's support in southern Ireland.[3]

When Toirdelbach died in 1156, Muirchertach Mac Lochlainn took up the claim to high kingship. Muirchertach emulated previous kings in presiding over a synod (at Mellifont, Co. Louth) in 1157 and through conspicuous patronage of the church.[4] Muirchertach, like his immediate predecessors, was more ruthless than pious. After Muirchertach blinded Eochaid Mac Duinn Sléibe, king of Ulaid, in

[2] Flanagan, 'High-kings', pp. 917–18.
[3] O'Byrne, 'Ua Conchobhair, Tairrdelbach'.   [4] Duffy, *Ireland*, pp. 54–5.

1166 many of his northern allies deserted him, and he was killed by Mac Duinn Sléibe's foster father, Ua Cerbaill of Airgíalla, in revenge. Ruaidrí Ua Conchobuir had been a thorn in Mac Lochlainn's side since 1156. In 1160 and 1161 he campaigned in Meath and southern Ireland, forging an alliance with Tigernán Ua Ruairc of Bréifne. In 1166 when Mac Lochlainn's grip on power was unravelling, Ruaidrí marched on Dublin to capture the strategically important settlement and then moved north and divided Mac Lochlainn's lands following his death. Diarmait Mac Murchada of Leinster had been an ally of Mac Lochlainn who opposed Ruaidrí's kingship. As a result, Ruaidrí's allies invaded Diarmait's territories, led by Tigernán Ua Ruairc, who had a personal score to settle with Diarmait for the abduction of his wife fourteen years earlier. The attack caused Diarmait to flee from Ireland in 1166. Diarmait returned with English mercenaries the following year and regained his lands in south Leinster in return for delivering hostages to Ruaidrí and a payment of gold to Tigernán to lessen the 'venom of his fury' for prior insults.[5] In 1169, Diarmait invited more troops from Britain to help him win back the kingdom of Leinster. In 1170, buoyed up by further forces from Britain, he directly challenged Ruaidrí Ua Conchobuir by marching towards Tara in a bid to claim the over-kingship of Ireland, and his forces plundered a strong of churches en route. Ruaidrí responded by killing the hostages Diarmait had previously granted to him. It was a high price to pay for ambition as the hostages included a son and a grandson of Diarmait. Ruaidrí would also outlive Diarmait and maintain his supremacy in Ireland until the arrival of Henry II.[6]

THE ENGLISH INVASION

When Diarmait lost his throne in 1166 it may have seemed natural for him to appeal to a powerful neighbour with whom he had previously enjoyed positive relations. Henry II and Diarmait had shared common interests in the Irish Sea trade, and common friends such as Robert fitzHarding in Bristol. Henry seemed to regard Diarmait as a safe leader for the strategically important Irish ports that faced England. When Muirchertach Mac Lochlainn seized direct control of Dublin in 1154, this prompted Henry to consider invading Ireland

[5] Scott and Martin, eds., *Expugnatio*, p. 25.
[6] Flanagan, 'High-kings with opposition', pp. 932–3.

to secure his concerns there. This plan found favour with the church of Canterbury, which sought to bring Dublin within its jurisdiction. Nevertheless, the plan was temporarily shelved and Diarmait regained his position.[7] In 1165 Henry hired the Dublin fleet for his Welsh campaigns. When Diarmait was chased from Ireland the following year, he travelled to Aquitaine and obtained Henry's permission to raise a mercenary force from among his subjects.[8]

Diarmait used the troops he recruited to regain control of Leinster. To formalise his alliance with Richard de Clare, lord of Strigoil and earl of Pembroke (popularly known as Strongbow), Diarmait granted the hand of his daughter Aífe in 1170. It seems unlikely that the bride came with the promise of a kingdom as Diarmait had three sons at the time (although one had been blinded by a political rival in 1169, and one would be killed later in 1170). Had Diarmait offered Strongbow succession to his kingship together with his daughter, he must have foreseen the imposition of foreign lordship over a large swathe of Ireland. Transmarine alliances were not unprecedented. Nearly seventy years earlier, a Munster over-king, Muirchertach Ua Briain, had married his daughter to Arnulf de Montgomery, who held lands in southwest Wales and Yorkshire. When Strongbow overrode the claims of Diarmait's male relatives and became king of Leinster in 1171, Henry II came to subdue this over-mighty subject and seize the Irish Sea ports for himself.[9]

Henry's navy arrived at Waterford in October 1171. Strongbow tendered his submission and surrendered Dublin, Waterford and Wexford for Henry's personal use. Dublin was then granted to the loyal subjects of Bristol with an eye to developing the economic potential of Irish Sea trade. Henry celebrated Christmas in Dublin where lavish entertainment was offered to Irish kings who came to recognise his authority.[10] One major player in Irish politics who refrained from this act was Ruaidrí Ua Conchobuir. Nevertheless, such a display of power by a mighty and charismatic foreign king must have caused grave concern to Ruaidrí. Henry's six-month visit to Ireland had an indelible impact and concluded with the speculative grant of Meath to Hugh de Lacy.[11] This grant brought the wealthiest

---

[7] Duffy, *Ireland*, p. 70.   [8] Flanagan, *Irish society*, p. 56.
[9] O'Byrne, *War*, pp. 7–12.   [10] Flanagan, *Irish society*, pp. 308–11.
[11] Mills and McEnery, eds., *Calendar of the Gormanston Register*, pp. 6, 177.

lands of Ireland into English hands and may have been intended as a check on the ambitions of Strongbow.

A full conquest of Ireland, however, was not on Henry's agenda. In 1173, he was faced with a rebellion from his two eldest sons supported by the king of France. Henry called on Strongbow to fight on his behalf in Normandy. The departure of English troops from Ireland prompted a Gaelic uprising against the English settlers in Leinster and Meath, whose presence was regarded as unwelcome and unjust.[12] A treaty was concluded between Henry and Ruaidrí, king of Connaught, at Windsor in 1175. It allowed Ruaidrí to hold his lands peacefully in return for obedience to the English king and a hefty annual tribute.[13] Ruaidrí was also obliged to keep his own subjects loyal to the English king. The Treaty of Windsor raised the possibility that there could be two kings in Ireland, one English over-king and one Gaelic sub-king, to divide the island between them. Nevertheless, the agreement may have been a short-term ploy by Henry to delay Ruaidrí from taking further military action. Henry II's followers disregarded the terms immediately, and in 1177 Henry granted away the lands of Munster to his followers.[14] The English conquests in Ireland would continue in a piecemeal and incomplete fashion, causing the island to remain politically segregated. For the next two centuries, English royal involvement in Ireland was normally indirect and focused on fiscal exploitation to fund wars in Britain and the Continent. The fact that Ireland remained divided may have initially suited English monarchs. It lessened the risk that over-mighty subjects would control the island contrary to their own interests. The incompleteness of the first stage of conquest was perhaps as much by design as through incompetence.

THE LORDSHIP OF IRELAND

In 1177, Henry sought to make his youngest son John, king of Ireland. Henry may have intended the Irish colony to pass down the cadet line of the royal house as a separate kingdom. A crown was even arranged with the pope, but the scheme was not put into effect because of the deaths of popes favourable to it. Instead John was made Lord of Ireland. In 1185 Henry sent John to assume his lordship in

---

[12] Duffy, *Ireland*, pp. 77–9; O'Byrne, *War*, p. 15.
[13] Flanagan, *Irish society*, pp. 312–13.   [14] Duffy, *Ireland*, p. 91.

person, but John's visit was troubled. On the one hand, John managed to secure the borders of Leinster through a programme of land grants and castle building. On the other, he was said to have insulted and alienated some Irish kings, and he fell out with Hugh de Lacy, the most powerful English magnate in the island.[15] King Henry may have sought to establish a counterweight to de Lacy by arranging the marriage of his trusted knight William Marshal to Isabel, heiress of Strongbow. The marriage took place with the support of the newly crowned Richard I in 1189.[16] Another great power in Ireland who caused concern to the English crown was John de Courcy, an adventurer who had carved out lands in Ulster in 1177. De Courcy styled himself *princeps Ulidiae* (prince of Ulster) and behaved in royal fashion, distributing lands, minting coin and marrying the Manx princess Affreca in 1180. In 1185 Henry appointed de Courcy, Justiciar of Ireland, to secure his loyalty.[17] When Henry II died and John became king of England, he sought to bring down the great men who had established themselves in Ireland under his father.

John's accession to the kingship of England united the lordship of Ireland with the English crown. During his reign, English power continued to expand through speculative grants and the exploitation of conflicts between Irish rulers. John took an interest in fortifying strategic sites and ordered magnificent castles to be built at Limerick and Dublin (see Figure 9.1). The loss of Normandy from English control in 1204 may have focused John's attention of the development of the royal administration in Dublin and the stimulation of the Irish economy. John introduced a mint and an exchequer. He also brought English common law to Ireland on his second visit to Ireland in 1210.[18] John may have intended there to be a single law for his English and Irish subjects. However English magnates took care to exclude the Gaelic Irish from access to English royal courts.

John's own dealings with Gaelic lords were not uniformly antagonistic. In 1210 Donnchad Cairprech Ua Briain, king of Thomond, formally submitted to John and was knighted.[19] In 1215 he offered a deal to Cathal Crobderg Ua Conchobuir that Cathal should hold all Connacht apart from Athlone for an annual payment of 300 marks; however, the charter was not executed.[20] Despite these manoeuvres

[15] Ibid., pp. 94, 99, 101–2. [16] Crouch, *William Marshal*, pp. 67–9.
[17] Martin, 'John', pp. 134–6. [18] Duffy, *Ireland*, p. 98.
[19] Martin, 'John', p. 130. [20] Frame, *Colonial Ireland*, p. 50.

Figure 9.1 King John's Castle, Limerick

John did not reach a settlement with the most powerful Gaelic rulers, and the island remained in a state of war. John also struggled to cultivate good relations with the major English vassals in Ireland. These included John de Courcy and Hugh II de Lacy. The king handed John de Courcy's lands in Ulster to de Lacy in 1205, which prompted de Courcy to rebel. De Courcy was later pardoned in 1210 and allied with the king against his former rival de Lacy. Hugh II de Lacy would later return to Ireland after King John's death and clash with his successor Henry III.[21]

John's later years were beset by military failure in France and disputes with the papacy and his magnates. In these circumstances authority in Ireland was delegated to Henry of London, who became Justiciar of Ireland and Archbishop of Dublin in 1213.[22] John died ignominiously in 1216 of dysentery while campaigning against his own barons in England. It is often said that John's successors had little interest in Irish affairs. While decision making fell into the hands of justiciars, English kings did maintain some involvement in Ireland

---

[21] Martin, 'John', pp. 136, 141–2.
[22] Frame, *Colonial Ireland*, p. 106; Duffy, *Ireland*, p. 105.

through the appointment of trusted officers and by sending junior members of the royal family to Ireland.[23]

John's son Henry was only nine years old when he became king. His regent William Marshal held extensive lands in Ireland, England and Wales, which helped to secure the loyalty of the Irish colony to the boy king. In 1217 Magna Carta was issued in Ireland, defining the limits of royal power and protecting the rights of barons and freemen.[24] However, no attempt was made to secure the rights of the native Irish, which were under increasing pressure. In 1217, it was ordered that no Irishman could be elected to any cathedral church, a position that was opposed by the papacy. Other abuses of the Church for political ends were rife. De Marisco who served as justicar from 1215 to 1221 intruded his nephew into the bishopric of Killaloe (Co. Clare) in 1216 without canonical election or papal provision, while William Marshal flouted threats of papal excommunication by appropriating lands from the bishopric of Ferns.[25]

The level of independence exercised by the English in Ireland could pose a threat to their king. Hugh II de Lacy of Ulster and Meath was in rebellion from Henry's accession until his earldom was restored in 1227.[26] Henry also came into conflict with Richard Marshal (son of William). Henry III followed the tactics of his father in setting his troublesome magnates against each other. De Lacy and Richard de Burgh, a former justiciar (who was regaining favour after his own disagreement with the king), opposed Richard Marshal, who was killed in 1234.[27] The power of English magnates in Ireland continued to grow with the intrusion of Richard de Burgh and Hugh de Lacy into Connacht in 1234 and 1235. Although Henry III sought to curb the power of individual magnates, he willingly delegated authority. He leased most of his demesne lands and promoted the development of an Irish chancery and a common bench in Dublin to oversee the administration of justice.

The greater magnates were subdued by problems of succession more than by the deeds of Henry III. Meath was divided between

[23] See for example Hartland, 'Household knights'.
[24] Stubbs, ed., *Select charters*, pp. 292–302.
[25] Martin, 'John', pp. 152–3; Duffy, *Ireland*, pp. 107–8.
[26] Frame, *Colonial Ireland*, p. 71.   [27] Lydon, 'Expansion', pp. 164, 168.

co-heiresses following the death of Walter de Lacy in 1241. The death of Walter's childless brother Hugh, the following year, brought Ulster under direct royal control. In Leinster, the death of the last son of William Marshal led to the division of his lands between five sisters.[28] While this may have relieved the king of over-mighty subjects, it also stored up problems for the future. The fragmentation of power in the English colony made it vulnerable to baronial infighting and Irish attacks. While Henry was maximising his income from Ireland, he was also seeking military backing from both Irish and English lords for his campaigns in Scotland and Wales. In 1245 Feidlimid Ua Conchobuir king of Connacht provided 3000 foot soldiers in Wales in return for a modest fee and an alleged promise of recognition of his lordship.[29] There is no evidence that Henry III granted to Feidlimid the security of tenure that he craved. The growing distrust of Irish lords towards the English king would also create problems for the future.

In 1254, Henry granted Ireland to his son and heir Edward, along with Chester, Bristol, the Channel Islands and lands in Gascony. Henry reserved to himself regalian rights over the Church and also took care to stipulate by charter that Ireland was never to be separated from the English crown. The colony remained loyal to Henry III and Edward during the barons' war that arose in England. In 1264, the English rebel Simon de Montfort had captured both Henry and Edward at the Battle of Lewes. In the following year, de Montfort sent letters ordering magnates in Ireland to disobey Edward. Nevertheless, Edward escaped and felled de Montfort in battle with Anglo-Irish support at Evesham in 1265.[30]

Under Edward I, private warfare flourished in Ireland, largely due to rivalries between the families of de Burgh and the Geraldines. This dispute was not resolved until the families of Richard de Burgh of Ulster and John FitzThomas of Offaly (of the Geraldines) were bound by marriage in 1298.[31] Edward's government was also undermined by frequent changes in leadership: no less than eleven justiciars served between 1254 and 1272.[32] Corruption within the administration did not help. Accusations of malpractice were made against local and central officials, including the de Fulbourn family who

---

[28] Frame, *Colonial Ireland*, p. 74.   [29] Lydon, 'Expansion', p. 177.
[30] Frame, *Ireland and Britain*, p. 62.   [31] Duffy, 'Turnberry band', pp. 128–30.
[32] Lydon, 'Years of crisis', p. 181.

served in the chancery and the treasury and who provided a justiciar in 1281.[33]

Alongside these problems were military challenges to the colony. A new generation of Gaelic lords were taking up arms to recover lost territory. In Munster the Meic Carthaig won victories at Callan (Co. Kerry) and Mangerton (Co. Kerry) in 1261 and 1262 that held the Fitzgeralds of Desmond in check. In Leinster a famine in the 1270s provoked Irish raids on English territory, and Meic Murchada of Leinster emerged as the leaders of a coalition of Irish lords. Despite the assassination of two leading members of Meic Murchada on the orders of the justiciar Stephen de Fulbourn, warfare continued in the 1280s and 1290s.[34] In 1297 a parliament was summoned in an attempt to bring peace to Ireland. It reinforced a requirement for local communities to provide manpower and costs for their defence. An insight into life on the marches is provided by the stipulation that private armies were to remain on the lands of their lord and not commit robbery.[35] It was also commanded that English lords could not make unauthorised truces with the Irish and that the Irish were not to be provoked into war by unwarranted attacks. The English were also forbidden to adopt Irish hairstyles, so that they would not be mistaken for Irishmen. Thus, the agreements of the parliament placed the burden of defence on local communities, but peacekeeping was centralised. The statutes were very difficult to enforce. Starved of money, the Irish government was struggling to bring any kind of peace to Ireland.

Edward I's Scottish and Welsh wars sucked cash, supplies and manpower from the Irish colony over the course of two decades. Edward's last major expedition to Scotland in 1303 engaged 173 ships to bring 3400 men from Ireland for 100 days.[36] The lack of money to pay the troops left many men facing starvation. Even after this ruinous expedition, large sums of money and supplies were drawn upon, which the colony could ill afford. A series of bad harvests also caused widespread distress. Edward II sought to improve conditions. In 1308 the royal favourite Piers Gaveston was sent to Ireland as justiciar. He enjoyed military successes at Leinster, although any gains were of a temporary nature. In 1311, Edward II attempted the staunch the flow of money

---

[33] Sweetman and Handcock, eds., *Calendar of documents relating to Ireland*, II: 551–3 (no. 2332), III: 1–15 (no. 2).
[34] Simms, 'Gaelic revival'.   [35] Connolly, ed. and trans., 'Enactments', pp. 154–5.
[36] Lydon, 'Edward I'.

from Ireland by allowing the revenues of the colony to be retained and spent there.[37] Nevertheless the ongoing wars in Scotland caused the continual requisition of supplies. It appears that English magnates were also embroiled in conflicts and corruption, which caused nearly as many problems to the colony as the Irish, but Edward could not afford to step in and alienate potential supporters.

The war in Scotland spread to Ireland in May 1315, when Edward Bruce, brother of the Scottish king, arrived with 6000 troops. He based himself on the Antrim coast, received the submission of local Irish kings and proclaimed himself king of Ireland. Later that year, Bruce campaigned in Meath and may have gained the support of the de Lacys. Bruce won a significant victory over government forces near Ardscull (Co. Kildare) in 1316, but returned to Ulster where he took Carrickfergus Castle after a prolonged siege. In 1317, both Edward and Robert Bruce marched on Dublin, but the city was prepared for a siege and the brothers turned westwards. Without finding widespread support from the Gaelic Irish, Robert returned to Scotland. Edward led a final fatal expedition to Meath in 1318. He was killed at Faughart, and his head was brought to Edward II by John de Bermingham who was granted the newly created earldom of Louth in return.[38]

Another leading magnate who had opposed the Bruce invasions was Roger Mortimer, lord of Trim (Co. Meath) and Wigmore (Herefordshire). He was made justiciar of Ireland in 1316 and again in 1319 and attempted with some success to restore order within the colony.[39] In 1321 Roger opposed Edward II over the favour he was granting to the Despenser faction in England. Political disputes in England had a knock-on effect in Ireland, and the magnates aligned themselves into opposing groups.[40] By 1327, Edward II was dead, Edward III was in the minority, and Mortimer was the lover of Queen Isabella. Mortimer used his influence in Ireland, becoming earl of March and overseeing the creation of earldoms for James Butler in Ormond and the Geraldine Maurice FitzThomas in Desmond.

The creation of the earldoms was not merely a quick fix for Mortimer to win favour in Ireland. It was part of a longer-term policy. The earldom of Kildare was created for John FitzGerald in 1316, and the short-lived earldom of Louth was created for de Bermingham in

---

[37] Lydon, 'Edward II and the revenues', pp. 52–3.
[38] McNamee, *Wars of the Bruces*, pp. 166–99; Duffy, 'Bruce invasion', p. 42.
[39] Dryburgh, 'Roger Mortimer', pp. 90–8.   [40] Lydon, 'Impact', p. 299.

1319.[41] While the English colony lost ground in the west, the Dublin government focused its control on the densely populated heartlands of the colony. Power on the margins was delegated to greater magnates who could secure them. The earls of Kildare, Ormond and Desmond, were men who moved between the worlds of Gaelic Ireland and England, adopting the cultures of both, while sporting a politically English identity.

In 1330, Edward III was able to take the government into his own hands, and he soon had Mortimer executed. The young king then planned a major expedition to Ireland. Preparations were nearly complete when the pope and parliament dissuaded him from going.[42] Edward would spend much of his reign preoccupied with the Hundred Years' War against France, but he sought tighter control in Ireland by seeking to reverse the policy of delegating power to local interests (see Figure 9.2). In 1341, he ordered a general resumption of all grants in Ireland that were made during the reign of his father. Furthermore, Edward commanded that all officials with property and personal connections in Ireland were to be replaced by Englishmen with lands and benefices in England. This order caused outrage. It revealed growing tensions between the English of Ireland and those of England. A petition was sent to the king, who accepted the loyalty and entitlements of his English subjects in Ireland, and the requirements were dropped.[43]

During the 1330s and 1340s, the colony faced many challenges. In 1333 the murder of William de Burgh, lord of Connacht and earl of Ulster, in a family feud weakened English rule. In Leinster, Laoiseach Ó Morda successfully regained their former territory of Leix (Co. Laois).[44] During this period the justiciarship of Ireland was held by John Darcy, a trusted member of Edward III's household, but he held his post as an absentee. In 1345 a new justiciar Ralph Ufford was given the task of restoring the earldom of Ulster, only to die the following year. The trauma wrought by the Black Death at the end of the 1340s exacerbated the growing crisis, and in 1360 the Great Council at Kilkenny appealed to Edward III, claiming that the colony was on the verge of collapse.[45]

---

[41] Frame, *Colonial Ireland*, p. 138.   [42] Watt, 'Approaches', p. 307.
[43] Watt, 'Anglo-Irish colony', p. 371.
[44] Williams, ed., *Annals of Ireland by Friar John Clyn*, s.a. 1342.
[45] Richardson and Sayles, *Parliaments*, no. 16; Lydon, 'Ireland and the English Crown', pp. 283–4.

Figure 9.2 Edward III on the throne, Great Charter Roll Waterford

The king dispatched his son Lionel of Clarence to serve as chief governor of Ireland in 1361 with a sizeable army funded from England. Lionel had a personal interest in Irish affairs through his wife Elizabeth, who was heiress to the earldom of Ulster. Clarence's arrival was the first in a series of sustained efforts to strengthen English rule in Ireland. The colony had long ceased to be a profitable enterprise and now turned into an unwelcome drain on English resources. Lionel served in Ireland until 1366 and made various attempts to shore up English power by recalling absentees to Ireland and by issuing the 'Statutes of Kilkenny' in 1366.[46] The statutes forbade the English born in Ireland to use the Irish language, marry Irish wives or observe Irish law. These regulations were not an innovation in Ireland, but they served as a definitive statement of opposition to 'degeneracy' among the English in Ireland. In practice, they did little to aid the fortunes of the colony.

William of Windsor was appointed chief governor after the death of Clarence, but his economic and military demands on the Anglo-Irish magnates made him deeply unpopular. Windsor struggled and failed to make the colony pay its way, and the justiciarship became a poisoned chalice.[47] In 1382, both the earls of Ormond and Desmond refused to take the post, and John Colton, the archbishop-elect of Armagh, was given the job despite his own protests.[48] The Irish colony was now dependent on support on England to meet its basic fiscal and military needs. The Anglo-Irish elite appealed for Richard II's direct intervention in Ireland to improve things. Richard responded by visiting Ireland on two occasions after he had secured peace with France and when opposition to his reign in England seemed under control.

Richard arrived at Waterford in October 1394 with a new justiciar called Richard Mortimer. The king rapidly obtained the submission of Art Mac Murchada of Leinster who had been taking protection money from the English.[49] In January 1395, Art and the leader of the Uí Broin of County Wicklow promised to surrender their lands in Leinster and serve as royal mercenaries. Soon after, Richard knighted Art and three other Irish kings in Christ Church cathedral, Dublin.

[46] Harbison, ed. and trans., _Statute_; Crooks, 'Hobbes'.
[47] Harbison, 'William of Windsor', pp. 156–9.
[48] Watt, 'Anglo-Irish colony', p. 392.
[49] O'Byrne, _War_, pp. 109–11; Duffy, _Ireland_, pp. 159–62.

Richard also attempted to include Gaelic rulers in the Irish parliament, but this effort failed.[50] The English in Ireland had a vested interest in excluding their neighbours from power and were too mistrustful to admit them. The Gaelic Irish continued to suffer exclusion from English common law, despite the statue of 1330 that offered access to all freeman.[51] The continued apartheid between Irish and English offered little prospect for lasting peace. The oaths of the Leinster kings were dishonoured after Richard's departure. A contingent of Art's troops along with the Uí Thuathail and the Uí Broin intercepted the justiciar Richard Mortimer on campaign in Leinster in 1398 and killed him.[52] This act is thought to have prompted King Richard's second expedition to Ireland in 1399. On this occasion, Art withdrew into the Leinster mountains and successfully conducted a guerrilla war against the English forces. The invasion of England of Henry Bolingbroke, duke of Lancaster and a rival claimant to the throne, forced Richard's withdrawal back to England; he was toppled from power in England in the same year.

Richard's gains in Ireland were of a temporary nature, a fact recognised by the contemporary chronicler, Adam of Usk.[53] Nevertheless, Richard's responsiveness to the requests of the Anglo-Irish won admiration and a degree of loyalty to the Yorkist cause. In 1399, the Dublin administration may have hoped that Richard would win back his crown. Henry IV found it necessary to command the chancellor and treasurer in Dublin to remove Richard's name from seals of the administration, ten weeks after he came to the throne.[54] In the years that followed, the earls of Desmond and Kildare tended to side with the deposed house of York, while the absentee earl of Ormond affiliated himself with the Lancastrians. Thus, once again, events in England exacerbated factional divisions in Ireland.

THE HOUSES OF YORK AND LANCASTER

In the fifteenth century, English royal control in Ireland was limited to the east Midlands, north Leinster and a string of coastal ports to which travel was perilous by land and sometimes by sea. The earliest reference to the 'Pale' – an area comprising Dublin, Meath, Louth

---

[50] Cosgrove, 'Emergence', p. 549; Johnston, 'Richard II'.
[51] Watt, 'Anglo-Irish colony', pp. 394–5.   [52] O'Byrne, *War*, p. 112.
[53] Gwen-Wilson, ed. and trans., *Chronicle of Adam of Usk*, pp. 18–19.
[54] Cosgrove, 'Emergence', p. 547.

and Kildare – was made in 1446–7.[55] Work was undertaken in 1454 to secure these counties through the construction of fortresses and trenches along their borders, which physically manifested territorial divisions and the emergence of a siege mentality. These fortifications proved successful in securing strategic lands under crown control and demarcating an area of strong English identity within Ireland. Beyond these four shires government functions were delegated to local lords over whom Dublin administration exercised little authority.

Royal concerns about the failure of the English colony in Ireland worsened the position of the Gaelic Irish and the Anglo-Irish alike. Henry IV made provisions against labourers leaving Ireland and absentee landlords. In 1413, Henry V ordered the expulsion of 'all Irish' from England at the risk of losing goods and facing imprisonment. In 1422, it was commanded that every Irish-born student wishing to enter Oxford or Cambridge required a letter of recommendation from the justiciar of Ireland. Expulsion orders were issued regularly during the reign of Henry VI, and those of Irish birth in England were subjected to a poll tax on aliens in 1440 that prompted complaints from the government in Dublin. In 1442 the alien status of the Anglo-Irish was dropped, but local attempts were still made to levy the tax on them.[56] These circumstances show the difficulties the English in Ireland faced in being recognised as English in England.

The demographic facts of Ireland in the fifteenth century made it increasingly difficult to maintain the laws of segregation between the English and the Irish. Licenses were granted to English landowners to allow them to take Gaelic tenants. Gaelic-named merchants were gaining growing influence in urban life, and more ecclesiastical benefices were passing to Irish clerics.[57] There are also increasing records of Irish individuals acquiring charters of denisation (citizenship) in the fifteenth century, so that they might be counted as English and enjoy equal rights in the colony. While a degree of Anglicisation was taking place among the Irish, the adoption of Gaelic customs was also proceeding apace among the English in Ireland.

Some of the English felt unease at the blurring of ethnic boundaries and feared the loyalties of the Irish in their midst. These worries were reflected in a statue of 1431 that ordered the imprisonment of

---

[55] Ibid., p. 533.   [56] Cosgrove, 'England and Ireland', p. 530.
[57] Cosgrove, 'Emergence', pp. 553–4.

Irish spies who dwelt among the English.[58] Attempts were made to limit Gaelic immigration and also to maintain physical distinctions between the Gaelic Irish and the Anglo-Irish, as men were required to shave their upper lip as a declaration of Englishness.[59] Such regulations, which seem faintly ridiculous with hindsight, show how problematic it could be to maintain difference. While the English in England saw little to distinguish Anglo-Irish and Gaelic Irish, the 'Annals of Connacht' for the year 1419 referred to a contingent of Gaelic and Anglo-Irish troops serving in France with Ormond as *Éireannach* 'Irish'. This common identity was, however, admitted only in a context outside Ireland.[60]

The royal efforts to shore up the English colony in Ireland in the late fourteenth century made little headway. In a bid to restore the colony's fortunes, Henry IV appointed his own son Thomas of Lancaster as chief governor of Ireland in 1401 with the promise of 12,000 marks annually to support his work. The promise of funds was not realised, and Thomas left two years later. He returned in 1408 on a smaller but more secure income and led a campaign in Leinster, but soon left to follow a military career in France.[61] After a few years John Talbot was made chief governor of Ireland. Talbot was chosen for his military prowess and his Irish connections: he had family in Malahide and a claim to the lordship of Wexford. He campaigned vigorously, but accumulated significant debts in Ireland. His belligerent personality also caused friction, not least with the fourth earl of Ormond. By 1417 Talbot and Ormond were openly hostile, and Ormond's land had been seized. In 1420, Ormond became chief governor, and in 1421 the Irish parliament petitioned the king criticising Talbot's lieutenancy. Talbot then accused Ormond of treasonable activities in Ireland, while Ormond complained of persecution.

Ormond's lieutenancy had its advantages from an English perspective. He was able to govern with minimal financial support as he could draw upon extensive lands and connections within Ireland. The policy of employing Anglo-Irish earls as justiciars would recur in the fifteenth century, for it allowed the English crown to scale down its commitments in Ireland. Nevertheless, Ormond faced stiff opposition from Richard Talbot, brother of John, who had been appointed

---

[58] Brewer and Bullen, eds., *Calendar of the Carew Manuscripts*, p. 290.
[59] Ellis, 'Civilising', p. 84.   [60] *A Conn, s.a.* 1419.
[61] Lydon, *Ireland*, p. 127; Cosgrove, 'Emergence', pp. 537–8.

archbishop of Dublin. In 1445 John Talbot was reappointed, but the feud with Ormond was ended soon after by the marriage of Talbot's son to Ormond's daughter. The Talbot-Ormond feud highlighted the difficulties of remote government as local interests could outweigh royal directives, and distance made it harder for the king to quell factional rivalries.[62]

The high-status appointment of Richard, duke of York as justiciar of Ireland followed in 1447. Richard was heir to the childless king Henry VI. He was welcomed by many in the colony who hoped for recovery after years of feuding and decline. Richard had a personal interest in Ireland. He had inherited a claim to lands in Ulster and Connacht from Lionel of Clarence, and lands in Trim and Leix through his uncle Edmund Mortimer. Richard enjoyed some success in Leinster, and in 1449 he was able to bring the northern potentate Henry Ua Néill into formal submission.[63] Lack of funds would frustrate Richard's further efforts in Ireland, and he was drawn into political events in England with the build-up to the Wars of the Roses. In 1452 the fifth earl of Ormond, a loyal supporter of Henry VI, was appointed as justiciar, which caused friction with the earls of Desmond and Kildare. Then in 1459, Richard fled to Ireland to escape the Lancastrians.

At this point, many in the Irish colony made a brave assertion of loyalty to the Yorkist cause. Richard's lands in England were forfeit, but the Irish parliament confirmed Richard in office and claimed it was not bound to English decisions, being 'corporate unto itself'.[64] In theory, English statues were binding but they required publication in Ireland, and until they were published they could not be enforced. The Irish colony proved to be strategically significant as a Yorkist base. Henry VI tried to outmanoeuvre the Anglo-Irish by trying and failing to win Gaelic lords to his side.[65] Richard of York crossed to England in 1460 and died in conflict, but a large and bloody battle fought at Towton in the following year secured the succession of his son Edward IV.

As the tables turned, the defeated Lancastrians now tried to use Ireland as a base for their interests, counting on the loyalty of the earl of Ormond. His party was, however, defeated by the earl of Desmond

[62] Crooks, 'James', p. 163.   [63] Cosgrove, 'Anglo-Ireland', pp. 557–9.
[64] Duffy, *Ireland* pp. 172–4; Lydon, *Ireland*, p. 147.
[65] Cosgrove, 'Anglo-Ireland', p. 567.

at Piltown (Co. Kilkenny) in 1462.[66] The Yorkist party in Ireland was rewarded for its loyalty, and the justiciarship of Ireland was regularly held by the earls of Kildare until the sixteenth century. Their long tenure in government allowed the Kildares to build up their power and recover lands on the northern march of Leinster. Their influence was sufficient that the restoration of a Lancastrian Henry Tudor to the English throne in 1485 did not bring an immediate end to the Kildare fortunes. The eighth earl, Gerald Mór, took the dangerous risk of backing Lambert Simnel, a Yorkist pretender, who was crowned Edward VI in Christ Church cathedral in 1487. Kildare provided a large force of Gaelic kerne for the invasion of England, but the Yorkist army was roundly defeated at Stoke by Newark. Henry VII deemed it necessary to retain Kildare as a strong magnate on the Irish marches, and he was pardoned.[67]

Kildare was later implicated in the activities of another Yorkist pretender, Perkin Warbeck, who landed at Cork in 1491. The Warbeck crisis coincided with the revival of a feud between the factions of Kildare and Ormond. Henry VII sought to promote Ormond as a counterweight to Kildare. Kildare outwardly co-operated with the king and his appointment of Sir Edward Poynings as justiciar to overhaul the Dublin government. Kildare was suspected of treason, but proved 'too big to fail' as a bastion of Anglo-Irish authority in Ireland. After Warbeck's siege of Waterford failed, the pretender fled to Scotland. A marriage was arranged between Elizabeth St John, first cousin of Henry VII, and the earl of Kildare to tie him to the Tudor cause.

The marriage alliances of Gerald FitzGerald, the eighth earl of Kildare, are instructive in demonstrating how Kildare played in the various fields of English, Gaelic and Anglo-Irish politics. His sister and daughters married into the Gaelic families of Uí Néill and Meic Carthaig Riabach; other daughters married the Anglo-Irish earls of Ormond, Sir Piers Butler of Polestown, and Christopher Fleming, baron of Slane, as well as the Gaelicised Finn Ulick de Burgh of Clanrickard.[68] A poet likened Kildare to an Irish over-king. It is notable that his court had the officers and trappings of both English and Gaelic culture.

---

[66] Quinn, 'Aristocratic autonomy', p. 599.   [67] Lydon, *Ireland*, p. 167.

[68] Ellis, 'Fitzgerald, Gerald'.

As justiciar of Ireland, Edward Poynings's mission was to restore English royal authority. In a parliament convened at Drogheda in 1494–5 a series of acts were passed. These included the resumption of royal grants made in Ireland since 1327 and the requirement for prior royal consent to hold a parliament or submit legislation to it.[69] This prevented any re-run of events in 1460 when parliament claimed to be 'corporate unto itself'. Poynings's Law marked the new determination of the Tudor monarchy to bring Ireland under tighter control. The partial conquest of Ireland by the English and the refusal to admit equal rights to Gaelic subjects doomed Ireland to instability. The creation of the Pale at the end of the Middle Ages was an attempt to secure a border within which royal control could be exercised directly. Beyond the Pale, the great earls of Kildare, Desmond and Ormond, were to protect Anglo-Irish interests with minimal crown intervention. This policy proved to be dangerous as Ireland became a base for rivals to the English throne. In the sixteenth century Ireland became more important to the English crown as its Continental possessions waned and the North European economy boomed. Ireland would again become a field for English colonisation and expansion.

A KINGSHIP OF GAELIC IRELAND?

The idea of a Gaelic kingship of all Ireland was never lost on bardic poets throughout the Middle Ages, who continually harkened back to this ideal. In 1175, the Treaty of Windsor had offered the prospect of a Gaelic monarchy under the Uí Chonchobuir of Connacht. However, English expansion into Connacht in the 1230s made this increasingly unlikely. In the 1250s there was a brief attempt to revive a high kingship of Ireland as both Feidlimid Ua Conchobuir of Connacht and Tadg Ua Briain of Munster recognised Brian Ua Néill of Tyrone as king of Ireland.[70] Despite his aspirations, Brian Ua Néill faced opposition closer to home from the Meic Lochlainn and within his own dynasty. He was killed in 1260 during an attack on the English in Ulster, and his head was sent to Henry III in London. Brian's supporters in Connacht then had little option but to accept English overlordship.

---

[69] Quinn, 'Early interpretation', pp. 242–3.
[70] Lydon, 'Land of war', p. 244; AConn, *s.a.* 1260; AI, *s.a.* 1261.

A renewed call for a kingship of Ireland was made when Edward Bruce arrived at Larne (Co. Antrim) in 1315. The English king Edward II appealed to Pope John XXII to condemn the supporters of the Scottish invasion. In response, a remonstrance was sent to the pope by Domnall Ua Néill. He described in impassioned language the wrongs that had been committed 'by some kings of England, their evil ministers and English barons born in Ireland' since the papal bull *Laudabiliter* was issued.[71] Domnall claimed himself to be the true heir to the kingdom of Ireland, but he surrendered his rights to Edward Bruce, 'who is sprung from our noblest ancestors'. The remonstrance failed to win papal recognition of Edward Bruce as king of Ireland, but it was powerful enough to move the pope to tell Edward II to deal more fairly with Ireland. The years 1315–18 witnessed much turmoil and loss of life.[72] In Connacht, Feidlimid Ua Conchobuir led a coalition of Gaelic forces against the Anglo-Irish, but he was killed and his side was heavily defeated. Feidlimid was lauded by contemporary chroniclers as the most suitable candidate for the kingship of all Ireland. In 1318, Edward Bruce fell in battle at Faughart, north of Dundalk (Co. Louth), and support for the Scottish cause collapsed.[73] Although the ideal of a Gaelic kingship of all Ireland had wide-ranging appeal as a poetic ideal, there was rarely consensus as to whom that king should be.

Provincial loyalties in Ireland remained strong. In 1403, the 'Annals of Ulster' praised Niall Óg Ua Néill as a man 'who would take the kingship of Ireland'.[74] Nevertheless the contemporary Welsh patriot Owain Glendywr had no success in attempting to call the Gaelic Irish together against the English. Gaelic leaders had greater success in reviving ancient ideas of provincial over-kingship that the Meic Murchada continued to assert in Leinster and the Uí Chonchobuir claimed in Connacht.[75] The 'Libelle of Englyshe Polycye', which was composed around 1437, expressed the fear that so much land now lay in the hands of the 'wild Irish' that they might raise a king of their own against the English. Alarm may have been raised by expeditions of the northern potentate Eógan Ua Néill. In 1430, he attacked Louth, burnt Dundalk and undertook a circuit of the

---

[71] Watt *et al.*, eds., *Scotichronicon*, VI: 385–403.
[72] Duffy, 'Bruce invasion', pp. 42–3; Lydon, 'Impact', p. 293.
[73] Duffy, *Ireland*, pp. 135–40.   [74] Simms, 'Ulster revolt', pp. 147–51.
[75] Cosgrove, 'England and Ireland', pp. 530–1.

midlands, enforcing submission from a number of Irish and English lords.[76] Nevertheless, Éogan and his son Henry would be enticed into alliance with the Anglo-Irish earls of Ormond and Kildare. There was no realistic prospect of united Gaelic rule in Ireland. Power had been too fragmented by the intrusion of English lordships and the complex political relations at a local level often caused strife between kin and Gaelic neighbours,while agreements with English lords compromised any attempts to forge a pan-Gaelic anti-English coalition. In 1541, the Irish parliament proclaimed Henry VIII king of Ireland (his predecessors had been styled 'lord of Ireland'). The concept of a Gaelic monarchy in Ireland had long been adhered to, but it was never to become a political reality.

PROVINCIAL HISTORY

Many of the Gaelic families who came to dominate provincial politics in the twelfth century were able to maintain or regain a position of status by 1500. This political longevity reflects the resilience and local strength of the Gaelic system of kingship despite the large-scale English conquests of the late twelfth and early thirteenth centuries. The impact of English settlement in Ireland varied greatly. Some regions including the extreme northwest were virtually untouched, while other areas – eastern Mide and the lowlands of Leinster and Munster – witnessed significant change. The political geography of the English lordship did not foster a strong central authority. Beyond the hinterlands of Dublin, liberties were granted to greater English lords who were able to hold power. These powerful lords became enmeshed in local politics like their Gaelic counterparts, and their activities transcended cultural divisions between English and Irish society.

CONNACHT

In the eleventh century, the two major dynasties of Connacht were the Uí Chonchobuir, who held the provincial over-kingship, and the Uí Ruairc, who contested it. In the twelfth century kings of Uí Chonchobuir consolidated their hold on the province and advanced their ambitions to be kings of all Ireland. The reign of Toirdelbach

---

[76] Cosgrove, 'Ireland beyond the Pale', p. 573.

Ua Conchobuir (r. 1106–56) brought significant investment in building projects and churches in Connacht. A new bridge and castle were built at the strategic river crossing at Athlone during the 1120s, which aided and protected communication between Connacht and the other provinces of Ireland. Toirdelbach also founded a fort at the mouth of the River Gaillimh that would develop into the successful port of Galway.[77] On the eastern margins of Connacht, the kingdom of Bréifne held a position of prominence during the reign of Tigernán Ua Ruairc from 1128 to 1172. Tigernán avoided conflict with Toirdelbach by focusing his ambitions on eastwards expansion into Mide.

Toirdelbach's son Ruaidrí Ua Conchobuir, and Tigernán Ua Ruairc, refused to submit to Henry II of England at his winter palace in Dublin in 1171. Ua Ruairc was treacherously killed by Hugh de Lacy in 1172, but Ruaidrí continued to oppose foreign colonisation in Leinster, Meath and Munster. In 1175 Henry II agreed to secure Ruaidrí's control over Gaelic Ireland at the Treaty of Windsor, but the English king showed little inclination to rein in the territorial ambitions of the colonists. The last years of Ruaidrí's reign were marred by the rivalry of his descendants, and he was forced to retire from power to the monastery of Cong.[78]

The divisions among Ruaidrí's progeny were exploited by the English colonists. Cathal Crobderg rose to power in 1189 with English support, and he held his lands through submission to King John. On Cathal's death in 1224 the rapprochement with English royal authority broke down. The province was granted to Richard de Burgh excepting five cantreds of strategic land in and around County Roscommon that could remain in the hands of native kings. Despite efforts to maintain good relations with the English kings during the reign of Feidlimid Ua Conchobuir (d. 1265), Uí Chonchobuir lands were further eroded by grants to English royal favourites. Feidlimid's son Áed followed a policy of military opposition, fighting successfully against Walter de Burgh, earl of Ulster and lord of Connacht. Áed's death in 1274 left the Ua Conchobuir dynasty in disarray and unable to build on his military success.[79]

---

[77] Ó Cróinín, *Early Medieval Ireland*, pp. 282–3.
[78] Ó Cróinín, *Early medieval Ireland*, pp. 289–90.
[79] Frame, *Colonial Ireland*, pp. 52–4.

The Bruce invasion caused further dissension in the early four-teenth century. One contender for the Connacht kingship, Feidlimid, supported Richard de Burgh against the invaders. Another con-tender, Ruaidrí, fought on their behalf. After Feidlimid had disposed of Ruaidrí he changed sides, but fell in battle against the forces of Richard de Bermingham at Athenry in 1316.[80] The conflict exacted a heavy toll on Feidlimid's vassals and allies. Divisions within Uí Chon-chobuir continued, but this did not stop Gaelic lords in Connacht from successfully wresting lands from English control. One group that rose in prominence in this period was the Uí Chellaig, which seized the Butler lordship of Omany.

English power in Connacht suffered after the assassination of the de Burgh earl of Ulster in 1333, which left a young daughter as heir. The English lords were themselves deeply divided, and rival lineages of de Burgh contested for influence over the family's lands in Connacht. These wars hastened the collapse of English royal control in Con-nacht. By the late fourteenth century, the borough of Roscommon was abandoned, and the demesne lands of de Burgh were taken over by Gaelic families and minor branches of de Burgh. Uí Chonchobuir were irreconcilably divided in 1384 between a 'red' and 'brown' fac-tion, each backed by rival lineages of the MacWilliams who were Gaelicised descendants of de Burgh.[81] During the fifteenth century these families of Upper and Lower MacWilliams (based, respectively, in Co. Galway and Co. Mayo) dominated Connacht, and the ancient title of provincial king gradually fell into disuse. The great distance of Connacht from Dublin meant that the English government wielded little authority there. The English lords of the area eventually went native as little benefit could be obtained from maintaining links with the English crown.

ULSTER AND THE NORTH

The northwest of Ireland also remained beyond the range of English royal government for much of the Middle Ages. The Northern Uí Néill had long been dominant in this region. The ambitions of Cenél nEógain to extend their power across Ireland had been thwarted in the eleventh century by the rise of the Munster over-king Brian Boru and his descendants, as well as internal rivalries between Uí Néill

---

[80] Nicholls, *Gaelic and Gaelicised Ireland*, p. 143.   [81] Ibid., pp. 145–8.

(based south of the Sperrin mountains) and Clann Domnaill (based to the north). In the twelfth century, the Mac Lochlainn dynasty of the Inishowen peninsula rose to prominence. Their king Muirchertach came to dominate Ireland for a decade after 1156. After Muirchertach's demise, the kingship of Cenél nEógain divided power between Muirchertach's son Niall and a rival claimant Áed Ua Néill. For the remainder of the Middle Ages the Meic Lochlainn clung onto a much-reduced power base on the Inishowen peninsula.

East of the River Bann lay the historic kingdom of Ulster. Its two main families were descended from Dál Fíatach, namely Meic Duinn Sléibe and Meic Áengusa. Succession disputes within Dál Fíatach and Cenél nEógain in the twelfth century provided the ideal circumstances for English intervention. In January 1177, John de Courcy seized Dál Fiatach lands with a band of 22 knights and about 300 other followers. De Courcy cemented his position by building castles at Carrickfergus (Co. Antrim) and Dundrum (Co. Down) and through patronage of the church, thus winning the approval of leading Irish clerics in the region. De Courcy also manipulated existing rivalries and worked with some Irish kings against others. De Courcy eventually fell from power not because of Gaelic resistance, but because of the hostility of the de Lacy family and King John. In 1205 Hugh II de Lacy received Ulster as an earldom from the king, although he too would fall from royal favour, five years later.[82]

By 1200, power west of the Bann had been secured by Áed mac Áeda Ua Néill of Cenél nEógain. After King John's visited Ireland in 1210, he ordered an assault on the unconquered lands of the north under the direction of John Grey, bishop of Norwich. Castles were built at various locations, but any gains were short-lived. Áed entered into an agreement with the English crown, and colonial settlement in Ulster remained restricted to coastal areas.[83] Later the de Burgh conquest of Connacht in 1236 would threaten the southwestern borders of Uí Néill influence. In 1263, King Henry made Walter de Burgh lord of Connacht and earl of Ulster. Walter's son Richard sought to extend his lands to the west, and built a castle at Northburgh (Co. Donegal) on the shores of Lough Foyle.[84]

---

[82] McNeill, 'County Down', pp. 107–8; Frame, *Colonial Ireland*, pp. 65, 67.
[83] Simms, 'Late medieval Tír Eoghain', pp. 132–5.
[84] Simms, 'Late medieval Donegal', p. 186.

Ulster would become closely involved with affairs in Scotland. In the early thirteenth century grants of land along the east coast were given to Scottish earls of Atholl and Carrick and the lord of Galloway. The troubled political circumstances of the thirteenth and fourteenth centuries prompted an influx of highland settlers to Ulster, who served as galloglasses (*gall-óclaig* 'foreign warriors') a class of mercenaries in the retinues of different Gaelic kings.[85] Ulster's proximity to Scotland made it a natural base for the Bruce campaign in Ireland between 1315 and 1318, which had a devastating impact on the region. Domnall Ua Néill of Tír Eógain made common cause with Edward Bruce. After his defeat, the lands of Tír Eógain were divided by de Burgh between Henry of Clann Áeda Buide (which was allied to de Burgh) and Áed, son of Domnall Ua Néill.

Earl William, son of Richard de Burgh, was murdered by his own vassals in 1333, and the earldom fell into the hands of absentees. This weakness aided Gaelic expansion. Despite ongoing wars of succession, Uí Domnaill of Cenél Conaill extended their lordship over Inishowen, and Clann Áeda Buide (Clandeboy) intruded into the areas of southern Co. Antrim and northern Co. Down, placing them in conflict with the Anglo-Irish Savage family and Uí Thuirtre (who had established themselves in the centre of Co. Antrim before 1169). From the fourteenth century, Uí Néill kings claimed for themselves the title 'kings of Ulster'. For the remainder of the Middle Age, English control was restricted to coastal enclaves including Ards and Lecale (Co. Down).[86]

Niall Mór Ua Néill (fl 1380s–1403), son of Áed Ua Néill, was one of the more remarkable leaders to emerge in the north. He gave homage to Richard II in 1395 during his Irish visit, despite contesting the claims of the Mortimer earls of March and Ulster, and he held significant sway in Ulster. Niall was a patron of poets who foretold that he would reclaim the ancient kingship of Tara. Vivid descriptions of Niall survive in the writings of the chronicler Jean Froissart and a Catalan pilgrim de Perellós that reflect on his military prowess, hospitality and eschewal of English culture.[87] He was eventually succeeded (after a dispute over succession) by his son Eógan, whose long career

---

[85] Nicholls, 'Scottish mercenary kindreds', p. 89.
[86] McNeill, 'County Down', p. 117.
[87] Simms, 'Late medieval Tír Eoghain', pp. 149–50.

included raids on the English Pale and wars against Uí Domnaill of Cenél Conaill.[88]

James Butler, the 'White' earl of Ormond, negotiated a series of treaties between Eógan and the English government, cementing an alliance through the marriage of his niece to Eógan's son Henry (Énri). It was Henry who would meet Richard, duke of York and earl of Ulster, when he arrived in Ireland in 1449 and render his submission. Some years later, Henry received a gold chain and scarlet cloth as livery from the Yorkist king Edward IV, who was also earl of Ulster.[89] Henry's co-operation with the Anglo-Irish government was further cemented by the marriage of his son Conn to Eleanor FitzGerald, daughter of the seventh earl of Kildare, and the grant of English common law to their offspring. After Conn was murdered in 1493 by his half-brother, the powerful earl of Kildare intervened to help raise the sons of Conn to power in Tír Eógain.[90] The English made little headway in bringing Ulster and the lands of Northern Uí Néill under their control. Ulster remained as an area of strong Gaelic culture and identity during the later Middle Ages. The province was later targeted for plantations in order to secure British cultural influence in the region.

MUNSTER

In 1100, Munster was home to the most powerful king of Ireland, Muirchertach Ua Briain, but by the end of the century much of the province was brought under English control. Gaelic rulers were able to regain some influence in the province by the fifteenth century, but Munster was the seat of two families of English earls, the Ormonds and the Desmonds, who were important players in Anglo-Irish government and society.

After the demise of Muirchertach Ua Briain, over-king of Munster, in 1119, the province was divided between the dynasties of Meic Carthaig and Uí Briain. Initially the two families cooperated in a bid to offset the growing power of the kings of Connacht, but the province failed to reunite in the long term. Both the lords of Meic Carthaig and Uí Briain submitted to Henry II in 1171, but within a

---

[88] Simms, 'Medieval Fermanagh', pp. 92–3.
[89] Simms, 'The king's friend', pp. 219–20, 223, 225.
[90] Simms, 'Late medieval Tír Eoghain', p. 154.

few years Henry granted some of their lands to his followers. Further speculative grants were made by King John in 1185. The eruption of succession disputes among the Uí Briain of Thomond in 1194 and among the Meic Carthaig of Desmond in 1206 compromised any attempts to resist English intrusion. As a result, the fertile regions of Munster were rapidly colonised. In southern Munster, only the mountainous areas of the southwest (in modern Co. Kerry) remained free from English control.[91] In northern Munster, Gaelic power was hemmed in north and west of the Shannon. The English colonisation was accompanied by rapid development of the agrarian economy and the southern coastal ports, from where the produce of their hinterlands was exported.

A number of colonial families benefitted from the rich pickings in Munster. Thomas FitzMaurice, ancestor of the Anglo-Irish house of Desmond – a cadet branch of the Geraldines of Leinster (Thomas's elder brother Gerald founded the house of Kildare) – obtained lands in western Limerick and married an Irishwoman Sadb. Their son John extended the family territories through marriage to the heiress Margery FitzAnthony, obtaining a royal grant of the lands of Decies and Desmond. Another prominent settler was Theobald Walter, butler to John, lord of Ireland, and ancestor of the Butlers of Ormond. In 1185 Theobald received a speculative grant of five and a half cantreds in north Munster south of the Shannon.[92]

In the Gaelic areas of north Munster, Donnchad, son of Domnall Mór Ua Briain, followed a policy of co-operation with the English crown. He was knighted by King John, but only held the lands of Munster north of the Shannon for which he paid rent. The further erosion of Ua Briain power through land grants made by Henry III prompted a war against the crown from 1257 that met with little success. In 1276, King Edward granted Thomond to Thomas de Clare.[93] De Clare initially allied with the king of Thomond, Brian Ua Briain, against his rival kinsman Toirdelbach; however, relations soon soured and Brian was brutally executed in 1277. Toirdelbach then entered an agreement with de Clare to hold Thomond apart from Bunratty (Co. Clare), for which he paid a yearly rent until his death in 1306. Warfare then ensued between the colonists as de Clare and de Burgh

[91] Frame, *Colonial Ireland*, pp. 44–5.
[92] Cunningham, *Anglo-Norman advance*, p. 55.
[93] Nally, 'Maintaining the marches', p. 36.

(whose power was based in Connacht) backed rival Ua Briain candidates for the lands of Thomond. The conflict culminated in the defeat and death of Richard de Clare at the hands of Muirchertach, son of Toirdelbach Ua Briain, at the battle of Dysert O'Dea (Co. Clare) in 1317.[94] The power of the de Clares ended in 1321 with the death of Thomas de Clare, and most of Thomond was taken from English control.

In southern Munster, political changes were also taking place. Domnall Got Mac Carthaig founded a new lordship of Mac Carthaig Riabach (Reagh) on lands taken from Uí Mathgamna in 1232. His son Fíngen Mac Carthaig became king of Desmond in 1260. Fíngen proceeded to destroy a string of English castles and won a decisive battle against the colonists at Callan in 1261. After the battle, areas of west Cork and south Kerry came under Mac Carthaig rule.[95] The minority of the Desmond Geraldines between 1298 and 1314 helped the Meic Carthaig consolidate their position.

As the English colony in Munster contracted, power became more focused in hands of two Anglo-Irish families: the Fitzgeralds, earls of Desmond (who held a noncontiguous swathe of territory in Kerry, Limerick, Cork and Waterford), and the Butlers, earls of Ormond (who had a more compact lordship in Tipperary and Kilkenny). The career of Maurice, first earl of Desmond, was marked by feuds with various Anglo-Irish families. His activities earned crown disapproval, especially when he made common cause with Brian Bán Ua Briain, king of Thomond. After a brief imprisonment, Maurice turned against Brian Bán, but he continued to flout English royal government, ironically becoming justiciar in the final year of his life (1355).[96] Maurice's son and eventual successor Gerald cultivated good relations with his Mac Carthaig neighbours. He suffered military defeat at the hands of Uí Briain of Thomond in 1370, but forged an alliance with them by 1388.[97] Although the earls of Desmond tended to look westward, Gerald's marriage into the powerful Ormond family should have secured good relations with his English neighbours. Nevertheless, a violent feud erupted between the families in the 1380s and 1390s.

The Butlers of Ormond were key players in Ireland during the late fourteenth and early fifteenth centuries. They compensated for the

[94] Nicholls, *Gaelic and Gaelicised Ireland*, p. 156.   [95] Ibid., p. 159.
[96] Waters, 'The earls of Desmond', pp. 19–97.   [97] Ibid., pp. 120, 127.

loss of lands in Munster by acquiring properties in Leinster, including Kilkenny Castle in 1393.[98] As their power shifted eastwards, the
Butler lands in County Tipperary fell under the control of cadet
branches. James the third earl (fl. 1385–1405) was a fluent speaker of
the Irish language and helped negotiate submissions for Richard II
when he visited Ireland in 1394–5. He was followed by James, the
fourth or 'White Earl' (fl.1411–52), who served on military expeditions to France and made frequent visits to England.[99] Although
the White earl had a keen interest in English affairs, his patronage of
Gaelic culture is witnessed in the 'Book of the White Earl' and the
praise poetry of Tadg Óg Ó hUiginn. His ability to transcend the
worlds of the English court and Gaelic Ireland made him an important figure in the Anglo-Irish administration.

In the late fifteenth century, the earls of Desmond and Ormond
took opposing sides in the Wars of the Roses, with Desmond in the
Yorkist camp. James, fifth earl of Ormond, was executed by the York-
ists in 1461 and had his head displayed on London Bridge.[100] Thomas
FitzGerald, seventh earl of Desmond, fell foul of royal government
and was executed in 1468. His death caused unrest in Ireland, and
the Desmonds seem to have had supporters among both the Irish
and Anglo-Irish. The power of the Desmond earls declined in the
last quarter of the fifteenth century as the Dublin administration
increasingly favoured the earl of Kildare.[101] Despite the early successes of English colonists in Munster, the province became increasingly detached from royal control as the Middle Ages wore on.

LEINSTER

Because of its proximity to England and its wealthy coastal ports,
Leinster was of great strategic importance during the later Middle
Ages. In the twelfth century, the leading dynasty of Leinster was the
Meic Murchada (a branch of Uí Chennselaig) in southern Leinster.
Their rule was not always popular, and typically Dublin sought a
degree of independence. In 1115, the people of Dublin allied with
Domnall Ua Briain of Munster to fight Donnchad Mac Murchada.
The king of Leinster died in the encounter and was later reported to

---

[98] Watt, 'Anglo-Irish colony', p. 355.   [99] Empey, 'Butler-Ormond'.
[100] Watts, 'Butler, James'.
[101] Quinn, 'Aristocratic autonomy', p. 598; Duffy, *Ireland*, p. 174.

have been buried with a dog in the centre of Dublin as an insult.[102] In 1126, Diarmait Mac Murchada succeeded to the kingship and lived until 1171. Diarmait has become one of the most ill-famed characters of Irish history for his role in bringing English adventurers to Ireland. Although Diarmait cannot bear full blame for the conquest, his character was not endearing. He was a brutal warrior and a rapist who abducted both an abbess of Kildare and the wife of his political rival Ua Ruairc. In the manner of many medieval kings, Mac Murchada saw no contradiction in combining a life of violence with patronage of the church. Among other deeds, he founded the Cistercian Abbey at Baltinglass (Co. Wexford) endowed St Mary's Abbey, Ferns (Co. Wexford), and All Hallows Priory in Dublin. It is likely that the 'Book of Leinster' was compiled with his support. On his death in 1171, the kingship of Leinster was taken by Strongbow. This prompted a fierce reaction from Diarmait's male relatives, and a succession dispute rumbled on until 1175. Thereafter leading members of the Mac Murchada dynasty served as officers to the Marshal heirs of de Clare.[103]

William I Marshal (d. 1219) married Strongbow's heiress Isabel de Clare in 1189. Extensive landholdings in England, as well as those acquired in Ireland, placed the Marshals in the top rank of colonial families. William I Marshal had a rocky relationship with the administration of King John, but remained loyal in his later years. His son William II Marshal (d. 1231) was a personal friend of Áed Ua Conchobuir of Connacht and opposed colonists who threatened his interests, including de Lacy. The Marshal family fostered economic development in Leinster through their towns of Kilkenny and New Ross and built a string of castles including at Carlow, Dunamase, Kildare, Kilkenny and Wexford. The last of the Marshal male line passed away in 1245, and their lands were divided among five co-heiresses.[104] The resulting fragmentation of power between the Bigods, de Clares, Mortimers, de Vescys and de Valences provided an opportunity for Gaelic lords in Leinster to flex their muscles from the late thirteenth century.

The FitzGeralds of Kildare and Offaly rose to prominence after the death of William II Marshal. They were descended from Maurice FitzGerald who had come to Ireland in 1169. The alliance of Maurice,

[102] *AU, s.a.* 1115; Martin, 'Allies', p. 76.   [103] O'Byrne, *War,* p. 15.
[104] Frame, *Colonial Ireland,* p. 74; Crooks, 'Marshal', pp. 322–3.

second baron of Offaly, with Richard de Burgh and Hugh de Lacy led to the acquisition of lands in Connacht and Ulster. Maurice also demonstrated his loyalty to Henry III, serving as justiciar from 1232 to 1245 and participating in the downfall of Richard Marshal whom Henry III opposed. Maurice was rewarded by marriage to the king's niece Agnes de Valence in 1266. The family's ascent was not without some glitches, however. In 1294, King Edward summoned John FitzGerald to Westminster and stripped him of the family's lands in Connacht and Ulster. John redeemed himself through military service and earned the title, earl of Kildare, shortly before his death in 1316.[105]

Although Leinster was the first region of Ireland to be brought under English control, Gaelic lords remained in the upland areas from where they could lead raids on English settlements when it was profitable to do so. The late thirteenth and fourteenth centuries witnessed a revival of Gaelic lordship in Leinster. In the northwest borders of the province, the Meic Gilla Pátraic, entrenched in the mountains of Slieve Bloom, recovered the lands of Upper Ossory, while Uí Morda took lands in Leix (Co. Laois) and extended their lordship into Slievemargy (Co. Laois). In northeast Leinster, the Uí Broin and Uí Thuathail successors to the Uí Dúnlainge kingship extended their base in and around the Wicklow mountains. The Meic Murchada also rose to prominence from the 1370s under Art Mór Cáemánach, who forged a kingdom in the areas of Carlow and north Wexford at the expense of the English. In 1394, Mac Murchada was obliged to submit to Richard II, but he defied royal authority during Richard's second expedition to Ireland in 1399. Jean Creton, a French diplomat who accompanied Richard in 1399, has left a vivid description of Art's horsemanship and military prowess.[106] The power of Meic Murchada declined after Art's death in 1416–17, partly due to the campaigns of the justiciar John Talbot. Art's descendants nevertheless retained the title 'king of Leinster' until the sixteenth century.

In the early fifteenth century, the English of Leinster were embroiled in a bitter feud between Talbot and James Butler, the fourth earl of Ormond, concerning the inheritance of the honour of Wexford. Ormond was supported by his father-in-law, the earl of

---

[105] Orpen, 'Fitz Geralds'.
[106] Lydon, *Ireland*, pp. 115–17, 121–3; Webb, trans., 'Translation of a French metrical history'.

Kildare. As a result, Kildare was arrested in 1418 on the accusation of plotting against Talbot.[107] The colonial infighting may have aided the rise of Uí Chonchobuir of Offaly in northern Leinster. From the 1420s, In Calbach Ua Conchobuir operated in alliance with the de Berminghams and Uí Ragallaig of Cavan to prey upon English settlers in Meath. John Talbot failed to keep In Calbach more than temporarily in check, and at his death in 1458, the 'Annals of Connacht' claimed that In Calbach 'got more of Leinster from the Galls and Gaels opposing him' than any previous lord.[108]

The late fifteenth century witnessed the meteoric rise of the earls of Kildare under the patronage of English kings. The seventh earl, Thomas, successfully defended the Pale and regained a large tract of territory in the Kildare Marches from Uí Chonchobuir of Offaly. Thomas's son Gerald, 'the Great earl', served as chief governor of Ireland on three occasions from 1478 until his death in 1513. Gerald was an able military strategist who reorganised the Pale's southern defences around his principal castles, including Maynooth, Kildare, Athy, Castledermot and Powerscourt. Remarkably, Gerald survived as the principal royal agent in Ireland despite accusations of treason for supporting two separate pretenders to the English throne. The lands of Leinster were too strategically significant to the English government, and Gerald was too influential to risk bringing him down and creating a power vacuum in Ireland.[109] It would be left to Henry VIII in the sixteenth century to enforce more direct English royal control in Leinster.

MEATH

The wealth and accessibility of Meath made it vulnerable to the ambitions of Irish over-kings in the twelfth century and to the ambitions of English colonists thereafter. The Uí Maíl Sechnaill erstwhile kings of Tara had fallen into relative obscurity by the twelfth century. On several occasions, contenders for the over-kingship of Ireland stepped in to determine who would rule in Mide. In the northeast of the province, the decline of Uí Maíl Sechnaill aided the rise of Donnchad Ua Cerbaill of the Airgíalla, although his death in 1168 after a

---

[107] Crooks, 'Background'.
[108] *AConn, s.a.* 1458; Nicholls, *Gaelic and Gaelicised Ireland*, p. 174.
[109] Ellis, 'Fitzgerald, Gerald'.

forty-year reign would leave something of a power vacuum.[110] The weakened province of Mide therefore made for relatively easy pickings for the English invaders. In 1172, Henry II granted the liberty of Meath to Hugh de Lacy for the service of fifty knights, along with custody of Dublin.[111] Hugh de Lacy built the fortress at Trim (Co. Meath) as the *caput* of English lordship in Meath among numerous other castles, and sought spiritual protection by founding a Benedictine Priory at Fore (Co. Westmeath). By 1178, Hugh had cultivated positive links with the Connacht over-king Ruaidrí Ua Conchobuir. His ensuing marriage to Ruaidrí's daughter without the permission of Henry II called his loyalty into question. Hugh would later be accused of preventing Gaelic lords from paying tribute to the crown. Nevertheless, he was not generally popular among Gaelic rulers, and he was assassinated in 1186 at the behest of the Gaelic king of Tethba.[112] Hugh was succeeded by his son Walter, who was born from his first 'official' marriage. Hugh's son William Gorm, born from his Ua Conchobuir bride, was judged illegitimate, although he would play an active role in Irish affairs in alliance with his English half-brothers.[113]

Walter gained control of his father's lands in Ireland in 1194 and soon after founded the borough of Drogheda. Walter and his brother Hugh would later incur the displeasure of the kings John and Henry III, which necessitated the payment of hefty fines in 1198, 1213 and 1225. These fines, along with de Lacy's ambitious programme of castle building and ecclesiastical patronage, led the family to become increasingly mired in debt. Walter died in 1241 without a male heir. His estates passed through two granddaughters, Margaret and Maud, to the families of John de Verdon and Geoffrey de Geneville.

Geoffrey de Geneville held the share of Meath centred on the castle of Trim and served as justiciar of Ireland from 1273 to 1276. His justiciarship was inglorious due to his military defeats at the hands of the Leinster Irish. In later years, Geoffrey was embroiled in disputes with royal officials in Dublin and only maintained his rights in Meath with difficulty. Geoffrey retired to the Dominican Priory of Trim in 1308, and his lands passed via his granddaughter to Roger Mortimer of Wigmore in Herefordshire.[114] Roger built up

[110] Smith, *Colonisation*, p. 15.
[111] Veach, 'Henry II's grant'; Veach, 'Relentlessly'.   [112] AU, *s.a.* 1186.
[113] Veach, 'King and magnate'; Veach and Verstraten Veach, 'William Gorm'.
[114] Prestwich, 'Geneville, Geoffrey'.

considerable power in Ireland, gaining custody over the de Verdon lands of western Meath during a minority, and extending his influence into Louth and Kildare, becoming earl of March in 1328. Mortimer's aggrandisement in Ireland was aided by the great influence he wielded in England and Wales. He was instrumental in the deposition of Edward II in 1327, and his status at court during the minority of Edward III caused resentment among magnates. Roger was executed on the young king's orders in 1330, but his grandson Edmund acquired through marriage and inheritance the earldoms of Ulster and March, as well as the lordships of Clare, Connacht, Kilkenny and Meath. This power bloc meant that the Mortimers became key agents of the crown, although their interests across the Irish Sea led to their long periods of absence from Ireland, which aided the rise of Gaelic families.[115]

Uí Maíl Sechnaill were unable to capitalise on the weakening of English power. They had been reduced to a marginal existence in Delvin (Co. Westmeath) where they fought a war of attrition against English settlers, particularly the local Tuit family. Meanwhile other Gaelic dynasties rose to prominence, including Uí Fergail of Annaly who destroyed the English settlements along the northwestern fringes of Meath, while the lands of Moycashell (Co. Westmeath) fell under the control of the Meic Eochagáin of Cenél Fiachach. From the late fourteenth century, the authority of Dublin was increasingly rejected by Gaelicised English families in west Meath, including the Daltons, Dillons, and Tyrrells.[116] The families of eastern Meath, which lay closer to Dublin, remained more loyal to English kings. During the late Middle Ages, landholders including the Flemings (who held estates in north Meath) and the Nugents (of Delvin in west Meath) held local government positions and jostled for influence in the central administration based in Dublin.

Upwardly mobile families would be continually drawn to the fertile and accessible lands of eastern Meath throughout the Later Middle Ages, and this helped keep the region under English royal control. In the fourteenth century, these families included the Darcys, Prestons and Plunketts, who acquired lands through marriage and purchase and held government positions of local and central significance in the fifteenth century and beyond.[117] The wealth and status of these

---

[115] Dryburgh, 'Mortimer'.   [116] Nicholls, *Gaelic and Gaelicised Ireland*, p. 177.
[117] Abraham, 'Upward mobility'.

families are reflected in the construction of tower houses and the addition of perpendicular features to local churches in the fifteenth century. The wealth, density of English settlement and proximity to Dublin made eastern Mide (Meath) the most culturally and politically Anglicised area of Ireland in the later Middle Ages.

The institutions introduced for colonial government in Ireland were based on English models. The headquarters of the English administration sat in Dublin, making it the capital of the English colony. Given the difficulties of communication between England and Ireland, it became necessary from an early stage to have a royal representative in post in Dublin. Thus, a great deal of power was vested in the justiciar or chief governor who exercised many royal prerogatives, including the right to summon parliament and issue writs in the king's name. He presided over the supreme court in Ireland and was the commander-in-chief of the royal army during all campaigns. Given that the purpose of colonial expansion was power and profit, an exchequer was one of the first governmental institutions to be established. This was presided over by a treasurer and chamberlain who kept a record of accounts and related business. In 1232, a chancery was created separate from the exchequer, with its own staff and records, and from 1250 escheators were regularly appointed to oversee the income of vacant bishoprics.[118]

The shiring of Ireland was a piecemeal endeavour, influenced by the boundaries of pre-existing Irish political units. County Dublin was forged in the late twelfth century, and the process continued through much of Ireland in the thirteenth century.[119] Large areas of the English lordship were organised into liberties where local lords were granted some immunity from royal jurisdiction (except taxation, representation in parliament and great councils and – apart from Meath – the four legal pleas of arson, rape, forestalling and treasure trove).[120] By the middle of the thirteenth century, the Irish judiciary had a sedentary bench of common pleas sitting in Dublin, while shire courts and liberty courts provided justice in the localities. The law administered in all of these courts was the common law of England

---

[118] Lydon, 'Expansion', p. 171.   [119] McGrath, 'Shiring of Ireland'.
[120] Frame, 'Lordship and liberties'.

(access to which was denied to most of the Gaelic Irish).[121] The justiciar was the highest court of appeal within the colony, and above
him cases could still be referred to the English king.

The justiciar was expected to take advice regarding the day-to-day
management of the colony from tenants in chief of the crown and
higher clergy, as well as salaried officials. Great Councils were held
to bring the greater magnates and the king's officers together to discuss issues, and these lay the foundations for the Irish parliament. The
first mention of an Irish parliament refers to a gathering at Castledermot in 1264.[122] The role of parliament was to settle disputes, deal with
petitions, formulate legislation, grant subsidies and obtain consent for
other measures. By 1297, when grave concerns merited wider representation, the parliament included not only secular and ecclesiastical
magnates but also two knights from each county and liberty, sheriffs
and a steward from each liberty. By 1299, cities and major boroughs
were also represented, although membership of a parliament could
still be tailored to suit the matters under discussion.[123] By the end
of the fourteenth century popular representatives of 'the commons'
and 'clerical proctors' representing the lower clergy were introduced.
Nevertheless, the Gaelic Irish who dwelt in the English colony continued to be excluded. The numbers attending parliament shrank as
the area under English jurisdiction in Ireland declined in the fourteenth and fifteenth centuries. The parliament represented the voice
of the Anglo-Irish elite in Ireland. It was distinct from the government in London, although it was expected to enforce its decisions in
an Irish context. In 1495 Poynings's Law sought to curtail the independence of the Irish parliament by requiring English royal approval
to summon a parliament or enact any item of legislation.

GAELIC INSTITUTIONS

Inauguration was an important institution for the public recognition
of a new leader in Gaelic Ireland. Often the ritual took place in an
open-air assembly. More than thirty sites have been identified in the
Irish landscape. A variety of features including earthen mounds, inauguration stones and sacred trees are associated with these sites. Their

[121] See the earlier discussion.
[122] Richardson and Sayles, *Irish Parliament*, pp. 58–60.
[123] Lydon, 'Land of war', p. 271.

use is witnessed in prose tracts, annals and bardic poetry from the twelfth century, but with increasing significance from the fourteenth century onwards. The success of Gaelic lords in regaining or extending their territories at the expense of English colonists enhanced the role of inauguration, not merely as a show of strength but also to assert claims over territory. Rites of inauguration, despite their archaic sentiment, were also influenced by European practices. The famous Tulach Óg inauguration chair of the Uí Néill (illustrated by Richard Bartlett and destroyed in 1602) may reflect a hybrid between a throne, as used by Continental and British kings, and an older inauguration stone, '*Lec na Riogh*', that is mentioned in Irish chronicles in 1432.[124] Thus in the rites of Irish kingship, as elsewhere, archaism and innovation were combined.

In addition to inaugural assemblies, other public and private gatherings were an essential feature of lordship. Public assemblies (*óenaig*) continued to be held, although the political significance of these gatherings declined and they were increasingly linked with festivals of the church.[125] Gatherings of the elite are also referred to, which might have had a legal role. The term *airecht*, later *oireachtas*, referred to meetings of the vassals of a Gaelic lord. These assemblies had a range of purposes including settling disputes, raising taxes and making proclamations.[126] Councils comprising a restricted group of advisors were also held. There was overlap in the purpose and nomenclature of consultative meetings. However, their display and exercise of leadership must have been as significant as councils and parliaments were for English colonists.

The members of a lord's council included a selection of close adherents and the officers of his own household. A lord was bound to his chief clients through a system of payments and stipends; land and gifts were also used to reward officials, including poets, judges, bodyguards, stewards and messengers. In the course of the Middle Ages, a shift has been discerned from ceremonial and hereditary roles within the royal household of Gaelic kings to a body of trained professionals, including the posts of marshal and constable adopted from Anglo-Norman culture; there was also a greater military emphasis.[127] Trained professional jurists or 'brehons' continued to be important figures

---

[124] FitzPatrick, *Royal inauguration*, pp. 139–41.
[125] Simms, *From kings to warlords*, pp. 62–3.   [126] Ibid., pp. 67, 75.
[127] Ibid., pp. 94–5.

in the retinue of Gaelic lords. Many English lords also employed brehons to adjudicate in cases among their Gaelic subjects. Famous legal dynasties, including the Meic Áedacáin of Connacht and the Uí Deoráin of Leinster, ran their own law schools The Gaelic legal system was based on inherited rules and principles, so that early law texts were preserved, copied and glossed, enabling a degree of uniformity in legal training across Ireland despite high levels of political fragmentation. Laws were reinterpreted and adapted over time so that they included elements of English, Roman and canon law by the fifteenth century. Serious crimes became less a matter of private arbitration as lords claimed shares of legal fines, and the death penalty was imposed more freely in cases that excited public censure.[128]

The role of poets as public officials continued in the Later Middle Ages. More is known about their careers in the later Middle Ages when the authorship of poems was more frequently preserved. The poet was the professional publicist, eulogiser and sometimes diplomat for important families and leaders. The transmission of oral memory and personal testimony was a significant aspect of maintaining agreements between powerful individuals, although written documentation increased in significance as the Middle Ages progressed. Gaelic land transactions were sometimes recorded in religious manuscripts such as the twelfth-century *notitiae* written into the 'Book of Kells'. From the twelfth century charters composed on European models came into use through the influence of Church reform, and they became more widespread following the English invasion.[129] The increased use of official documentation (primarily linked to the church) led the greater Gaelic lords to have their own chancellors or secretaries and to draw on the services of a favoured ecclesiastical institution.[130] Written agreements could also be authenticated by notaries who served a secular and ecclesiastical role in Gaelic Ireland.[131]

By the end of the Middle Ages, many features of Gaelic lordship had been incorporated into the houses of greater English magnates. Similarly, English and Continental practices influenced the governance of the Gaelic elite. This interchange reflected the close

[128] Nicholls, *Gaelic and Gaelicised Ireland*, pp. 53–4.
[129] Flanagan, 'Irish royal charters'.   [130] Simms, *From kings to warlords*, p. 94.
[131] McInerney, *Clerical and learned lineages*, p. 97.

proximity of Gaelic and English cultures as well as Continental links through trade, war and the Church.

CONCLUSION

In the decades prior to the English invasion of Ireland, power was increasingly centralised in the hands of Irish provincial over-kings. However, any bids to establish a Gaelic monarchy were cut short by the invasion of Henry II of England. During the late twelfth and thirteenth centuries, large areas of eastern and southern Ireland were colonised by the English. The incompleteness and piecemeal nature of this conquest would leave the island divided as Gaelic kings continued to rule beyond the boundaries of English power. As the English colony waned in the fourteenth century, Gaelic lords were able to increase their landholdings, and there was greater acculturation between the Gaelic Irish and English colonists. During the fifteenth century, the English elite in Ireland developed loyalties and interests that might diverge from the parliament in London. English royal government became focused in the regions of Dublin and Drogheda, and royal authority was increasingly devolved to the Anglo-Irish earls of Desmond, Ormond and Kildare. Despite the growing authority of Gaelic lords in the fifteenth century, their power remained fragmented at a regional level. The long-held notion of a Gaelic kingship of all Ireland would remain a poetic aspiration and an unfulfilled prophecy.

10

RELIGION AD 1100–1500

In the memorable words of Richard Southern, 'When historians write of the Church as if it could be separated from secular history, they are simply repeating the mistake made by medieval ecclesiastical reformers, who were never more clearly captives of their environment than when they spoke of their freedom from it.'[1] In Ireland as elsewhere in late medieval Christendom, Church, society and politics were intimately enmeshed. The Church continually adapted in response to, and shaped, broader historical developments. From the late eleventh century, the impact of the so-called Gregorian reform movement would be felt in Ireland, initiating a process of religious renewal and institutional restructuring. The rivalries between Irish over-kings would help mould the outcome of these developments. The English invasion brought further changes, hastening conformity with external ecclesiastical mores in some regions and inhibiting their development in others. Later influences on the medieval Church included the growth of the mendicant orders and the political and cultural changes of the fourteenth century that brought a greater share of Irish territory under Gaelic control. At the end of the period under discussion, the Church was a powerful and widely respected institution in Irish society. There was, it seems, little appetite for the dramatic changes that would reshape the Church in Ireland during the sixteenth century.

[1] Southern, *Western society*, p. 16.

The Church in early medieval Ireland was complex patchwork of religious institutions often combining pastoral and monastic functions at a single location. In the late eleventh century, interest in the currents of contemporary Church reform, the conquest of England by William the Conqueror, and the reluctance of towns that claimed a Scandinavian identity to be incorporated within Irish dioceses prompted links to develop between a number of Irish churches and the see of Canterbury. The archbishops of Canterbury consecrated bishops of Dublin and Waterford in the late eleventh century. The Uí Briain kings of Munster were interested in cultivating relations with these powerful primates of the English Church who recognised their position as kings of Ireland. However, in the early twelfth century, the Irish Church developed its own self-contained episcopal hierarchy. Irish kings and leading churchmen worked together to create an island-wide diocesan system for the provision of pastoral care. At the same time, Continental religious orders were given patronage to establish houses in Ireland.

In 1101, Muirchertach Ua Briain, over-king of Munster, granted the Rock of Cashel, capital of his Munster rivals, to the Church in perpetuity. This act symbolised a combination of political and religious interests.[2] Muirchertach presented himself as a pioneer of reform, and the decrees of the synod at Cashel in 1101 show an attempt to introduce precepts of clerical celibacy and canon laws of marriage into Irish society.[3] Muirchertach worked to win the friendship of the archbishops of Armagh who could aid him in wielding influence over the lands of Northern Uí Néill. The primates would, however, remain sympathetic to Uí Néill interests under the guise of peacemaking. In 1101, Domnall Mac Amalgada, *comarba* of Armagh, arranged a truce between Ua Briain and the northern Uí Néill ruler Mac Lochlainn, for one year. The archbishop may have been influenced by the contemporary continental Peace of God movements of the continent. A further truce was arranged in 1109 by Cellach, the new *comarba* of Armagh and an ardent reformer.

Soon after Cellach was consecrated, a new bishopric was created at Limerick under the auspices of Muirchertach Ua Briain. The burgeoning Hiberno-Scandinavian town had become the Ua

[2] AT, *s.a.* 1101.   [3] Ó Corráin, 'Synod'; Bray, ed., *Records of convocation*, pp. 79–80.

Briain ruler's principal residence. Muirchertach bypassed the earlier policy of allowing bishops of Hiberno-Scandinavian sees to be consecrated in Canterbury. Instead, the new bishop, Gille(bertus), appears to have been consecrated in Ireland. Gille went on make an important theoretical contribution to Church reform in Ireland with his tract *De Statu Ecclesiae*, which laid down a pattern for the secular church hierarchy.[4] He presided as papal legate over the Synod of Ráith Bresail in 1111 where a diocesan structure of twenty-six sees was laid down, with two archdioceses of Armagh and Cashel (Co. Tipperary).[5] This significantly reduced the number of bishops active in Ireland, but the number was still large in comparison to many parts of western Europe.[6] This restructuring of the Church was a major achievement, although politically biased towards Munster through the significance given to Cashel.

As political circumstances changed, another synod was held in 1152 at Kells-Mellifont.[7] This meeting provided two further archdioceses at Dublin and Tuam (Co. Galway), with primacy awarded to Armagh and an increase in the overall number of sees to thirty-eight. The proceedings at Kells-Mellifont were sanctioned by the papal legate, Cardinal John Paparo, and the arrangements effectively quelled English claims of ecclesiastical supremacy in Ireland. There had been rivalry between the archbishops of Canterbury and Armagh over control of Dublin in 1121. The effective snub to Canterbury's position posed by the Kells-Mellifont synod may have led certain members of the English clerical hierarchy to support an English invasion of Ireland. In 1154, John of Salisbury helped secure from Pope Hadrian IV the bull *Laudabiliter* for King Henry II. This authorised the invasion of Ireland in return for ecclesiastical taxes and Church reforms, although it would not be acted upon for another seventeen years.

The enthusiasm for reform in Ireland was not restricted to a handful of kings and bishops. A wider level of support was required to implement decisions made at the reform synods. This enthusiasm was also witnessed by the patronage of new religious orders. In the twelfth century, the lifestyle of monks and nuns would be brought into greater uniformity when the rules of St Benedict and

---

[4] Fleming, *Gille*.

[5] Dumville, *Councils*, pp. 38, 43; MacErlean, 'Synod of Ráith Bresail'.

[6] Dolley, *Anglo-Norman Ireland*, p. 14.

[7] Comyn and Dinneen, eds. and trans., *History of Ireland by Geoffrey Keating*, III: 314–17; Bray, ed., *Records*, p. 85.

St Augustine were popularised, often replacing diverse local practices and traditions. The drive for new religious orders in Ireland
was spearheaded by Cellach, archbishop of Armagh, and his chosen
successor. Máel Máedoc, better known as St Malachy. Malachy introduced the Continental religious observances of the Augustinians and
the Cistercians to Ireland. The Augustinian canons had spread rapidly
in Europe since they had received papal sanction in 1059. Their way
of life combined conventual life with pastoral duties.[8] The Cistercians emerged at the very end of the eleventh century as an order
that advocated strict adherence to the rule of St Benedict. In 1139–40
Malachy travelled to Rome via France and stayed at the Cistercian
house of Clairvaux. It was here that he learnt about the order and
befriended Bernard of Clairvaux, one of the leading churchmen in
twelfth-century Europe. The Augustinians and Cistercians were the
most popular of the continental religious orders in Ireland. Before the
English invasion more than ten Cistercian houses and forty houses of
Augustinian canons had been established.[9] The majority of reformed
houses were founded for male religious, but a significant minority
were for women, including the foundation of two convents by Diarmait Mac Murchada. There was also support for education. In the
1160s Ruaidrí Ua Conchobuir, king of Connacht, provided an annual
endowment of ten cows to support the lector of Armagh in teaching
students from Ireland and Scotland.[10]

The degree of reform achieved in Irish churches and lay society
before the English arrived was a matter of debate. The invaders came
in the words of Pope Alexander III 'to root out the weeds of vice from
the Irish'. According to Jocelin of Furness writing in the 1180s, the
Irish credited St Malachy with the restoration of the Irish Church to
Christian laws, but the English claimed all the credit for themselves.[11]
Bernard of Clairvaux is often quoted for his commentary on the
barbarity of the Irish in his 'Life of St Malachy'. He denounced their
reluctance to pay first fruits or tithes, their lack of confession and
penance, unlawful marriages and the lack of preaching and devotional music in churches, declaring them to be 'Christians in name,
pagans in fact'. However, this negative portrayal served to highlight
his portrayal of Malachy's achievements in reviving Christian customs

[8]   Preston, 'Canons', p. 24.
[9]   Watt, *Church in medieval Ireland*, pp. 43, 49–50; Flanagan, *Transformation*, p. 243.
[10] *AU, s.a.* 1169, cf. 1162, 1174.   [11] Watt, *Church in medieval Ireland*, p. 155.

and rebuilding churches. Bernard of Clairvaux claimed that the Irish had changed: 'Which before was not my people, now is my people.'[12]

Nevertheless, such radical changes could not happen quickly. Some tenets of reform, such as the separation of ecclesiastical and lay interests and the celibacy of priests, caused recurrent difficulties throughout Christendom. The nonconformity of the Irish to ecclesiastical marriage laws was, among other things, enthusiastically condemned by apologists for the English invasion. In 1172, a synod was held at Cashel under the auspices of the English king Henry II where Irish bishops supported his reform agenda. A set of Latin decrees from the council was recorded by Gerald of Wales, which reiterated the concerns over tithes and marriage laws that had been voiced in earlier councils.[13] Letters from Pope Alexander III endorsed the decisions made at Cashel and enjoined the Irish to be obedient to Henry II.[14]

The English conquerors were generous in their patronage of new religious orders, founding around eighty new priories, monasteries and nunneries by 1230. However, this new elite, as did the old one, could take from the Church with one hand and give with the other. William I Marshal, who seized lands from Ferns Abbey, was the founder of two Cistercian abbeys in Ireland at Duiske (Co. Kilkenny) and Tintern (Co. Wexford), as well as Cartmel Priory in England.[15] Another noble who had an ambivalent relationship to the Church was William de Burgh. He plundered the monasteries of Abbeyknockmoy, Clonfert, Meelick and Clonmacnoise in 1202–4, but was also the founder of the Augustinian house of Athassel (Co. Tipperary).[16] The orders favoured by the incoming elites were the Augustinians, the priory-hospitals of the *Fratres Cruciferi*, and the Knights Templar. The Benedictines and the Cistercians also received significant amounts of support from the colonists.

By 1230 it has been estimated that there were around 200 religious houses for men, and around 40 nunneries in Ireland. The majority of these institutions had been founded under Gaelic patronage.[17] The twelfth-century reforms brought Ireland an impressive number of religious houses in relation to its size, wealth and population. The

---

[12] Ibid., pp. 17–18.
[13] Scott and Martin, eds. and trans., *Expugnatio*, pp. 98–101; Bray, ed., *Records*, ed. Bray, pp. 91–4.
[14] Sheehy, *When the Normans came*, pp. 25–31.
[15] Crouch, *William Marshal*, pp. 212–13.
[16] Watt, *Church in medieval Ireland*, p. 48.   [17] Hall, 'Towards a prosopography', p. 3.

categorisation of houses according to the ethnic identity of their founders, obscures the fact that patronage of religious foundations did not need to be ethnically exclusive. For example, in the late thirteenth century, a Gaelic Irishman, William Ua Ceallaig, gave land in Meath to the canons of Llanthony Secunda, an English house with extensive estates in Ireland.[18]

In addition to diocesan and monastic reform, a key organisational development of the twelfth century was the formation of territorially defined parishes. The complex system of pastoral care witnessed in the early Middle Ages was, over the course of time, simplified into a single system, whereby territorially defined parishes lay under the direct jurisdiction of diocesan bishops. It is not clear to what extent this process was in train before the English invasion owing to the nature of the sources, but the settlers appear to have accelerated this development. It was convenient for English lords to have parishes coterminous with units of lordship.[19] These often preserved the boundaries of pre-existing secular territorial units. In Gaelic areas, customary loyalties to familial churches or mother churches and the distribution of church lands (or *termonn*) may have slowed the process of change. Nevertheless, there is archaeological evidence of a marked expansion of church building in western parts of Ireland from the late twelfth century. This may reflect parochial reorganisation contemporary with developments in the English colony.[20]

THE IMPACT OF REFORM ON THE GAELIC CHURCH

Institutional reform based on external models was not welcomed by all. In the 1150s and 1160s Abbot Flaithbertach Ua Brolcáin, leader of the Columban *familia* based at Derry, sought to reform his churches.[21] However, in 1203 the conversion of the Columban community of Iona to Benedictine rule prompted a violent reaction from the abbots of Derry and Armagh and the bishops of Derry and Raphoe, who unsuccessfully attempted to oust the Benedictines.[22] Some local bishops also refused to yield to their new archbishops within the reorganised diocesan system. These dioceses could be downgraded to rural deaneries as a result.[23] Sometimes the changes were smoothed over through compromise or by facilitating less

---

[18] Hogan, *Priory of Llanthony*, pp. 145–7.   [19] Flanagan, *Transformation*, p. 87.
[20] Ní Ghabláin, 'Origin of medieval parishes', p. 39.
[21] Herbert, *Iona, Kells and Derry*, pp. 109–23.   [22] *AU, s.a.* 1204.
[23] McInerney, *Clerical and learned lineages*, p. 76.

disruptive changes. Many ecclesiastical settlements were converted to the Augustinian rule. In so doing churches could continue to perform parochial duties and observe the religious life. The Augustinians were less hierarchic and allowed more local autonomy than other new orders. The Augustinian rule also gave scope for local variations in lifestyle that could reflect former practices.[24] A sense of continuity with the past is reflected in Augustinian houses through the cults of Irish saints that they often promoted.[25]

It has been noted at Clones (Co. Monaghan) and Ballysadare (Co. Sligo) that church lands were divided between the new religious orders and incumbent *erenagh* families. This hints that some churches witnessed a territorial divorce settlement between members of the religious community who supported reform and those who opposed it.[26] A few communities opted to remain as they were and survived into the later Middle Ages, including the Culdees of Armagh. In 1366, the Dublin diocesan decrees refer to churches that neither observed the rules of Benedict nor Augustine, which might suggest that traditional forms of religious life continued even in the southeast of Ireland where English influence was strong.[27] Other communities conformed to European norms at a fairly late stage. For example, the church at Mayo only became a house of Augustinian canons in 1386.[28]

Within the new orders, some Gaelicisation of customs may be observed. Attitudes towards women was one element that reflected this Gaelicisation. Some houses took the form of double monasteries. These were regarded as suspect by the incoming English, and the practice was soon suppressed. However, it did not stop aristocratic women from being admitted to male houses as residents in retirement. In 1181, Gerald of Wales denounced the Cistercian abbey of St Mary's, by Dublin, for admitting a benefactress. He would probably have also disapproved of the retirement of Derbforgaill, benefactress of Mellifont, who died at that monastery in 1193.[29] Despite Gerald's censure, women of status were not kept out of male houses. In 1476 Ailbe, daughter of Áed Mac Uidhir, retired to Lisgoole (Co. Fermanagh), a house of Augustinian canons, where she died one year later.[30]

---

[24] Preston, 'Canons', p. 25.   [25] McInerney, *Clerical and learned lineages*, pp. 85–6.

[26] Nicholls, 'Gaelic society', p. 436.   [27] Gwynn, ed., 'Provincial', p. 103.

[28] Nicholls, 'Gaelic society', p. 435.   [29] Flanagan, *Transformation*, pp. 200–1.

[30] Nicholls, 'Gaelic society', p. 436.

In Irish society, church lands were often held as kin-land by cadet branches of leading dynasties. These families often held positions within the Church. The twelfth-century reforms meant that church land was often alienated from kin groups, which might only remain on these lands as tenants subject to episcopal control. Hereditary *coarbs* and *erenaghs* continued to function in areas of Gaelic landholding, but their status and function varied.[31] The reforms were not rapidly or uniformly applied. In the later Middle Ages, *coarbs* and *erenaghs* not infrequently held quasi-ecclesiastical posts as rectors or archdeacons. In these roles, they could continue their duties to provide hospitality and look after the physical possessions of the church.[32] To sustain their work, they might claim customary dues from peoples who dwelt on church lands.[33] Erenaghships continued to be established in Gaelic areas after the twelfth century. For example, the Uí Chatháin *erenaghs* were introduced from Dungiven Abbey (Co. Derry) to the lands of Corcomroe Abbey (Co. Clare) in the fourteenth century.[34] They became permanent tenants on mensal lands and may have assisted in the management of the abbey's ecclesiastical estates following the loss of population after the Black Death. In the sixteenth century, a number of *erenagh* lineages continued in Gaelic areas, often descended from the families of late medieval bishops.[35]

The persistence of pre-invasion ecclesiastical lineages and other features of early Irish churches demonstrate that Church reform in Ireland was never complete. The English invasion might be blamed for interrupting this process. However, it can be questioned whether institutional religious reform could have been uniformly achieved without the political unification of Ireland. Whether that political unity would have been realised free from foreign intervention is unknowable.

THE CONSPIRACY OF MELLIFONT

While tensions may have arisen in the twelfth century between communities who embraced reform and those who opposed it, difficulties could also arise within the ecclesiastical hierarchy of reformed communities. The most infamous conflict of this nature was the

---

[31] For the definitions of coarb and erenach see the earlier discussion; Ó Scea, 'Erenachs'.

[32] McInerney, *Clerical and learned lineages*, pp. 16–17, 75.   [33] Ibid., pp. 65–9.

[34] Ibid., pp. 78, 121.   [35] Nicholls, 'Gaelic society', p. 434.

so-called Conspiracy of Mellifont. Mellifont was the mother house of twenty Cistercian abbeys with Gaelic associations. Trouble began in 1216 when a Cistercian visitation to Mellifont (Co. Louth) authorised by the General Chapter was refused entry, and a riot took place at her daughter house at Jerpoint (Co. Kilkenny). In 1217, the abbots of both houses were removed, and a further investigation of the Irish Cistercian monasteries was commissioned by the General Chapter of the Order. The breakdown in discipline at Mellifont happened in an area and time of political turmoil that was more about authority than ethnicity.[36] The contemporary rebellion of Hugh II de Lacy against the English crown was opposed by William II Marshal, Áed Ua Conchobuir, king of Connacht, and the Munster kings of Meic Carthaig and Uí Briain. On his side, Hugh was supported by Áed Ua Néill of Tír Eógain. It was not until 1227, that Hugh II de Lacy was fully restored to his lands in Ireland. The conditions were not conducive to disciplined or harmonious religious life.

In 1226, two French abbots were sent to visit the Mellifont filiation in Ireland. Their visit faced resistance, rendering it ineffective and incomplete. The abbot of Owney (Co. Limerick) was deputed to finish the job, but he suffered persecution including robbery and the murder of some servants. In 1227 the Cistercian Order regarded the actions of the Mellifont filiation as a conspiracy against the Order. A number of Mellifont's daughter houses were reassigned to English and Welsh monasteries, and an English abbot, Stephen of Lexington, was sent to restore discipline. His letter book has survived, telling of his dangerous mission.[37] Abbeys were reconciled with difficulty and sometimes with threats of force. A number of abbots were deposed, but their replacements were not always welcome. In 1228, the new abbot of Mellifont resigned, while that assigned to Fermoy (Co. Cork) was murdered in 1230.[38] In a bid to prevent further trouble, Stephen of Lexington ordered that future monks had to be conversant in French and Latin (perhaps reflecting difficulties in communication between the Cistercian central authorities and monks in Ireland). Stephen also forbade the appointment of Irish abbots until 'they may in due time be more capable masters'. This could indicate racism on Stephen's part, although some abbeys were exempted from the ruling.[39] A group of Irish bishops appealed against Stephen and gained a

[36] O'Dwyer, *Conspiracy*, pp. 17–18.   [37] O'Dwyer, trans., *Stephen of Lexington.*
[38] O'Dwyer, *Conspiracy*, p. 21.   [39] Watt, *Church in Medieval Ireland*, p. 58.

sympathetic hearing from Gregory IX, who appointed them as visitors to the Irish Cistercian abbeys. Accusations of racial exclusion in monasteries would continue to be made from both a Gaelic Irish and an Anglo-Irish perspective throughout the later Middle Ages.

MENDICANT ORDERS

A new wave of religious foundations took place in Ireland from the 1220s with the arrival of mendicant preachers in Ireland. These new orders were characterised by their adherence to poverty, thereby living on charity and shunning the accumulation of property. They also combined public ministry with communal observance of the liturgical hours, and thus became popular among the laity. The four main mendicant orders that emerged in the thirteenth century were the Dominicans, Franciscans, the Carmelites and the Augustinian Friars. All would find support from both English and Gaelic communities in Ireland.

Initially the mendicants had an urban focus, and their earliest houses were in the more populous eastern and southern parts of the island. The first Dominican foundations in 1224 were in Dublin and Drogheda (Co. Louth), soon to be followed by communities in Kilkenny, Waterford, Limerick and Cork in the 1220s. In the following decade, Franciscan communities were established at Dublin, Athlone (Co. Roscommon) and perhaps at Youghal (Co. Cork).[40] From these initial foundations, the Friars spread west with some vigour, so that there were twenty-three Dominican houses by 1291 and thirty-two Franciscan friaries in Ireland by 1336, although most of these foundations were in place by the 1270s.[41] The Carmelites, Augustinian Friars and Friars of the Sack came to Ireland in the last third of the thirteenth century, and despite worsening economic conditions, twenty-eight friaries were founded between them by 1341. Compared to monastic orders the mendicant houses were relatively cost effective to endow, which may have been a factor in their popularity.

Patronage of the friars transcended ethnic boundaries. At Athenry (Co. Galway) the Dominican friary was founded by Meiler de Bermingham in 1241, but much of the claustral complex was built through the largess of Gaelic families, including the Uí Chonchobuir,

---

[40] Ó Clabaigh, *Friars*, pp. 9, 12.   [41] Ibid., p. 8.

Uí hEidhin and Uí Chellaig. Similarly, in Cork, the Dominican friary was founded in 1229 by Philip de Barry, but it was supported by the Meic Carthaig.[42] Mixed ethnic communities were promoted as a matter of principle within the Franciscan order in Ireland. This ideal was espoused on occasion by the English government as a way to promote peace. However, in 1310 and 1366. attempts were made to exclude the Gaelic Irish from religious houses in English areas, although the policy was not observed.[43] Gaelic friars were able to represent an influential minority in some Anglo-Irish houses, while in areas on the frontiers of English landholding, the balance between friars of different identities could be equitable, as revealed by the necrology of the Dominican house of Athenry dated 1394×1452.[44]

Despite the evidence of peaceful coexistence, tensions did erupt on numerous occasions among friars and their patrons. In 1291, there is record of a violent confrontation between Irish and English friars at a Franciscan chapter in Cork, in a dispute over the rights of the Gaelic brethren.[45] Furthermore the Franciscan bishop of Kildare, Nicholas Cusack complained to Edward I in a letter dated 1283×99 that the Gaelic Irish were often incited to violence by the Irish-speaking religious of various orders.[46] These suspicions came to a head during the years of the Bruce invasion when Edward II asked the justiciar to consider removing Irish friars out of areas of English jurisdiction.[47] In the 'Remonstrance of the Princes' sent to the pope in 1317, an Anglo-Irish Franciscan was singled out for promoting the heresy that it was not sinful to kill a Gaelic Irishman. For his part, Edward II complained to the pope about Gaelic friars who preached against him. As a result, legislation issued at the Franciscan provincial chapter in Dublin in 1324 ordered that the most distrusted Gaelic friars should be moved from eight convents to other houses. The fiscal prejudice of the English government was revealed in 1327 when the annual royal alms granted to Athlone friary (Co. Roscommon) was transferred to Cashel (Co. Tipperary) as no English friars remained at Athlone. The house was, however, restored to favour in 1354.[48] From the late fourteenth century, the political focus of the friars shifted towards Gaelic areas. This was in part owing to the consequences of the Black Death,

[42] Watt, *Church in medieval Ireland*, pp. 64–5.   [43] Ibid., pp. 82–4.
[44] Ó Clabaigh, *Friars*, pp. 31, 261–2.   [45] Watt, *Church in medieval Ireland*, pp. 78–9.
[46] Ó Clabaigh, *Friars*, p. 31.   [47] Watt, *Church in medieval Ireland*, p. 80.
[48] Ó Clabaigh, *Friars*, pp. 38, 91.

but it also reflected a more general shift of political control in Ireland into Gaelic hands.

Given their frequent activities and contacts outside the cloister, the mendicant orders would be badly affected by the Black Death of the mid-fourteenth century and recurrent episodes of plague that followed. One of the expedients adopted that reflected a crisis of personnel was that Augustinian Friaries were permitted to appoint local friars without knowledge of Latin.[49] The difficulties of procuring food and ministry in the wake of the plague are reflected in the right granted by the English crown to friars of Ennis (Co. Clare) to preach and beg in English districts in 1375.[50] Nevertheless, despite these straitened conditions a handful of new friaries continued to be founded in the 1350s.[51]

From the late fourteenth century, the friars in Ireland enjoyed continued popularity, with almost forty new houses of different mendicant orders being founded in the fifteenth and early sixteenth centuries, mainly in the west of Ireland, as well as forty-nine houses of lay adherents of the tertiary order (discussed later).[52] Success brought its challenges, however, and the friars attracted criticism for lapses in their standards. This was voiced most vigorously in Ireland by Richard FitzRalph, archbishop of Armagh in the late 1350s. In the fifteenth century, stricter adherence to mendicant ideals was promoted through the Observant reform movement.[53] This movement could be construed as pulling away from English authority because the houses that professed strict observance were exempted from ordinary provincial jurisdiction and given a greater degree of autonomy.

A movement away from English control can also be perceived more widely among the mendicants in the fifteenth century. Constitutionally the Irish Franciscans had enjoyed a greater independence as a separate province within the order. The first Gaelic minister provincial was William Ua Ragallaig, who acquired a charter of denisation as a condition of being confirmed in his post by King Henry VI in 1445. His appointment was opposed by a group of Anglo-Irish friars, and Henry VI withdrew his approval. Nevertheless, his position was upheld by Pope Eugenius IV, and William would be eventually succeeded by another Gaelic friar.[54] The Dominicans in Ireland sought

[49] Ó Clabaigh, *Friars*, p. 42.   [50] McInerney, *Clerical and learned lineages*, p. 84.
[51] Ó Clabaigh, *Friars*, pp. 42–3.   [52] Ibid., pp. 59–73.
[53] See the later discussion.   [54] Ó Clabaigh, *Friars*, pp. 70–2.

and failed to establish a separate province in the fourteenth century. In 1484 this concession was granted, and Maurice Ua Mocháin was appointed as prior provincial. However in 1491, the English Dominicans secured the reduction of the Irish province to its former subordinate status.

During the fifteenth century, the Observant movement and growing constitutional independence of the friars promoted closer ties to Continental houses and the papacy. These links proved to be significant during the reformations of the sixteenth century.[55] The emergence of Third Order mendicants among the laity in the fifteenth century was further demonstration of the success of the friars in winning popular support. The friars' espousal of life in imitation of Christ proved to be inclusive, both ethnically and across social boundaries.

SECULAR CLERGY AD 1180–1400

Within the secular church, tensions quickly emerged between Irish and English factions. These divisions have led to a debate whether the Church in later medieval Ireland was an agent of division or reconciliation. There has been a danger of imposing contemporary perspectives onto medieval materials. The surviving sources shed insights on moments when ethnic tensions may have added fuel to the fire of ideological and political conflict. The papacy strove to promote peace between Christians who obeyed its commands, regardless of nation, while advocating political obedience to kings of England.

Ethnic tensions are said to have arisen during the Dublin diocesan synod of 1186.[56] The decrees of the council have survived, as have two accounts written by Gerald of Wales who participated in the event. According to Gerald, Ailbe Ua Máile Muaid, abbot of Baltinglass (Co. Wicklow) and later bishop of Ferns who was favoured by John, lord of Ireland, preached a sermon that condemned the lack of chastity among English and Welsh priests who had settled in Ireland. This was backed up in the conciliar legislation issued by the English archbishop John Cumin, which praised the chastity of the Irish clergy and condemned 'the foul contagion of strangers' and forbidding all clergy from keeping concubines. Gerald, a man given to strong prejudices, followed Ailbe's sermon with his own condemnation of the Irish clergy for their drunkenness and neglect of pastoral care, which

---

[55] Walsh, 'Clerical estate', p. 367.   [56] Bray, ed., *Records*, pp. 96–105.

caused the laity to wallow in vice. Irish saints, he argued, were not people willing to die for their faith, for there had been few martyrs in Ireland. Gerald reported that the sermon was approved by his countrymen. He also recorded the response of the Irish archbishop of Cashel, who pointed out that Ireland lacked martyrs since the people were not wont to show force to their churchmen, 'but now a people has come to our country who know how to make martyrs'.[57] Gerald may have recorded the retort, both as a clever response, and as a dig against king Henry II regarding the English martyr Thomas Becket who was killed allegedly on his orders. The council of 1186, illustrates how ill feeling could be stirred up by sermons that highlighted the moral shortcomings of one people compared to another. Fiery characters like Gerald of Wales and Ailbe Ua Maíl Muaid were not inclined to promote harmony.[58]

Ailbe Ua Maíl Muaid would later excommunicate William I Marshal for seizing lands of the church from his diocese of Ferns. William's actions sparked another controversy. In 1216, King John had given Ailbe, bishop of Ferns, control of the temporalities of the diocese of Killaloe (Co. Clare) as his favourite candidate for the vacant see. However, the king died soon after, and William Marshal was appointed as regent of England for the nine-year-old King Henry III. Marshal was determined that Ailbe would not succeed to the diocese. In 1217 a veto against the promotion of Irishmen to Irish sees was promulgated under the name of William Marshal for the juvenile king. A complaint was sent to Pope Honorius III, who responded with letters condemning the exclusion of Irishmen from benefices as well as their inequality in law.[59] The English lords who had a vested interest in Ireland were perhaps most inclined to discriminate against the Gaelic Irish in ecclesiastical matters.

The years after 1180 were characterised by the Anglicisation of the episcopate in Ireland. The spread of English settlement was reflected in the selection of prelates. In 1181 Lorcán Ua Tuathail (Laurence O'Toole), archbishop of Dublin, died and he was replaced by an English royal nominee, John Cumin. Meath had an English prelate from 1192 and Waterford by 1195, followed by Down, Leighlin and Ossory, which came into English hands around 1202. Lismore and Limerick received English bishops from 1215–16. By 1216 the

---

[57] O'Meara, trans., Gerald of Wales, *History and topography*, pp. 115–16.
[58] Watt, *Church in medieval Ireland*, pp. 100, 152–7.   [59] Ibid., pp. 99–104.

diocese of Glendalough (an area largely under Gaelic control) was united with Dublin. William Marshal's attempt to install an English bishop at Killaloe in 1217 ultimately failed, although the dispute continued on after his death. Ferns and Kildare had English bishops from 1223.[60] The number of English bishops in Ireland had peaked by the mid-fourteenth century. Most of the bishoprics in the west of Ireland remained in Gaelic hands. Others switched between prelates of different backgrounds.

Sometimes friction can be observed between candidates from different cultures. Armagh was the most powerful archdiocese in Ireland, and it became the locus of a struggle for power in 1201, on the death of Archbishop Tomaltach Ua Conchobuir. Two rival elections were held. King John sought to buy off the Irish candidate, Echdonn (aka 'Eugenius') Mac Gille Uidhir, with a pension of 20 marks a year and the promise of another bishopric, but Echdonn took his case to Rome, where his election was upheld. Eventually Echdonn was reconciled with King John.[61] The conflict in Armagh indicated that the English of the diocese were unwilling to accept a Gaelic archbishop, although it was not until the mid-fourteenth century that Gaelic archbishops ceased to be appointed to Armagh. The diocese was divided for linguistic and political reasons. The archbishop was usually based in County Louth assisted by an Anglo-Irish archdeacon, while the dean of Armagh who was usually Gaelic Irish resided in Armagh. This arrangement continued into the sixteenth century.[62] Many sees in the later Middle Ages alternated between Irish and English prelates. It may be too simple to see rivalries over ecclesiastical power in national terms. Often rival claimants for episcopal office possessed a common ethnic identity, but where one representing local interests might be in contention with a prelate who lacked a local power base.[63]

The Church was powerful because of its physical resources, but the preaching of religious leaders could also wield more power over the laity than the mandates of political leaders. The anxieties wrought by the decline of English lordship at the end of the thirteenth century were expressed through suspicion of Gaelic churchmen, both within English-held areas and outside them. In 1324, Edward II asked the pope to support a programme that could help boost English

[60] Mooney, *Church*, p. 7.   [61] Watt, *Church and the two nations*, pp. 226–30.
[62] Mooney, *Church*, p. 6.   [63] Walsh, 'Clerical estate', pp. 363–4.

royal authority in Ireland. The plans were intended to ensure that all clergy preached loyalty to the English crown, that reluctance to accept English novices into Gaelic religious houses should be condemned, and that dioceses with an annual income of less than sixty pounds should be united with a larger diocese. The last suggestion would have removed many cathedrals from Gaelic areas and placed more power into the hands of bishops whose sees were located in Anglo-Irish towns. Shortly after Edward's petition, the papacy united the diocese of Cloyne and Cork, but went no further in implementing the requested diocesan changes.[64]

The demographic and political crises faced by the English lordship in the fourteenth century had ramifications for the secular Church. Many Anglo-Irish clerics seem to have left Ireland to work in England in the 1360s and 1370s. Political conditions may have made ministry in Ireland less attractive, while the impact of the Black Death in England opened up new opportunities to obtain benefices or gain employment as chantry priests. Their departure may have increased the numbers of Gaelic Irish clergy ministering in English districts. The Dublin diocesan decrees of 1367 required that all Gaelic priests within the English lordship swear an oath of fidelity to the king.[65] In the 'Statutes of Kilkenny, priests were required to minister in the English language, although they were given a period of time to learn the language if they had not already mastered it.[66] The 'Statutes of Kilkenny' further enjoined that in the future 'no Irishman of the nations of the Irish' should be allowed to join any cathedral, collegiate church or religious house, or hold any benefices. This rule proved to be unworkable, and exemptions were made through granting licences to Gaelic clergy.[67] Nevertheless intolerance and suspicion towards Gaelic clergy resurfaced in later legislation, while the departure of Anglo-Irish priests to England provoked further concern in the fifteenth century.

The papal schism that shook Europe from 1378 to 1417 stirred up divisions in Ireland. In 1378, Urban VI was elected pope, but shortly after the cardinal electors claimed that their choice had been influenced by a Roman mob. A new election was held and Clement VII was selected. Urban VI refused to stand down, and in the following

---

[64] Watt, *Church and the two nations*, pp. 193–5.
[65] Gwynn, ed., 'Provincial', pp. 100–2; Bray, ed., *Records*, pp. 171–89.
[66] Hardiman, ed., *A Statute*, §3.   [67] Ibid., §§13, 14.

months different rulers in Europe aligned themselves with one pope or the other. Richard II of England pronounced in favour of Urban VI, while the French and the Scots favoured Clement VII, who based himself at Avignon.[68] Most of Ireland supported Urban VI, but there were pockets of support for Clement VII in the archdioceses of Tuam, Armagh and Cashel – in areas under Gaelic control. That the schism may have stirred up ethnic tensions is hinted at by Clement's suspension of the Anglo-Irish bishop Robert of Killala who campaigned against him in Connacht. Some of the papal revenues collected in Ireland in the 1380s were diverted away from Urban VI to support the work of Clement VII. However, support for the Avignon papacy had fizzled out before the papal schism ended in 1417.[69]

The surviving evidence concerning the secular Church in late medieval Ireland focuses on moments of friction and irregularity. This casts a rather unedifying shadow on the state of the Church. It has perhaps been too easy to overplay the notion that there were two opposed nations in medieval Ireland. Undoubtedly there were difficulties in provision of a single Church hierarchy across two cultures and a fragmented political landscape. However, on a day-to-day basis the Church continued to function, and practical solutions were reached to address the pastoral needs of the laity.

THE CLERICAL ESTATE IN THE FIFTEENTH CENTURY

Although it has been conventional across Europe to portray the pre-Reformation era as one of decline, the fifteenth century witnessed religious enthusiasm in Ireland. This was expressed through considerable investment in church buildings across Ireland. The period also witnessed growing links with the papacy, particularly outside the English lordship. It also saw closer involvement between Gaelic Irish and Anglo-Irish communities. Within Gaelic churches the bonds between local families and churches were cemented by growing evidence for hereditary control of benefices and religious houses. The lack of clerical celibacy and the practice of nepotism within the Irish church would later receive much criticism. However, the argument can be made that that this was a practical method of securing clerical education and pastoral care in areas where parochial incomes were low by European standards.

[68] Barrell, *Medieval Scotland*, p. 239.   [69] Burns, trans., 'Papal letters'.

Architectural and archaeological studies have demonstrated that a major programme of church building, remodelling and ornamentation took place across Ireland in the fifteenth century. The majority of Irish medieval cathedrals were modified in this period through the addition of decorated doorways and windows to suit contemporary tastes. In the Pale, approximately twenty towers were added to churches to provide priestly accommodation, along with the construction and re-ornamentation of the majority of parish churches. These developments were not confined to prosperous Anglo-Irish areas. In Co. Clare, at least thirty-four churches were rebuilt in the fifteenth and sixteenth centuries, while in Fermanagh the archaeological evidence of church renovation and construction is complemented by chronicle evidence.[70] In 1480, the 'Annals of Ulster' recorded the death of Tomás Óg Mac Uidhir, lord of Fermanagh, describing him as 'a man that made churches and monasteries and Mass chalices and was once in Rome and twice in the city of St James on pilgrimage'. The programme of church rebuilding and ornamentation corresponded with the spread of the mendicant observant movement and religious fraternities among the laity. These developments show the strength of religious faith throughout Ireland and reflect displays of wealth during a time of relative economic prosperity.

In England, the parliament had sought to curtail papal involvement in the Church through the 'Statute of Provisors' of 1351. This limited the scope of papal appointments to clerical offices and the referral of litigation on Church matters to Rome. By the fifteenth century, these provisions were implemented in the English lordship of Ireland but not outside it. An increasing number of cases in Gaelic areas were referred to Rome in the fifteenth century.[71] Procurators were employed to transact business with the curia, and public notaries also exercised their office in Ireland by papal and/or imperial authority.[72] Occasionally supplicants travelled to Rome directly to present their case, accompanying pilgrims on their long journey south. An increase in the number of visitors to Rome prompted John Swayne, archbishop of Armagh, to plan a hostel there for both Anglo-Irish and Gaelic visitors in the early fifteenth century.[73]

---

[70] Jefferies, 'A Church in decline?'
[71] McInerney, *Clerical and learned lineages*, p. 95.
[72] Ibid., p. 97.   [73] Walsh, 'Clerical estate', p. 372.

The Gaelicisation of the Church was reflected in some of the matters brought before the pope. For example, during the pontificate of Boniface IX (1389–1401), Donald Magluay sought to displace William Wylde and John Tathe from benefices at Rathwire and Castlericard (Co. Westmeath) on the basis of their inability to understand the language of the majority of their flock. The matter was judged in Magluay's favour.[74] In 1482, Sixtus IV did not uphold the complaint of the people of Waterford, who refused to accept Nicholas Ua hÁengusa as their bishop of the grounds that he could not speak English.[75] The Gaelicisation of the Church is also apparent from other sources from the fourteenth century. These include the poem 'Land of Cockaygne' found in the British Library, manuscript Harley 913. It was composed in Middle English probably by a Franciscan author in Leinster. It is a satire on the luxurious life of Gaelic Cistercians. However, the text displays Irish linguistic features, revealing a context of two cultures in contact. In the fifteenth century, Irish churches became increasingly dependent on Gaelic families for recruitment. For example, between 1421 and 1520 more than half of the appointments made to Dublin benefices in Rome were given to men bearing Gaelic names.[76]

The principle of hereditary succession that had a strong place in the early medieval Church flourished with renewed vigour at the end of the Middle Ages. High levels of concubinage and clerical illegitimacy were present within Gaelic society. A survey of papal registers for the period 1400–86 indicates that one-third of priests who were issued mandates for benefices in the diocese of Kilfenora (Co. Clare) had clerical fathers.[77] In Gaelic Scotland similarly high levels of clerical offspring entering the Church are recorded. The marriage of clergy appears to have been more socially acceptable in Gaelic society than it was among the Anglo-Irish.[78] The fact that certain Gaelic lineages were able to monopolise local benefices could have had a practical value, given that clerical incomes in Gaelic areas tended to be inadequate. As there was no university in Ireland and travel abroad was prohibitively expensive, many clergy were trained within the family or at institutions with familial connections. From a pragmatic perspective,

[74] Ibid., p. 365.   [75] Theiner, ed., *Vetera monumenta*, pp. 487–8.
[76] Coleman, 'Obligationes pro annatis'.
[77] McInerney, *Clerical and learned lineages*, p. 98.
[78] Cosgrove, 'Armagh registers', pp. 314–15.

ecclesiastical lands and buildings could be maintained to greater effect in the knowledge that they were passing on to the next generation.

In the fifteenth century, there is increasing evidence for powerful Gaelic lineages obtaining church appointments. In some churches, the practice had been continuous throughout the later Middle Ages. For example, the nunnery of Kilcreevanty (Co. Galway) was founded by Cathal Crobderg Ua Conchobuir around 1200, and all known abbesses of that community were members of the same dynasty.[79] Meanwhile the Uí Briain of County Clare occupied high-status posts in the dioceses of Killaloe and Kilfenora.[80] In the diocese of Clogher the Mac Uidhir family dominated the bishopric, along with their Mac Cathmáil kinsmen.[81] The increasing practice of papal provision may have encouraged the development of a clerical oligarchy that could offer economic benefits both to the curia and to the families involved. The meagre nature of clerical incomes in Gaelic areas encouraged families to hold their benefices in plurality.[82] These apparent clerical abuses did not necessarily mark a decline in religious fervour, for there is plenty of evidence for lay piety and church building in the fifteenth century. Rather these deviations from institutional ideals may have been regarded as practical and acceptable within local society.

RESOURCES

The Church in Ireland was supported by a variety of sources including lands, rents, tithes, fees for services and customary payments, as well as donations and bequests. Despite this wide range of income streams many religious houses and parishes were poor by western European standards, and there was a notable distinction between the wealth of churches that lay securely within the English lordship and those outside it.

A great deal of land in Ireland was held by the Church. The archbishops of Dublin, who were probably the wealthiest churchmen in Ireland, held around 53,200 acres of land in County Dublin at the end of the Middle Ages (nearly one-quarter of the county). In the west, Cistercian abbeys tended to rank among the larger landholders. Corcomroe Abbey was the largest landholding unit in County Clare.

[79] Hall, 'Towards a prosopography', pp. 8–9.
[80] McInerney, *Clerical and learned lineages*, pp. 138, 142–3.
[81] Watt, 'The papacy and Ireland', pp. 136–7.
[82] McInerney, *Clerical and learned lineages*, p. 186.

In addition to the rents and rights of landholding, the larger churches held livestock, fisheries, mills and other buildings. In the fourteenth century, economic decline lessened donations of land to the Church, and changing political conditions caused some Anglo-Irish monasteries to lose outlying estates. Warfare and plague led to a decline in revenues for the archbishop of Dublin, who in 1352 obtained a grant from the pope to hold three or more benefices to compensate for losses.[83] However, other ecclesiastical estates in the English lordship continued to return healthy profits. In 1381, it was recorded that the proctors of the Irish lands of Llanthony Secunda Priory in Gloucester could regularly send £80 a year to England.[84] In the fifteenth century economic growth raised the incomes of church estates, which along with increased donations from the laity underpinned a contemporary boom in church building.

Tithes were the principal source of income for the secular Church. The 1172 Synod of Cashel had enjoined the laity to pay tithes on animals, crops and other produce to their church. The promulgation of this edict indicates that regularisation was sought across Ireland. The payment of tithes on other incomes was nevertheless variable. In 1453 the provincial synod of Cashel ordered the payment of tithes on the possessions of doctors, poets and craftsmen, which had not been customary before.[85] Not all the tithes collected in a parish went to support local pastoral work. A high percentage of parishes were impropriated by 1500, which meant their income was used to support religious institutions or individuals elsewhere in the Church.[86] Parish incomes in Ireland were often split between a rector (who received the greater share) and a vicar. In the province of Tuam and part of that of Armagh, bishops also received one-third or one-quarter of the tithes collected locally.[87]

With the exception of the dioceses of Dublin and Meath, parishes were generally underfunded. Priests would have been heavily dependent on customary offerings and payments from the laity. One positive effect may have been that clergy needed to cultivate good relations with their parishioners and minister effectively to secure donations. On the other hand, clerical poverty may have led to less educated or able priests providing pastoral care; it may have cultivated

---

[83] Down, 'Colonial society' p. 452.   [84] Ibid., p. 453.
[85] Begley, *Diocese of Limerick*, pp. 37–9.   [86] Ellis, 'Economic problems', p. 255.
[87] Nicholls, 'Gaelic society', p. 435.

undue subservience to wealthier parishioners and encouraged some
clerics to find other sources of income.[88] Efforts to safeguard the
incomes of parish priests can be seen in the decrees of the provincial
synod of Cashel in 1453. These stipulate that mendicants should not
beg on feast days when secular priests expected to receive church
offerings and that mendicants should give a quarter of any funeral
donations to the local parish priest.[89] These decrees also highlight
how vulnerable church tenants and property were to depredations
and lay exactions. A line had to be drawn between the hospitality that was provided voluntarily by the church and the hospitality that a secular lord might exact from his subjects.[90] Churches,
particularly in Gaelic areas, were expected to provide sustenance
for travellers and the needy. In 1479, Maurice Ua Fáeláin, a cleric
of Cloyne, complained to the pope that he could not subsist and
maintain hospitality according to the Irish manner on the income
of his rectory of Mahoonagh (Co. Limerick).[91] While the resources
of the Church in late medieval Ireland were vast, it maintained a
large number of clerics and temporalities to provide spiritual services (preaching, confession, sacraments and prayers). In addition, the
Church was relied upon for provisions for the poor, sick and travellers.
It was also a tool of government, preaching obedience and providing diplomatic and administrative manpower. For all these reasons,
both spiritual and pragmatic, the medieval Church was a prestigious
and useful institution that attracted devotion and donations from the
laity.

DONATIONS

Donations to the Church brought esteem in this world and promised
support in the next. Patrons of the Church came from all levels of
society, but it was those who gave the most who are best documented.
At the top of the hierarchy were kings. English kings did not found
many religious houses in Ireland, but they did offer letters of protection and gifts.[92] Gaelic rulers were prominent as founders of churches
in the west of Ireland, as powerful English lords were in the south
and east.[93] The wealth generated by new boroughs in Ireland funded

---

[88] *Cal. Papal letters*, V: 315; XIII: 162–3; Preston, 'Canons', p. 39.
[89] Begley, *Diocese of Limerick*, pp. 291–2, 433.
[90] Simms, 'Guesting and feasting', p. 84.   [91] *Cal. Papal Letters*, XIII: 76, 123.
[92] Ó Clabaigh, *Friars*, pp. 88–91.   [93] See the earlier discussion.

religious patronage by the urban elites. One example is the construction of the Lady Chapel in the Franciscan church of Dublin by the mayor, John le Decer, in the early fourteenth century.[94] Other religious sponsors included Margaret Athy, wife of the mayor of Galway, who initiated the construction of an Augustinian friary.[95] Wealthy individuals secured their commemoration by commissioning monuments within churches. These included tombs, statues and windows. Patrons of more middling status might provide furnishings or liturgical vessels or cloth for altars and statues.[96] Many gifts were linked with death and the afterlife. Places of burial were socially ranked, ideally close to the altar of a powerful church. Wealthy patrons often gave bequests in their will to cover their funeral expenses, including a procession, the funeral service, candles, a feast for the mourners and food to distribute among the poor.[97] The social elite could also fund prayers and masses to ease their soul's journey to heaven.[98]

While death may have provided a sobering focus for investment in the soul and social remembrance, piety was also demonstrated in life through charity. Within Gaelic society hospitality had long been a duty expected from the elite as well as from the Church. It was often praised alongside virtues in eulogies of pious men and women. In 1433, Margaret Ní Cherbaill was celebrated by poets and annalists for offering lavish feasts during a time of famine.[99] Ramon de Perellós, who left a vivid description of his visit to Ireland in 1397, reported that the court of the Ua Néill king was followed by a great number of poor who were fed on beef.[100] Such lavish hospitality was a mark of status in Gaelic society and might be prized as a form of social display more than the accumulation of material goods. Conspicuous charity could also help the donor through the prayers of the poor, which might help salve the souls of the rich.

The religious orders that were most dependent on charity were the mendicant friars for they shunned (at least in theory) the accumulation of property. The limits of questing for each friary and the scope of their pastoral work had to be licensed by bishops to avoid conflicts with secular clergy.[101] To help protect against temptation and

[94] Ó Clabaigh, *Friars* p. 97.   [95] Lyons, 'Lay female piety', p. 60.
[96] Ó Clabaigh, *Friars*, p. 107; Hall, *Women*, pp. 26–7.   [97] Hall, *Women*, p. 40.
[98] Mac Niocaill, ed., 'Registrum Cantariae'; Byrne *et al.*, ed. and trans., *Register of St Saviour's*.
[99] Simms, 'Guesting and feasting', pp. 91–2.
[100] Haren and de Pontfarcy, eds., *Medieval pilgrimage*, p. 110.
[101] Ó Clabaigh, *Friars*, p. 136.

other dangers, friars travelled in pairs on their quests and preaching tours. Their preaching had to appeal to the laity to win their support, as well as to provide edification. We have a direct insight into their words thanks to the survival of *Liber Exemplorum*, a thirteenth-century book of anecdotes to be used in preaching. It was put together by an English friar who spent much of his life in Ireland, and a number of sensational stories are included. These shed light on the fears and hopes of the Irish laity, as well as an element of salesmanship on the part of the friars when it came to describing the spiritual benefits of gifts and indulgences.[102]

RELIGIOUS GUILDS, CONFRATERNITIES AND TERTIARIES

Guilds and parish fraternities facilitated the communal organisation of charity and religious activities. In common with those of other European towns, urban craft guilds in Ireland had a strong religious dimension. In Dublin each guild had a chantry priest to pray for its members and a patron saint whose feast day was celebrated. In addition, the city guilds contributed to the annual Corpus Christi pageant. This was a major event in which each guild enacted scenes from the Bible that reflected their craft.[103] In the fifteenth century, the vogue for men and women to band together to secure commemorative masses and prayers became widespread. A large number of parish fraternities were founded in eastern Ireland for this purpose. The best documented is the Guild of St. Anne at St Audoen's church in Dublin, which was formally established in 1431, but chantries also flourished in rural parishes in the fifteenth and sixteenth centuries.[104]

Larger religious institutions also offered prayers and hospitality for their lay supporters, who could obtain the privilege of burial in the religious habit of their order.[105] By the fifteenth century it was common for letters of confraternity to be offered by religious houses to their benefactors. A formula letter for this purpose is preserved in the chapter book of the Franciscans of Youghal dating to 1491–2.[106] Lay engagement with mendicant ideals could also be expressed by wearing the cord of the Franciscan habit and by daily recitation of certain prayers and spiritual exercises. Gerald FitzGerald, the ninth earl of

---

[102] Jones, trans., *Friars' tales*, §§46, 166.
[103] Webb, 'Guilds of Dublin', p. 510.   [104] Lennon, 'Parish fraternities'.
[105] Hall, *Women*, pp. 25–6; Ó Clabaigh, *Friars*, p. 48.
[106] Ó Clabaigh, *Friars*, pp. 302–4.

Kildare, displayed his affiliation with the mendicants by owning two gold chains adorned with friar's knots, although this seems somewhat ironic given the order's devotion to poverty.[107]

Wealthy layfolk who wished to emulate the religious life could endow a private chapel or use a portable altar in their home, and there is evidence that this practice increased during the fifteenth century.[108] Lay folk could also adopt a more rigorous religious lifestyle by joining the tertiary order of mendicants. The tertiary orders of Franciscans and Dominicans had become well established in Ireland by the early fifteenth century.[109] Membership entailed commitment to an ascetic regime, celebrating the liturgy of the hours and observing fasts. Females were expected to wear veils while men were forbidden to bear arms, but otherwise they could continue to be married and work, living halfway between the secular and religious worlds. Between 1426 and 1539, approximately forty-nine houses were founded for tertiaries to live a communal life, a phenomenon that was markedly more popular in the north and west of the island.[110] While piety among the laity was conspicuous throughout the Middle Ages through donations to the Church, good works and prayer, the fifteenth century witnessed a greater expression of piety through membership of fraternal organisations.

SAINTS' CULTS AND PILGRIMAGE

One medium by which piety could be expressed was through devotion to the saints. Throughout Ireland, local saints represented local interests and identities as mediators between the living and the divine. Their feast days were important events for celebration within the community, as in some places they continue to be today. A common belief that saints and relics were channels of divine power is found in annalistic records, as well as in religious texts. For example, in 1411, the 'Annals of Ulster' reported that the holy cross of Raphoe (Co. Donegal) shed blood. Irish miracles are recorded in the early thirteenth-century Franciscan *Liber Exemplorum*, including the tale of a man from Wexford saved from hell because his sister used to dedicate two gallons from each brewing to the Virgin Mary.[111]

---

[107] Ibid., p. 305.   [108] Hall, *Women*, p. 23.
[109] Ó Clabaigh, *Friars*, pp. 306–7.   [110] Ibid., p. 311.
[111] Jones, trans., *Friars tales*, §46, cf. §§62, 99, 117, 142, 146, 166, 180, 183.

Hagiographical material was included in great manuscript collections. The twelfth-century *Lebor na hUidre* contains a poetic eulogy of St Columba, the 'Vision of Adomnán' and a tale concerning St Patrick's conversion of King Lóegaire. Hagiographical works provide a fascinating insight into devotional practices and religious culture.[112] A large number of Saints' Lives were composed or updated in the twelfth century, prompted by the spiritual and organisational impact of Church reforms.[113] The cults of Irish saints were popular not only among the Gaelic Irish but they were also adopted by the English and remained popular abroad.[114] The twelfth century witnessed the creation of new saints – Malachy of Armagh and Lorcán Ua Tuathail (Laurence O'Toole), brother-in-law of Diarmait Mac Murchada – whose cults were promoted by the Gaelic Irish and Anglo-Irish. International saints were venerated in Ireland, and the relics of Continental saints in Irish churches, such as the finger of St Ann at St Audoen's in Dublin, brought pilgrims from far and wide. While Saints' cults provided a focus for local identity, they could also unite individuals across Christendom in common devotion.

Many prominent Irish churches became sites of pilgrimage. In the mid-twelfth century Toirdelbach Ua Conchobuir commissioned the highly ornate 'Cross of Cong' to be made to hold a fragment of the True Cross.[115] One of the largest relic collections in Ireland was held at Christ Church, Dublin, which attracted visitors from Ireland and abroad.[116] However, the most renowned pilgrimage site in Ireland was St Patrick's Purgatory located in Lough Derg (Co. Donegal). A cave on Station Island in the lake was regarded as a place of spiritual healing. From the twelfth century, it attracted pilgrims across Europe at a time when the notion of purgatory as a physical place became popular in Western Christendom.[117] A number of pilgrims have left a written record of their visit. These include the twelfth-century *Tractatus de Purgatorio Sancti Patricii* by Henry of Saltrey, describing the otherworldly encounters of an Irish knight, and the mid-fourteenth-century 'Vision of Louis of France'. Some accounts hint that visitors came to Lough Derg out of curiosity and adventure as much as for spiritual enlightenment. Concerns that the entrance to purgatory was a hoax led Pope Alexander VI to close the site temporarily in 1497.[118]

[112] Herbert, 'Medieval collections'. [113] Flanagan, *Transformation*, pp. 14–15.
[114] Bartlett, 'Cults', pp. 68–77; Buckley, '*Peregrini*'. [115] Murray, 'Cross of Cong'.
[116] Preston, 'Canons', p. 36; Hall, *Women*, p. 29. [117] Le Goff, *Birth*.
[118] Ryan, 'Saint Patrick's Purgatory', p. 24.

Pilgrims from Ireland ventured overseas to the great shrines of Rome, Santiago de Compostela and Jerusalem. Chronicles name prominent individuals who undertook the arduous journey to foreign lands.[119] Some pilgrims left written accounts. The most detailed account of an Irish pilgrim to the Holy Land is that of Friar Simon Simmonds who set out from Clonmel (Co. Tipperary) in 1323.[120] From his many new experiences on this journey he concluded, 'Everyone who makes the journey to our Lord's sepulchre needs three sacks; a sack of patience, a sack of silver, a sack of faith.'[121] Pilgrims were not always members of the secular elites or clergy. In the thirteenth century, mention is made of a tavern owner from Leinster called Palmer because he had been to the Holy Land.[122] The study of saints' cults and pilgrimage in Ireland illustrates high standards of piety and orthodoxy in late medieval Ireland. However, these standards were not universally adhered to, and the Church faced various challenges to its property and to its theological tenets over time.

CHALLENGES TO THE CHURCH

The rules of the Church permeated every aspect of medieval life. This generated a constant challenge to both the religious and the laity to uphold its ideals in their conduct. Apart from the general problem of 'sin' and the agency of demons, the Church was also concerned to root out lay attitudes that undermined its authority. Prominent among these concerns was lack of respect for the resources of the Church. Seizure of assets, withholding of dues, governmental taxation, payment of protection money, warfare and theft were risks that churches faced at various times from powerful lay figures. Devotional writings often contained cautionary tales for those who might plan to rob the Church or violate its sanctuary. These criminals are often shown to fail in their goals, be miraculously struck with remorse or come to a sticky end.[123] The inclusion of such miracles indicates that church property was perceived to be in continual need of saintly protection. Diocesan decrees and Episcopal registers demonstrate the use of ecclesiastical censures (including excommunication)

---

[119] *AConn, s.aa.* 1300, 1445, 1462; *AU, s.aa.* 1450, 1451, 1480, 1484, 1491.
[120] Esposito, ed. and trans., *Itinerarium.*   [121] Chareyron, *Pilgrims*, p. 16.
[122] Jones, trans., *Friars tales*, §99.
[123] Heist, ed., *Vitae Sanctorum*, p. 295; Jones, trans., *Friars tales*, §§115, 117–18.

and peer pressure to remedy infringements against the Church and its tenants.[124]

In addition to problems posed by incursions and depredations on ecclesiastical resources, the Church was intolerant of noncanonical beliefs that bordered on magic and undermined its authority. The late thirteenth-century Franciscan *Liber Exemplorum* reports the confession of a tavern keeper's wife in Leinster who had added part of a communion wafer to a cask of wine on the advice of a witch to magically increase its value. The plan backfired as the wine disappeared. This prompted the woman to seek penance, and the wine was then miraculously restored. A similar confusion of religion and magic is represented in one of the acts of John Colton, archbishop of Armagh. In 1383–9 he condemned the belief that the blood of a hare caught on a Good Friday could serve as a remedy for various diseases, and he banned hunting on that day.[125] *Maleficium*, or harmful magic, is mentioned in chronicle accounts, which may imply its existence was taken for granted. Famously in 1414 the death of John Stanley, governor of Ireland, was attributed to the satirical powers of the poet Niall Mór Ua hUiginn, whose lands had been plundered by Stanley. The demise of another political figure, Tadg Ua Briain, king of Thomond, in 1466 was attributed to the evil eye.[126]

Noncanonical beliefs and *maleficium* came to be increasingly defined as heresy in the later Middle Ages. While occasional references are made to heresy in Ireland in the twelfth and thirteenth centuries, hardening papal definitions and intolerance towards noncanonical belief made heresy a more pressing issue in the fourteenth century.[127] Although heresy remained uncommon in Ireland, a few cases, notably that of Alice Kyteler, have received widespread attention. The case of Alice Kyteler might not have received such widespread notoriety had it not been for the dogged pursuit of heresy accusations by Richard Ledrede, bishop of Ossory. The English cleric had trained at Avignon. His patron, Pope John XXII, was zealous in the definition and pursuit of sorcery. On Ledrede's arrival in Ossory in 1317, he quickly sought out any evidence for heretical beliefs among his flock. A few years later some of the stepchildren of Alice Kyteler, a successful Kilkenny businesswoman, carried charges of sorcery against

[124] E.g. Smith, ed., *Register of Nicholas Fleming*, nos 12, 19, 34–5, 44, 50–51, 58, 131, 134.
[125] Reeves, ed., *Acts of Archbishop Colton*, p. xvii.   [126] *AConn, s.aa.* 1414, 1466.
[127] Flanagan, *Transformation*, p. 107; Williams, 'Heresy'.

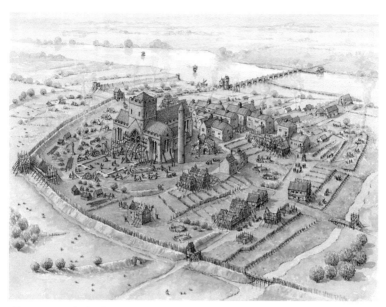

Figure 10.1 The building of St Canice's Cathedral, Kilkenny, with the older round
tower in situ (by Philip Armstrong)

her. Alice had been widowed three times, and her fourth husband
was ill. Her stepchildren felt disinherited and suspected Alice of hastening their fathers' deaths. Nevertheless, Alice had powerful allies
who attempted to block Ledrede's pursuit of her case. Alice successfully escaped the country, but it was her associates who would suffer.
Her maid, Petronilla of Meath, was burnt at the stake in 1324 after
confessing under torture that Alice had sex with a demon, denied
Christ and practised witchcraft. Arnold le Poer, seneschal of Kilkenny,
died in prison, while Alice's son William Outlaw had to undertake
penance and pay for lead for the roof of Kilkenny cathedral (iron-
cally the cathedral roof later collapsed under the weight of the lead;,
see Figure 10.1).[128] Ledrede would also fall foul of powerful figures
during the witchcraft trial and, later on in his career, faced periods
of imprisonment, exile and excommunication. Ledrede still held the
see of Kilkenny at his death in 1360, but a letter drafted by the archbishop of York a few years before his demise claimed that Ledrede was

---

[128] Shinners, ed. *Medieval popular religion*, pp. 238–41.

suffering from senility and madness and did not cease from persecuting his parishioners.[129]

Accusations of heresy were rarely motivated by religious principles
alone. The suppression of the Knights Templar had begun through
the political concerns of King Philip IV of France, but was later
endorsed by Pope Clement V. This led to members of the order being
imprisoned in Dublin in 1308.[130] Heresy was an emotive slur that
could be employed against political enemies. The burning of Gaelic
Irish lords by English authorities in 1326 and 1353 had a clear political
edge. Accusations could fly in both directions. In 1317 the 'Remonstrance of the Princes' accused the English in Ireland of heresy, while
in 1331 a letter from the justiciar and council of Ireland appealed for a
crusade against Gaelic heretics and the English rebels who supported
them.[131]

On a local scale, accusations of heresy were occasionally made by
high-ranking clerics who sought to bring wayward subordinates to
heel or to bring rivals for high office into disrepute.[132] A few clerics
came to adopt heretical or semi-heretical positions through theological enquiry and personal reflection. Richard FitzRalph, archbishop
of Armagh (d. 1360), was not a heretic but his views, which included
challenging the friars' claim that Christ was a mendicant, and that
divine grace alone should be the basis of secular power, influenced
later followers of Wycliffe and Huss.[133] Other anti-mendicant scholars, Henry Crumpe (d. 1401) and Philip Norris (d. 1467), faced accusations of heresy in their lifetimes. However, evidence for widespread
intellectual engagement with heresy in late medieval Ireland is lacking. The ultimate failure of the Protestant Reformations of the sixteenth century in Ireland may reflect on the level of stability and
orthodoxy of the Church in the fifteenth century.

CONCLUSION

In Ireland, as elsewhere in late medieval Christendom, religion permeated many aspects of life. This is particularly apparent during the
twelfth century when a movement for Church reform was sweeping

---

[129] Raine, ed., *Historical papers*, pp. 403–6.
[130] Wood, 'Templars', pp. 348–50.
[131] Watt, 'Negotiations', pp. 14–15, 20; Gleeson, 'Fourteenth century'.
[132] E.g. Smith, ed., *Register of Nicholas Fleming*, nos 73, 129.
[133] Ó Clábaigh, *Friars*, p. 155; Walsh, *Richard FitzRalph*.

through Europe. Irish rulers supported reform to advance their own status and avoid claims of English primacy, while Henry II used the same means to justify his invasion of Ireland. The twelfth century witnessed the arrival of new monastic rules and diocesan reorganisation. English attempts to modernise the Church in the guise of colonialism may have stunted reform in Gaelic-held areas. Even within reformed institutions, tensions could arise between English and Gaelic churchmen. However, it is possible to over-exaggerate ethnic divisions within the medieval Church. The mendicant houses founded from the thirteenth century often included friars and attracted patronage from both nations. From the late fourteenth century, the proportion of Gaelic clerics holding benefices in the English colony increased, reflecting greater changes in Irish society. The Church gained economic support from a wide variety of sources including lands, rents, tithes, fees and donations. Nevertheless, many individual institutions in Ireland were poor by western European standards, and they suffered from time to time from warfare and exploitation by secular or ecclesiastical figures in authority. Despite the challenges faced by the medieval Irish church, its overall stability and orthodoxy lent little popular support to the Protestant Reformations in the sixteenth century.

II

THE ARTS AD 1100–1500

————————— • —————————

Ireland's cultural achievements from AD 1100–1500 have tended to be seen as a decline from an early medieval 'Golden Age', but this has detracted attention from many creative and beautiful works of art. Early studies emphasised the backward-looking character of Gaelic culture and its distinction from English culture. Nevertheless, Gaelic society both honoured inherited traditions and was open to innovation in the fields of education, literature, music, decorative arts and architecture. Considerable regional and chronological variations are displayed in the work of scribes, artists and builders. Too often, late medieval Irish art is measured against external benchmarks of English and European culture, such as conformity with a specific art-historical or literary movement. However, in recent years there has been growing appreciation for the abundant cultural resources of late medieval Ireland and their inherent and unique qualities.

EDUCATION

For centuries, the ecclesiastical schools of Ireland provided a wide-ranging education that extended beyond religious matters and excelled in scholarship in Irish and Latin. Latin scholarship was flourishing at major ecclesiastical centres including Glendalough (Co. Wicklow), Lismore (Co. Waterford) and Armagh (Co. Armagh) in the twelfth century. Manuscript evidence shows that these schools were in contact with mainstream European trends.[1] During the 1160s

[1] Byrne, 'Trembling', pp. 40–1.

Ruaidrí Ua Conchobuir gave his support to the cathedral school at Armagh, but any plans to develop a university there were scuppered by the political changes that were wrought in Ireland in the following decade. Dublin was to be the centre of English authority, and it was here in 1192 that a secular college of clerks was founded at St Patrick's cathedral. An attempt was made to found a university in Dublin in the early fourteenth century. However, this was perhaps ill timed in terms of the economic and political well-being of the English colony. Although papal permission for the project was confirmed and a constitution was drawn up in 1320, the university never got off the ground. In 1475 a petition was sent to the pope for the foundation of a university teaching theology and the arts, but despite Vatican approval, the plan came to nothing.[2]

Despite the absence of a university, a scholarly education could be obtained by other means by the few who had the ability and resources to pursue it. A continuous stream of Irish students went to study at foreign universities. Eminent among these was Richard FitzRalph, a native of Dundalk, who became chancellor of Oxford University in 1332 and archbishop of Armagh in 1346. Another example was Muiris Ua Fithchellaig, who was regent of studies at Milan and Padua before becoming archbishop of Tuam in 1506. Education was available in Ireland through schools associated with religious houses. The mendicant orders were prominent educators, with schools of theology founded at Dublin, Athenry (Co. Galway), Galway and Drogheda (Co. Louth) during the later Middle Ages.[3]

In Gaelic areas, lay schools also flourished under noble patronage. Before the twelfth century, dynasties of scholars in poetry, history and law fostered knowledge and oversaw the creation of schools. However, it is for their activities in the later Middle Ages that learned families and lay schools of western Ireland are best known. From the twelfth century, Church reform effectively marginalised Irish vernacular education, whose traditions were assumed by learned lineages. These lineages might also number clerics among their ranks, but their power bases remained outside the church. Quite often, learned families had a strong local affiliation due to the lands and resources provided by their patrons. An example is the Meic Áedacáin legal family who maintained a law school at Ballymacegan (Co. Tipperary)

---

[2] Bhreathnach and Ó Flóinn, 'Ireland', pp. 583–4.
[3] Scott, 'Latin learning', pp. 937–52; Mooney, *Church*, p. 24.

where they received patronage from Uí Chennéitig. Their library displayed wide-ranging interests including homilies and passions, and their alumni pursued careers in history and genealogy as well as law.[4] The longevity of some scholarly families is fascinating. The poet Cú Chonnacht Ua Dálaig, who died at the church of Clonard (Co. Meath) in 1139, was the ancestor to the various dynasties of Uí Dálaig who pursued careers as poets and educators across Ireland and Scotland until the seventeenth century.[5] While chances for university education were limited in Ireland, opportunities to gain knowledge and excel within well-established fields of learning were highly prized.

LITERATURE IN IRISH

A large body of literature composed in Irish survives from the period AD 1100–1500. This reflects the activities of learned lineages and the care with which a number of manuscripts were preserved and copied over time. A striking feature of these texts is the emergence of a standard literary version of the Irish language at the end of the twelfth century. Classical Irish, or Early Modern Irish as it is also known, was the main mode or literary communication until the seventeenth century.[6] The regularisation of the language reflects a conscious desire among the literati of Ireland and Scotland to share a common register of writing that reflected high educational standards. Classical Irish had the advantage of being easily comprehensible across dialectal and regional boundaries. Another striking feature of the late medieval literary output is the dominance of verse. Students of different schools, including history, law and medicine, as well as poetry, were trained to compose verse in a metrical pattern involving fixed numbers of syllables per line. Professional praise poets were required to master the most difficult form called *dán díreach* (or 'straight verse'). Use of verse therefore permeated all areas of composition alongside prose, including genealogical literature, versified religious and secular narratives, teaching and mnemonic poems for law and medicine.[7]

Perhaps the most famliar output of the Irish literati of the late Middle Ages was praise poetry. This was verse directed to members of the nobility in return for payment, and it was often intended for public recitation. It continued an earlier tradition of poetic eulogies. Many

---

[4] Follett, 'Religious texts'.   [5] Henry and Marsh-Micheli, 'Manuscripts', p. 790.
[6] Carney, 'Literature in Irish', p. 689.   [7] Simms, *Medieval Gaelic sources*, pp. 57–9.

of these works have been preserved in manuscript anthologies dating from the fourteenth to the seventeenth centuries. Much more was doubtlessly lost. Stock themes were employed to praise poetic patrons, including impeccable ancestry, generosity, physical beauty, courage in war, and suitability to rule a wider territory, if not all of Ireland. Flattering comparison might also be made to historical figures or to the fecundity of lands under the patron's rule, which reflects supernatural approval of their status. The selection and presentations of these themes were personalised for their patron. Books of poems were also put together for particular families of patrons. A notable example is the *Duanaire Mhéig Shamhradháin* ('Book of Magauran') of the fourteenth century, of which thirty-three poems survive. Careful reading of praise poems can provide an insight into the political aspirations of a named ruler or family at a given time.[8]

Patronage of bardic poetry was not restricted to the Gaelic elites, although the incongruity of writing praise poems for patrons with opposing interests was commented on by the poet Gofraid Finn Ua Dálaig in the fourteenth century. In a humorous confession to Gerald FitzGerald, son of Maurice, earl of Desmond, he wrote, 'In poems to the English we promise the expulsion of the Gaels from Ireland; in those to the Gaels we promise the expulsion of the English east overseas!'[9] His patron Gerald FitzGerald was a prolific amateur in the composition of Irish poetry, and more than sixty poems attributed to him have survived. In addition to conventional praise poetry, other genres of bardic poem included laments, love poems, satire and religious poems. One of the best-known religious poets was the fifteenth-century Franciscan, Philip Bocht Ua hUiginn, of whom twenty-nine works survive. The poems of Ua hUiginn combined bardic convention with Latin learning. For example, his poems devoted to St Francis drew heavily on the thirteenth-century *Legenda maior* of the saint written by the Italian Franciscan and theologian, St Bonaventure.[10] While studies of bardic poetry have tended to stress their conservatism, it is clear that poets were open to a variety of influences in shaping their work.

Claims to noble ancestry appear prominent in praise poems. It is therefore not surprising that genealogies in prose and verse were an important part of the literary output of Gaelic authors in the

---

[8] Carney, 'Literature in Irish', p. 695; Simms, *Medieval Gaelic sources*, pp. 70–71.
[9] Carney, 'Literature in Irish', p. 696.   [10] Ó Clabaigh, *Friars*, p. 185.

later Middle Ages. Often these works were compiled over a long period. The genealogies preserved in the 'Book of Leinster' had been reworked and updated several times between the seventh and twelfth centuries.[11] These works should not be considered as entirely factual. They might telescope generations or take on board oral tradition and invention over time. One of the renowned genealogical works of the later Middle Ages was *Triallam timcheall na Fódla* ('Let us travel around Ireland'). The poem describes each regional lordship of Ireland and gives the name of the traditional ruling dynasty. This work was begun by Seán Mór Ua Dubhagáin in the fourteenth century, who covered Connacht, Ulster, the Midlands and Leinster. It was completed by Gilla na Náem (Giolla na Naomh) Ua hUidhrín in the fifteenth century, who described the southern provinces. The absence of reference to English lords has created the false impression that these poets sought to describe Ireland as it was before 1169. However, the authors' aim was to establish the claims of Gaelic lords to particular lands. Where new Gaelic families had risen to power replacing old dynasties, up-to-date information was included in their verse. The presentation of the past was important in Irish literature because it helped to promote current causes.[12]

Another type of composition that compiled and supplemented existing texts was chronicling. Notable collections of annals that have survived include the 'Annals of Ulster', which were compiled by Cathal Óg Mac Magnusa of Belleisle (Co. Fermanagh) in 1497. The 'Annals of Loch Cé' and the 'Annals of Connacht' appear to originate in a text compiled and maintained by the Ua Maíl Chonaire school in Connacht in the Later Middle Ages.[13] Gaelic schools also preserved older prose narratives, and often these were reworked. For example, new versions were made of *Táin Bó Cúailnge* ('The Cattle Raid of Cooley') known as Recension IIb (Stowe) and Recension III.[14] Another well-loved story, *Longes mac nUislenn* ('The Exile of the Sons of Uisliu', more widely known as 'the Deirdre story'), was rewritten in the fourteenth or fifteenth century under the title *Oidheadh Chlainne Uisnigh* ('The Violent Death of the Sons of Uisneach').[15]

[11] Simms, *Medieval Gaelic sources*, p. 44.
[12] Carney, 'Literature in Irish', p. 690; Simms, *Medieval Gaelic sources*, pp. 45–6.
[13] Simms, *Medieval Gaelic sources*, p. 23; Ó. Muraíle, 'Cathal Óg.
[14] Carney, 'Literature in Irish', p. 700.
[15] Mac Giolla Léith, ed. and trans., *Oidheadh chloinne hUisneach*.

Fresh prose compositions often looked back to older themes while catering to contemporary tastes and literary fashions. A significant body of literature from the late Middle Ages concerns the legendary pre-Christian hero Finn mac Cumaill (Finn McCool). Tales about Finn had been in circulation since the ninth century. By the twelfth century, Fenian narrative could be described as a literary industry.[16] As Finn and his followers formed a mobile band, the popularity of the tales could relate to an emerging national consciousness. He was a hero who could be associated with all the provinces of Ireland. The longest prose narrative that survives from the Middle Ages is *Acallam na Senórach* ('Colloquy of the Ancients'). It consists of heroic tales about Finn and his followers from all around Ireland, set within a framing narrative of conversations between Finn's retainer Caílte and St Patrick. The religious and political concerns of the text hint at its origins in Connacht in the first decades of the thirteenth century. Additional prose narratives concerning Finn and his outlaw companions were created in the Later Middle Ages, and they remained enduringly popular into modern times.[17]

A number of sagas composed in the later Middle Ages concerned historical or pseudo-historical kings. The genre of king tales includes *Aided Muirchertaig mac Erca* ('The Death of Muirchertach mac Erc'), which can be dated to the twelfth century. It relates how the king, Muirchertach, disowns his wife and children after meeting a beautiful otherworldly woman, Sín. However, Sín uses her magic to hasten the downfall of the king.[18] Another genre of tales focused on the triumphant battles of great rulers. Foremost among these is the early twelfth-century *Cogad Gáedel re Gallaib* ('The War of the Gaels and the Foreigners'). This describes how the Munster over-king Brian Boru battled against vikings, ultimately sacrificing his life at the Battle of Clontarf. The saga would provide inspiration for other texts including *Caithréim Thoirdhealbhaigh* ('The Battle Career of Toirdelbach') that describes internecine conflict in Munster at the turn of the fourteenth century.[19]

Devotional works continued to be written in Irish and Latin during the later Middle Ages. A flurry of Latin and Irish Saints' Lives were reworked or freshly composed in the twelfth century that

---

[16] Dooley and Roe, trans., *Tales of the elders*, p. xvi.
[17] Ibid., p. xli; Carney, 'Literature in Irish', p. 701.   [18] Herbert, 'Death'.
[19] Nic Ghiollamhaith, 'Dynastic warfare'.

mirror the tensions and concerns inherent in contemporary Church reform.[20] Hagiography often combined a devotion to local saints with political interests; for example, the fourteenth-century 'Life of St Berach' of Cloonbarry (Co. Roscommon) appears to reflect on a controversy between the Church and bardic poets.[21] A number of homilies and sermons that were written for popular edification have survived and give insight to late medieval piety.

Another genre was functional prose, including legal and scientific texts. Older works continued to be copied and glossed in secular schools, which enabled them to be preserved, while the glosses give a rich insight into scholarly developments. Tracts on the rights of secular lords cast light on the burdensome character of late medieval lordship through exactions of rents, tributes and seigneurial entitlements.[22] Medical texts are also a rich and under-researched body of information about scientific throught from the later Middle Ages, often combining folk medicine and Latin scholarship.

Literature in Irish also embraced narratives from abroad. Translations of English texts were popular in the fifteenth century. Sometimes these were translated from a French composition or translation via English, into Irish. It may be fairer to call some of these adaptations rather than direct translations. Examples include *Lorgaireacht an tSoidhigh Naomhtha* ('The Pursuit of the Holy Grail'), which represents a lost English version of the Arthurian 'Quest for the Holy Grail'. The travels of Marco Polo were translated from an English text by Fíngin Ua Mathgamna at the end of the fifteenth century. Another notable work was *Stair Ercuil agus a bás* ('The History of Hercules and his Death'), which was adapted from Caxton's *The recuyell of the historyes of Troye*, printed around 1474.[23]

Translations from Latin tended to be more direct, showing familiarity among the Gaelic literati with Latin. Religious works figure prominently within this category. One of the more popular works was *Smaointe Beatha Chríost*, a fifteenth-century translation of the 'Meditationes vitae Christi' (falsely attributed to St Bonaventure). Other works included a mid-fifteenth-century version of *De contemptu mundi* by Pope Innocent III, undertaken by William Mac Duibne of Bréifne while recovering from a sword wound.[24] Apocryphal texts were also translated from Latin, including stories

[20] Flanagan, *Transformation*, p. 15.   [21] Simms, *Medieval Gaelic sources*, p. 85.
[22] Ibid., p. 97.   [23] Carney, 'Literature in Irish', p. 706.   [24] Mooney, *Church*, p. 33.

from the highly popular Italian hagiographic compilation, *Legenda Aurea* ('The Golden Legend').[25] Translations of scientific works were also made for practical use. Prominent among these was a fifteenth-century translation of the *Regimen sanitatis* that was composed in the thirteenth century by Magninus of Milan.[26]

A great variety of literature was written in Irish in the Later Middle Ages. While often this has been characterised as backward looking or archaic in character, closer examination reveals continuous engagement with European intellectual trends and literary fashions alongside the veneration of past traditions. The engagement of the Gaelic literati with the outside world is best exemplified by translations of foreign works, which became increasingly popular towards the end of the Middle Ages.

NON–IRISH LITERATURE

A number of different languages were spoken in the English colony. These included Norman French, Latin, Welsh, Flemish and Irish, but English was the dominant vernacular. Legislation from the fourteenth century shows that the Irish language was making headway among the English, and the government sought to stamp down on it. Although the literary heritage that survives from the late Middle Ages in the Irish language is spectacular, the non-Gaelic languages of Ireland have left a modest legacy that is also worthy of exploration.

Little remains of Norman French literature in Ireland. The two main literary works are 'The Song of Dermot and the Earl' written in the early thirteenth century and a poem of some 200 lines describing the fortifying of the town of New Ross in 1265.[27] Apart from these, there are only a few minor fragments, including verses attributed to the first earl of Desmond. In the 'Red Book of Ossory' two fragments of French songs have survived that speak of the pain of love. The reason for their inclusion is because the bishop of Ossory, Richard Ledrede (1317–c. 1361) was campaigning against his clergy's penchant for 'vile secular songs'. He sought to replace them (although one wonders with what success) with edifying Latin hymns of his own composition.[28] This small body of literature suggests that there was some interest in French literature and culture.

---

[25] McNamara, *Apocrypha*, p. 64. [26] Nic Dhonnchadha, 'Medical writing'.
[27] Bliss and Long, 'Literature', pp. 715–19. [28] Bliss and Long, 'Literature', p. 711.

French and English were used for governmental business and some economic transactions. This is beautifully illustrated by an early fifteenth-century sketch in the 'Red Book of the Exchequer'. The picture depicts the court and its officials around the chequered table speaking in French.[29] French was also used in acts of parliament from 1310 to 1472, alternating occasionally with Latin. The high status of Norman French in the thirteenth century is reflected in its use along with Latin on some tombstone inscriptions from New Ross. However, by the fifteenth century, French was of diminishing cultural significance. English came to replace French and Latin in official and personal documents.

English was used for day-to-day communication in colonised areas. The English spoken and written in Ireland had obtained a distinctive patois by the fourteenth century. It drew distinctive elements from a combination of influences, including western English dialects and Irish. The main source of Hiberno-English literature in Ireland is BL Harleian MS 913, which can be dated to around AD 1330 and may originate from a Franciscan milieu. There are seventeen pieces preserved in English, scattered between texts in Latin and Old French. These mainly comprise religious and satirical verses. A religious poem by Friar Michael of Kildare is outstanding for its metrical complexity and social conscience in highlighting the difficulty for the rich of obtaining a place in heaven. Among the satirical poems, the best known is the 'Land of Cockaygne', which dwells on the theme of a secular paradise. The poem creatively engages with Irish, Hiberno-Latin and other European literatures. It draws inspiration from the Book of Revelation, and it lampoons early Irish otherworld tales. Specifically, it is a critique of the lax ways of monastic clergy. The monks who dwell in Cockayne wear Cistercian habits. However, they pass their time feasting and seducing the nuns who dwell nearby and use their gift of flight to race each other. The 'Land of Cockaygne' is said to be better than heaven. The idea of undertaking penance to short-cut time in purgatory is also parodied. The poet states that to reach the Land of Cockaygne one must wallow up to the neck in pig dung for seven years.[30]

Beyond Harleian MS 913, a few fragments of Hiberno-English composition survive. One notable example is found in the register of John Swayne (archbishop of Armagh, 1418–39), which berates

---

[29] Moss, ed., *Art*, p. 450.
[30] Bliss and Long, 'Literature', pp. 727–9; Glaser, ed., *Middle English poetry*, pp. 149–54.

women's love of fashion and particularly of horned headdresses with the words, 'God that berreth the crone of thornes, Destru the prude of wome[n] hornes'.[31] Apart from satire, other compositions include a 'treatise on gardening' from the fourteenth century and a handful of medical recipes. Hiberno-English was also used in a number of translations and transcriptions of texts composed elsewhere. These include the devotional writings of the English mystic, Richard Rolle, and the 'Expugnatio Hibernica' of Gerald of Wales. The literary tastes of the English elite in Ireland are suggested by the library holdings of Gerald, earl of Kildare. More than a hundred titles were catalogued in 1526. There were thirty-four items in French, thirty-four in Latin, twenty-one in English (mainly romances and histories), and nineteen in Irish.[32]

Latin was the language of the church, education and some areas of government. The many Latin texts relate to day-to-day record-keeping, correspondence, laws, annals and regulations. More literary works included hagiography, edificatory writings, scholarship and satire, mirroring the type of composition found in English. Generally speaking, late medieval Latin texts from Ireland did not possess such a pronounced Irish flavour as had their early medieval counterparts.[33] This may reflect a conscious effort by authors born in Ireland to fit with the norms of Latin culture in west European intellectual life. The process of conforming to mainstream European culture began prior to the English invasion, influenced by growing contacts abroad and the papally inspired movement for ecclesiastical reform. A model for secular Church reorganisation was outlined in the treatise entitled *De Statu Ecclesiae* penned by Bishop Gille(bertus) of Limerick in the early twelfth century. The mid-twelfth century witnessed renewed composition of Latin lives of Irish Saints. These include Lives of two Munster saints, Mochuille and Flannán, which were coloured by the reforming agenda to outline the rights and privileges of the Church.[34]

The aftermath of the English invasion prompted further hagiographic outpourings. This was a time when many new churches were being built in Ireland. The great 'Life of St Patrick' that was composed by Jocelin of Furness in the 1180s supported the interests of John de Courcy, who sought to establish himself in Ulster. It also defended some features of early Irish churches while upholding

---

[31] Bliss and Long, 'Literature', p. 733.   [32] Byrne, 'Earls of Kildare'.
[33] Scott, 'Latin learning', p. 935.   [34] Ó Corráin, 'Foreign connections'.

reform ideas. Jocelin's work probably reflected the interests of his ecclesiastical patrons, Archbishop Tommaltach of Armagh and Bishop Malachy of Down.[35] The early thirteenth-century 'Life of St Gerald of Mayo' presented an Englishman as a religious hero in eighth-century Connacht. This story may have been intended to appeal to both Gaelic and English audiences.[36]

Latin plays were a more vivid way or communicating religious ideas in the medieval world, but much of them has been lost. An Easter drama survives in two fourteenth-century manuscripts that originated in the parish of St John the Evangelist, Dublin.[37] Hymns and poetic recitals were another means to convey religious principles. A small body of Latin religious poems survive of Irish provenance, and there is a larger corpus of hymns. Perhaps the most industrious author of Latin verse in Ireland was Richard Ledrede, the heretic-hunting bishop of Kilkenny.[38] The expressions of love, peace and joy in these compositions imply the complex character of a man who had a maidservant tortured and burnt at the stake. Closely associated with the cult of saints was pilgrimage, and travel accounts then as now, appealed to people's curiosity regarding the world around them. The best-known pilgrimage account from late medieval Ireland is Simon Simmonds's journey to the Holy Land in the 1320s. He gives an account of his journey through England, France, Italy and Egypt to Jerusalem where the account breaks off.[39]

Edificatory compilations represent another grouping of Latin compositions from Ireland. A *Vademecum* was a small formal book composed by friars and other clerics for personal use that included model sermons, exempla, biblical excerpts, notes and advice. A number of these survive ranging in date from the thirteenth to the fifteenth centuries.[40] More generic pastoral aids include two thirteenth-century texts from a Franciscan milieu: *Liber Exemplorum* and *Promptuarium morale*. The first is a series of moralising tales put together by an English friar in Ireland. The work draws on a wide range of sources, but also includes some tales particular to Ireland that were gathered orally. *Promptuarium* is a concordance of scriptural, liturgical and patristic sources. The addition of sermon notes relating to Irish

[35] Flanagan, 'Jocelin of Furness'.   [36] Ní Mhaonaigh, 'Of Saxons', p. 426.
[37] Scott. 'Latin learning', p. 978.
[38] Ó Clabaigh, *Friars*, pp. 291–92; Colledge, ed., *Latin poems*.
[39] Esposito, ed. and trans., *Itinerarium*.   [40] Ó Clabaigh, *Friars*, p. 288.

saints suggests the author was associated with the Franciscan community of Downpatrick.[41] Related to these edificatory works is a treatise written on the seven deadly sins by 'Friar Malachy of Ireland' around AD 1300. This provides engaging commentary on the perceived vices of contemporary society.[42]

A number of scholars who travelled from Ireland to foreign universities became acclaimed authors of theological and philosophical works. Prominent among these were Richard FitzRalph and Muiris Ua Fithchellaig mentioned earlier. FitzRalph was a prolific author associated with no less than twenty separate compositions.[43] His career is well documented through his time at the University of Oxford and the papal court in Avignon to the deanery of Lichfield and archbishopric of Armagh. The details of his life are supplemented by his own 'sermon diary' that recorded his travels and the issues that concerned him. His most influential work was *De pauperie Salvatoris*, which dealt with concepts of lordship, property and possession. Ua Fithchellaig's origins are less certain, but he was a Gaelic Franciscan who taught philosophy in two Italian universities before his appointment to the archbishopric of Tuam in 1506. His work includes three commentaries on the works of John Duns Scotus and a metrical paraphrase of Peter Lombard's 'Sentences', which was a standard textbook of medieval theology.[44]

An impressive amount of literature survives from late medieval Ireland. Much of this is in Irish, but works composed in Norman French, English and Latin are also notable. This rich and intriguing body of literature reveals much about Irish society, scholarship and cultural influences.

GAELIC MANUSCRIPTS

A manuscript is both a repository of texts and a cultural artefact in its own terms. The twelfth century witnessed the creation of three large compilations in the Irish language. *Lebor na hUidre* is the earliest, containing all or part of thirty-seven texts. It is estimated that only half of the contexts survive. Another manuscript, Oxford, Bodleian MS B502, consists of two parts: the first dates to around AD 1100

---

[41] Ibid., pp. 291–2.   [42] Scott, 'Latin learning', pp. 969–71.
[43] Sharpe, *Handlist*, pp. 478–81.
[44] Scott. 'Latin learning', pp. 952, 962; Sharpe, *Handlist*, p. 375.

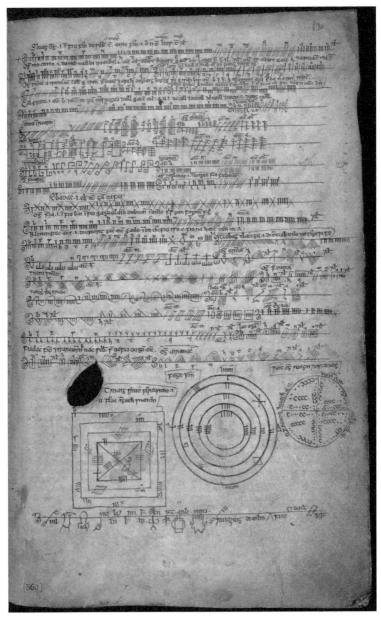

Figure 11.1 Book of Ballymote (Royal Irish Academy, MS 23 P 12, folio 170r 'Tract on Ogam')

and the second dates to c. 1125. The latest of the three is the 'Book of Leinster', which dates to the second half of the twelfth century. All three manuscripts combine religious and secular literature, with a prominent place given to epics, poems and historical and pseudo-historical literature. The manuscripts are illuminated with zoomorphic initials and interlace, with details heightened by the use of colour including vivid reds and yellows. The investment in twelfth-century manuscripts reflects not only the wealth accrued by the Irish Church but may also reflect anxieties about the preservation of traditions and status wrought by ecclesiastical restructuring and reform.

After the twelfth century, there was a hiatus in the production of Irish-language manuscripts. Their production shifted geographically away from Leinster and the Midlands and from monastic scriptoria to the schools of learned families in Gaelic-held areas. Nevertheless, continuity was observed in the style of script and decoration of Gaelic manuscripts in the fourteenth and fifteenth centuries and in the wide range of contents.[45] From the late fourteenth century a series of large compilations were made that preserved knowledge of medieval Irish literature for future generations. The 'Book of Ballymote', which dates to the end of the fourteenth century, is one great example (see Figure 11.1). The contents include Irish genealogical, topographical, biblical, and hagiographical material; adaptations of Classical literature; and a tract on ogam. It is richly decorated with illuminated initials, while drawings of animals, hands and figures accompany the text to serve as reading aids. Of similar date and significance are the 'Yellow Book of Lecan', 'Great Book of Lecan' and the 'Book of Uí Maine'.[46]

The production of large-scale manuscripts continued in the fifteenth century. The political trend towards decentralisation in that century placed more resources in the hands of Gaelic and English lords that could then be invested in scholarly activities and the arts. *An Leabhar Breac* is one of the best preserved due to its care in the Mac Áedacáin learned family of Duniry (Co. Galway). It was compiled c. 1411 and contains a mixture of Irish and Hiberno-Latin religious writings. The manuscript is simply decorated, with coloured zoomorphic patterns interwoven through important initials and two diagrams. *Liber Flavus Fergusiorum* is a simply illustrated manuscript

---

[45] Henry and Marsh-Micheli, 'Manuscripts', pp. 789–92.
[46] Carey, 'Compilations'.

dated to c. 1440 of Connacht provenance. It mainly comprises religious tracts but also includes some saga materials.[47]

The majority of these great Irish books may be linked with Gaelic schools or patrons, but names of colonial families are also invoked in their creation. The important compilation of religious and secular texts known as the 'Book of Lismore' was compiled for Fíngin Mac Carthaig Riabach, lord of Carbery (Co. Cork), and his wife Caitlín, who was the daughter of Thomas, seventh earl of Desmond. The 'Book of Pottlerath' contains two manuscripts of miscellaneous prose, verse and genealogies.[48] The first manuscript was compiled in the early fifteenth century for James Butler, fourth earl of Ormond, A second was added in the mid-fifteenth century at the behest of his nephew Edmund. The earlier manuscript is of higher quality, and its illustrated initials combine animals' bodies and geometric motifs reminiscent of eighth- and ninth-century Irish art.[49] Another composite volume, the 'Book of Fermoy', combines manuscripts from the fourteenth to the sixteenth centuries. This is linked with the Roche family of County Cork.[50] The association of colonial families with Gaelic manuscripts demonstrated that appreciation of Irish literature and learning could cross cultures in medieval Ireland.

The large compilations just discussed represent only part of the work of Gaelic scribes in the later Middle Ages. Numerous compendia of praise poetry, law and medical manuscripts have also survived. These works tend to be sparsely illustrated as befits their workaday purpose, and their survival is due to the care afforded by Gaelic learned families.[51] The Reformation and English conquests would curtail the work of Gaelic bards and scholars in the early modern era. However, the process of copying and interpreting texts was continued by scribes and hedge-school masters until they came into vogue for academic study. Many textual relics from the later Middle Ages remain unpublished and provide much scope for future scholars.

MANUSCRIPTS IN THE LATIN LANGUAGE

The impact of Continental influences on the twelfth-century Irish Church can be observed in two biblical manuscripts: the 'Gospels

[47] Herbert, 'Medieval collections'; Carney, 'Literature in Irish', p. 690.
[48] Oxford, Bodleian, Laud Miscellany 610; Carney, 'Literature in Irish', pp. 692–3.
[49] Moss, ed., *Art*, p. 422.   [50] Dublin, Royal Irish Academy, MS 23 E 29.
[51] Moss, ed., *Art*, p. 116; Kelly, *Guide to early Irish law*, pp. 225–31.

of Máel Brigte' and 'Cormac's Psalter'.[52] 'Cormac's Psalter' of the late twelfth century includes Gallican psalms, Vulgate canticles and related materials. A possible reference to St Bernard of Clairvaux on a page heading suggests a Cistercian provenance. The text was composed in Irish script, and the major initials are richly decorated with zoomorphic initials using knotted wire and interlaced ribbon designs with effective use of contrasting colour. The early twelfth-century 'Gospels of Máel Brigt' is a pocket-sized manuscript whose ornament shows the influence of Scandinavian Ringerike design. The opening initials of each gospel are ornamented with interlace and blocks of colour and two evangelist portraits also survive. The work was written in Armagh, but it contains annotations that reflect the scholarship of the cathedral school at Paris during the late twelfth century.[53] This little book is an important window onto Continental influences in Ireland prior to the English invasion.

The twelfth-century movement for Church reform placed renewed emphasis on conformity with Continental and English liturgical observance.[54] This is reflected in surviving missals or service books from late medieval Ireland.[55] After 1170, Gaelic scribes produced Latin manuscripts that tended to imitate English manuscripts in style and decoration. These include collections of Lives of Irish saints. The earliest surviving example was probably made at the Augustinian monastery of Saints' Island (Co. Longford). It dates from the early fourteenth century. The script is of English style, decorated with conventional European thread-like patterns and palmettes in blue and red. However, the Gaelic provenance of the manuscript is denoted by the use of Irish abbreviations and flourishes on some of the letters.[56] The 'Codex Salmanticensis' of the fourteenth century and the 'Codex Kilkenniensis' of the fifteenth century are also famous repositories of hagiographic literature. They have English-style script, but little decoration.[57]

The survival of manuscripts from an English milieu in Ireland clusters around the coastal towns and the new religious communities whose cultural activities looked overseas for inspiration. Survivals from Christ Church cathedral, Dublin, include the 'Black Book',

---

[52] Moss, ed., *Art*, pp. 243, 248. [53] Cf. *AU* 1174.
[54] Flanagan, *Transformation*, p. 129. [55] Moss, ed., *Art*, pp. 249–53.
[56] Oxford, Bodleian, Rawlinson B485 and B505; Henry and Marsh-Micheli, 'Manuscripts', p. 788; Sharpe, *Medieval Irish Saints' Lives*, pp. 253–4.
[57] Dublin, Marsh's Library, MS Z3. 1. 5.

which began life in England and came to Dublin at the turn of the
fourteenth century where material was added relating to the history
of the cathedral.[58] A finely illuminated psalter was commissioned in
England by the cathedral prior Stephen de Derby in the late fourteenth century.[59] There are several books from other churches in
County Dublin, including three musical manuscripts from the church
of St John the Evangelist on Fishamble St. A scatter of manuscripts
survives from institutions in Meath and Leinster, Limerick cathedral
and Armagh. Most of these books are ornamented with conventional
blue or red initials accompanied by loose thread-like patterns. Human
heads and figures sometimes appear, for example on the terminals or
loops of the initials.

Non-ecclesiastical manuscripts in Latin include charters, government documents and town registers. The most striking of these is
the 'Great Charter Roll of Waterford'.[60] It consists of a long roll of
vellum put together in the late fourteenth century. The text comprises copies of charters granted to the city, illustrated with key figures
from the history. These include coloured depictions of Prince John
holding a falcon, Edward III (see Figure 9.2), and Henry of London,
archbishop of Dublin. Illustrations of minor figures in blue and red
costumes are also peppered through the text. The naturalism and ele-
gance of the illustrations show close adherence to the 'international
Gothic' style of late fourteenth-century Europe. The late medieval
Latin manuscripts from Ireland reflect close contact with the outside world, both in Gaelic and English communities. However, they
also exhibit an interest in the preservation of local heritage, whether
through the Lives of native Saints or the records of local events and
charters. There is a significant change in the character of illustra-
tion found in Latin manuscripts after the English invasion, with a
departure from Insular styles towards the imitation of English and
Continental models.

MUSIC

Ireland had an acclaimed musical tradition in the twelfth century. It
was distinctive from much of Britain. but shared strong similarities
with Scotland. Gerald of Wales described the main instruments of

---

[58] Gwynn, 'Some unpublished texts', p. 285.
[59] Moss, ed., *Art*, p. 248.   [60] Henry and Marsh-Micheli, 'Manuscripts', p. 786.

the Irish as the harp (*citharia*) and the lyre (*tympanum*) in which the Irish were 'more skilled than any nation'. Ireland's proficiency in 'intricate polyphony' was singled out for praise, as were the quickness and liveliness of Irish music.[61] In addition to the string instruments mentioned by Gerald, wind instruments are also mentioned in early sources as a standard accompaniment to the harp. Harpists were among the most prestigious of Irish musicians. The *cláirseach*, or 'modern' triangular framed harp became popular in Ireland from the fourteenth century. The 'Brian Boru' harp on display in Trinity College Dublin may be the most famous example, and it dates from the fifteenth century.[62] The English in Ireland also enjoyed music, as evidenced by Bishop Ledrede of Ossory's attempts to stop his clergy singing inappropriate secular songs in the fourteenth century. Music also naturally crossed ethnic boundaries. The 'Statutes of Kilkenny' sought to curb the employment of Irish pipers, lyre players and harpists by the English. Much as today, musicians might pursue their hobby for its own sake, gain casual employment or become renowned professionals. The best musicians were often employed in the retinues of great lords and were valued members of their household.

Music was integral to social gatherings with both religious and secular purposes. Gerald of Wales informs us that Irish clerics often carried harps. In the eleventh and twelfth centuries, Ireland's ecclesiastical links with England and southern Germany brought new musical influences. From the late twelfth century, there was a shift towards Anglo-centric music in the Church.[63] All of the surviving manuscript sources for music in medieval Ireland are liturgical books. Resources for understanding secular music are rare, and many musicians would have played from memory or emulation without the need for notation. Surviving literary sources highlight the importance of music in medieval Ireland and hint at how different musical cultures influenced each other.

DECORATIVE ARTS

Visual arts were expressed in many different media including metalwork, stone, leather, bone, wood and paint. However, there were common stylistic developments over time that can be briefly summarised. One striking feature in Irish art is that themes and

---

[61] O'Meara, trans., Gerald of Wales, *History and topography*, pp. 103–4.
[62] Gleason, 'Music'.   [63] Lawrence, 'What did they sing?' p. 119.

motifs from early Insular art continued to be productive, particularly in artworks of Gaelic provenance. Comparison can therefore be made between the abstracted human ornament in the 'Book of Kells' (c. AD 800), the twelfth-century 'Book of Leinster' and the fourteenth-century 'Book of Ballymote', although these later examples were less accomplished. Similarly, animal interlace patterns show continuity in concept, albeit with different stylistic details from early medieval art to the fourteenth- or fifteenth-century 'Cross of Clogher'.[64] The combination of conservatism and innovation may reflect the reverence shown towards early artworks that survived into the later Middle Ages and their continued status as artistic sources of inspiration. Individual objects were sometimes worked on in different periods, including numerous shrines that were repaired and updated over time. The cultivation of distinctive Irish art styles that drew upon established ideas and new fashions could serve as an expression of identity and dialogue between different artistic traditions.

Scandinavian-derived art styles were well established in Ireland before AD 1100, but their popularity would continue into the twelfth century, particularly on Church metalwork, manuscripts and stone sculpture. The Urnes style was the latest of the so-called Viking art styles that originated in eleventh-century Scandinavia. It is characterised by slender lizard-like representations of creatures bearing large almond-shaped eyes. The bodies of the animals and the foliate tendrils that emerge from them curl around each other in wide loops. In Ireland, the style was modified into more compact, symmetrical designs. This can be observed on the 'Cross of Cong', which dates to the 1120s. The cross was made at the behest of Toirdelbach Ua Conchobuir, king of Connacht, to enshrine a relic of the True Cross. The cross has an oak core covered by sheets of brass overlain with gilt bronze openwork plaques. It is decorated with spirals of gold filigree and niello and blue and white glass bosses. A polished rock crystal at the junction of the arms was placed to protect the (now-missing) relic.[65] Another fine example of Urnes style can be seen on St Lachtin's arm-shrine, which is nearly contemporary with the 'Cross of Cong', but was produced in Munster under Mac Carthaig patronage. The shrine consists of a wooden core with decorative bronze plates. It is covered in Urnes-style interlace inlaid with silver and outlined with niello to give a contrasting colour effect.

[64] Moss, ed., *Art*, pp. 56–7, 59.   [65] Murray, *Cross*.

Panels of gilded filigree, enamel, and glass studs add to its visual impact. Although lavishly covered with Urnes-style ornament, the shape of the shrine may rely on German or Byzantine inspiration.[66]

Romanesque art looked to Continental and English models and was introduced to Ireland in the twelfth century. As the name implies, there were Classical elements to this design, and it may have been an ideological accompaniment to the movement for papally inspired Church reform. The style was represented in Irish sculpture, metalwork and painting of the twelfth and thirteenth centuries, often combined with other stylistic elements. Romanesque influence is exemplified on free-standing crosses of the twelfth century that bear full-length representations of Christ. These include the Glendalough Market Cross that shows Ottonian influence in its use of moulded terminals and naturalistic figural representation, combined with Irish Urnes-style ornament.[67] The Cashel Cross appears to emulate the 'Volto Santo', a wooden crucifix kept at Lucca in Italy. The form of the free-standing crosses revived a fashion of the ninth and tenth centuries; thus innovative design is represented on an archaic medium.[68]

Gothic art refers to a range of late medieval styles that began in twelfth-century Europe and came to Ireland with the English invasion. Gothic art continued to develop and influence Irish design throughout the Middle Ages. The style is most readily linked with architecture, but it was expressed across the range of Irish visual arts. The principles of Gothic design includ: vertical emphasis, drawing the eyes upwards with narrow columns and pointed arches; elaborate foliage patterns with elongated barbed stems and tendrils; and figurative sculpture that conveys more movement and emotion than Romanesque depictions. These ideas were effectively displayed in Irish metalwork. A very fine example is the Lislaughtin or Ballylongford cross from County Kerry (see Figure 11.2). According to its Gothic inscription, this ornate processional cross was made in 1479 by an Irish craftsman under Ua Conchobuir patronage. The cross was made of silver gilt. The stem is taken up with a full-length representation of Christ. At the end of the cross arms and the centre are quatrefoils, each of which contained an evangelist symbol, although the central one is now lost. The cross-arms are occupied by the

[66] Moss, ed., *Art*, p. 291.
[67] Cf. Continental links with Irish churches, discussed earlier.
[68] Moss, ed., *Art*, pp. 47, 155–8.

Figure 11.2 Lislaughtin Cross (Ballylongford, Co. Kerry)

inscription interspersed with interlace patterns, foliage and small animals that symbolise virtue and vice. The whole cross is edged with
delicate foliage patterns. The work is a masterpiece of mainstream
Gothic art. However, the stylised depiction of Christ may hearken
back to pre-invasion Irish design.[69]

---

[69] Hourihane, *Gothic*, pp. 103–5, 152–3.

In the fourteenth and fifteenth centuries, there was a concern to refurbish earlier book shrines to create composite works of art. A fine example is the *Domnach Airgid*, which consists of a yew box covered with decorative metal plates. In the mid-fourteenth century, the front plate was replaced with four silver gilt panels, and a central cross was adorned with a cast of the crucified Christ, a rock crystal and a shield illustrating the instruments of the Passion. The gilt plates depict a range of Irish and international saints seated and standing under Gothic arcades. The spaces around the gilt panels are occupied with interlace, foliage designs and an inscription that identifies the abbot of Clones (Co. Monaghan) as the patron and John Ua Bárdáin as producer of the work. The corners of the box are decorated with mounts showing running animals in Gothic style.[70] Earlier decoration remained on the top and sides of the shrine, allowing the coexistence of old and new visual imagery.

Visual arts also included wall paintings and fabrics that enlivened the interiors of many medieval elite dwellings and churches. However, these types of art works are vulnerable to deterioration over time, so only a few survive. The earliest surviving frescoes in Ireland are the fragments of figurative scenes, patterns of ashlar masonry and patterns of Romanesque style found in the chancel of Cormac's chapel (Co. Tipperary). Some of the best-preserved medieval wall paintings can be viewed at Abbeyknockmoy Abbey (Co. Galway). These date to the early fifteenth century and include the figure of St Michael holding the scales of judgement beside the crucified Christ, the martyrdom of St Sebastian and a scene of three living and three dead kings reflecting on the theme of mortality.[71] Fine textiles that have survived from the late Middle Ages represent imported goods, including the lavish vestments and copes from Christ Church cathedral, Waterford that date from the fifteenth century. They include the 'Passion cope' of green velvet on a cloth of gold with embroidered scenes from the Passion and crucifixion of Christ. The Waterford vestments reflect the wealth and contacts of the medieval church.[72]

Throughout the later Middle Ages Irish artists and craftsmen drew upon foreign fashions, but many also revered earlier Irish artwork that they preserved or imitated. The retrospective element in Irish design was more apparent in Gaelic areas and has been interpreted as an

---

[70] Moss, ed., *Art*, pp. 294–5.   [71] Ibid., pp. 91–3.
[72] McEneaney, 'Politics and devotion', pp. 40–5.

expression of regional or ethnic identity.[73] It echoes a respect for the past that is also seen in Irish architecture.

SECULAR ARCHITECTURE

A striking feature of the Irish rural landscape is the scattered ruins of medieval buildings. These encompass a great variety of structures from ringforts to tower houses, showing considerable dynamism in late medieval Irish architecture. While ringforts are the most characteristic site of early medieval domestic settlement, the extent to which their use continued after 1100 has been hotly debated. In areas that fell under English control, a minority of ringforts were adapted for ringworks, mottes and manorial centres, but the majority were abandoned. In Gaelic areas, settlement reorganisation may have led some sites to be vacated in the eleventh and twelfth centuries. Béal Boru (Co. Clare) was occupied into the late eleventh century. It was then reused by English settlers in the thirteenth century who heightened the banks to create a ringwork or bailey.[74] A dozen or so sites in Gaelic areas have yielded finds of glazed pottery that denote occupation or reoccupation of sites in the thirteenth and fourteenth centuries. The ringfort is a practical and flexible enclosed space, so this does not seem surprising. The historical prestige of some ringforts could promote their continued occupation or reuse by upwardly mobile families as an appropriation of authoritative space in the landscape. A few ringforts in Gaelic areas were constructed in the later Middle Ages.[75] Crannógs are another early medieval-type site whose use continued into the later Middle Ages, and their late occupation is well attested. However, there is no evidence as yet that crannógs were built anew in the late medieval era.[76]

As the construction of ringforts declined after AD 1000, there may have been a shift towards unenclosed lowland settlement. References to *caislén* and *caistél* in twelfth-century Ireland indicate that Irish kings were familiar with castle-building technology and sought to introduce them to defend key areas of their lordship. A boom in ringwork and motte construction came with the English invasion. These earth and wooden constructions were relatively cheap and quick to construct. An estimated 400 mottes were built in the expanding English

[73] Hourihane, *Gothic*, p. 160.
[74] Barry, *Archaeology*, pp. 48–9; O'Keeffe, *Medieval Ireland*, p. 21.
[75] Glasscock, 'Land', p. 228.   [76] O'Keeffe, *Medieval Ireland*, p. 24.

colony c. 1170–1230.[77] Mottes were a prime means by which English lords asserted control over newly conquered land. Their worth had been proven during the first wave of Norman settlers in England and Wales a century before. A few were built in frontier areas by Gaelic patrons to match English military tactics. Once English lords had consolidated their position, they tended to replace strategically located mottes with stone castles, while others were left to decay.

As the construction of mottes waned, moated rectangular enclosures emerged as a new form of defended settlement in the period 1250–1300. Up to 750 of these may have been built in English areas of Leinster and Munster, but they are rare in Ulster. Moated sites are often found in frontier regions and may reflect a secondary wave of English colonisation into marginal areas. The tenuous nature of some of these moated enclosures may be observed at Rigsdale (Co. Cork), where three stone structures were begun (a possible gatehouse, hall and garderobe), but not completed before the site was abandoned.[78] Literary evidence suggests that some moated sites were built or occupied by Gaelic lords. A poem by Áengus Rúad Ua Dálaig composed around 1306, celebrates Áed Ua Conchobuir's palace at the moated site of Cloonfree (Co. Roscommon).[79]

For those English colonists who could afford it, construction in stone offered the best security to them in Ireland. The first stone fortresses were built with rectangular tower keeps. The most impressive examples still stand at Trim and Carrickfergus. These castles were built for display as well as defence. At Trim, Christian symbolism and social hierarchy seem integral to the castle's design (see Figure 11.3).[80] Advances in European castle design meant that the royal castles built at Dublin and Limerick in the early thirteenth century lacked a central donjon, but consisted of cylindrical towers and gatehouses flanking a courtyard. The trend for round towers was also observed c. 1200 at Dundrum (Co. Down) and Nenagh (Co. Tipperary). Keepless castles, featuring a massive curtain wall, gatehouse and hall, were popular in the central decades of the thirteenth century, as can be seen at Liscarroll (Co Cork).[81] The development of castle building in Edwardian Wales also brought new influences to Ireland. In the

---

[77] Barry, *Archaeology*, pp. 37–8; O'Keeffe, *Medieval Ireland*, p. 16.
[78] Barry, *Archaeology*, p. 91.   [79] O'Conor and Finan, 'Moated site'.
[80] O'Keeffe, *Medieval Ireland*, p. 37.
[81] Barry, *Archaeology*, p. 59; Glasscock, 'Land', p. 219.

Figure 11.3 Trim Castle, Co. Meath

1270s, the royal castle at Roscommon was reconstructed on a rectangular plan with D-shaped angle towers and a massive twin-towered gatehouse. Its design shows that English architecture in Ireland was at the cutting edge of development. It is similar to Harlech castle in Gwynedd, which was built shortly thereafter. Castle building and enhancement continued on a smaller scale into the early fourteenth century, but as the English colony waned, a number of fortresses fell into disrepair.[82]

From c. 1300, the English no longer had a monopoly on the ownership of stone castles. Ballintober (Co. Roscommon) was built in imitation of Roscommon Castle in the early fourteenth century. Its patron has been identified as either Richard de Burgh (Burke) or Cathal Ua Conchobuir.[83] From the fourteenth century some castles taken from the English were used as dwelling places for Gaelic lords. These include Ferns (Co. Wexford) where fifteenth-century pottery denotes later occupation by the Meic Murchada Cáemánach.[84] From the late fourteenth century until the sixteenth century, tower houses were built under Gaelic and English patronage. More than

---

[82] Barry, *Archaeology*, pp. 62, 68.
[83] Glasscock, 'Land', pp. 219–20; Barry, *Archaeology*, p. 68; Moss, ed., *Art*, p. 351.
[84] Barry, *Archaeology*, p. 62.

three thousand have been recorded.[85] Tower houses usually consisted of two or three lofted storeys over a vaulted basement. Often the roof was covered with thatch or wooden shingles. There are regional variations in their design. Tower houses remain familiar sights in most parts of Munster and Connacht, but much less so in areas of Ulster.[86] They were also common within the English lordship where construction was encouraged in 1429 by a subsidy of £10 for each tower built by the liegemen of Dublin, Meath, Kilkenny and Louth. The success of this policy is indicated by subsequent restrictions imposed on the erection of tower houses in 1449.[87]

Tower houses were not originally the isolated features they appear to be in the landscape nowadays. They were usually accompanied by a courtyard or bawn that might accommodate subsidiary buildings of wood and wattle, as well as provide protection for livestock, guests and dependants at times of uncertainty. A key feature of these dwellings was the hall for entertainment and feasting, which might be an ancillary building or integral to the tower. We are lucky to have visitor accounts from the sixteenth and seventeenth centuries of the hall and chambers of tower houses that enliven our understanding of late medieval Irish life.[88] The popularity of the tower house meant that few large-scale castles were built in the fifteenth century, perhaps reflecting a general trend in the decentralisation of power. The compact rectangular form of the tower house was also adapted for urban environments; for example, Skiddy's Castle, Cork, built in 1445.

While castles and fortified dwellings were the strongholds of the aristocratic elites in medieval Ireland, towns were also important places of secular architectural patronage. Dublin was the largest pre-invasion town, and its importance was marked c. 1100 by the construction of a stone wall around the city. This was remarked upon as one of the wonders of Ireland. The wall consisted of a rubble core with mortared stone facing. Its width was an impressive 1.5 metres, and it extended up to 3.5 metres in height.[89] Pre-invasion walls are also recorded at Waterford and Wexford.[90] From the thirteenth century until the end of the Middle Ages, walls were added to around fifty towns, many of which had been founded by English settlers. Impressive examples can be seen at several sites in Ireland including

[85] Ibid., p. 69.   [86] Nicholls, 'Gaelic society', p. 406.   [87] Barry, *Archaeology*, p. 186.
[88] O'Keeffe, *Medieval Ireland*, p. 46.   [89] Barry, *Archaeology*, p. 121.
[90] Scott and Martin, eds. and trans., *Expugnatio*, pp. 33, 35, 67.

Fethard (Co. Tipperary) and Athenry (Co. Galway). Funds were raised for these building projects through murage grants that allowed tolls to be imposed on a range of market goods for fixed periods. The design of walls and towers varied over time, as may be observed at Waterford where six mural towers survive of differing shapes and styles. The evolution of town wall designs can be seen to reflect contemporary developments in castle building.[91]

Urban housing varied in style and quality according to the wealth of the inhabitants. In Dublin a level of continuity has been noted between the housing styles of the twelfth and the thirteenth century, although the quality of the carpentry appears to have declined after 1170.[92] The type 1 longhouse that had dominated the urban landscape from the tenth century was gradually superseded by sill-beam and other types of construction. In the thirteenth century, fully framed timber buildings were introduced. Otherwise known as cage-work houses, they continued to be built into the sixteenth century.[93] Stone was not commonly used for urban domestic structures, although the appearance of tower houses in the urban landscape has already been noted. By the fifteenth century, towns such as Dingle, Sligo and Galway flourished under Gaelic control. Sligo was said to possess many 'splendid' stone and wooden buildings when it was burnt in 1396.[94]

Less is known of rural housing in Ireland. Halls and huts of wattle construction are referred to as dwelling houses of the Irish in the twelfth and thirteenth centuries. Excavations of English manorial sites suggest a standard house was rectangular in plan with a cattle byre (cowshed) at one end and a dwelling at the other. Along the western seaboard, stone building was more common, and some of the circular or beehive huts that are well known to anyone who has visited the Dingle peninsula (Co. Kerry) were used during in the later Middle Ages. The poorest housing may have been temporary ovoid huts of clay and wattle work with roofs of thatch or sod, without windows or chimneys. This type of structure is illustrated on Irish maps from the sixteenth and seventeenth centuries.

While Gaelic and English populations in Ireland had inherited different building traditions, there was a process of synthesis and importation of new architectural styles during the later Middle Ages that fostered common elements in the architecture of both communities.

[91] Moss, ed., *Art*, p. 373.   [92] Barry, *Archaeology*, p. 120.
[93] Moss, ed., *Art*, pp. 377–8.   [94] *AFM, s.a.* 1396.

In particular, the tower houses, of which many ruined examples haunt the Irish landscape, symbolise the fusion of a common design concept with regional building traditions. The tower houses represented a great investment of wealth. However, the effort lavished on church architecture often outranked that of domestic structures during the later Middle Ages.

RELIGIOUS ARCHITECTURE

From the late eleventh century, the impact of papally inspired Church reform can be seen in the introduction of new architectural forms as well as new ideas of Church organisation. The Irish reform synods of the early twelfth century laid out new structures for dioceses, which elevated the status of some churches and repressed others. The patrons of churches who sought to raise their status expressed their ambitions through architectural display, demonstrating affiliation with European reform ideas through the adoption of features of Romanesque architecture. The term 'Romanesque' was coined in the nineteenth century, but it describes a style that drew inspiration from the Latin past, and it was dominant in European churches during the eleventh and twelfth centuries.[95]

Royal patronage as well as ecclesiastical authority would be significant in the deployment of Romanesque architecture. One of the finest and earliest examples of this style in Ireland is Cormac's chapel in Cashel (Co. Tipperary). It was built under the patronage of Cormac Mac Carthaig, king of Munster in 1127 × 1134. Its Romanesque features included a rib-vaulted chancel and characteristic round arches and arcading along its walls. Nevertheless, the small scale of the church and its high stone roof reflect Irish building traditions.[96] Similarly at Killeshin (Co. Laois) a fine Romanesque church was built under the patronage of Diarmait Mac Murchada, king of Leinster around AD 1150.[97] During the early twelfth century the facades of Roscrea (Co. Tipperary), and Ardfert (Co. Kerry) were constructed incorporating Romanesque and earlier Irish architectural traditions. A few other churches added Romanesque elements to an earlier core. The extravagant Romanesque portal added at Clonfert (Co. Galway) in the third quarter of the twelfth century is one such example (see the cover image).[98]

---

[95] Moss, ed., *Art*, p. 46.   [96] O'Keeffe, *Medieval Ireland*, p. 134.
[97] Stalley, 'Hiberno-Romanesque', p. 92.   [98] Moss, ed., *Art*, p. 161.

The patronage of new religious orders further promoted the adoption of new architectural ideas. The Cistercians, who first arrived at Mellifont (Co. Louth) in 1142, favoured large, pre-existing cruciform churches with aisled naves. Continental models were followed at some of their churches, including Mellifont and Jerpoint (Co. Kilkenny). However, the resources available to Irish church builders often led to the construction of smaller and simpler rectangular churches that incorporated Romanesque principles. The Nun's church at Clonmacnoise is of modest proportions, but it includes many exquisite Romanesque sculptural details. It was completed in 1167 under the patronage of Derbforgaill, daughter of Murchad Ua Maíl Sechnaill, king of Meath, and affiliated with the Arrouaisian order of Augustinian canons.[99]

The English invasion prompted a spate of church building, including parish churches, cathedrals and monasteries. While the colonists sought to impose their mark, they did not espouse a complete break with the ecclesiastical past, whose authority could add prestige to their own institutions. New cathedral buildings at Cloyne, Rosscarbery, Cashel and Kilkenny preserved round towers as a symbol of their former heritage.[100] The new buildings adopted elements of European Gothic style. The characteristics of Gothic art included pointed arches, ribbed vaults and flying buttresses to allow greater height and light. English influences can be identified at a number of churches. At Christ Church cathedral in Dublin, Archbishop John Cumin (1181–1212) replaced the earlier church with a lavish construction. It was built on a cruciform plan with an aisled nave, two-stage elevation and stone-ribbed vaulting throughout. The early stages of building, visible in the transepts, included Romanesque historiated capitals similar to those at Wells cathedral in Somerset.[101] The nave, which was built from c. 1230, was unmatched in Ireland for the quality of its Gothic architecture and included the work of English masons.

In the last decade of the twelfth century, the emergence of a 'School of the West' represented a Gaelic cultural response to Romanesque and Gothic architectural influences. A group of fifteen to twenty buildings in Connacht and Thomond constructed around AD 1200 presented common features, including pointed arches, triple shafts and window splays framed by continuous mouldings, tubular

---

[99] Ní Ghradaigh, 'But what exactly did she give?'
[100] Moss, ed., *Art*, p. 12.   [101] Ibid., p. 163.

chevrons and highly stylised plant ornament.[102] The Cistercian abbey of Boyle (Co. Roscommon) is one of the earliest to display these characteristics, which were shared by other reformed abbeys and more modest buildings including Drumacoo church (Co. Galway).[103] The creative fusion of Hiberno-Romanesque, English and Gothic features show that Gaelic patrons drew upon the latest architectural developments to foster a distinctive and sophisticated regional style.

The years from 1150 to 1250 witnessed the construction of some of the finest ecclesiastical buildings in Ireland. Substantial investment in architectural patronage continued into the fourteenth century, with additions to existing churches, the reconstruction of cathedrals at Downpatrick (Co. Down) and Tuam (Co. Galway) around 1300, and the erection of friaries. The mendicant orders tended to occupy sites with humble architectural beginnings that developed in piecemeal fashion over time according to a claustral plan. Churches tended to be relatively plain, narrow halls as at Ennis (Co. Clare) and Nenagh (Co. Tipperary). 'Decorated' style tracery appeared on some churches from the fourteenth century, as has survived in the south wall of the choir at Fethard friary (Co. Tipperary) and in the east windows at Athenry (Co. Galway).[104]

The Black Death limited the construction of new churches for nearly half a century. Nevertheless, in the fifteenth century a wave of church building and renovation was witnessed in regions of Gaelic lordship. Additions were also made to existing churches. For example, at Ardfert cathedral (Co. Kerry) a south transept was added, and the walls were raised and crenellated. The features that marked out Gothic architecture in fifteenth-century Ireland included small window openings giving rise to large expanses of unarticulated walls, and squared framework above doors and towers that might be adorned with battlements. The austere, militaristic appearance of many late Gothic churches in Ireland stood in contrast to churches in contemporary England.[105] Perpendicular features, which may be regarded as quintessentially English, were adopted in the adornment of doorways and wall panels, but the designs were localised, fusing styles and motifs from different periods and regions.[106] These independent stylistic developments reflect growing confidence among the

---

[102] O' Keeffe, *Medieval Ireland*, p. 140.   [103] Moss, ed., *Art*, p. 499.
[104] O' Keeffe, *Medieval Ireland*, p. 149.   [105] Moss, ed., *Art*, pp. 51, 169.
[106] Hourihane, *Gothic*, pp. 90, 98.

Irish elites. Just as the English construction of mottes on Irish ecclesiastical sites was evocative of societal change in the twelfth century,
the building of Gaelic friaries on land reclaimed from English lords
tells its own story. When Quin friary (Co. Clare) was constructed
under Mac Conmara in 1433, the symbolism was overt. It overlay and
incorporated remains of a thirteenth-century castle built by the de
Clares.[107]

Parish churches in Ireland tended to be simple rectangular buildings built of local stone. Their numbers expanded in the thirteenth century as the population grew, and many older churches
were extended. Large aisled parish churches were built anew at
New Ross (Co. Wexford), Carrickfergus (Co. Antrim) and Gowran
(Co. Kilkenny) reflecting the ostentation of their thirteenth- and
fourteenth- century patrons. In the fifteenth century, a surge in
patronage for the church was reflected in new features added to old
churches. Within the English lordship the addition of windows with
perpendicular tracery and bell towers was fairly common.[108] Wealthy
families commissioned structures to display their status and piety. For
example, the St Laurence family added an aisle to St Mary's, Howth
(Co. Dublin) in the late fifteenth century, while the FitzGeralds added
a college to St Mary's, Youghal (Co. Cork) in 1464.[109] Examples
of new parish churches in Gaelic areas included Carrick (Co. Fermanagh), built under the auspices of Gilbert Ua Flannacáin and Margaret Nic Uidhir, and Aghalurcher (Co. Fermanagh), also founded
with Meic Uidhir support.[110]

Gaelic and English families reinforced their ties with a particular
church by commissioning funerary monuments. The sarcophagus in
Cormac's chapel Cashel (Co. Tipperary), is one of the finest examples of Irish Romanesque carving. It dates to the 1120s and was commissioned for one of the Meic Carthaig kings. Its form combined
an international outlook with Irish Urnes-style ornament. From the
early thirteenth century, cross-carved slabs and coffins were made
in areas of English settlement. Effigial sculpture was adopted across
cultural boundaries. One of the earliest sculptures of a knight in
Ireland is at Timolin church (Co. Kildare), which dates from the early
thirteenth century. King Feidlimid Ua Conchobuir at Roscommon
and King Conchobar Ua Briain at Corcomroe (Co. Clare) also had

---

[107] Barry, *Archaeology*, p. 194.   [108] O' Keeffe, *Medieval Ireland*, p. 150.
[109] Moss, ed., *Art*, pp. 174, 176.   [110] Barry, *Archaeology*, p. 195.

funerary effigies made around AD 1300. In the fifteenth century, elaborate tomb chests became fashionable. The Plunketts of Meath were particularly active in commissioning these works with chests decorated with scenes of the Passion, saints and heraldic devices surmounted by effigies of knights and ladies. In Gaelic areas chest tombs were often set within canopied recesses as may be seen at Ennis Friary (Co. Clare).[111]

The enormous vitality and dynamism of the Church in late Middle Ages were expressed in relatively large-scale constructions and a range of architectural styles. While architectural expression in Ireland is more modest in scale than other parts of western Europe, it is no less intriguing or diverse. The architecture of the later Middle Ages was shaped by impulses from abroad, including Church reforms, the English invasion, European fashions and the Black Death. These impulses combined with local building traditions, pragmatism and tastes to create forms of expression that were distinctively Irish.

CONCLUSION

The educational opportunities and wealth available to support artistic and architectural creativity in late medieval Ireland were limited in comparison to other west European countries. Nevertheless, a large body of literature, church metalwork and architecture has survived, albeit often in an incomplete state. The cultural background of the patrons and craftspeople exercised some influence on artistic expression. Thus, reverence for earlier Irish artistic traditions is more apparent in Gaelic-held areas, while Anglo-Irish artists tended to look to Britain for inspiration. These cultural divisions were also blurred in many places. The intermingling of English, Gaelic and Continental cultures in late medieval Ireland created new and distinctive works of art. These can be appreciated for their differences from mainstream art styles and movements rather than being criticised for their aesthetic nonconformity.

---

[111] Moss, ed. *Art*, pp. 466–73; O'Keeffe, *Medieval Ireland*, p. 162.

CONCLUSION

———————— • ————————

This book attempts to show how Ireland altered over the course of eleven hundred years from AD 400 to AD 1500. While the Middle Ages is popularly perceived as a period of stagnation and limited intellectual horizons, closer study reveals it to be a period of remarkable change and creativity. Furthermore, the long-standing trope that Irish institutions were archaic and only forced to change through foreign interventions has come under increasing criticism in recent years.[1] Irish society has been perceived as backward looking for different reasons. Anti-Irish prejudice proclaimed that the Irish were naturally primitive, while some nationalists desired to portray Irish society as resilient to change and unsullied by foreign influence.[2] Stereotypes of Ireland as an archaic society still exert a strong influence on popular perceptions of the Irish past. The watersheds that have conventionally divided medieval Irish history have been linked with external forces, namely the arrival of St Patrick from Britain in the late fifth century, the arrival of vikings at the end of the eighth century, and the English invasions of 1169–71. In this book, emphasis has been given to innovation and adaptation within medieval Irish society, and a less segregated view of the island's history has been promoted.

This book has skimmed over developments in economic, social, political, religious and art history over an extended time frame. Its

---

[1] Flanagan, *Irish society*, pp. 1–3; Duffy, *Ireland in the Middle Ages*, p. 2; Bhreathnach, *Ireland*, p. 241.
[2] Binchy, 'Passing'.

purpose has been to provide a brief introduction to medieval Ireland. This has meant a more detailed narrative of change has had to be omitted. Many interesting complexities and debates in medieval Irish history have not been touched on. The reader is encouraged to find out more and consult a wider range of material. Beyond the existing historical literature, there is also much potential for the further study of the abundant but under-researched primary sources for medieval Irish history. Future research will not only fill in details and contribute to existing debates but will also explore new lines of argument and continue to reshape our overall impression of events.

The story of change in Irish history begins with the first written sources. In Late Antiquity, the adoption of literacy accompanied innovations in farming practices and population growth. In the fifth century, there is evidence of the spread of Christianity and growing competition for lands and status that encouraged migration and the emergence of new political dynasties, including Uí Néill and Eóganachta. One of the overarching themes in the abundant literary heritage of early medieval Ireland is the preoccupation with rank and status. Written sources demonstrate that opportunities for social advancement in early medieval Ireland were limited, and the risk of downward social mobility among the elite created fierce competition. Military endeavour and patronage were means by which powerful dynasties could enhance their status. Some of this patronage was expressed in great works of art that remain as iconic symbols of Irish identity to this day.

By the end of the eleventh century, the identity of the different provinces of Ireland had been firmly established. Power had become focused into the hands of several leading dynasties and major churches. The process of centralisation had been aided by economic growth and the symbiotic relationship of church and government. Yet, despite the existence of a clearly defined Irish ethnic identity, no single royal dynasty was to establish overarching power to make the imagined community of Ireland a nation-state.[3] The island would remain disunited. The years after the invasion of Henry II in AD 1171, witnessed widespread redistribution of lands to English immigrants and the political marginalisation of Gaelic royal dynasties. The incomplete and devolved nature of the English conquest would lead to contested ownership of lands. The English colony declined in

---

[3] Dumville, 'Did Ireland exist?'

the fourteenth century as a consequence of heavy taxation to fund English wars against the Welsh, Scots and French and of famines, epidemics and warfare. A significant amount of land was taken back into Gaelic control. English royal government was, by the end of the Middle Ages, reduced to the areas around Dublin and Drogheda. The Irish dynasties of Uí Néill, Uí Briain, Uí Chonchobuir and Meic Murchada were able to reclaim something of their former glories.

From the end of the twelfth century, society in Ireland was characterised by a division between Gaels and 'the English born in Ireland'. This dualism was initially enforced through legal apartheid. However, the rules were widely flouted. Gaelic, Anglo-Irish, or English factions struggled for power in Ireland, but there is evidence for widespread acculturation. Frequent conflicts during the Middle Ages nurtured long-standing grievances, frustrated ideals and broken promises. The narrative of Irish history is therefore different from the triumphalist accounts of some other European nation-states. The prejudices against the Gaelic Irish, to whom the whole island once belonged, were intensified in the tumultuous events of the early modern period when the English crown sought to impose direct rule and religious change on the Gaels and Anglo-Irish alike. In each century after AD 1500, writers of different political persuasions would look back to the Middle Ages to interpret and spin the origins of ongoing political divisions. Perhaps there is no greater reason to study the past, apart from its inherent fascination, than to question the stories told by later generations to justify their opinions. While the events of the past are unchanging, the significance assigned to them and the way they are narrated are constantly open to fresh evaluations and new approaches.

APPENDIX: A GUIDE TO SURNAMES

——————— • ———————

Throughout this book the policy has been adopted of spelling Irish words and names according to Middle Irish century conventions, rather than reflecting changing patterns of orthography through the Middle Ages. This allows a degree of conformity and should be sufficient to enable students to identify the same words and names in medieval primary sources. Exceptions to this rule are made for the titles of well-known texts, which are spelt according to scholarly convention for ease of identification in other contexts. A concordance is given here to help identify the link between medieval Irish surnames used in this book and their modern Irish and English equivalents. Irish surnames may be spelt in different ways (like English ones), and they can give rise to variant forms in modern English spelling and pronunciation. The first elements of Irish surnames are often Mac, meaning 'son of'; Ua/Ó, meaning 'grandson of' or 'descendant of'; or Ní(c), the female equivalent of both. This element may be dropped when a name is Anglicised. To take an example, the surname Ua Ruairc gives rise to the modern English variants O'Rourke, O'Rorke, Roarke, Roark, Rouark, and so on. For the sake of space, one or two common English spellings are given for each name to serve as a guide.

Middle Irish	Contemporary	English version
Cáemánach	Caomhánach	Kavanagh
Mac Áedacáin	Mac Aodhagáin	MacKeegan
Mac Áengusa	Mac Aonghusa	MacGuiness
Mac Amalgada	Mac Amalgadha	MacAuley
Mac Carthaig	Mac Carthaigh	MacCarthy
Mac Cathmáil	Mac Cathmaoil	McCaul
Mac Cerbaill	Mac Cearbhaill	MacCarroll/Carvill
Mac Domnaill	Mac Domhnaill	Mac Donnell
Mac Duibne	Mac Dhuibhne	Mac Givney/McAvinue
Mac Duinn Sléibe	Mac Duinnshléibhe	Mac Dunleavy
Mac Eochada	Mac Eochadha	MacGeogh
Mac Eochagáin	Mac Eochagáin	Mageoghegan
Mac Flannchada	MacFhlannchadha	MacClancy
Mac Gilla Pátraic	Mac Giollaphádraig	Gilpatrick
Mac Gilla Epscoip	Mac Giolla Easpaig	MacGillespie
Mac Murchada	Mac Murchadha	MacMurrough/Murphy
Mac Ruaidrí	Mac Ruaidhrí	Mac Rory
Mac Suibne	Mac Suibhne	Mac Sweeney
Mac Tigernáin	Mac Tighearnáin	MacTiernan
Mac Uidhir	Mac Uidhir	Maguire
Ua Bresláin	Ó Breasláin	O'Breslan
Ua Briain	Ó Briain	O'Brien
Ua Broin	Ó Broin	O'Byrne
Ua Brolcáin	Ó Brolcháin	O'Brallaghan/Bradley
Ua Canannáin	Ó Canannáin	O'Cannon
Ua Catháin	Ó Catháin	O'Kane
Ua Cellaig	Ó Ceallaigh	O'Kelly
Ua Cennéitig	Ó Cinnéide	O'Kennedy
Ua Cennselaig	Ó Cinnsealaigh	Kinsella
Ua Conchobuir	Ó Conchúir	O'Connor
Ua Dálaig	Ó Dálaigh	O'Daly
Ua Deoráin	Ó Deoráin	O'Doran
Ua Dúnlainge	Ó Donnghaile	O'Donnelly
Ua Fergail	Ó Ferghail	O'Farrell
Ua Fithchellaig	Ó Fithcheallaigh	O'Fihely
Ua Flaithbertaig	Ó Flaithearta	O'Flaherty
Ua hEidin	Ó hEidhin	O'Hyne
Ua hUidrín	Ó hUidhrín	O'Heerin
Ua hUiginn	Ó hUiginn	O'Higgin

Middle Irish	Contemporary	English version
Ua Lochlainn	Ó Lochlainn	O'Loughlin
Ua Maíl Chonaire	Ó Maolchonaire	O'Mulconry
Ua Maíl Muaid	Ó Maolmhuaidh	O'Molloy
Ua Maíl Ruanaid	Ó Maolruanaidh	O'Moroney
Ua Maíl Sechnaill	Ó Maeleachlainn	O'Melaghlin
Ua Mathgamna	Ó Mathúna	O'Mahony
Ua Mocháin	Ó Mocháin	O'Mohan
Ua Morda	Ó Mordha	O'Moore
Ua Néill	Ó Néill	O'Neill
Ua Rónáin	Ó Rónáin	O'Ronayne
Ua Ragallaig	Ó Raghallaigh	O'Reilly
Ua Ruairc	Ó Ruairc	O'Rourke
Ua Seasnáin	Ó Seasnáin	O' Shasnan/Sexton
Ua Tuathail	Ó Tuathail	O'Toole

BIBLIOGRAPHY

——————— • ———————

Abraham, K., 'Upward mobility in later medieval Meath', *History Ireland*, 5.4 (1997), 15–20.

Andersen, P., 'When was regular, annual taxation introduced in the Norse islands of Britain? A comparative study of assessment systems in north-western Europe', *Scandinavian Journal of History*, 16 (1991), 73–83.

Anderson, A., and M. Anderson, eds. and trans., *Adomnán's Life of Columba*, rev. edn (Oxford: Clarendon Press, 1990).

Andrews, J., 'The mapping of Ireland's cultural landscape. 1550–1650', in P. J. Duffy *et al.* eds, *Gaelic Ireland, c. 1250–1650* (Dublin: Four Courts Press, 2001), pp. 153–80.

  Shapes of Ireland: maps and their makers 1564–1839 (Dublin: Geography Publications, 1997).

Baillie, M., *New light on the Black Death: the cosmic connection* (Stroud: Tempus, 2007).

  'Proposed re-dating of the European ice core chronology by seven years prior to the 7th century AD', *Geophysical Research Letters*, 35 (2008) available online at http://onlinelibrary.wiley.com/doi/10.1029/2008GL034755/full.

Barrell, A., *Medieval Scotland* (Cambridge: Cambridge University Press, 2000).

Barry, T., *The archaeology of medieval Ireland* (London: Batsford, 1994).

  'Rural settlement in Ireland in the Middle Ages: an overview', *Ruralia*, 1 (1996), 134–41.

Bartlett, R., 'Cults of Irish, Scottish and Welsh saints in twelfth-century England', in B. Smith ed., *Britain and Ireland, 900–1300: insular responses to medieval European change* (Cambridge: Cambridge University Press, 1999), pp. 67–86.

  The making of Europe: conquest, colonisation and cultural change (London: Penguin, 1994).

Bateson, J., 'Roman material from Ireland: a reconsideration', *Proceedings of the Royal Irish Academy. Section C*, 73 (1973), 21–97.

Begley, J., *The Diocese of Limerick, ancient and medieval* (Dublin: Browne and Nolan, 1906).

Bemmer, J., 'The early Irish hostage surety and inter-territorial alliances', *Historical Research*, 89 (2016), 191–207.

Bennett, I., *Excavations 1990: summary accounts of archaeological excavations in Ireland* (Bray: Wordwell, 1991).

Best, R., ed., 'Some Irish charms', *Ériu*, 16 (1952), 27–32.

Bhreathnach, E., *Ireland in the medieval world, AD 400–1000: landscape, kingship and religion* (Dublin: Four Courts Press, 2014).

Bhreathnach, E., and R. Ó Flóinn, 'Ireland: culture and society', in S. Rigby ed., *A companion to Britain in the later Middle Ages* (Oxford: Blackwell, 2003), pp. 558–95.

Bieler, L., ed. and trans., *The Patrician Texts in the Book of Armagh* (Dublin: Dublin Institute for Advanced Studies, 1979).

   ed. *St Patrick's Confessio*, available online at www.confessio.ie (Dublin: Royal Irish Academy, 2011).

Bill, J., *Welcome on board! The Sea Stallion from Glendalough: a viking longship recreated* (Roskilde: Viking Ship Museum, 2007).

Binchy, D., ed. and trans., 'Bretha Crólige', *Ériu*, 12 (1938), 1–77.

   'Bretha Déin Chécht', *Ériu*, 20 (1966), 1–66.

   ed., *Corpus Iuris Hibernici*, 6 vols (Dublin: Dublin Institute for Advanced Studies, 1978).

   Críth Gablach (Dublin: Dublin Institute for Advanced Studies, 1941).

Bitel, L., *Isle of the Saints: monastic settlement and Christian community in early Ireland* (Cork: Cork University Press, 1993).

Blakelock, E. 'Early medieval cutting edge technology: an archaeometal-lurgical, technological and social study of the manufacture and use of Anglo-Saxon and viking knives', 2 vols, unpublished PhD diss. (University of Bradford, 2013).

Bliss, A., and J. Long, 'Literature in Norman French and English to 1534', *NHI2*, pp. 708–36.

Borsje, J., 'The monster in the river Ness in *Vita Sancti Columbae*: a study of a miracle', *Peritia*, 8 (1994), 27–34.

   'Rules and legislation on love charms in early medieval Ireland', *Peritia*, 21 (2010), 172–90.

   'The second spell in the Stowe Missal', in C. Hambro and L. Widerøe, eds, *Lochlann: Festskrift til Jan Erik Rekdal* (Oslo: Hermes, 2013), pp. 12–26.

Bourke, A., *et al.* eds, *The field day anthology of Irish Writing Vol. IV: Irish women's writings and traditions* (Cork: Cork University Press, 2002).

Bourke, E., 'Life in the sunny south-east – housing and domestic economy in viking and medieval Wexford', *Archaeology Ireland*, 9.3 (1995), 33–6.

Bray, A., *The friend* (Chicago: University of Chicago Press, 2003).

Bray, D., 'The study of folk-motifs in early Irish hagiography: problems of approach and rewards at hand', in J. Carey *et al.* eds, *Studies in Irish hagiography: saints and scholars* (Dublin; Four Courts Press, 2001), pp. 268–77.

Bray, G., ed., *Records of Convocation, XVI: Ireland, 1101–1690* (Woodbridge: Boydell and Brewer, 2006).

Breatnach, L., ed. and trans., 'The first third of *Bretha Nemed Tóisech*', *Ériu*, 40 (1989), 1–40. 'Irish collective and abstract nouns, the meaning of *cétmuinter* and marriage in early medieval Ireland', *Ériu* 66 (2016), 1–29.

  A Companion to the Corpus Iuris Hibernici (Dublin: Dublin Institute for Advanced Studies, 2005).

  ed. and trans., *Uraicecht na Ríar: the poetic grades in early Irish law* (Dublin: Dublin Institute for Advanced Studies, 1987).

  'Varia VI: 3. *Ardrí* as an old compound', *Ériu*, 37 (1986), 192–3.

Brewer, J., and W. Bullen, eds, *Calendar of the Carew Manuscripts preserved in the Archiepiscopal Library at Lambeth, 1515–74* (London: Longmans, 1867).

Bridge, M., 'Locating the origins of wood resources: a review of dendroprovenancing', *Journal of Archaeological Science*, 39.8 (2012), 2828–34.

Britnell, R., *Britain and Ireland 1050–1530: economy and society* (Oxford: Oxford University Press, 2004).

Brooks, E. St. John, ed., *Register of the Hospital of S. John the Baptist without the New Gate, Dublin* (Dublin: Irish Manuscripts Commission, 1936).

Buckley, A., 'Music and musicians in medieval Irish society', *Early Music*, 28 (2000), 165–90.

  '*Peregrini pro Christi*: The Irish Church in medieval Europe as reflected in liturgical sources for the veneration of its missionary Saints', *De Musica Disserenda*, 4.1 (2008), 93–105.

Bull, M., 'Criticism of Henry II's expedition to Ireland in William of Canterbury's miracles of St Thomas Becket', *Journal of Medieval History*, 33 (2007), 107–29.

Burns, C., trans., 'Papal letters of Clement VII of Avignon (1378–94) relating to Ireland and England', *Collectanea Hibernica*, 24 (1982), 7–44.

Butler, W., *Gleanings from Irish history* (London: Longmans, 1925).

Byrne, A., 'The earls of Kildare and their books at the end of the Middle Ages', *Library*, 14.2 (2013), 129–53.

Byrne, F.J. 'Ireland and her neighbours, c. 1014–c. 1072', *NHI* 1, pp. 862–98.
  Irish kings and high kings (London: Batsford, 1973).

  'The trembling sod: Ireland in 1169', *NHI2*, pp. 1–42.

  'Tribes and tribalism in early Ireland', *Ériu*, 22 (1971), 128–66.

Byrne, N., *et al.*, eds and trans. *Register of St Saviour's Chantry of Waterford* (Dublin: Irish Manuscripts Commission, 2013).

Cahill, T., *How the Irish saved civilisation* (London: Hodder and Stoughton, 1996).

Cahill Wilson, J., *Late Iron Age and Roman Ireland* (Dublin: Wordwell, 2014).

Campbell, E., 'Were the Scots Irish?' *Antiquity*, 75 (2001), 285–92.

Candon, A., 'Muirchertach Ua Briain, politics and naval activity in the Irish Sea, 1075–1119', in G. Mac Niocaill and P. F. Wallace, eds, *Keimelia: papers in memory of Tom Delaney* (Galway: Galway University Press, 1988), pp. 397–415.

Carey, J., 'Compilations of lore and legend: Leabhar na hUidhre and the books of Uí Mhaine, Ballymote, Lecan and Fermoy', in B. Cunningham and S. Fitzpatrick, eds, *Treasures of the Royal Irish Academy Library* (Dublin: Royal Irish Academy, 2009), pp. 17–31.

The Irish national origin legend: synthetic pseudohistory, Quiggin Pamphlet (Cambridge: University of Cambridge, 1994).

'Varieties of supernatural contact in the Life of Adomnán', in J. Carey *et al.*, eds, *Studies in Irish hagiography: Saints and scholars* (Dublin; Four Courts Press, 2001), pp. 49–62.

Carlin, N., 'Ironworking and production' in N. Carlin, L. Clarke and F. Walsh, eds, *The archaeology of life and death in the Boyne Floodplain* (Bray: Wordwell, 2008), pp. 87–112.

Carney, J., 'Language and literature to 1169', *NHI1*, pp. 451–510.

'Literature in Irish, 1169–1534', *NHI2*, pp. 688–707.

ed. and trans., 'The Ó Cianáin miscellany', *Ériu*, 21 (1969), 122–47.

Cave, R., and H. Coulson, ed. and trans., *A source book for medieval economic history* (New York: Biblo and Tannen, 1965).

Chareyron, N., *Pilgrims to Jerusalem in the Middle Ages*, trans. W. D. Wilson (New York: Columbia University Press, 2005).

Charles-Edwards, T., trans., *The Chronicle of Ireland*, 2 vols (Liverpool: Liverpool University Press, 2005).

'A contract between king and people in early medieval Ireland? *Críth Gablach* on kingship', *Peritia*, 8 (1994), 107–19.

Early Christian Ireland (Cambridge: Cambridge University Press, 2000).

Early Irish and Welsh kinship (Oxford: Oxford University Press, 1993).

'Early Irish Law', *NHI1*, pp. 331–70.

'Irish warfare before 1100', in T. Bartlett and K. Jeffery, eds, *A military history of Ireland* (Cambridge University Press: Cambridge, 1996), pp. 26–51.

'Lebor na Cert and clientship', in K. Murray, ed., *Lebor na Cert: reassessments* (London: Irish Texts Society, 2013), pp. 13–33.

'The Penitential of Columbanus', in M. Lapidge, ed., *Columbanus: studies on the Latin writings* (Woodbridge: Boydell and Brewer, 1997), pp. 217–39.

'The structure and purpose of Adomnán's Vita Columbae' in J. Wooding *et al.*, eds, *Adomnán of Iona: theologian, lawmaker, peacemaker* (Dublin: Four Courts, 2010), pp. 205–18.

Childs, W., and T. O'Neill, 'Overseas trade', *NHI2*, pp. 492–524.

Christiansen, S., 'Infield-outfield systems – characteristics and developments in different climatic environments', *Geografisk Tidsskrift*, 77 (1978), 1–5.

Clancy, T., 'Iona v. Kells: succession, jurisdiction and politics in the Colum-ban familia in the later tenth century', in F. Edmonds and P. Russel, eds, *Tome: studies in medieval Celtic history and law in honour of Thomas Charles-Edwards* (Woodbridge: Boydell Press, 2011), pp. 89–103.

Clancy, T., *et al.*, trans., *Triumph Tree: Scotland's earliest poetry AD 550–1350* (Edinburgh: Canongate, 1998).

Clarke, H., 'The 1192 charter of liberties and the beginnings of Dublin's municipal life', *Dublin Historical Record*, 46 (1993), 5–14.

'Christian cults and cult centres in Hiberno-Norse Dublin and its hinter-land', in A. MacShamhráin, ed., *The Island of St Patrick: church and ruling dynasties in Fingal and Meath, 400–1148* (Dublin: Four Courts Press, 2004), pp. 140–58.

Conversion, church and cathedral: the diocese of Dublin to 1152', in J. Kelly and D. Keogh, eds, *History of the Catholic Diocese of Dublin* (Dublin: Four Courts, 2000), pp. 19–50.

Coleman, A., 'Obligationes pro annatis Diocesis Dublinensis, 1421–1520', *Archivium Hibernicum* 2 (1913), app. ii, pp. 1–72.

Colgrave, B., ed. and trans., *The Life of Bishop Wilfrid by Eddius Stephanus* (Cambridge: Cambridge University Press, 1927).

Colgrave, B., and R. Mynors, eds and trans., *Bede's ecclesiastical history of the English people* (Oxford: Clarendon Press, 1969).

Colledge, E., ed., *The Latin poems of Richard Ledrede O.F.M. Bishop of Ossory, 1317–1360* (Toronto: Pontifical Institute of Medieval Studies, 1974).

Comber, M., 'Trade and communication networks in early historic Ireland', *Journal of Irish Archaeology*, 10 (2001), 73–91.

Comyn, D., and P. S. Dinneen, eds and trans., *The history of Ireland by Geoffrey Keating*, 4 vols (London: Irish Texts Society, 1902–14).

Connolly, P., 'The enactments of the 1297 parliament', in J. Lydon, ed., *Law and disorder in thirteenth century Ireland* (Dublin: Four Courts Press, 1997), pp. 139–62.

Connolly, P., and G. Martin, eds, *The Dublin Guild Merchant Roll, c. 1190–1265* (Dublin: Dublin corporation, 1992).

Connon, A., 'The "Banshenchas" and the Uí Néill queens of Tara', in A. P. Smyth, ed., *Seanchas: studies in early and medieval Irish archaeology, history and literature in honour of Francis J. Byrne* (Dublin: Four Courts, 2000), pp. 98–108.

Cooper, A., 'The King's four highways: legal fiction meets fictional law', *Journal of Medieval History*, 26 (2000), 351–70.

Cosgrove, A., 'Anglo-Ireland and the Yorkist cause, 1447–60', *NHI2*, pp. 557–68.

'The Armagh registers: an under-explored resource for late medieval Ireland', *Peritia* 6–7 (1987–88), 307–20.

'The emergence of the Pale, 1399–1447', *NHI2*, pp. 533–56.

'England and Ireland, 1399–1447', *NHI2*, pp. 525–33.

'Ireland beyond the Pale, 1399–1460', *NHI2*, pp. 569–90.

Crooks, P., 'The background to the arrest of the fifth earl of Kildare and Sir Christopher Preston in 1418: a missing membrane', *Analecta Hibernica*, 40 (2008), 1–15.

'Constructing a "laboratory for Empire": colonial Ireland from the Statutes of Kilkenny to Poynings Law', *SHISO*, 1063 (2012), 9–43.

'"Hobbes", "dogs" and politics in the Ireland of Lionel of Antwerp, c. 1361–6: The Denis Bethell Prize Essay 2005', *Haskins Society Journal*, 16 (2005), 117–48.

'James the Usurper of Desmond and the origins of the Talbot-Ormond feud', in S. Duffy, ed., *Princes, prelates and poets in medieval Ireland: essays in honour of Katharine Simms* (Dublin: Four Courts Press, 2013), pp. 159–84.

'Marshal,' in S. Duffy, ed., *Medieval Ireland: an encyclopedia* (New York: Routledge, 2005), pp. 322–3.

Cross, T., and C. Slover, trans., *Ancient Irish tales* (New York: Henry Holt, 1936).

Crouch, D., *William Marshal: knighthood, war and chivalry, 1147–1219* (Harlow: Pearson, 2002).

Crotty, P., *et al.*, trans., *The Penguin Book of Irish Poetry* (London: Penguin, 2010).

Cullinan, F., ed., *Thirty-Eighth Report of the Deputy Keeper of the Public Records of Ireland* (Dublin: Public Record Office, 1906).

Cunningham, G., *The Anglo-Norman advance into the South-West Midlands of Ireland 1185–1221* (Roscrea: Parkmore, 1987).

Curran, M., *The antiphonary of Bangor and the early Irish monastic liturgy* (Dublin: Irish Academic Press, 1984).

Curtis, E., *History of medieval Ireland, from 1086 to 1513* (London: Methuen, 1923).

Curtis, E., and R. McDowell, trans., *Irish historical documents 1172–1922* (London: Methuen, 1943).

Davidson, L., and J. Ward, eds and trans., *The sorcery trial of Alice Kyteler: a contemporary account* (Binghamton, NY: Medieval and Renaissance Texts and Studies, 1993).

Dillon, M., *Early Irish literature* (Chicago: University of Chicago Press, 1948).

ed. and trans., *Lebor na Cert: the Book of Rights* (Dublin: Irish Texts Society, 1962).

Doherty, C. 'Donnchad Donn mac Flainn (d. 944)', *Oxford dictionary of national biography* (Oxford: Oxford University Press, 2004) available online at www.oxforddnb.com/view/article/50107.

'Exchange and trade in early medieval Ireland', *Journal of the Royal Society of Antiquaries of Ireland*, 110 (1980), 67–89.

'The monastic town in early medieval Ireland', in H. B. Clarke and A. Simms, eds, *The comparative history of urban origins in non-Roman Europe* (Oxford: British Archaeological Reports, 1985), pp. 45–75.

'A road well travelled: the terminology of roads in early Ireland', in E. Purcell *et al.*, eds, *Clerics, kings and vikings: essays on medieval Ireland in honour of Donnchadh Ó Corráin* (Dublin: Four Courts Press, 2015), pp. 21–30.

'Vikings in Ireland: a review', in H. B. Clarke, M. Ní Mhaonaigh and R. Ó Floinn, eds, *Ireland and Scandinavia in the Early Viking Age* (Dublin: Four Courts Press, 1998), pp. 288–330.

Dolley, M., *Anglo-Norman Ireland* (Dublin: Gill and Macmillan, 1972).

'Coinage to 1534: the sign of the times', *NHI2*, pp. 816–26.

Dooley, A., and H. Roe, trans., *Tales of the elders of Ireland: Acallam na Senórach* (Oxford: Oxford University Press, 1999).

Down, K., 'Colonial society and economy in the high Middle Ages', *NHI2*, pp. 439–91.

Downham, C., 'The Battle of Clontarf in Irish history and legend', *History Ireland* (September/October 2005), pp. 19–23.

'The break-up of Dál Riata and the rise of Gallgoídil', in H. B. Clarke and R. Johnson, eds, *The Vikings in Ireland and beyond: before and after the Battle of Clontarf* (Dublin: Four Courts, 2015), pp. 189–205.

'The career of Cearbhall of Osraige', *Ossory, Laois and Leinster*, 1 (2004), 1–18.

'England and the Irish Sea zone in the eleventh century', *Anglo-Norman Studies*, 26 (2003), 55–73.

'Religious and cultural boundaries between vikings and Irish: the evidence of conversion', in J. Ní Ghradaigh and E. O'Byrne, eds, *The march in the islands of the medieval West* (Leiden: Brill, 2012), pp. 15–34

'Viking camps in ninth-century Ireland' in S. Duffy, ed., *Medieval Dublin*, 10 (Dublin: Four Courts, 2010), pp. 93–125.

Viking kings of Britain and Ireland: the dynasty of Ívarr to AD 1014 (Edinburgh: Dunedin Academic Press, 2007).

'The Viking slave trade', *History Ireland*, 17.3 (2009), 15–17.

'The vikings in Southern Uí Néill until 1014', *Peritia* 17–18 (2003–04), 233–55.

'Vikings' settlements in Ireland before 1014', in J. V. Sigurðsson and T. Bolton, eds, *Celtic-Norse relationships in the Irish Sea in the Middle Ages 800–1200* (Leiden: Brill, 2014), pp. 1–21.

Dryburgh, P., 'Mortimer', in S. Duffy, ed., *Medieval Ireland: an encyclopedia* (New York: Routledge, 2005), pp. 339–42.

'Roger Mortimer and the governance of Ireland, 1317–20', in B. Smith, ed., *Ireland and the English world in the later Middle Ages* (Basingstoke: Palgrave Macmillan, 2009), pp. 89–103.

Dryburgh, P., and B. Smith, eds, *Handbook and select calendar of sources for medieval Ireland in the National Archives of the United Kingdom* (Dublin: Four Courts Press, 2005).

Duffy, S., *Brian Boru and the Battle of Clontarf* (Dublin: Gill and Macmillan, 2013).

'The Bruce invasion of Ireland: a revised itinerary and chronology', in S. Duffy, ed., *Robert the Bruce's Irish Wars: the invasions of Ireland 1306–1329* (Stroud: Tempus, 2002), pp. 9–45.

'The career of Muirchertach Ua Briain in context', in D. Bracken and D. Ó Riain-Raedel, eds. *Ireland and Europe in the twelfth century: reform and renewal* (Dublin: Four Courts, 2006), pp. 74–105.

Ireland in the Middle Ages (Basingstoke: Macmillan, 1997).

'The Turnberry band', in S. Duffy, ed., *Princes, prelates and poets in medieval Ireland: essays in honour of Katherine Simms* (Dublin: Four Courts Press, 2013), pp. 124–38.

Dumville, D., *Councils and synods of the Gaelic Early and Central Middle Ages*, Quiggin Pamphlet (Cambridge: Department of Anglo-Saxon, Norse and Celtic, 1997).

'Did Ireland exist in the twelfth century?' in E. Purcell *et al.*, eds, *Clerics, kings and Vikings: essays on medieval Ireland in honour of Donnchadh Ó Corráin* (Dublin: Four Courts Press, 2015), pp. 115–26.

'Ireland and North Britain in the earlier Middle Ages: contexts for Míniugud senchasa fher nAlban', in C. Ó Baoill and N. McGuire, eds, *Rannsachadh na Gàidhlig* (Aberdeen: An Chló Gaidhealach, 2002), pp. 209–42.

Dumville, D., *et al.*, *Saint Patrick AD 493–1993* (Woodbridge: Boydell, 1993).

Dyer, C., *Making a living in the Middle Ages: the people of Britain 850–1520* (New Haven, CT: Yale University Press, 2002).

Earwood, C., 'Turned wooden vessels of the early historic period from Ireland and western Scotland', *Ulster Journal of Archaeology*, 3rd ser. 54/55 (1991–92), 154–9.

Eastwood, B., 'The astronomy of Macrobius in Carolingian Europe: Dungal's letter of 811 to Charles the Great', *Early Medieval Europe*, 3 (1994), 117–34.

Edwards, N., *The archaeology of early medieval Ireland* (London: Batsford, 1990).

'The archaeology of early medieval Ireland, c. 400–1169: settlement and economy', *NHI1*, pp. 235–300.

Ellis, S., 'Civilising the natives: state formation and the Tudor monarchy', in S. G. Ellis and Lud'a Klusáková, eds. *Imagining frontiers, contesting identities* (Pisa: Pisa University Press, 2007), pp. 77–92.

'Economic problems of the church: why the Reformation failed in Ireland', *Journal of Ecclesiastical History*, 41 (1990), 239–65.

'Fitzgerald, Gerald, eighth earl of Kildare (1456?–1513)', *Oxford dictionary of national biography* (Oxford: Oxford University Press, 2004) available online at www.oxforddnb.com/view/article/9554.

The Pale and the Far North: government and society in two early Tudor borderlands. The O'Donnell lecture 1986 (Galway: National University of Ireland, 1988).

Reform and revival: English government in Ireland, 1470–1534 (London: Royal Historical Society, 1986).

'Taxation and defence in late medieval Ireland: the survival of scutage', *Journal of the Royal Society of Antiquaries of Ireland*, 107 (1977), 5–28.

Empey, A., 'Butler-Ormond', in S. Duffy, ed., *Medieval Ireland: an encyclopedia* (New York: Routledge, 2005), pp. 59–60.

Eska, C., ed. and trans., *Medieval law and its practice: Cáin Lánamna, an Old Irish tract on Marriage and Divorce Law* (Leiden: Brill, 2009).

Esposito, M., ed. and trans., *Itinerarium Symonis Semeonis ab Hybernia ad Terram Sanctam* (Dublin: Dublin Institute for Advanced Studies, 1959).

Etchingham, C., *Church organisation in Ireland, AD 650 to 1000* (Maynooth: Laigin Publications, 1999).

    'Skuldelev 2 and Viking Age ships and fleets in Ireland', in E. Purcell, P. MacCotter, J. Nyan and J. Sheehan, eds, *Clerics, kings and Vikings: essays on medieval Ireland in honour of Donnchadh Ó Corráin* (Dublin: Four Courts Press, 2015), pp. 79–90.

Etchingham, C., and C. Swift, 'English and Pictish terms for brooch in an eighth century Irish law text', *Medieval Archaeology*, 48 (2004), 31–49.

Evans, N., 'Annals and chronicles' in S. Duffy, ed., *Medieval Ireland: an encyclopedia* (New York: Routledge, 2005), pp. 20–2.

Farr, C., 'The Incipit pages of the MacRegol gospels', in R. Moss, ed., *Making and meaning in Insular art: proceedings of the fifth International conference on Insular Art held at Trinity College Dublin* (Dublin: Four Courts, 2007), pp. 275–87.

FitzPatrick, E., *Royal Inauguration in Gaelic Ireland c. 1100–1600: a cultural landscape study* (Woodbridge: Boydell and Brewer, 2002).

Fitzsimons, F., 'Fosterage and gossiprid in late medieval Ireland: some new evidence', in P. J. Duffy, D. Edwards and E. Fitzpatrick, eds, *Gaelic Ireland: land, lordship and settlement c. 1250–c. 1650* (Dublin: Four Courts Press, 2001), pp. 138–49.

Flanagan, D., 'A summary guide to the more commonly attested ecclesiastical elements in place names', *Bulletin Ulster Place Names Society*, 2nd ser. 4 (1981–2), 69–76.

Flanagan, M.T., 'High-kings with opposition', *NHI1*, pp. 899–933.

    ed. and trans., *Irish Royal Charters: texts and contexts* (Oxford: Oxford University Press, 2005).

    'Irish royal charters and the Cistercian order', in M. T. Flanagan and J. Green, eds, *Charters and Charter Scholarship in Britain and Ireland* (Basingstoke: Palgrave and Macmillan, 2005), pp. 120–39.

    Irish society, Anglo-Norman settlers, Angevin kingship: interactions in Ireland in the late twelfth century (Oxford: Oxford University Press, 1989).

    'Jocelin of Furness and the cult of St Patrick in twelfth-century Ulster', in C. Downham, ed., *Jocelin of Furness: proceedings of the 2011 conference* (Donington: Shaun Tyas, 2013), pp. 45–66.

    The transformation of the Irish Church in the twelfth century (Woodbridge: Boydell Press, 2010).

Fleming, J., *Gille of Limerick c. 1070–1145: architect of a medieval Church* (Dublin: Four Courts, 2001).

Foley, A., 'Chieftains, betaghs and burghers: the Irish on the royal manors of medieval Dublin', in S. Duffy, ed., *Medieval Dublin XI* (Dublin: Four Courts Press, 2011), pp. 202–18.

Follett, W., 'Religious texts in the Mac Aodhagáin library of Lower Ormond', *Peritia*, 24–5 (2013–14), 213–29.

Forester, T., trans., *Giraldus Cambrensis: The topography of Ireland* (Cambridge, ON: In Parenthesis, 2000).

Frame, R., *Colonial Ireland, 1169–1369*, 2nd edn (Dublin: Four Courts Press, 2012).

'The defence of the English lordship, 1250–1450', in T. Bartlett and K. Jeffery, eds, *A military history of Ireland* (Cambridge: Cambridge University Press, 1996), pp. 76–98.

'Exporting state and nation: being English in medieval Ireland', in L. Scales and O. Zimmer, eds, *Power and the nation in European history* (Cambridge: Cambridge University Press, 2005), pp. 143–65.

Ireland and Britain 1170–1450 (London: Hambledon, 1998).

'"Les Engleys Nées en Irlande": the English political identity in medieval Ireland', *Transactions of the Royal Historical Society*, sixth series, 3 (1993), 83–103.

'Lordship and liberties in Ireland and Wales, c.1170–c.1360', in H. Pryce and J. Watts, eds, *Power and identity in the later Middle Ages: essays in memory of Rees Davies* (Oxford: Oxford University Press, 2007), pp. 125–38.

Freeman, P., *Ireland and the classical world* (Austin: University of Texas Press, 2001).

Fulford, M., M. Handley, and A. Clarke, 'An early date for Ogham: the Silchester ogham stone rehabilitated', *Medieval Archaeology* 44, (2000), 1–23.

Gantz, J., trans. *Early Irish myths and sagas* (Harmondworth: Penguin, 1981)

Geber, J., 'Comparative study of perimortem weapon trauma in two early medieval skeletal populations (AD 400–1200) from Ireland', *International Journal of Osteoarchaeology*, 25 (2015), 253–64.

Gerriets, M., 'Economy and society. Clientship according to the Irish laws', *Cambridge Medieval Celtic Studies*, 6 (1983), 43–61.

Gilbert, J., and R. Mulholland, eds, *Calendar of the Ancient Records of Dublin in the possession of the Municipal Corporation*, 19 vols (Dublin: J. Dollard, 1889–1944).

Gillingham, J., 'The context and purpose of Geoffrey of Monmouth's "History of the Kings of Britain"', *Anglo-Norman Studies*, 13 (1991), 99–118.

Given-Wilson, C., ed. and trans., *The Chronicle of Adam of Usk, 1377–1421* (Oxford: Clarendon Press, 1997).

Glaser, J., ed. and trans., *Middle English poetry in modern verse* (Indianapolis, IN: Hackett, 2007).

Glasscock, R., 'Land and people, c.1300', *NHI2*, pp. 205–39.

Gleason, A., 'Music', in S. Duffy, ed., *Medieval Ireland: an encyclopedia* (New York: Routledge, 2005), pp. 346–48.

Gleeson, D., 'A fourteenth century Clare heresy trial', *Irish Ecclesiastical Record*, 89 (1958), 36–42.

Godfrey, C.J., *The Church in Anglo-Saxon England* (Cambridge: Cambridge University Press, 1962).

Goedheer, A., *Irish and Norse traditions about the Battle of Clontarf* (Haarlem: H. D. Tjeenk Willink and Zoon, 1938).

Graham-Campbell,J., 'An early medieval horse-harness mount, of Irish manufacture, from Yorkshire', in E. Purcell *et al.*, eds, *Clerics, kings and Vikings: essays on medieval Ireland in honour of Donnchadh Ó Corráin* (Dublin: Four Courts Press, 2015), pp. 247–50.

'A Viking Age gold hoard from Ireland', *Antiquaries Journal*, 54 (1974), 269–72.

Gray, E., ed. and trans., *Cath Maige Tuired: The second battle of Mag Tuired* (Kildare: Irish Texts Society, 1982).

Greene, D., ed., *Fingal Rónáin and other stories* (Dublin: Dublin Institute for Advanced Studies, 1955).

'The influence of Scandinavian on Irish', in B. Almqvist and D. Greene, eds, *Proceedings of the Seventh Viking Congress, Dublin, 15–21 August 1973* (Dublin: Viking Society for Northern Research, 1976), pp. 75–82.

Griffiths, D., *et al.*, *Meols: the archaeology of the north Wirral coast* (Oxford: Oxford University School of Archaeology, 2007).

Gwynn, A., 'The first synod of Cashel', *Irish Ecclesiastical Record*, 66 (1945), 81–92; 67 (1946), 109–22.

'Irish monks and the Cluniac reform', *Studies: An Irish Quarterly Review*, 29 (1940), 409–30.

ed., 'Provincial and diocesan decrees of the diocese of Dublin during the Anglo-Norman period,' *Archivium Hibernicum*, 11 (1944), 31–117.

'Some notes on the history of the Book of Kells', *Irish Historical Studies*, 9 (1954), 131–61.

ed., 'Some unpublished texts from the Black Book of Christ Church, Dublin', *Analecta Hibernica*, 16 (1946), 281–337.

Gwynn, E., ed. and trans., *Metrical Dindshenchas*, 3 vols (Dublin: Royal Irish Academy, 1903–13).

ed. and trans., 'Rule of the Céli Dé', *Hermathena*, 44 (1927), 127–64.

Gwynn, E., and W. Purton, eds and trans., 'The monastery of Tallaght', *Proceedings of the Royal Irish Academy. Section C*, 29 (1911–12), 115–79.

Hall, D., 'Towards a prosopography of nuns in medieval Ireland', *Archivium Hibernicum*, 53 (1999), 3–15.

Women and the Church in medieval Ireland, c. 1140–1540 (Dublin: Four Courts Press, 2008).

Hall, V., *The making of Ireland's landscape* (Cork: Collins Press, 2011).

Halpin, A., 'Coinage', in S. Duffy, ed., *Medieval Ireland: an encyclopedia* (New York: Routledge, 2005), pp. 96–8.

'Weapons and warfare in Viking-Age Ireland', in J. Sheehan and D. Ó Corráin, eds, *The Viking Age: Ireland and the West* (Dublin: Four Courts, 2005), pp. 124–35.

Halpin, A. and C. Newman, *Ireland: an archaeological guide* (Oxford: Oxford University Press, 2006).

Hand, G., *English law in Ireland, 1290–1324* (Cambridge: Cambridge University Press, 1967).

Harbison, P., 'Early Irish pilgrim archaeology in the Dingle peninsula', *World Archaeology*, 26. 1 (1994), 90–103.

Harbison, S., 'William of Windsor, the court party and the administration in Ireland', in J. Lydon, ed., *England and Ireland in the later Middle Ages: essays in honour of Jocelyn Otway-Ruthven* (Blackrock: Irish Academic Press, 1981), pp. 153–74.

Hardiman, J., ed., *A Statute of the fortieth Year of King Edward III, Enacted in A Parliament Held in Kilkenny, A.D. 1367, before Lionel Duke of Clarence, Lord Lieutenant of Ireland* (Dublin: Irish Archaeological Society, 1843).

Haren, M., and Y. de Pontfarcy, eds, *The medieval pilgrimage to St Patrick's Purgatory. Lough Derg and the European Tradition* (Enniskillen: Clogher Historical Society, 1988).

Harrington, C., *Women in a Celtic Church, Ireland 450–1150* (Oxford: Oxford University Press, 2002).

Hartland, B., 'The household knights of Edward I in Ireland', *Historical Research*, 77 (2004), 161–77.

Heist, W., ed., *Vitae sanctorum Hiberniae: ex codice olim Salamanticensi nunc Bruxellensi* (Brussels: Société de Bollandistes, 1965).

Henry, F., and G. Marsh-Micheli, 'Manuscripts and illuminations, 1169–1603', *NHI2*, pp. 781–815.

Herbert, M., 'Charter material from Kells', in F. O'Mahony, ed., *The Book of Kells: proceedings of a conference at Trinity College Dublin* (Dublin: Scolar Press, 1994), pp. 60–77.

'The death of Muirchertach mac Erca: a twelfth-century tale', in F. Josephson, ed., *Celts and Vikings: proceedings of the Fourth Symposium of Societas Celtologica Nordica* (Göteborg:Novum Grafiska AB, 1997), pp. 27–39.

Iona, Kells and Derry: the history and hagiography of the monastic familia of Columba (Oxford: Clarendon Press, 1998).

'Medieval collections of ecclesiastical and devotional materials: Leabhar Breac, Liber Flavus Fergusiorum and The Book of Fenagh' in B. Cunningham and S. Fitzpatrick, eds, *Treasures of the Royal Irish Academy Library* (Dublin: Royal Irish Academy, 2009), pp. 33–43.

'The Vita Columbae and Irish hagiography: a study of Vita Cainnechi' in J. Carey *et al.*, eds, *Studies in Irish hagiography: Saints and scholars* (Dublin; Four Courts Press, 2001), pp. 31–40.

Herbert, M., and M. McNamara, eds and trans., *Irish biblical Apocrypha: selected texts in translation* (Edinburgh: T. and T. Clark, 1989).

Hillam, J., 'A medieval oak tree-ring chronology from south-west England', *Tree-ring Bulletin*, 40 (1980), 13–22.

Hogan, A., *The Priory of Llanthony Prima and Secunda in Ireland, 1172–1541* (Dublin: Four Courts Press, 2008).

Holland, M., 'Dublin and the reform of the Irish church: eleventh and twelfth centuries', *Peritia*, 14 (2000), 111–60.

'Were early Irish church establishments under lay control?' in D. Bracken and D. Ó Riain-Raedel, eds, *Ireland and Europe in the twelfth century: Reform and Renewal* (Dublin: Four Courts Press, 2006), pp. 128–42.

Holm, P., 'The naval power of Norse Dublin' in E. Purcell, P. MacCotter, J. Nyan and J. Sheehan, eds, *Clerics, kings and Vikings: essays on medieval Ireland in honour of Donnchadh Ó Corráin* (Dublin: Four Courts Press, 2015), pp. 67–78.

'The slave trade of Dublin, ninth to twelfth centuries', *Peritia*, 5 (1986), 317–45.

Hourihane, C., *Gothic art in Ireland, 1169–1550: enduring vitality* (New Haven, CT: Yale University Press, 2003).

Hore, H., and J. Graves, eds, *The social state of the southern and eastern counties of Ireland in the sixteenth century* (Dublin: Royal Historical and Archaeological Association of Ireland, 1870).

Hudson, B., 'The changing economy of the Irish Sea province', in B. Smith, ed., *Britain and Ireland 900–1300: insular responses to medieval European change* (Cambridge: Cambridge University Press, 1999), pp. 39–66.

Hughes, K., *Early Christian Ireland: introduction to the sources* (Ithaca, NY: Cornell University Press, 1972).

'The Church in Irish society, 400–800', *NHI1*, pp. 301–30.

Iogna-Prat, D., 'Churches in the landscape', in T. Noble and J. Smith, eds, *Cambridge history of Christianity, III: early medieval Christianities c. 600–c. 1100* (Cambridge: Cambridge University Press, 2008), pp. 363–79.

James, D., 'Two medieval Arabic accounts of Ireland', *Journal of the Royal Society of Antiquaries of Ireland*, 108 (1978), 5–9.

Jefferies, H., 'A Church "in decline"? The pre-reformation Irish Church', *History Ireland*, 6 (2006), 13–18.

Jenkinson, F., ed, *The Hisperica famina* (Cambridge: Cambridge University Press, 1908).

Johnson, M., '"Vengeance is mine": saintly retribution in medieval Ireland', in S. A. Throop and P. Hyams, eds, *Vengeance in the Middle Ages: emotion, religion and feud* (Abingdon: Routledge, 2016), pp. 5–50.

Johnston, D., 'Richard II and the submissions of Gaelic Ireland', *Irish Historical Studies*, 12 (1980), 1–20.

Johnston, E., *Literacy and identity in medieval Ireland* (Woodbridge: Boydell Press, 2013).

Jones, D., trans., *Friars' Tales: thirteenth century exempla from the British Isles* (Manchester: Manchester University Press, 2011).

Jordan, W., *The Great Famine: northern Europe in the early fourteenth century* (Princeton, NJ: Princeton University Press, 1997).

Kelly, F., 'Agriculture', in S. Duffy, ed., *Medieval Ireland: an encyclopedia* (New York: Routledge, 2005), pp. 7–9.

A guide to early Irish law (Dublin: Dublin Institute for Advanced Studies, 1988).

Early Irish farming: a study based mainly on the law texts of the 7ᵗʰ and 8ᵗʰ centuries AD (Dublin: Dublin Institute for Advanced Studies, 2000).

ed. and trans., *Marriage disputes: A fragmentary Old Irish law-text* (Dublin: Dublin Institute for Advanced Studies, 2015).

Kelly, M., *The Great Dying: the Black Death in Dublin* (Stroud: Tempus, 2003).

The history of the Black Death in Ireland (Stroud: Tempus, 2001).

Kenney, J., *The sources for the early history of Ireland: introduction and guide. Volume one: ecclesiastical* (New York: Columbia University Press, 1929).

Kenny, G., 'Anglo-Irish and Gaelic marriage laws and traditions in late medieval Ireland', *Journal of Medieval History*, 32 (2006), 27–42.

Anglo-Irish and Gaelic women in Ireland c. 1170–1540 (Dublin: Four Courts Press, 2007).

Kenny, M., 'Coins and coinage in pre-Norman Ireland', *NHI1*, pp. 842–51.

'A hoard of Hiberno-Norse coins from Clonmacnoise, Co. Offaly', in H. King, ed., *Clonmacnoise studies vol. I: seminar papers 1994* (Dublin: Dúchas, 1998), pp. 133–48.

Kerr, T., F. McCormick and A. O'Sullivan, *The Economy of Early Medieval Ireland*, EMAP Report 7.1 (2013) available online at www.emap.ie/documents/Early_Medieval_Archaeology_Project_Final_Report.pdf.

Kerr, T., G. Swindles and G. Plunkett, 'Making hay while the sun shines? Socio-economic change, cereal production and climatic deterioration in early medieval Ireland', *Journal of Archaeological Science*, 36 (2009), 2868–74.

King, H., 'Economy and Industry of Early Medieval Clonmacnoise: a preliminary view', in N. Edwards, ed., *The archaeology of the early medieval Celtic churches* (Leeds: Maney, 2009), pp. 333–49.

Kinsella, T., trans., *The Táin, translated from the Irish epic Táin Bó Cuailnge* (Dublin: Dolmen, 1969).

Knott, E., trans., *Irish classical poetry*, rev. ed. (Cork: Mercier Press, 1966),

Koch, J., J. Carey, *et al.*, trans., *The Celtic Heroic Age. Literary sources for ancient Celtic Europe and early Ireland and Wales* (Aberystwyth: Celtic Studies Publications, 2003).

Krusch, B., ed., 'Vita Columbani', in B. Krusch and W. Levison, eds, *Monumenta Germaniae historica: scriptores rerum Merovingicarum*, 7 vols (Hanover: Hahn, 1884–1920) IV: 822–44.

ed., *Venanti Honori Clementiani Fortunati Presbyteri Italici Opera Pedestria, Monumenta Germania Historia, Scriptores Rerum Merouingicarum Auctores Antiquissimi*, 4.2 (Berlin: Weidmann, 1885).

Lacey, B., *Cenél Conaill and the Donegal Kingdoms, AD 500–800* (Dublin: Four Courts Press, 2006).

Laing, L., *The archaeology of Celtic Britain and Ireland* (Cambridge: Cambridge University Press, 2006).

Lawrence, F., 'What did they sing at Cashel in 1172? Winchester, Sarum and Romano-Frankish Chant in Ireland', *Journal of the Society for Musicology in Ireland*, 3 (2008), 111–25.

Le Goff, J., *The birth of Purgatory*, trans. A. Goldhammer (Chicago: University of Chicago Press, 1986).

Lennon, C., 'The parish fraternities of County Meath in the late middle ages', *Ríocht na Midhe*, 19 (2008), 85–101.

Levison, W., ed. 'Vita Filiberti', in B Krusch and W. Levison, eds, *Monumenta Germaniae historica: scriptores rerum Merovingicarum*, 7 vols (Hanover: Hahn, 1884–1920), V: 566–604.

Lionard P. and F. Henry, 'Early Irish grave-slabs', *Proceedings of the Royal Irish Academy, C*, 61 (1960/1961), 95–169.

Lucas, A., 'Irish food before the Potato', *Gwerin*, 3.2 (1960), 3–43.
  'The plundering and burning of churches in Ireland, 7th to 16th century', in E. Rynne, ed., *North Munster studies: essays in commemoration of Monsignor Michael Moloney* (Limerick: Thomond Archaeological Society, 1967), pp. 172–229.

Ludlow, F., *et al.*, 'Medieval Irish chronicles reveal persistent volcanic forcing of severe winter cold events, 431–1649', *Environmental Research Letters*, 8 (2013) available online at http://iopscience.iop.org/1748-9326/8/2/024035.

Lydon, J., 'Edward I, Ireland and the war in Scotland, 1303–1304', in P. Crooks, ed., *Government, war and society in medieval Ireland* (Dublin: Four Courts, 2008), pp. 200–15.
  'Edward II and the revenues of Ireland in 1311–12', *Irish Historical Studies*, 14 (1964), 39–57.
  'The expansion and consolidation of the colony, 1215–54', *NHI2*, pp. 156–78.
  'The impact of the Bruce invasion, 1315–27', *NHI2*, pp. 275–302.
  'Ireland and the English Crown, 1171–1541', *Irish Historical Studies*, 29 (1995), 281–94.
  Ireland in the later Middle Ages (Dublin: Gill and Macmillan, 1973).
  'A land of war', *NHI2*, pp. 240–74.
  The lordship of Ireland in the Middle Ages (Dublin: Gill and Macmillan, 1972).
  'The years of crisis, 1254–1315', *NHI2*, pp. 179–204.

Lynn, C., 'Recent archaeological excavations in Armagh city: an interim summary', *Seanchas Ardmhacha* 8 (1977), 275–80.

Lyons, M., 'Lay female piety and church patronage in late medieval Ireland' in B. Bradshaw and D. Keogh, eds, *Christianity in Ireland: revisiting the story* (Blackrock: Columba, 2002), pp. 44–75.
  'Weather, famine, pestilence and plague in Ireland, 900–1500', in E. M. Crawford, ed., *Famine: the Irish experience 900–1900* (Edinburgh: John Donald, 1989), pp. 31–74.

MacCotter, P., *Medieval Ireland: territorial, political and economic divisions* (Dublin: Four Courts Press, 2008)

Macdonald, P., 'An archaeological evaluation of the inaugural landscape of Crew Hill (Cráeb Telcha), Co. Antrim', *Ulster Journal of Archaeology*, 67 (2008), 84–106.

MacErlean, J., 'Synod of Ráith Bresail. Boundaries of the diocese of Ireland (A.D. 1110 or 1118)', *Archivium Hibernicum*, 3 (1914), 1–33.

Mac Giolla Léith, C., ed. and trans., *Oidheadh chloinne hUisneach: The violent death of the children of Uisneach* (London: Irish Texts Society, 1993).

MacHugh E., *et al.*, 'Early medieval cattle remains from Scandinavian settlement in Dublin; genetic analysis and comparison with extant breeds', *Philosophical Transactions of the Royal Society of London B*, 354 (1999), 100–9.

Mac Neill, J., 'Early Irish population groups: their nomenclature, classification and chronology', *Proceedings of the Royal Irish Academy. Section C*, 29 (1911/1912), 59–114.

Mac Niocaill, G. 'Fitzgerald, Gerald fitz Maurice, third earl of Desmond (1338?–1398)', *Oxford dictionary of national biography* (Oxford: Oxford University Press, 2004) available online at www.oxforddnb.com/view/article/9553.

  ed. 'Registrum Cantariae S. Salvatoris Waterfordensis', *Analecta Hibernica*, 23 (1966), 135–222.

  ed., 'Tír Cumaile', *Ériu*, 22 (1971), 81–6.

Maginn, C., 'Gaelic Ireland's English frontiers in the late Middle Ages', *Proceedings of the Royal Irish Academy, Section C*, 110 (2010), 173–90.

Mahaffy, J., ed., 'Two early tours in Ireland', *Hermathena*, 18 (1914), 1–16.

Manning, I., 'Piracy and sixteenth-century Ireland: a social history of Ireland's contribution to pre-Golden Age piracy', unpublished PhD diss. (University of Liverpool, 2016).

Martin, F. X., 'Allies and an overlord, 1169–1172', *NHI2*, pp. 67–97.

  'Diarmait Mac Murchada and the coming of the Anglo-Normans', *NHI2*, pp. 43–66.

  'John, lord of Ireland, 1185–1216', *NHI2*, pp. 127–55.

Mason, L., *Food culture in Great Britain* (London: Greenwood, 2004).

McCarthy, D., 'The origins of the *Latercus* paschal cycle', *Cambrian Medieval Celtic Studies*, 28 (1994), 25–49.

McCone, K., 'Werewolves, cyclopes, *díberga*, and *Fíanna*: juvenile delinquency in early Ireland', *Cambridge Medieval Celtic Studies*, 12 (1986), 1–22.

McCormick, F., 'Cows, ringforts and the origins of Early Christian Ireland', *Emania*, 13 (1995), 33–7.

McDonald, A., 'Aspects of the monastic landscape in Adomnán's Life of Columba', in J. Carey *et al.*, eds, *Studies in Irish hagiography: saints and scholars* (Dublin; Four Courts Press, 2001), pp. 15–30.

McDonough, C., trans. *Moriuht: a Norman-Latin poem from the early eleventh century* (Toronto: Pontifical Institute of Medieval Studies, 1995).

McEneaney, E., 'Politics and devotion in late fifteenth-century Waterford', in R. Moss *et al.*, eds, *Art and devotion in late medieval Ireland* (Dublin: Four Courts Press, 2006), pp. 33–50.

McErlean, T., and N. Crothers, *Harnessing the tides: The early medieval tide mills at Nendrum monastery, Strangford Lough* (Belfast: Stationery Office, 2007)

McErlean, T., R. McConkey and W. Forsythe, *Strangford Lough: an archaeological survey of the maritime landscape* (Belfast: Blackstaff Press, 2003)

McGrath, G., 'The shiring of Ireland and the 1297 parliament', in J. Lydon, ed., *Law and disorder in thirteenth century Ireland: the Dublin parliament of 1297* (Dublin: Four Courts Press, 1997), pp. 107–24.

McInerney, L., *Clerical and learned lineages of medieval Co. Clare: a survey of the fifteenth century papal registers* (Dublin: Four Courts Press, 2014).

McKenna, L., ed. and trans., 'Poem to Cloonfree castle', *Irish Monthly*, 51 (1923), 639–45.

McLaughlin, R., *Early Irish satire* (Dublin: Dublin Institute for Advanced Studies, 2008).

McLeod, N., 'Interpreting early Irish law: status and currency (Part 1)', *Zeitschrift für Celtische Philologie*, 41 (1986), 46–65.

　'Interpreting early Irish law: status and currency (Part 2)', *Zeitschrift für Celtische Philologie*, 42 (1987), 41–115.

　'Kinship', *Ériu*, 51 (2000), 1–23.

McManus, D., *A Guide to ogam* (Maynooth: An Sagart, 1997).

McNamara, M., *The apocrypha in the Irish Church* (Dublin: Dublin Institute for Advanced Studies, 1975).

McNamee, C., *The Wars of the Bruces: Scotland, England and Ireland, 1306–1328* (East Linton: Tuckwell Press, 1997).

McNeill, T., 'County Down in the later Middle Ages' in L. Proudfoot, ed., *Down: History and Society* (Dublin: Geography Publications, 1997), pp. 103–21.

Meehan, B., *The Book of Kells: an illustrated introduction to the manuscript in Trinity College Dublin* (London: Thames and Hudson, 1994).

Melczer, W., ed. and trans., *The pilgrim's guide to Santiago de Compostela* (New York: Italica Press, 1993).

Meyer, K., ed. and trans., *Aislinge Meic Conglinne: the vision of MacConglinne, a Middle Irish wonder tale* (London: David Nutt, 1892).

　ed. and trans., *The triads of Ireland* (Dublin: Royal Irish Academy, 1906).

Mills, J., and M. J. McEnery, eds, *Calendar of the Gormanston Register* (Dublin: Royal Society of the Antiquaries of Ireland, 1916).

Mitchell, L., 'Gender(ed) identities? Anglo-Norman settlement, Irish-ness and the Statues of Kilkenny of 1367', *Historical Reflections*, 37.2 (2011), 8–23.

Mooney, C., *The Church in Gaelic Ireland: thirteenth to fifteenth centuries* (Dublin: Gill and Macmillan, 1969).

Moore, R., *The formation of a persecuting society: authority and deviance in Western Europe 950–1250*, 2nd edn (Oxford: Wiley-Blackwell, 2007).

Moran, D., *The philosophy of John Scottus Eriugena: a study of idealism in the middle ages* (Cambridge: Cambridge University Press, 1989).

Morrissey, J., 'Cultural geographies of the contact zone', *Social and Cultural Geography*, 64 (2005), 551–66.

Moss, R., ed., *Art and architecture of Ireland, volume 1: Medieval, c. 400–c. 1600* (Dublin: Royal Irish Academy, 2014).

Moylan, T., 'Vagabonds and sturdy beggars: poverty, pigs and pestilence in medieval Dublin', *Dublin Historical Record*, 1.1 (1938), 11–18.

Mullally, E., ed. and trans., *The deeds of the Normans in Ireland: La geste des Engleis en yrlande: a new edition of the chronicle formerly known as The Song of Dermot and the Earl* (Dublin: Four Courts, 2002).

Murphy, M., and K. O'Conor, 'Castles and deer parks in Anglo-Norman Ireland', *Eolas*, 1 (2006), 53–70.

Murphy, M., and M. Potterton, *The Dublin region in the Middle Ages: settlement, land-use and economy* (Dublin: Four Courts Press, 2000).

Murray, G., *The Cross of Cong: a masterpiece of medieval Irish art* (Dublin: Irish Academic Press, 2014).

Mynors, R., *et al.*, eds and trans. *William of Malmesbury, Gesta Regum Anglorum, The History of the English Kings*, 2 vols (Oxford: Clarendon Press, 1998–9).

Mytum, H., *The origins of early Christian Ireland* (London: Routledge, 1992).

Nally, D., 'Maintaining the marches: seigneur, sept and settlement in Anglo-Norman Thomond', in M. Lynch and P. Nugent, eds, *Clare history and society* (Dublin: Geography Publications, 2008), pp. 27–59.

Nic Dhonnchadha, A., 'Medical writing in Irish, 1440–1700', in. J. B. Lyons, ed., *Two thousand years of Irish medicine* (Dublin: Eireann Health Publications, 1999), pp. 21–6.

Nic Ghiollamhaith, A., 'Dynastic warfare and historical writing in North Munster, 1276–1350', *Cambrian Medieval Celtic Studies*, 2 (1981), 73–89.

Nicholls, K., *Gaelic and Gaelicised Ireland in the Middle Ages* (Dublin: Gill and Macmillan, 1972).

   Gaelic and Gaelicised Ireland in the Middle Ages, 2nd edn (Dublin: Lilliput Press, 2003).

   'Gaelic society and economy', *NHI2*, pp. 397–438.

   'Scottish mercenary kindreds in Ireland, 1250–1600', in S. Duffy, ed. *The world of the Galloglass: kings, warlords and warriors in Ireland and Scotland, 1200–1600* (Dublin: Four Courts Press, 2007), pp. 86–105.

Ní Chonaill, B., 'Child centred law in medieval Ireland', in R. Davis and T. Dunne, eds, *The empty throne: childhood and the crisis of modernity* (Cambridge: Cambridge University Press, 2008), 1–31.

Ní Dhonnchadha, M., 'On Gormfhlaith daughter of Flann Sinna and the lure of the sovereignty goddess', in A.P. Smyth, ed., *Seanchas: studies in early and medieval Irish archaeology, history and literature in honour of Francis J. Byrne* (Dublin: Four Courts Press, 2000), pp. 225–37.

   'The guarantor list of *Cáin Adomnáin* 697', *Peritia*, 1 (1982), 178–215.

Ní Ghabláin, S., 'The origin of medieval parishes in Gaelic Ireland: the evidence from Kilfenora', *Journal of the Royal Society of Antiquaries of Ireland*, 126 (1996), 37–61.

Ni Ghradaigh, J., 'But what exactly did she give?' Derbforgaill and the Nuns' Church', in H. King, ed., *Clonmacnoise Studies II: seminar papers 1998* (Dublin: Stationery Office, 2003), pp. 175–207.

Ní Mhaonaigh, M., *Brian Boru: Ireland's greatest king?* (Stroud: Tempus, 2007).
   'Of Saxons, a Viking and Normans: Colmán, Gerald and the monastery of Mayo', in J. Graham-Campbell and M. Ryan, eds, *Anglo-Saxon/Irish relations before the Vikings* (Oxford: Oxford University Press, 2009), pp. 411–26.

Nock, A.D., *Conversion: the old and the new in Religion from Alexander the Great to Augustine of Hippo* (Oxford: Clarendon Press, 1933).

O'Brien, A., 'Politics, economy and society: the development of Cork and the Irish south coast region c. 1170 to c. 1583', in P. O'Flanagan and C. Buttimer, eds, *Cork: history and society* (Dublin: Geography Publications, 1993), pp. 83–156.

O'Brien, E., 'Pagan or Christian? Burial in Ireland during the 5th to 8th centuries AD', in N. Edwards, ed., *The archaeology of the early medieval Celtic churches* (Leeds: Maney, 2009), pp. 135–54.

O'Brien, M., ed. and trans., 'A Middle-Irish poem on the Christian kings of Leinster', *Ériu*, 17 (1955), 35–51.

O'Byrne, E., *War, politics and the Irish of Leinster, 1156–1606* (Dublin: Four Courts Press, 2003).
   'Ua Conchobair, Tairrdelbach (1088–1156)', in S. Duffy, ed., *Medieval Ireland: an encyclopedia* (New York: Routledge, 2005), pp. 471–74.

Ó Carragáin, T., *Churches in early medieval Ireland: architecture, ritual and memory* (New Haven, CT: Yale University Press, 2010)

Ó Clabaigh, C., *The friars in Ireland, 1224–1540* (Dublin: Four Courts Press, 2012).

O'Connor, R., *The destruction of Da Derga's Hostel: kingship and narrative artistry in a medieval Irish saga* (Oxford: Oxford University Press, 2013).

O'Conor, K., 'Housing in later medieval Gaelic Ireland', *Ruralia*, 4 (2002), 201–10.
   The archaeology of medieval rural settlement in Ireland (Dublin: Royal Irish Academy, 1998).

O'Conor, K., and T. Finan, 'The moated site at Cloonfree, Co. Roscommon', *Journal of the Galway Archaeology and History Society*, 54 (2002), 72–87.

Ó Corráin, D., 'The career of Diarmait mac Máel na mBó, king of Leinster: pt 2', *Old Wexford Society Journal*, 4 (1972–3), 17–24.
   'The early Irish churches: some aspects of organisation', in D. Ó Corráin, ed., *Irish antiquity: essays and studies presented to Professor M.J. O'Kelly* (Cork: Tower Books, 1981), pp. 327–41.
   'Foreign connections and domestic politics: Killaloe and the Uí Briain in twelfth-century hagiongraphy', in D. Whitelock *et al.*, eds, *Ireland in*

early medieval Europe (Cambridge: Cambridge University Press, 1982), pp. 213–31.

Ireland before the Normans (Dublin: Gill and Macmillan, 1972)

'Ireland c. 800: aspects of society', *NHI1*, pp. 549–608.

'Muirchertach Mac Lochlainn and the Circuit of Ireland', in A. Smyth, ed., *Seanchas: studies in early and medieval Irish archaeology, history and literature in honour of Francis J. Byrne* (Dublin: Four Courts Press, 2000), pp. 238–50.

'Nationality and kingship in pre-Norman Ireland', in T. W. Moody, ed., *Historical studies XI: nationality and the pursuit of national independence, papers read before the conference held at Trinity College, Dublin, 26–31 May 1975* (Belfast: Appletree Press, 1978), pp. 1–35.

'The synod of Cashel, 1101: conservative or innovative?', in D. Edwards, ed., *Regions and rulers in Ireland, 1100–1650* (Dublin: Four Courts, 2004), pp. 13–19.

Ó Cróinín, D., *Early medieval Ireland, 400–1200* (Harlow: Longman, 1995).

'Hiberno-Latin literature to 1169', *NHI1*, pp. 371–404.

'Ireland, 400–800', *NHI1*, pp. 182–234.

Ó Cuív, B., ed. and trans., 'A poem composed for Cathal Croibhdhearg Ó Conchubhair', *Ériu*, 34 (1983), 157–74.

O Daly, M., ed. and trans., 'A Poem on the Airgialla', *Ériu*, 16 (1952), 179–88.

O'Donovan, J., ed. and trans., *The circuit of Ireland by Muircheartach Mac Neill, Prince of Ailech* (Dublin: Irish Archaeological Society, 1841).

O'Dwyer, B., *The conspiracy of Mellifont, 1216–31* (Dublin: Dublin Historical Association, 1970).

trans., *Stephen of Lexington, Letters from Ireland 1228–9* (Kalamazoo, MI: Cistercian Publications, 1982).

Ó Floinn, R., 'The Anglo-Saxon connection: Irish metalwork AD 400–800', in J. Graham-Campbell and M. Ryan, eds, *Anglo-Saxon-Irish relations before the Vikings* (Oxford: Oxford University Press, 2011), pp. 231–52.

'The archaeology of the early Viking age in Ireland', in H. Clarke, M. Ní Mhaonaigh and R. O'Floinn, eds, *Ireland and Scandinavia in the Early Viking Age* (Dublin: Four Courts Press, 1998), pp. 132–65.

'Beginnings: early medieval Ireland, AD 500–850', in P. F. Wallace and R. Ó Floinn, eds, *Treasures of the National Museum of Ireland: Irish antiquities* (Dublin: Gill and Macmillan, 2002), pp. 171–212.

'Handmade medieval pottery in S E Ireland – 'Leinster ware' in G. Mac Niocaill and P. F. Wallace, eds, *Keimelia: studies in medieval archaeology and history in memory of Tom Delaney* (Galway: Galway University Press, 1988), pp. 325–49.

O'Grady, S., ed. and trans., *Silva Gadelica*, 2 vols (London: Williams and Norgate, 1892).

Ó hAodha, D., ed. and trans., *Bethu Brigte* (Dublin: Dublin Institute of Advanced Studies, 1978).

O'Keeffe, J., ed., 'Dál Caladbuig', in J. Fraser *et al.*, eds, *Irish Texts Fasciculus 1* (London: Sheed and Ward, 1931), pp. 19–21

  ed. and trans., 'The Rule of Patrick', *Ériu* 1 (1904), 216–24.

O'Keeffe, T., *Medieval Ireland; an archaeology* (Stroud: Tempus, 2000).

  'Rural settlement and cultural identity in Gaelic Ireland, 1000–1500', *Ruralio*, 1 (1996), 142–53.

O'Leary, A., 'Mog Ruith and apocalypticism in eleventh-century Ireland', in J. Nagy, ed., *The individual in Celtic literatures*, Celtic Studies Association of North America Yearbook 1 (Dublin: Four Courts, 2001), pp. 51–60.

Ó Lochlainn, C., 'Roadways in ancient Ireland', in J. Ryan, ed., *Féil-sgríbhinn Eóin Mhic Néill: essays and studies presented to professor Eoin MacNeill on the occasion of his seventieth birthday, May 15th 1938* (Dublin: Three Candles, 1940), pp. 465–74.

O'Loughlin, T., 'The library of Iona in the late seventh century: the evidence from Adomnán's *De locis sanctis*', *Ériu*, 45 (1994), 33–52.

O'Meara, J., ed., 'Giraldus Cambrensis in Topographia Hibernie', *Proceeding of the Royal Irish Academy*, 52 (1948–50), 113–78.

  trans., *The history and topography of Ireland* (Portlaoise: Dolmen, 1951).

  The voyage of St Brendan: a journey to the promised land (Portlaoise: Dolmen, 1976).

Ó. Muraíle, N., 'Cathal Óg Mac Maghnusa: his time, life and legacy', *Clogher Record*, 16.2 (1998), 45–64.

Ó Murchadha, D., 'Carmen, site of Óenach Carmain: a proposed location', *Eigse*, 33 (2002), 57–70.

O'Neill, P., '*Peregrinatio*: punishment and exile in the early Irish church', *Australian Celtic Journal*, 9 (2010), 37–48.

Ó Néill, P., and D. Dumville, eds and trans., *Cáin Adomnáin and Canones Adomnani* (Cambridge: Department of Anglo-Saxon, Norse and Celtic, 2003).

O'Rahilly, T., 'On the origin of the names Érainn and Ériu', *Ériu*, 14 (1946), 7–28.

Ó Riain, P., 'St. Finnbarr: a study in a cult', *Journal of the Cork Historical and Archaeological Society*, 82 (1977), 63–82.

Ó Riain-Raedel, D., 'The question of "pre-Patrician" Saints of Munster', in M. A. Monk and J. Sheehan, eds, *Early medieval Munster: archaeology, history and society* (Cork: Cork University Press, 1998), pp. 17–22.

Ó Ríordáin, S., 'The excavation of a large earthen ringfort at Garranes, Co. Cork', *Proceedings of the Royal Irish Academy. Section C*, 47 (1942), 77–150.

  'Roman material in Ireland', *Proceedings of the Royal Irish Academy. Section C*, 51 (1945–8), 35–82.

Orpen, G., 'The Fitz Geralds, barons of Offaly', *Journal of the Royal Society of Antiquaries of Ireland*, 4 (1914), 99–113.

Oschema, K., 'Blood-brothers: a ritual of friendship and the construction of the imagined barbarian in the Middle Ages', *Journal of Medieval History*, 32 (2006), 275–301.

Ó Scea, C., 'Erenachs, erenachships and church landholding in Gaelic Fermanagh, 1270–1609', *Proceedings of the Royal Irish Academy. Section C*, 112 (2012), 271–300.

Oskamp, H., ed. and trans., 'Echtra Condla', *Études celtiques*, 14 (1974), 207–28.

O'Sullivan, A., and C. Breen, *Maritime Ireland. An archaeology of coastal landscapes* (Stroud: Tempus, 2007).

O'Sullivan, A., *et al.*, *Early medieval dwellings and settlements in Ireland AD 400–1100*, BAR International Series (Oxford: Archaeopress, 2014).

   Early medieval Ireland AD 400–1100: The evidence from archaeological excavations (Dublin: Royal Irish Academy, 2014).

O'Sullivan, W., 'Manuscripts and palaeography', *NHI1*, pp. 511–48.

Otway-Ruthven, A., 'The native Irish and English law in medieval Ireland', *Irish Historical Studies*, 7 (1950), 1–16.

Patterson, N., *Cattle lords and clansmen: the social structure of early Ireland* (New York: Garland Press, 1991).

Picard, J-M., 'The cult of Columba in Lotharingia (9th to 11th centuries): the manuscript evidence', in J. Carey *et al.* eds, *Studies in Irish hagiography: Saints and scholars* (Dublin; Four Courts Press, 2001), pp. 221–36.

Plummer, C., ed. and trans., *Irish litanies* (London: Henry Bradshaw Society, 1925).

   ed. and trans., *Miscellanea Hagiographica Hibernica: vitae adhuc ineditae sanctorum Mac Creiche, Naile, Cranat*, Subsidia Hagiographica 15 (Brussels: Société des Bollandistes, 1925).

Prendergast, J., 'The Ulster creaghts', *Proceedings and Transactions of the Kilkenny and South-East of Ireland Archaeological Society*, 3 (1855), 420–30.

Preston, S., 'The canons regular of St Augustine: the twelfth century reform in action' in S. Kinsella ed., *Augustinians at Christ Church* (Dublin: Christ Church Cathedral, 2000), pp. 23–40.

Prestwich, M., 'Geneville, Geoffrey de, first Lord Geneville (1225x33–1314)', *Oxford dictionary of national biography* (Oxford: Oxford University Press, 2004) available online at www.oxforddnb.com/view/article/37448.

Prosper, *Chronicon Minora*, in T. Mommsen, ed., *Chronica Minora saec IV, V, VI, VII: Monumenta Germaniae Historica auctorum antiquissimorum IX*, 3 vols (Berlin: Weidmannm, 1892), I, 341–485.

Public Record Office, eds, *Calendar of state papers, foreign and domestic: Henry VIII, 1509–47*, 40 vols (London: Public Record Office, 1863–1950).

Purser, J., 'Reconstructing the River Erne horn', *Ulster Journal of Archaeology*, 61 (2002), 17–25.

Quinn, D., 'Aristocratic autonomy, 1460–94', *NHI2*, pp. 591–618.

'The early interpretation of Poynings' law, 1494–1534', *Irish Historical Studies*, 2 (1941), 241–54.

'The Irish parliamentary subsidy in the fifteenth and sixteenth centuries', *Proceedings of the Royal Irish Academy, Section C*, 42 (1934–5), 219–46.

Raftery, B., 'Iron Age Ireland', *NHI1*, pp. 134–81.

Raine, J., ed., *Historical papers and letters from the Northern Registers* (London: Longmans, 1873).

Rance, P., 'Attacotti, Déisi and Magnus Maximus: the case for Irish federates in late Roman Britain', *Britannia*, 32 (2001), 243–70.

Redknap, M., 'Glitter in the dragon's lair: Irish and Anglo-Saxon metalwork from pre-viking Wales, c. 400–850' in J. Graham-Campbell and M. Ryan, eds, *Anglo-Saxon-Irish relations before the Vikings* (Oxford: Oxford University Press, 2011), pp. 281–310.

Reeves, W., ed., *Acts of Archbishop Colton in his metropolitan visitation of the Diocese of Derry* (Dublin: Irish Archaeological Society, 1850).

Reynolds, A., *Anglo-Saxon deviant burial customs* (Oxford: Oxford University Press, 2009).

Richardson, H., and G. Sayles, *The Irish Parliament in the Middle Ages* (Philadelphia: University of Pennsylvania Press, 1952).

Parliaments and councils of medieval Ireland, I (Dublin: Stationery Office, 1947).

Richter, M., 'The European dimension of Irish history in the eleventh and twelfth century', *Peritia*, 4 (1985), 328–45.

Round, J., *Feudal England: historical studies on the eleventh and twelfth centuries* (London: Swan Sonnenschein, 1909).

Ruhaak (in press), 'An alternative Black Death narrative for Ireland: ecological and socio-ecological divides on the medieval European frontier'.

Russell, I., and M. F. Hurley, eds., *Woodstown: a Viking Age settlement in Co. Waterford* (Dublin: Four Courts Press, 2014).

Russell, P., ed. and trans., 'Nósa Ua Maine. The Customs of the Uí Mhaine', in T. Charles-Edwards *et al.*, eds, *The Welsh king and his court* (Cardiff: University of Wales Press, 2000), pp. 527–51.

Russell, P., S. Arbuthnot and P. Moran, 'Early Irish Glossaries Database', available online at www.asnc.cam.ac.uk/irishglossaries/.

Ryan, J., 'Saint Patrick's Purgatory, Lough Derg', *Clogher Record*, 3 (1975), 13–26.

Rynne, C., and C. Manning, 'How early Irish horizontal-wheeled mills really worked', *Archaeology Ireland*, 21 (2007), 21–3.

Schot, R., 'Uisneach Midi a medón Érenn: a prehistoric 'cult' centre and 'royal site' in Co. Westmeath', *Journal of Irish Archaeology*, 15 (2006), 39–71.

Schroeder, H., ed. and trans., *Disciplinary decrees of the General Councils: text, translation and commentary* (St. Louis, MO: Herder, 1937).

Scott, A., 'Latin learning and literature in Ireland, 1169–1500', *NHI1*, pp. 934–95.

Scott, A., and F. Martin, eds, *Expugnatio Hiberniae: the conquest of Ireland by Giraldus Cambrensis* (Dublin: Royal Irish Academy, 1978)

Sharpe, R., 'Armagh and Rome in the seventh century', in P. Ní Chatháin and M. Richter, eds, *Irland und Europa: Die Kirche im Frühmittelalter* (Stuttgart: Klett-Cotta, 1984), pp. 58–72.

'Churches and communities in early medieval Ireland: towards a pastoral model', in J. Blair and R. Sharpe, eds, *Pastoral care before the parish* (Leicester: Leicester University Press, 1992), pp. 81–109.

A handlist of the Latin writers of Great Britain and Ireland before 1540 (Turnhout: Brepols, 2001).

Medieval Irish Saints' Lives: an introduction to Vitae Sanctorum Hiberniae (Oxford: Clarendon Press, 1991).

'St Patrick and the see of Armagh', *Cambridge Medieval Celtic Studies*, 4 (1982), 33–59.

Sheehan, J., 'Early Viking age silver hoards from Ireland and their Scandinavian elements', in H. B. Clarke, M. Ní Mhaonaigh and R. Ó Floinn, eds, *Ireland and Scandinavia in the Early Viking Age* (Dublin: Four Courts Press, 1998), pp. 166–202.

'A Great Famine discovery of viking gold', in J. Crowley, W. J. Smyth and M. Crowley, eds, *The atlas of the Great Irish Famine 1845–50* (Cork: Cork University Press, 2012), pp. 630–1.

'Hiberno-Scandinavian broad-band arm-rings', in J. Graham-Campbell, ed., *The Cuerdale Hoard and related Viking-age silver and gold from Britain and Ireland in the British Museum* (London: British Museum, 2011), pp. 94–100.

'Ireland's early Viking Age silver hoards: components, structure and classification', *Acta Archaeologica*, 71 (2000), 49–73.

'A Peacock's Tale: excavations at Caherlehillan, Kerry, Ireland', in N. Edwards, ed., *The archaeology of the Celtic churches* (Leeds: Maney, 2009), pp. 191–206.

Sheehy, M., *When the Normans came to Ireland*, 2nd edn (Cork: Mercier Press, 1998).

Shinners, J., ed., *Medieval popular religion 1000–1500: a reader* (Ontario: Broadview, 1997).

Simms, K., 'Changing patterns of regal succession in late medieval Ireland', in F. Lachaud and M. Penman, eds, *Making and breaking the rules: succession in medieval Europe, c. 1000–c. 1600. Proceedings of the colloquium held on 6–7-8 April 2006, Institute of Historical Research* (Turnhout: Brepols, 2008), pp. 161–72.

From kings to warlords: the changing political structure of Gaelic Ireland in the later Middle Ages (Woodbridge: Boydell Press, 1987).

'Gaelic revival', in S. Duffy, ed., *Medieval Ireland: an encyclopedia* (New York: Routledge, 2005), pp. 189–90.

'Guesting and feasting in Gaelic Ireland', *Journal of the Royal Society of Antiquaries of Ireland*, 108 (1978), 67–100.

"'The king's friend": O Neill, the crown and the earldom of Ulster', in J. Lydon, ed., *England and Ireland in the later Middle Ages: essays in honour of Jocelyn Otway-Ruthven* (Blackrock: Irish Academic Press, 1981), pp. 214–36.

'Late medieval Donegal', in W. Nolan, L. Ronayne and M. Dunlevy, eds, *Donegal: history and society* (Dublin: Geography Publications, 2004), pp. 183–201.

'Late medieval Tír Eoghain', in C. Dillon and H. A. Jefferies, eds, *Tyrone: history and society* (Dublin: Geography Publications, 2000), pp. 127–62.

'The legal position of Irishwomen in the later Middle Ages', *Irish Jurist*, 10 (1975), 96–111.

'Medieval Fermanagh', in E. Murphy and W. Roulston, eds, *Fermanagh: history and society* (Dublin: Geography Publications, 2004), pp. 77–103.

Medieval Gaelic sources (Dublin: Four Courts Press, 2009).

'Nomadry in medieval Ireland: the origins of the creaght or caoraigheacht', *Peritia*, 5 (1986), 379–91.

'The Ulster revolt of 1404 – an anti-Lancastrian dimension', in B. Smith, ed., *Ireland and the English world in the late Middle Ages* (London: Palgrave Macmillan, 2009), pp. 141–60.

Simpson, L., 'Forty years a-digging: a preliminary synthesis of archaeological investigations in medieval Dublin', in S. Duffy, ed., *Medieval Dublin I* (Dublin: Four Courts Press, 2000), pp. 11–68.

Skre, D., 'Commodity money, silver and coinage in Viking-Age Scandinavia', in J. Graham-Campbell *et al.*, eds, *Silver economies, monetisation and society in Scandinavia, AD 800–1100* (Aarhus: Aarhus University Press, 2011), pp. 67–92.

Slavin, P., 'Crusaders In crisis: towards the re-assessment of the origins and nature of the "People's Crusade" of 1095–1096', *Imago Temporis. Medium Aevum*, 4.(2010), 175–99.

Smith, B., *Colonisation and conquest in medieval Ireland: the English in Louth 1170–1330* (Cambridge: Cambridge University Press, 1999).

Smith, B., 'The concept of the march in medieval Ireland: the case of Uriel', *Proceedings of the Royal Irish Academy, Section C*, 88 (1988), 257–69.

The English in Louth, 1170–1330 (Cambridge: Cambridge University Press, 1999).

'Late medieval Ireland and the English connection: Waterford and Bristol, ca. 1360–1469', *Journal of British Studies*, 50 (2011), 546–65.

ed., *The Register of Nicholas Fleming, Archbishop of Armagh 1404–1416* (Dublin: Irish Manuscripts Commission, 2003).

Southern, R., *Western society and the Church in the Middle Ages* (London: Penguin, 1970).

Sperber, I., L. Bieler and C. Downham, eds and trans., *The Life of St Patrick by Jocelin of Furness* (in press).

Stacey, R. Chapman, *Dark speech: The performance of law in early Ireland* (Philadelphia, PA: University of Pennsylvania Press, 2007).

Stalley, R., 'Ecclesiastical architecture before 1169', *NHI1*, pp. 714–43.

'Hiberno-Romanesque and the sculpture of Killeshin', in P. Lane and W. Nolan, eds, *Laois: history and society* (Dubin: Geography Publications, 1999), pp. 89–122.

Stancliffe, C., 'Columbanus's monasticism and the sources of his inspiration', in F. Edmonds and P. Russell, eds, *Tóme: studies in medieval Celtic history and law in honour of Thomas Charles-Edwards* (Woodbridge: Boydell, 2011), pp. 17–28.

'Religion and society in Ireland', in P. Fouracre, ed., *The new Cambridge medieval history, volume I: c. 500–c. 700* (Cambridge: Cambridge University Press, 2005), pp. 397–425.

Stevens, P., 'Clonfad: an industrious monastery', in P. Stevens and J. Channing, eds *Settlement and community in the Fir Tulach kingdom* (Dublin: Wordwell, 2012), pp. 107–34.

Stewart, A., trans., *The history of Jerusalem AD 1180 by Jacques de Vitry* (London: Palestine Pilgrims' Text Society, 1896).

Stocker, D., 'Aristocrats, burghers and their markets: patterns in the foundation of Lincoln's urban churches', in D.M. Hadley and L. ten Harkel, eds, *Everyday life in Viking-Age towns: social approaches to towns in England and Ireland, c. 800–1100* (Oxford: Oxbow, 2013), 119–43.

Stokes, W., ed. and trans., *Félire Óengusso Céli Dé: the martyrology of Oengus the Culdee* (London: Henry Bradshaw Society, 1905).

ed. and trans., *Lives of Saints from the Book of Lismore* (Oxford: Clarendon Press, 1890).

ed. and trans., 'The prose tales in the Rennes dindshenchas', *Revue Celtique*, 15 (1894), 272–336, 418–84; Revue Celtique, 16 (1895), 31–83, 135–67, 269–312, 468.

ed., *The Saltair na rann: a collection of early Middle Irish poems* (Oxford: Bodleian library, 1883).

Stokes, W. and J. Strachan, eds, *Thesaurus Palaeohibernicus*, 2 vols (Cambridge: Cambridge University Press, 1903).

Stothers, R., 'Volcanic dry fogs, climate cooling, and plague pandemics in Europe and the Middle East', *Climatic Change*, 42 (1999), 713–23.

Stout, M., 'The distribution of early medieval ecclesiastical sites in Ireland', in P. J. Duffy and W. Nolan, eds, *At the anvil: essays presented to Professor William J. Smyth* (Dublin: Geography Publications, 2012), pp. 53–80.

'Early Christian Ireland: settlement and environment', in T. B. Barry, ed., *A history of settlement in Ireland* (London: Routledge, 2000), pp. 81–109.

The Irish ringfort (Dublin: Four Courts Press, 1997).

Stubbs, W., ed., *Select charters and other illustrations of English constitutional history*, 9th edn rev. H. W. C. Davis (Oxford: Clarendon Press, 1921).

Sweetman, H., and G. Handcock, eds, *Calendar of documents relating to Ireland, 1171–1307*, 5 vols (London: Public Record Office, 1875–86).

Swift, C., 'Dating Irish grave-slabs: the evidence of the annals', in C. Bourke, ed., *From the Isles of the North – early Medieval art in Ireland and Britain* (Belfast: Stationery Office, 1995), pp. 245–9.

'Early Irish priests within their own localities', in F. Edmonds and P. Russell, eds, *Tome: studies in medieval Celtic history and law in honour of Thomas Charles-Edwards* (Woodbridge: Boydell, 2011), pp. 29–40.

'Forts and fields: a study of "monastic towns" in seventh and eighth century Ireland', *Journal of Irish Archaeology*, 9 (1998), 105–25.

'Óenach Tailten, the Blackwater valley and the Uí Néill kings of Tara', in A. Smyth, ed., *Seanchas: studies in early and medieval Irish archaeology, history and literature in honour of Francis J. Byrne* (Dublin: Four Courts Press, 2000), pp. 109–20.

Ogam stones and the earliest Irish Christians (Maynooth: St Patrick's College, 1997).

'Sculptors and their customers: a study of Clonmacnoise grave slabs', in H. King, ed., *Clonmacnoise studies volume 2: seminar papers* (Dublin: Stationery Office, 2003), pp. 105–23.

'Taxes, trade and trespass: the Hiberno-Norse context of the Dál Cais empire in Lebor na cert', in K. Murray, ed., *Lebor na Cert: reassessments* (London: Irish Texts Society, 2013), pp. 34–61.

Szaciłło, J., 'The O'Donohue group of saints' lives in the Codex Salmanticensis', unpublished PhD diss. (Queen's University Belfast, 2013).

Theiner, A., ed., *Vetera Monumenta Hibernorum et Scotorum Historiam Illustrantia* (Rome: Typis Vaticanis, 1864).

Thomas, C., *Christianity in Roman Britain to A.D.500* (London: Batsford, 1981).

Thorpe, L., trans., *Einhard: the life of Charlemagne* (London: Folio Society, 1970).

Thurneysen, R., ed. and trans. *Irisches Recht* (Berlin: Akademie der Wissenschaften, 1931).

Thurston, T. and G. Plunkett, 'A dynamic sociology of Iron Age, medieval and early modern Ulster, Northern Ireland', in L. Giosan, ed., *Climates, past landscapes, and civilizations* (Washington, DC: American Geophysical Union), pp. 177–91.

Todd, J., ed. and trans., *Cogadh Gaedhel re Gallaibh: the war of the Gaedhil with the Gaill*, Rolls Series (London: Longmans, Green, Reader, and Dyer, 1867).

Toner, G., '*Baile*: settlement and landholding in medieval Ireland', *Éigse*, 34 (2004), 25–43.

Valante, M., 'Reassessing the Irish "monastic town"', *Irish Historical Studies*, 31 (1998), 1–18.

'Taxation, tolls and tribute: the language of economics and trade in Viking Age Ireland', *Proceedings of the Harvard Celtic Colloquium*, 18–19 (1998–99), 242–58.

Veach, C., 'Henry II's grant of Meath to Hugh de Lacy in 1172: a reassessment', *Ríocht na Mídhe*, 18 (2007), 67–94.

'King and magnate in medieval Ireland: Walter de Lacy, King Richard and King John', *Irish Historical Studies*, 37 (2010), 179–202.

'Relentlessly striving for more: Hugh de Lacy in Ireland', *History Ireland*, 15.2 (2007), 18–23.

Veach, C., and F. Verstraten Veach, 'William Gorm de Lacy, "cheifest champion in these parts of Europe"' in S. Duffy, ed., *Princes, prelates and poets in medieval Ireland: essays in honour of Katharine Simms* (Dublin: Four Courts, 2013), pp. 63–84.

Verstraten Veach, F., 'Anglicisation in Medieval Ireland: was there a Gaelic Irish "Middle Nation"?', in S. Duffy and S. Foran, eds, *The English Isles: cultural transmission and political conflict in Britain and Ireland* (Dublin: Four Courts Press, 2013), pp. 118–38.

Walker, G., ed., *Sancti Columbani Opera* (Dublin: Dublin Institute for Advanced Studies, 1957).

Wallace, P., 'The archaeology of Ireland's Viking-Age towns', *NHI1*, pp. 813–51.

'The economy and commerce of Viking Age Dublin,' in K. Düwel *et al.*, eds, *Untersuchungen zu Handel und Verkehr der vor- und frühgeschichtlichen Zeit in Mittel – und Nordeuropa IV* (Göttingen: Vandenhoeck und Ruprecht, 1987), pp. 200–45.

'Viking Age Ireland, AD 850–1150', in P. F. Wallace and R. Ó Floinn, eds, *Treasures of the National Museum of Ireland: Irish antiquities* (Dublin: Gill and Macmillan, 2002), pp. 213–56.

Viking Dublin: the Wood Quay excavations (Newbridge: Irish Academic Press, 2016).

Walsh K., 'The clerical estate in later medieval Ireland: alien settlement or element of conciliation?', in J. Bradley, ed., *Settlement and society in medieval Ireland* (Kilkenny: Boethius Press, 1998), pp. 361–77.

Richard FitzRalph in Oxford, Avignon and Armagh: a fourteenth century scholar and primate (Oxford: Clarendon Press, 1981).

Walsh, M., and D. Ó Cróinín, eds and trans., *Cummian's Letter: De controversia Pashali* (Toronto: Pontifical Institute of Medieval Studies, 1988).

Wamers, E., 'Insular finds in Viking Age Scandinavia and state formation of Norway', in H. B. Clarke, M. Ní Mhaonaigh and R. Ó Floinn, eds, *Ireland and Scandinavia in the Early Viking Age* (Dublin: Four Courts Press, 2008), pp. 131–65.

Ware, J., *The antiquities and history of Ireland*, trans. by John Davies (Dublin: A. Crook, 1705).

Warntjes, I., 'Regnal succession in early medieval Ireland', *Journal of Medieval History*, 30 (2004), 377–410.

Warren, F., and J. Stevenson, *Liturgy and ritual of the Celtic church*, rev. edn (Woodbridge: Boydell, 1987).

Waters, K., 'The earls of Desmond in the fourteenth century', unpublished PhD diss. (University of Durham, 2004),

Watt, D., *et al.*, eds, *Scotichronicon: Walter Bower* (Aberdeen: Aberdeen University Press, 1993–98) VI, 385–403.

Watt, J., 'The Anglo-Irish colony under strain, 1327–99', *NHI2* pp. 352–96.

'Approaches to the history of fourteenth century Ireland', *NHI2*, pp. 303–13.

The Church and the two nations in medieval Ireland (Cambridge: Cambridge University Press, 1970).

The Church in medieval Ireland (Dublin: Gill and Macmillan, 1972).

'Gaelic polity and cultural identity', *NHI2*, pp. 314–51.

'Negotiations between Edward II and John XXII concerning Ireland', *Irish Historical Studies*, 10 (1956), 1–20.

'The papacy and Ireland in the fifteenth century', in B. Dobson, ed., *The Church, politics and patronage in the fifteenth century* (Gloucester: St Martin's Press, 1984), pp. 133–45.

'Butler, James, first earl of Wiltshire and fifth earl of Ormond (1420–1461)', in *Oxford dictionary of national biography* (Oxford University Press, 2004) available online at www.oxforddnb.com/view/article/4188.

Webb, J., 'The guilds of Dublin', *Irish Monthly*, 45 (1917), 507–14.

ed. and trans., 'Translation of a French metrical history of the deposition of King Richard the Second, written by a contemporary', *Archaeologia*, 20 (1824), 1–423.

Webster, J., 'Creolizing the Roman provinces', *American Journal of Archaeology*, 105 (2001), 209–25.

White, N., ed., *The Red Book of Ormond from the fourteenth century original preserved at Kilkenny castle* (Dublin: Stationery Office, 1932).

Whitfield, N., 'Dress and accessories in the early Irish tale, "The Wooing of Becfhola"', *Medieval Clothing and Textiles*, 2 (2006), 1–34.

'More like the work of fairies than of human beings': the filigree on the 'Tara' brooch, a masterpiece of late Celtic metalwork', *ArchéoSciences*, 33 (2009), 235–41.

Williams, B., ed. and trans., *The Annals of Ireland by Friar John Clyn* (Dublin: Four Courts Press, 2007).

Williams, B., 'Heresy in Ireland in the thirteenth and fourteenth centuries', in S. Duffy, ed., *Princes, prelates and poets in medieval Ireland: essays in honour of Katharine Simms* (Dublin: Four Courts Press, 2013), pp. 339–51.

'The sorcery trial of Alice Kyteler', *History Ireland*, 4.2 (1994), 20–4.

Winterbottom, M., ed. *Three Lives of English saints* (Toronto: Pontifical Institute of Medieval Studies, 1972).

Wood, H., 'The Templars in Ireland', *Proceedings of the Royal Irish Academy. Section C*, 26 (1906–7), 327–77.

Woods, A., 'Economy and authority: a study of the coinage of Hiberno-Scandinavian Dublin and Ireland', 2 vols, unpublished PhD diss. (University of Cambridge, 2013).

'Monetary activity in Viking-Age Ireland: the evidence of the single-finds' in R. Naismith, M. Allen and E. Screen, eds, *Medieval monetary history: studies in memory of Mark Blackburn* (Farnham: Ashgate, 2014), pp. 295–330.

Wormald, J., *Lords and men in Scotland: bonds of manrent, 1442–1603* (Edinburgh: John Donald, 1985).

Wright, R. and K. Jackson, 'A late inscription from Wroxeter', *Antiquaries Journal*, 48. 2 (1968), 296–300.

Wright, T., ed. *Political poems and songs relating to English history, Composed during the period from the accession Of Edward III to that of Richard III*, 2 vols, Rolls Series (London: Longman, Green, Longman and Roberts, 1861).

Wyatt, D., *Slaves and warriors in medieval Britain and Ireland, 800–1200* (Leiden: Brepols, 2009).

Young, S., 'Donatus, bishop of Fiesole 829–76, and the cult of St. Brigit in Italy', *Cambrian Medieval Celtic Studies*, 35 (1998), 13–26.

Youngs, S., 'Anglo-Saxon, Irish and British relations: hanging-bowls reconsidered', in J. Graham-Campbell and M. Ryan, eds, *Anglo-Saxon-Irish relations before the Vikings* (Oxford: Oxford University Press, 2011), pp. 205–30.

INDEX

●